Stanley Kubrick Produces

Stanley Kubrick Produces

JAMES FENWICK

Rutgers University Press
New Brunswick, Camden, and Newark, New Jersey, and London

Library of Congress Cataloging-in-Publication Data

Names: Fenwick, James (Film historian), author.
Title: Stanley Kubrick produces / James Fenwick.
Description: New Brunswick : Rutgers University Press, [2020] | Includes bibliographical references and index.
Identifiers: LCCN 2020009761 | ISBN 9781978814882 (cloth) | ISBN 9781978814875 (paperback) | ISBN 9781978814899 (epub) | ISBN 9781978814905 (mobi) | ISBN 9781978814912 (pdf)
Subjects: LCSH: Kubrick, Stanley. | Kubrick, Stanley—Criticism and interpretation. | Motion picture producers and directors—Great Britain—Biography. | Motion pictures—History—20th century.
Classification: LCC PN1998.3.K83 F46 2020 | DDC 791.4302/32092—dc23
LC record available at https://lccn.loc.gov/2020009761

A British Cataloging-in-Publication record for this book is available from the British Library.

Copyright © 2021 by James Fenwick
All rights reserved

No part of this book may be reproduced or utilized in any form or by any means, electronic or mechanical, or by any information storage and retrieval system, without written permission from the publisher. Please contact Rutgers University Press, 106 Somerset Street, New Brunswick, NJ 08901. The only exception to this prohibition is "fair use" as defined by U.S. copyright law.

∞ The paper used in this publication meets the requirements of the American National Standard for Information Sciences—Permanence of Paper for Printed Library Materials, ANSI Z39.48-1992.

www.rutgersuniversitypress.org

Manufactured in the United States of America

For mum and dad, and all your support over the years.

Contents

Introduction ... 1

Part I   The Emergence of a Film Producer, 1928–1955

1 The Beginning, 1928–1951 ... 11
2 The Unknown Early Years, 1951–1953 ... 26
3 The New York "Film School," 1953–1955 ... 44

Part II   The Harris-Kubrick Pictures Corporation, 1955–1962

4 The New UA Team, 1955–1956 ... 63
5 New Modes of Producing, 1957–1959 ... 79
6 Swords, Sandals, Sex, and Soviets, 1959–1962 ... 98

Part III   Polaris Productions and Hawk Films, 1962–1969

7 The Establishment of a Producing Powerhouse, 1962–1964 ... 119
8 Kubrick versus MGM, 1964–1969 ... 131

Part IV   The Decline of a Film Producer, 1970–1999

9 Kubrick and Warner Bros., 1970–1980 ... 155
10 The End, 1980–1999 ... 178
   Epilogue ... 197

Appendix A: *World Assembly of Youth* Credits	201
Appendix B: Filmography	203
Acknowledgments	207
Notes	209
Select Bibliography	243
Index	249

Stanley Kubrick Produces

Introduction

●●●●●●●●●●●●●●●●●●●●●

Stanley Kubrick wanted control. Control and information. These were the twin pillars on which he built his career and forged a power base for himself as an independent film producer, director, and writer in Hollywood across a fifty-year period. He'd always wanted control and information, even when working as a photographer throughout his late teens and early twenties at *Look* magazine. To relinquish control meant that Kubrick would have to do things other people's way, and that just wasn't *his* way. The narrative of Kubrick's life is all about control and was from the very beginning. And while far from suggesting that Kubrick did not collaborate (he certainly did, particularly on set with other artists, often facilitating extreme experimentation), he remained in control, particularly in his role as a producer, over every aspect of his productions, from development through distribution. By the 1970s onward, most of Kubrick's time was spent overseeing distribution and regional marketing campaigns, dubbing, cover designs for VHS releases, and more. In fact, Kubrick was far more often working as a producer than as a director, searching for stories or looking to ensure that his films achieved their full commercial potential.

This book highlights the narrative of control by looking specifically at the production contexts in which Kubrick operated, largely through his role as a producer. It details how Kubrick first emerged as a producer, how he obtained control over his productions (both business and creative), and the impact that control ultimately had on his career. What emerges is a portrait of a filmmaker overwhelmed by control to the point that he could no longer move his projects out of development and into production. This book does not provide a film-by-film production account or detail the minutiae of how films like *2001: A Space Odyssey* (1968) were made but rather depicts the industrial conditions that allowed

Kubrick to accrue the power that he did and the ways in which he wielded that power. If someone expects to read this book as an account of the productions, they will be disappointed, and I refer them to other books that have already done that.[1] This book also privileges Kubrick's early years—the decades of the 1940s, 1950s, and 1960s—over his later career due to the relative lack of scholarship in this regard.

What is largely missing from studies of Kubrick is how he came to be the powerful producer that he did by the end of the 1960s, the industrial and production conditions that facilitated his rise to power, and the ways in which the desire for and use of the control he obtained shaped and even, I would argue, contributed to his decline as a filmmaker. By this, I must clarify, I do not mean Kubrick's quality as an artist declined; rather his ability to successfully produce a film from development through distribution diminished. After all, in the final twenty-five years of his career he produced only four films, in contrast to the first twenty-five years of his career, in which he produced or directed nine.

But in examining the narrative of control, we can also begin to understand how, in many ways, it was also a myth partially constructed by Kubrick himself. To obtain the control he needed to make films—in fact, to even be able to enter the Hollywood mainstream—Kubrick had to construct the illusion of a powerful, maverick auteur. It was an image I would suggest that he purposely cultivated (evidence of which Filippo Ulivieri has developed through exhaustive empirical research).[2] From the earliest days of his career, producing and directing *Fear and Desire* (1953), Kubrick would be in close contact with journalists at newspapers like the *New York Times*, providing copy and undergoing interviews that positioned him as a controlling producer. It's an image that Kubrick developed as a means of furthering his status within the industry and of cementing his power base. But it's also a pernicious myth within Kubrick studies, one that has obstructed a holistic view of Kubrick's career and how he evolved as a producer in mainstream Hollywood. Therefore, by analyzing the industrial and production contexts in which he worked, we can begin to scratch away at his carefully crafted image to understand the wider structural forces in the American (and, to some extent, British) film industry, including industrial and economic logic, to understand just how Kubrick operated as a producer.

The success of the controlling image of Kubrick was clear in the outpouring of analysis by critics, scholars, and fans as to his impact, importance, and legacy on cinema and Hollywood following his death on March 7, 1999. In the obituaries and newspaper columns that ensued, a theme emerged that the *Guardian*'s Derek Malcolm perhaps best encapsulated. Malcolm described how Kubrick had spent half of his career fighting and beating Hollywood, "getting its money to make his expensive films but only on condition that no one interfered with him or them in any way. His power thus became greater than any of his contemporaries and most of the great filmmakers of the past."[3] The critics were largely effusive in their praise of Kubrick's artistic prowess and stressed, as Malcolm did, Kubrick's producing authority and control over every facet of his productions.

But there was, and continues to be, little contextual understanding as to where this control came from, instead confusing it with Kubrick's image as the ultimate auteur. Take Jonathan Romney's assessment of Kubrick's filmmaking power, comparing it to the supernatural forces that gripped the Overlook Hotel in *The Shining* (1980): "It's hard not to see Jack's struggle with the Overlook as an image of Kubrick's own peculiar relationship with Warner Bros. With any director, no matter how powerful, it's always the House, the Studio, that's ultimately in control but perhaps Kubrick, like Jack, really did have the run of the House. With his unique, still mysterious command of Warner's goodwill, he must have had either a power verging on the satanic (biographies often wax eerie about his eyes), or perhaps he just knew where the bodies are buried."[4] Romney equates Kubrick's power as a filmmaker to forces beyond comprehension, removing him and his work from the industrial realities of Hollywood and elevating Kubrick to the mythical status of the "auteur as superstar," to borrow a phrase from Joseph Gelmis's 1970 work *The Director as Superstar*, in which Kubrick featured.

What was lacking from the obituaries of Kubrick was any attempt to understand his work and role as a producer and how he obtained control. Nor was there any real attempt to truly understand Kubrick's impact on Hollywood, beyond his artistic influences. When it came to the issue of his control, Kubrick's myth once more came to dominate. Ronald Bergan asserted that Kubrick's autonomy and power were never "absorbed into the system on which he was financially dependent,"[5] while Janet Maslin argued that Kubrick's filmmaking and his "landmark films" were always delivered "at a safe distance from Hollywood whims."[6] Taking it to the extreme, Romney once more highlighted Kubrick's supposed godlike supremacy in Hollywood, saying that no other filmmaker could equal his power: "Even [Martin] Scorsese is held back by the fact of being human, with human neuroses."[7]

What many of the obituaries and summaries of Kubrick's life and legacy appeared to be doing was to perpetuate the myth of the auteur and, in the process, to fail and neglect to understand the industrial, production, and economic contexts in which he worked. Kubrick was very much a part of the Hollywood system upon which he relied, as this book demonstrates and as testified to by his business partner and producer at Harris-Kubrick Pictures Corporation, James B. Harris. In an interview in the wake of Kubrick's death, Harris asserted that "[Kubrick] always knew what was going on in Los Angeles, he would always read the trade press."[8] While Harris's comments alone may not be proof of Kubrick's intimate connection to and knowledge of Hollywood and the British and American film industries, they do reveal a voice trying to break through the Kubrick myth that had formed in both the critical mind and the public perception.

What is perhaps necessary in order to move away from this auteur myth is the decentering of Kubrick:[9] scholars and critics need to look beyond Kubrick as an insular case study to those contexts I have already mentioned. These were concerns that were raised by, among others, Peter Krämer and myself at the workshop "Life and Legacy, Studying the Work of Stanley Kubrick" held at the University of Leiden in July 2019. In a position paper that I delivered at that workshop, titled "Kubrick's Legacy," I argued that Kubrick was not as important as scholars and critics believed, by which I was suggesting we need to move beyond the auteur myth and begin to understand *why* Kubrick has come to be viewed as uniquely influential and powerful and to what extent it is a valid claim. For example, if Kubrick was an all-powerful producer by the 1970s, then just how unique was he? Were there other similarly powerful producers? Or, for example, if we continue to claim that Kubrick is somehow influential, just what does this mean? Citing quotes or references to Kubrick in other filmmakers' work, without an extensive empirical and comparative analysis of other filmmakers who are similarly quoted and referenced, does not necessarily tell us anything useful about the reach, extent, or uniqueness of Kubrick's influence. To decenter Kubrick means to think about, research, and write about Kubrick in a way that considers his position within the American and British film industries. And when we talk about his legacy, for example, we really need to rethink the questions we are asking and instead consider *who* has constructed that legacy, ranging from the studios he worked with to his family, his fans, the Stanley Kubrick Archive at the University of the Arts London, and, of course, Kubrick himself. After all, while Kubrick was undoubtedly an artist motivated by intellectual and philosophical curiosity, he was also a business and brand manager working within a profit-orientated industry.

Tracing Kubrick's role as a producer and understanding the external forces he was working and negotiating with (studios, distributors, private financiers, etc.) are arguably easier than determining his role as a director, mainly because of the archival material he has left behind. And it is in film archives that we can begin to find the role of the producer (a role discussed in more detail below), through the notes, budgets, business reports, and correspondence left behind. The Stanley Kubrick Archive is a treasure trove to learn how he operated and, more generally, how Hollywood operated. But the scale of material, spread over eight hundred linear meters of shelving,[10] speaks to Kubrick's desire for control and how it was underpinned by information. This was Kubrick's greatness as an artist, but his fatal flaw as a producer. Realizing that information gave him *ever more* control, Kubrick requested *ever more* information until it overwhelmed him and all those who worked with him. In the end, maybe he just had too much control and was unwilling to surrender.

The Stanley Kubrick Archive is a unique insight into the totality of Kubrick's career and surrounding industrial structures. And while it is not the only archive that documents Kubrick's career (see the Select Bibliography for a list of all the archives that have been consulted for this book), it is the most complete. The archive reveals Kubrick's interactions with industry figures, the way he produced his films (including developing ideas, securing contracts, and obtaining financing), and, perhaps most important, just what he was up to during those increasing gaps between films in his later years. For a man who was determined to remain a private figure during his life, it is remarkable that he left behind an archive that is so revealing. Kubrick's motivations, if any, in keeping the archive (did he envisage it being curated to serve as a historical record, for example?) will perhaps never be known. Instead, it was probably a further extension of the element of control that he needed, while it was left to others around him to file and organize the documents. Did they ever consult the reams of correspondence from, say, *Dr. Strangelove* (1964) ever again? Doubtful. But one can learn more about Kubrick's methods as a producer from consulting a source like the hundreds of boxes of correspondence than from any interview he gave. More important, even if the intention was *not* for the archive to serve as a historical record, it inevitably has become so, shedding a unique light onto one of the most turbulent and transformative periods of the post–World War II American film industry, from the late 1940s through the 1990s. Kubrick kept records not only about his own productions but also of competing films, constantly commissioning research on how other films at studios like MGM and Warner Bros. were being marketed and distributed. There are policy documents from United Artists, Columbia, MGM, and other studios. There are business records that read as a guide on how to produce an independent film in the 1950s. There is correspondence with some of the most noted actors in Hollywood history, from Laurence Olivier to Ingrid Bergman. There are business reports on emerging industrial trends, such as the move to base American productions abroad in the late 1950s and the increase in Hollywood productions being filmed in the former Soviet Bloc in the early 1990s. There is political and union correspondence, shedding light on a greatly underresearched component of mainstream film producing and the need to interact with and even compromise with industrial labor. To that end, it is perhaps time we recognized that the Stanley Kubrick Archive can serve as an archival source not just for the insular study of Stanley Kubrick but for research relating to the wider American and British film industries from the 1940s to the 2000s. In short, the Stanley Kubrick Archive, indeed Kubrick studies as a whole, doesn't have to be just about Stanley.

It's useful at this point to briefly consider what we mean by the role of the producer. It's a role that remains equivocal by nature, in spite of the growing research in producer studies.[11] It's quite possible that because of how the role has changed over the decades, each study of individual producers will lead to differing results as to how they should be defined. Jon Lewis's recent edited collection *Producing* (2016) attempts to provide a comprehensive history of the role, but even here it is a muddied account as to who or what a producer is, with the role transforming from era to era. As Lewis sums up in the introduction to the collection, "Of all the job titles listed in the opening and closing screen credits, 'producer' is certainly the most amorphous. There are businessmen producers (and businesswomen producers), writer-director and movie-star producers; producers who work for the studio or work as a liaison between a production company and the studio; executive producers whose reputation and industry clout alone gets a project financed (though their day-to-day participation in the project may be negligible); and independent producers whose independence is at once a matter of industry structure (as the studios no longer produce much of anything anymore)."[12] What Lewis constructs is an argument of how intrinsically the role of the producer, arguably more so than any other film role, is linked to the industrial conditions of Hollywood and is shaped by its changing economic structures. Therefore, when we think of Kubrick's role as a producer, it inevitably leads to a discussion of the industrial factors that shaped him and impacted on his work.

For Kubrick, the role is further muddied by how his roles as director and writer were often blurred with that of producer. But when we turn to the archive, and when we consider his career as a whole, he predominantly *did not* work as a director. Instead, between 1950 and 1999, a forty-nine-year period, Kubrick more often was a producer; during that time frame he was seldom on a film set or writing film scripts, but instead was developing ideas, seeking out new collaborations, negotiating contracts, devising marketing strategies, and supervising distribution campaigns. More than anything, Kubrick was a producer first and foremost, always looking to protect his business and creative interests and to ensure the maximum commercial return for his films.

This book uncovers Kubrick's role as a producer, and the producers whom he worked with, and considers the ways in which industrial contexts shaped his creative processes. It is a career survey, but also a history of the industrial transformations in producing, marketing, and distribution that took place in Hollywood from the 1950s onward. With a chronological structure, the book provides a narrative across four parts: (1) Kubrick's emergence as a producer in the early 1950s and the conditions that facilitated his transition from photographer at *Look* magazine to independent filmmaker; (2) his business and creative partnership with James B. Harris and their collaborations with Kirk Douglas; (3) Kubrick's establishment of a producing power base in the 1960s following the incorporation of Polaris Productions and Hawk Films and his move to the United Kingdom; and (4) Kubrick's final years at Warner Bros. and his decline as a producer able to move projects out of development and into production. What emerges is almost a tragic narrative, Kubrick's rise and fall as it were. Even though he eventually obtained full producing control of his productions, it ultimately led to debilitating levels of control that left him unable to successfully function as a producer. Indeed, by the end of his career, Kubrick repeatedly considered abdicating his responsibilities as director and in effect decentralizing elements of his control to other filmmakers.

Along the way, the book charts previously unexplored aspects of Kubrick's life and work. This includes his "unknown" early years in the 1950s when he worked closely with producers like Richard de Rochemont on documentaries and television series such as *World Assembly of Youth* (1952) and *Mr. Lincoln* (1952). The book also examines many of Kubrick's "lost" projects and raises questions as to the cultural and industrial logic behind these unmade films. By utilizing archival research and interviews with those who worked with Kubrick, the book works toward answering why Kubrick became the producer that he did, why he worked in the way that he did, and what the industrial forces were that shaped his career. It is hoped that by the end you, the reader, will begin to see Kubrick from a new perspective: as a producer fully entrenched within the structures of the American and British film industries.

Part 1

The Emergence of a Film Producer, 1928–1955
●●●●●●●●●●●●●●●●●●●●●●

1
The Beginning, 1928–1951

••••••••••••••••••••

Kubrick's early years—the twenty-seven-year period between his birth in 1928 and the incorporation of the Harris-Kubrick Pictures Corporation in 1955—are perhaps the least well known of his biography. But it is a period that is vital to understanding how he emerged as a film producer, why he made the move into the film industry, and the conditions that allowed him to do so. In the process of trying to map these early years, we must think about three interrelated aspects of Kubrick's personality, both business and personal: ambition, self-promotion, and, once again, control. As this chapter shows, these three pillars of Kubrick's approach to film producing were manifest from the very beginning.

This chapter, along with the others in this first section of the book, charts these early years. It starts with a brief overview of Kubrick's childhood in New York City, before exploring his formative teenage and twentysomething years, first working at *Look*, a biweekly photojournalism magazine, and then, crucially, transitioning to work in film. This is, I would suggest, an overlooked moment in Kubrick's life: Kubrick quit *Look* magazine, a secure job with a livable wage envied by his unemployed friends in Greenwich Village, to move into a decade-long period of financial precarity, career uncertainty, and search for autonomy. This chapter focuses on the production of his two short films, *Day of the Fight* and *Flying Padre*, both produced in 1950, followed by an attempt to understand his move into feature filmmaking, culminating in the privately financed effort *Fear and Desire*, filmed in 1951 and discussed in chapter 2. The chapter concludes that Kubrick was learning not so much the art of filmmaking in these years, but rather the art of self-promotion and preservation in order to advance his own career aims and to secure future work, with varying degrees of success.

Formative Interests

Kubrick was born on Thursday, July 26, 1928, at Manhattan's Society for the Lying-In Hospital, 305 Second Avenue, just north of Stuyvesant Square. His childhood was spent growing up in the Bronx. His parents, Jack Kubrick and Gertrude Kubrick (née Perveler), were both the children of Jewish immigrants. They raised Stanley and his sister, Barbara, born in 1934, in an apartment block on the Bronx's Clinton Avenue. The Bronx underwent rapid change in the early decades of the twentieth century, and its population grew exponentially from just over 200,000 in the 1900s to over 1.2 million by 1930. Indeed, Kubrick grew up in a borough that was largely well-to-do (contrary to the Bronx's modern image), with restaurants, shops, and department stores flourishing. It is also where Kubrick learned to play baseball as a teenager under the tutelage of Gerald Fried, a high school friend and future collaborator, who invited Kubrick to join the local team, the Barracudas.[1]

Kubrick's neighborhood had numerous movie palaces, many of them architectural delights. Most notable was the Loew's Paradise Theater on the Grand Concourse, a few blocks from Fordham Road and several blocks west of the Kubrick residence. The Paradise Theater was extravagant, with a capacity of four thousand seats, baroque decor, and "a ceiling painted dark blue to resemble a nighttime sky, with small light bulbs added to resemble stars and simulated clouds blown across the ceiling by a cloud machine"—this was the famed Atmospheric style of architect John Eberson.[2] The young Stanley would almost certainly have found himself on Fordham Road, being a short ride on the Webster and White Plains Avenues Streetcar Line. Fordham Road and the Grand Concourse was where many of the cinemas were located, from the above-mentioned Loew's Paradise Theater to the RKO Fordham and the Valentine. In fact, the streetcar lines often acted as a path along which cinemas were built, a yellow brick road for a film fan. The Webster and White Plains Avenues Line was no different, with a movie house at virtually every tram stop, including the Wakefield, Laconia, BB, Burke, and Allerton theaters. We can't be sure what films he saw or what impact they had on his understanding of film history and filmmaking, but it would have been in the cinemas of the Bronx that he was introduced to the films of Hollywood. However, Kubrick seems to ascribe more influence to the years he spent in the 1940s and 1950s when he says he developed a "fantasy image" of films:[3] "I really was in love with movies. I used to see everything at the RKO in Loew's circuit, but I remember thinking at the time that I didn't know anything about movies, but I'd seen so many movies that were bad, I thought, 'Even though I don't know anything, I can't believe I can't make a movie at least as good as this.' And that's why I started, why I tried."[4] Kubrick's comments, given in an interview in 1987, align with his notebooks from the 1950s, which reveal his at times utter contempt for the kind of generic, mainstream films being produced by Hollywood. But what is clear is that Kubrick had a developing passion for film by the time he was a teenager.

His early school days were spent at the less than inspiringly named Public School 3 and later Public School 90. He also had a brief period of private home schooling at age eight. Despite his parent's ambitions that he become a doctor, Kubrick simply did not fit into an academic lifestyle. He disrupted other students by repeatedly talking in class and was often disciplined. His time at the William Howard Taft High School was no different in terms of his performance. Located at Sheridan Avenue and 172nd Street, opposite the Bronx's Claremont Park, the school opened in the early 1940s and possessed a gray, drab air about it. The academic environment proved unstimulating, with an education program for boys focused on physical education to prepare them for war—the United States had entered World War II by the time of Kubrick's entry to high school. In many respects, Kubrick's poor education record reflected that of those around him, with more than half of the population completing no higher than eighth grade by 1940 and eight out of ten boys who graduated high school joining the war effort. By 1945, as few as 51 percent of seventeen-year-old boys were high school graduates. Kubrick says he always felt like a "misfit" in high school. His poor grades were largely due to his absenteeism, and in 1945 he was reported to the attendance bureau for his abysmal record. Seeing that their son was disillusioned with school, Jack and Gertrude sent Kubrick to spend a summer with his uncle from his mother's side, Martin Perveler, in Burbank, California, a few miles northeast of Hollywood.

Perveler would prove a key figure in the fledgling filmmaking career of Kubrick, providing the necessary financing to allow him to produce his first full feature, *Fear and Desire*, in 1951 (see chapter 2). Perveler became incredibly wealthy following his founding of Perveler's Pharmacy in the San Gabriel Valley in the late 1930s, growing into a chain of stores across Los Angeles over the next few years. Whether the city of Burbank stirred the cinematic soul of Kubrick, we'll probably never know. But it was a place with a rich cinematic heritage and headquarters to many important production companies and studios, including Warner Bros., the company that would fund and distribute Kubrick's films from the 1970s onward. Surely the visit would have impacted Kubrick's imagination and his growing "fantasy image" of filmmaking and Hollywood.

It was during this period that Kubrick developed an interest in visual imagery and photography, arguably influenced by a range of factors, one of which could have been the visit to Burbank. In addition, his father was a keen amateur photographer, while his friends at Taft had similar interests. Marvin Traub had his own darkroom, and Alexander Singer had an interest in painting and, by 1945, an interest in film directing.[5] Kubrick's growing interest in photography was expanded by the use of his father's Graflex camera.[6] He would, by his own account, fool around with the camera and even took it into William Taft High School, where he reputedly took photographs "of an English teacher, a *rara avis*, 'who read hamlet and acted out the play for the class.'"[7]

If we return to the three aspects of Kubrick's personality that were, I believe, central to his evolution as a filmmaker—ambition, self-promotion, and control—it is ambition that was the most prominent during the 1940s and 1950s. In the autumn of 1944, while he was still at Taft High and only sixteen years old, Kubrick submitted a set of photographs he took in Greenwich Village to *Look* magazine. His submission was rejected by the picture editor, Helen O'Brian, with his photographs being described as "fine" and his ideas as "good."[8] Kubrick's ideas seem to have been a combination of photography and portraiture, with a series of photographs of a young girl accompanied by a final drawing of her. Whether this was a collaboration with Alexander Singer, given his interest in drawing and painting, isn't clear, but the final idea was deemed to be substandard. Still, O'Brian was impressed and advised Kubrick that he should keep in contact and forward a revised project in due course.[9]

What is important here is not so much the rejection but the fact Kubrick had the ambition and the gall at age sixteen—*sixteen*—to submit his work to a major American magazine. He was displaying innovation and aspiration and a level of self-confidence that his work was good enough to be published in a professional outlet. It is also the first indication that this was a career path that Kubrick wanted to pursue. A year later, in 1945, he once again submitted a photograph to *Look*. It was a photograph of a depressed looking newsvendor, with a headline announcing the death of Franklin D. Roosevelt attached to his stall. Kubrick was paid twenty-five dollars for the image and, shortly thereafter, was recruited to work on a permanent basis at the magazine.

Transition

Kubrick spent nearly six years working at *Look* magazine, though his official dates working as a permanent staff photographer are unclear. Philippe Mather suggests Kubrick commenced working at the magazine sometime in April 1946,[10] initially on a freelance "apprentice" basis.[11] He then became a permanent member of staff from January 7, 1947 and published on a regular, monthly basis.[12] Kubrick suggests that he worked there for a period of four years, until the age of twenty-one.[13] This would correlate with archival documentation, which suggests Kubrick resigned from *Look* in early July 1950, prior to his twenty-second birthday.[14] The Kubrick estate, however, believes Kubrick was legally employed by *Look* until September 12, 1950.[15]

Kubrick's time at *Look* provided him with a degree of creative autonomy—though this was within limits. The organizational structure of the magazine under editor-in-chief Mike Cowles and executive editor Dan Mich was fairly informal; Mather has referred to Mich's style as being "fluid."[16] As former staff photojournalists have commented, collaboration throughout the production process was encouraged, including from the photojournalists.[17] Despite the collaborative atmosphere, there was still substantial editorial supervision, and ideas, text, and layout could still be vetoed by the respective editor.[18] Indeed, Kubrick seems to have wanted to push the limits of the creative freedom he was offered at the magazine. His attempts to broaden his autonomy were noted by the editorial team, particularly how he attempted to invest his own personality into his work. This invariably led to conflict with his editors, as was reflected following his decision to leave the magazine: "Believe it or not I enjoyed arguing with you about how to tackle a story. I think our stories were improved that way. I'm inclined to think you have gone as far as you can go at *Look*. I think that at any other magazine you might have less freedom, but also do better financially."[19]

Kubrick's decision to leave *Look* magazine to commence filmmaking does raise several questions: Why did he want to become a filmmaker? What were the financial conditions that allowed him to make the transition, moving from a position of financial security to (presumably) financial precarity? And what were the industrial conditions that facilitated this transition? Kubrick's desire to transition from photography to filmmaking may have partially been influenced by his high school friend, Alex Singer, who worked in an administrative role for producer Richard de Rochemont's "The March of Time" short film series.[20] Along, of course, with his growing passion for films more generally. But the question of the financial logic of transitioning to filmmaking is much more complicated given that Kubrick had a substantial and stable income at *Look*. His initial starting salary as an apprentice was $50 a week (an inflation adjusted value of approximately $656 in 2019), but by 1950 Kubrick claimed his salary had risen to around $105 a week (over $1,100 in 2019).[21]

Kubrick's salary at *Look* is important to consider, first because it shows he was making a substantial amount of money, particularly for a man of his age, and second because it shows that he was willing to leave secure, permanent employment in order to enter a period of employment uncertainty and financial insecurity. He may have had savings accrued while working at *Look* and a safety net of his family and friends, but he was still making a significant gamble in resigning from the magazine. He clearly thought he had the potential to succeed and, moreover, that there was money to be made. This is demonstrated following an encounter between Kubrick and Alex Singer. Singer had suggested to Kubrick that it cost $40,000 to produce a one-reeler short (approximately nine minutes of film) for "The March of Time" series. The cost surprised Kubrick, who believed he could produce a one-reeler for less. He recounted the story in an interview with Jeremy Bernstein in 1966, hinting toward his burgeoning understanding of film budgets and how to produce at a low cost. He apparently phoned a variety of local companies, including Eastman Kodak, camera rental companies, and film printing laboratories in New York to obtain quotes. Following his research,

Kubrick wagered that he could make a documentary film for around $3,500. As he told Bernstein, "I thought, 'Gee, if they're making these pictures for $40,000 and I can make them for $3,500, surely I must be able to sell them and at least get my money back, and probably make a profit.' In fact, we thought we could make a considerable profit."[22]

Profit seemed to be a key motivating factor for Kubrick's transition from photography to filmmaking. Following his research into the costs of making a film for "The March of Time" series, Kubrick clearly had the self-confidence that he could make a film at a much lower cost and that the industrial conditions for independent producing and the utilization of private financing made production possible. Indeed, following his decision to transition to filmmaking, he was soon presented with a variety of opportunities to make films, with the financial barrier seemingly not a hurdle to him at this early stage. Take for example how in August 1950 Kubrick was approached by independent producer Rex Carlton of Laurel Films with a tempting offer: an adaptation of Henrik Ibsen's *Enemy of the People*, for distribution with Eagle Classics.[23] Carlton was the president of Laurel Films, a New York–based Production company, and had produced two notable low-budget crime films: *C-Man* (Lerner, 1949) and *Guilty Bystander* (Lerner, 1950). Carlton's method of funding Laurel Films was through loans from the Chemical Bank; they had contributed over 50 percent of the $400,000 budget for *Guilty Bystander* on the back of a distributor agreement with Film Classics.[24] The latter was a distribution company incorporated by film producer and importer Irvin Shapiro, specializing in reissues of classic Hollywood films and newly produced, independent New York features.

Carlton's use of bank loans to finance his productions was uncommon practice for independent producers by 1949. Only the Bank of America in Los Angeles and the Chemical Bank in New York were actively involved in financing independent productions by the end of the 1940s. This had led to a downturn in independent production between 1948 and 1949. But Chemical Bank maintained what it called a "liberal policy" on loans to low-budget and medium-low-budget film producers based in the New York region who had agreements with Film Classics.[25] This included producer Louis de Rochemont, brother of Richard de Rochemont; Chemical partially funded his feature film *Lost Boundaries* (Werker, 1949). Rex Carlton now proposed a similar arrangement for the adaptation of *Enemy of the People*, with Kubrick as the director and coproducer. Carlton suggested that Kubrick incorporate his own production company and take ownership of a third of the film. He proposed a budget of approximately $150,000, with the Chemical Bank to loan around $75,000, or half of the budget. Kubrick was to raise the remaining $50,000 from a second investor (who would be repaid only after the bank had recouped its investment), and the remaining $25,000 would be through credit and deferments.[26] Carlton attempted to persuade Kubrick of the prestige of the project and how they could attract a leading Hollywood star. More important, he claimed the project would be a commercial hit:

"I think there is a wonderful chance that this picture will make a lot of profit. The banks don't gamble and your second money people will receive their original investment immediately after the bank."[27] Kubrick didn't agree to the deal, and a year later Laurel Films had collapsed following bankruptcy.[28]

The financial situation for independent producers was improving by the time Kubrick had made the decision to transition from photography to film producing in late 1949 and early 1950. In fact, according to industry sources quoted in *Variety* there had been a 25 percent increase in independent production by September 1949, with the main source of financing coming from wealthy private donors who were seemingly "attracted by the glamor of Hollywood, as well as by the chance of making a few more bucks."[29] As discussed in chapters 2 and 3, this was a particularly important context for how Kubrick funded his own projects in the early 1950s.

Also important to Kubrick's transition was his growing (though still limited) cultural network, the vital source of industry contacts—or sponsors—including producers, financiers, and distributors, who had access to the resources he needed in order to make his films and to progress his career. The increase in independent production in the early 1950s meant that many more producers were basing themselves outside of Los Angeles, with New York City becoming a fertile ground for independent producers wanting to shoot cheaply on its streets or as a site to base their production companies. Kubrick was now coming into contact with these individuals. As noted above, it is more than likely that Rex Carlton approached Kubrick through the mutual contact of the de Rochemont brothers. In turn, Kubrick had been introduced to the de Rochemonts through Alex Singer. Kubrick's career at *Look* magazine had also brought him into contact with a range of important filmmaking associates. This included Walker Evans and Helen Levitt.[30] The latter may even have contributed to Kubrick's desire to transition to filmmaking. Levitt worked on a series of independent films in the late 1940s, including collaborating with Janice Loeb and James Agee on two-reeler documentary *In the Street* (1948). The black-and-white silent film was shot in East Harlem and was based heavily on Levitt's own street photography, surreptitiously capturing New York street life. The importance of this New York–based cultural network to Kubrick's career development is apparent when noting that James Agee, a close collaborator of Levitt's, would serve as the screenwriter to Richard de Rochemont's *Mr. Lincoln* project in 1952, a project that Kubrick was also involved with (see chapter 2). The cultural connections of New York and its growing independent filmmaking scene were therefore of crucial importance to Kubrick's transitioning. Without this citywide network, it is arguable that he would have struggled to successfully make the transition. Indeed, the use of cultural networks and industrial sponsors was vital for Kubrick's survival in the film industry, right through to the end of the 1950s.

As for the commercial conditions that facilitated Kubrick's transition from photography to filmmaking, they centered on the documentary newsreel, epitomized by "The March of Time" series launched in 1935. The series was a successful form of screen journalism that revolutionized the form. Specifically, it crafted an approach in which "the questions of factual reportage and filmed re-enactment had to be answered not only in terms of *content* but also ... in terms of style."[31] Rather than merely recounting facts, the series experimented with drama, form, and content and inspired competition from other companies, not least RKO-Pathé and its "This Is America" series launched in 1942. By the time the United States had entered World War II, the genre was reaching estimated audiences of twenty million people each week.[32] The format maintained a steady popularity until the late 1940s and briefly the early 1950s, before television began to offer alternatives to the newsreel medium. Still the genre remained viable as a means for independent producers to enter commercial filmmaking and would have appeared lucrative to Kubrick, who was, after all, working in the equivalent genre within the print industry, the photo magazine.[33] This is not to say he wanted to work in documentary, but rather it was a means in which to begin working in the audiovisual medium and to prove his worth as a director and producer.

The final condition crucial to Kubrick's career transition was his family connections. His father Jack clearly wanted him to have a successful career, initially utilizing his own alumni contacts to attempt to enroll him at New York University, despite Kubrick not having the appropriate qualifications. But since it was obvious that Kubrick did not want to pursue an academic career, Jack instead supported his son's efforts to develop a career in the film industry and had the financial collateral with which to back him. This would be vital in the production of his first film, the short *Day of the Fight*.

Day of the Fight

Kubrick's first production was *Day of the Fight*, released in 1951. The documentary—the term is used loosely, as many of the scenes were staged—was an adaptation of sorts of Kubrick's photo story "Prizefighter" published in the January 18, 1949, issue of *Look* magazine.[34] The film documented a middleweight fight between the boxers Walter Cartier and Bobby James that took place on April 17, 1950. The film centers on Cartier and his routine in the days and hours leading up to the fight and on his relationship with his twin brother, Vincent, who helps him in his preparations.

The development of *Day of the Fight* possibly commenced as early as December 1949, when Kubrick devised a shooting schedule and wrote an outline for the film, and Alex Singer, who worked as Kubrick's assistant director, storyboarded the film.[35] The aim was for a five-day shoot.[36] Kubrick's outline focused on the dressing room scenes, as Cartier prepares to enter the boxing ring at Laurel Gardens Sports Arena in Newark, New Jersey. These scenes had to show Cartier in the dressing room two hours before the fight getting dressed, with the accompanying storyboards detailing the close-ups and establishing shots that were required. But in this draft form, Kubrick gave serious consideration to filming the dressing room scenes at a boxing camp at Greenwood Lake.

Located just outside of Warwick, New York, Greenwood Lake was used by many boxing champions as a training ground prior to major fights. This included Rocky Graziano, a boxer whom Kubrick had frequently photographed for *Look* magazine and someone he wanted to feature in *Day of the Fight*. The aim was to show Cartier sparring with Graziano. But Kubrick was put off filming in Greenwood Lake for several logistical reasons, not least the need to transfer the entire cast and crew from Newark to Greenwood at considerable cost. Kubrick was weighing up artistic desire against financial reality. He detailed the problems of shooting at Greenwood Lake in a draft shooting schedule, devising three categories of problems: props, actors, and equipment.[37] Props included trunks, gloves, and other items of boxing clothing for the shoot. The actors involved would include not only Cartier, but Graziano and two other men to participate in the training. Kubrick sensed the complexity of the logistics, including the need to locate a day in which all the actors were free to travel to Greenwood Lake. As for equipment, Kubrick needed to ensure he and Singer had enough rolls of film, along with appropriate lighting, extension cords, fuses, bulbs, and bulb outlets. Moving the production out of Newark would prove far too costly if Kubrick was to keep his budget down to around $3,500.

Kubrick's approach to producing *Day of the Fight* was very much hands-on, undertaking most of the roles himself, from directing and producing to sound recording and photography. He was assisted on the latter by Singer, the only other crew member, with the pair using two rented Eymo cameras for the boxing scenes. A total of four cameras were rented from the Camera Equipment Company throughout the course of the production. But despite the small crew size, the final production costs came to $3,896.41, nearly $400 over the planned budget.[38]

A version of *Day of the Fight* was most likely completed by July 1950, if not earlier, and was submitted to Richard de Rochemont's "The March of Time" series in August of that year. Kubrick's intention was to sell the film and make a profit.[39] De Rochemont gave the film considered attention but rejected it on August 31, 1950, deeming it theatrically unattractive.[40] De Rochemont's production assistant, Thomas Orchard, wrote to Kubrick to explain that de Rochemont had considered ways to make the film more attractive for the series but that "the surgery we suggested for the end won't quite do the trick—at least that's the word Mr. de Rochemont gave me after returning from Columbia this afternoon."[41] Rather than purchase the film for "The March of Time," de Rochemont attempted to sell it to Columbia; this was a studio that his brother, Louis, had signed an exclusive contract with in January 1950 to produce feature fiction, documentary films, and educational shorts based on material adapted from *Reader's Digest*.[42] It may well have been that de Rochemont had approached his brother to see whether he was interested in *Day of the Fight*.

It is not clear why de Rochemont believed *Day of the Fight* to be commercially unviable for "The March of Time" series. The series was still going strong and would not cease operation until a year later in July/August 1951.[43] Whatever the circumstances, *Day of the Fight* in the form it was presented to de Rochemont in August 1950 was rejected. But the producer was impressed by Kubrick's ambition and what he had achieved with his first ever film. De Rochemont advised Kubrick to remain in contact, with the hope that he could offer him work soon that might be of interest to him.[44]

Kubrick next turned to RKO-Pathé and its vice president of non-newsreel production, Jay Bonafield. RKO-Pathé was largely focused on short subjects for its "This Is America" and "Sportscopes" series, but also began feature filmmaking in the late 1940s. Bonafield was instrumental in this regard, steering the company toward greater production within New York, further building on the city's growing independent filmmaking scene. Bonafield had produced the company's first feature, the crime film *The Tattooed Stranger* (Montagne, 1949), which had been shot entirely in New York for just over $124,000.[45] The company owned a studio in East Harlem, on 106th Street and Park Avenue, sharing the overhead with NBC Television to reduce production costs.[46] The modest success of *The Tattooed Stranger* led Bonafield to initiate a two-a-year feature film production strategy for the company, with all films to be shot in New York.[47]

RKO-Pathé offered to purchase *Day of the Fight* from Kubrick sometime in the early autumn of 1950, at a cost of $4,000.[48] Once the production costs had been covered, Kubrick was left with $103.59 profit, of which he received only 50 percent—hardly the financial reward he had assumed filmmaking could offer. But RKO-Pathé's offer came with a caveat: the film had to be recut to fit the company's "This Is America" series. It is important to clarify that *Day of the Fight* as presented to de Rochemont in August 1950 was most likely different from the eventual released version put out by RKO-Pathé. In agreeing to the deal, Kubrick presumably lost a degree of creative autonomy of *Day of the Fight*, with RKO-Pathé revising it to conform to the stylistic conventions and "house style" of the "This Is America" series.[49] The voice-over narration was most probably added as part of the revision process. But *Day of the Fight* differed from other short films in the "This Is America" series; whereas the narration for *Day of the Fight* was provided by Douglas Edwards, the majority were narrated by Dwight Weist (the exception being *Lone Star Roundup*, narrated by Bob Hite). While it cannot be confirmed, it may be that Kubrick pushed for the option to choose his own narrator rather than use RKO-Pathé's in-house one.

In addition to the narration, a film soundtrack was also added. Gerald Fried was chosen by Kubrick to compose the film's score (again, suggesting he managed to retain an element of creative autonomy), and when recollecting his experiences of working on *Day of the Fight*, Fried confirms that he was contracted to RKO-Pathé and that the recording took place in their studio on Park Avenue.

Fried had around five months to work on the soundtrack, which would suggest that it needed to be ready by March 1951 at the latest, in time for the film's premiere the following month.[50]

The film was also expanded by RKO-Pathé to include a brief prologue detailing the history of boxing. Whereas most versions of the film presented today run to around about twelve minutes, the version screened in cinemas in the 1950s ran to just over sixteen minutes.[51] More importantly, and perhaps to Kubrick's frustration given the work he had put into the film, the latter version had a shared producing credit given to Bonafield. In contrast, the twelve-minute version of the film—potentially the version Kubrick had submitted to de Rochemont—lists only Kubrick as a producer and labels the film as being "A Stanley Kubrick Production."

Under its "This Is America" series, RKO-Pathé released an average of thirteen short films a year, with a focus on small-town America and an underlying theme of patriotism and wholesome family values.[52] There were a total of nine series, commencing in 1942 through to its closure in 1951. *Day of the Fight* was the eighth release of the final series. By April 26, 1951, the film was finally ready for release, some fourteen months since Kubrick had commenced development. It premiered as part of a package with RKO Radio Pictures' Robert Mitchum and Ava Gardner feature *My Forbidden Past* (Stevenson, 1951) in New York.

The production of *Day of the Fight* demonstrates how Kubrick was facing the financial realities of the industry into which he was transitioning. If his intention had been, as he indicated, to make a substantial profit, he instead made next to nothing. And he was faced with the need to compromise and negotiate with a range of external stakeholders who could interfere with his creative autonomy. What he did achieve though was the opportunity to make another short documentary.

Flying Padre

Kubrick's second film, *Flying Padre*, was made in the months following *Day of the Fight*'s purchase from RKO-Pathé, between October 1950 and January 1951. Once again it was based on a *Look* photo article, but this time one photographed by a colleague, George Heyer. Titled "Flying Priest" and published in October 1946, the article documented the life of Father Fred Stadtmueller, the titular flying priest. Stadtmueller's parish was the rural St. Joseph's in Mosquero, New Mexico, though he also served the El Carrizo community. In order to travel around the vast area to deliver communion, baptisms, weddings, and funerals, Stadtmueller would fly a plane, the so-called Spirit of St. Josephs.

Kubrick reached out to Stadtmueller in the early autumn of 1950 to explain his idea. It left Stadtmueller somewhat taken aback—"shocked" is how he described his reaction in a letter to Kubrick—as he merely thought Kubrick wanted to follow up on Heyer's 1946 article with more photographs.[53] But he was enthusiastic about the prospect of making a film and provided Kubrick with details of the churches he would be visiting throughout Harding County, New Mexico, in October 1950, including Genova, Gallegos, Sabinoso, Barney, and Hayden. He also offered Kubrick accommodations while making the film, allowing him to reduce his production costs.

On October 5, 1950, a deal between Kubrick and RKO-Pathé was finalized for him to shoot a "one reel short subject on the activities of a priest in New Mexico who flies his own plane to visit and aid the members of his parish."[54] Kubrick had suggested the idea for *Flying Padre* to RKO-Pathé and probably selected the *Look* story as the basis of adaptation due to his own overriding interest in aviation, along with the added need to produce a film that would "inform and entertain."[55] The film would be produced for the "Screenliners" series produced by Burton Benjamin (later to become vice president of CBS News). The series was eclectic in its range of topics, but all were mostly one-reeler documentaries, in contrast to how "Sportscope" and "This Is America" could be two-reelers.

The deal with RKO-Pathé left Kubrick with little producing control. Jay Bonafield set out the conditions of Kubrick's employment. Kubrick was to provide RKO-Pathé a rough cut of the picture.[56] If the rough cut was deemed acceptable, Kubrick would receive a fee of $1,500 for worldwide rights. The final cut of the film would then be supervised by Burton Benjamin, with no input from Kubrick. The initial outlay for the production costs had to be picked up by Kubrick, though he did receive a $1,000 advance. However, should the rough cut of the film be rejected, Kubrick had to repay $625 of the advance. The only cost RKO-Pathé would assume was for laboratory expenses, provided Kubrick used their facilities in New York. Finally, the only on-screen credit Kubrick would receive was director, despite the fact he was picking up a lot of the producing work, including arranging consent forms for all participants in the film.

Kubrick's evolving producing style and the way he was approaching negotiations on *Flying Padre* are apparent from archival correspondence. Take the tone, for example, of his letters to the Camera Equipment Company in October 1950. The Eymo camera he had rented from the company had malfunctioned, leading Kubrick to complain about the inconvenience and expense this had caused his production, including a detour to Los Angeles to collect a new camera. It is not clear whether Kubrick attempted to negotiate for a refund on the faulty equipment, but the tone of his letter suggested that this was something he expected.[57]

More intriguing, however, is the working relationship he developed with Stadtmueller. Kubrick wrote a contract of agreement for Stadtmueller in October 1950, in which he agreed to pay him 10 percent of the net profits of any sale of *Flying Padre*. Presumably, this would be a share of the $1,500 that RKO-Pathé had agreed they would pay Kubrick should they approve the rough cut. Why Kubrick should have agreed to share 10 percent of this fee with Stadtmueller is unclear.[58] The agreement caused considerable conflict when Kubrick later reneged on the arrangement. Kubrick's poor management of the *Flying Padre* budget, which led to a slight profit loss against the overall production costs, meant he was not able to share the proceeds of the fee. Stadtmueller reacted angrily on hearing this news and blamed Kubrick's mismanagement of the *Flying Padre* production: "The way you managed things I do not doubt that you lost part of your shirt on [*Flying Padre*]. BUT you signed a little paper saying you would provide me a copy of the sale contract and an itemized breakdown of the expenses involved."[59] Stadtmueller believed Kubrick was being disingenuous in his claims that there would be greater recompense to the church from the publicity that the film would bring.

Stadtmueller lodged an official complaint about Kubrick's behavior with RKO-Pathé and demanded that he receive a complimentary copy of the film in lieu of the fee promised to him. Stadtmueller felt that Kubrick had somehow taken away any kind of creative input he could have had on the documentary, requesting that he be allowed to preview the narration of the film before it was released. His complaint concluded that Kubrick was unfit to work for a company like RKO-Pathé and that he should be dismissed, saying that he could not be "depended upon to get everything straight and a company like RKO should not take a chance on being embarrassed."[60]

Stadtmueller clearly thought Kubrick had somehow double-crossed him in order to make the film. However, it was much more likely that Kubrick, once again, had been overambitious in his production plans and in devising a budget. The final production costs came to $1,673.79, with Kubrick again operating at a loss.[61] How Kubrick was covering his costs at this stage isn't clear. He may still have been receiving backing from his father. There may also have been further fees paid to Kubrick by RKO-Pathé, including a suggestion that they would pay him for the further rights to screen *Day of the Fight* in the "Sportscope" series, not just the "This Is America" series, for a total of $3,000.[62]

Flying Padre premiered on March 23, 1951 and, despite being produced after *Day of the Fight*, became Kubrick's first official and professional film release. It received good reviews and was described as "interesting and informative."[63] But Kubrick had worked for over a year in filmmaking and perhaps sensed he needed to take a more proactive approach in the way he promoted both his films and himself to gain a foothold in the industry. He was interviewed in January 1951, prior to the release of both *Day of the Fight* and *Flying Padre*, by Thomas Pryor of the *New York Times*. The article was vital in the creation of a mythology, as it were, about Kubrick's producing ability. Titled "Young Man with Ideas and a Camera," the piece positioned Kubrick as someone different from the usual Hollywood player, describing him as "no ordinary tyro" and "an adventuresome young man."[64] Kubrick provided Pryor with detailed biographical information, commencing with his time at *Look* and talking up his abilities as a photographer.

Kubrick stressed his own importance in producing the short films and the number of crew roles that he undertook. He also exaggerated the price for which the short films were purchased for distribution.

Kubrick was setting out a portrait of how he wanted to be seen in the industry, describing his maverick producing style and his ambitious personality, including his "determination to make a name for himself in the movie world."[65] It was a construct, positioning himself as the author of not only his own films but his own career. By allowing himself to be interviewed by Pryor—it is likely that Kubrick had approached Pryor for the interview—he clearly sensed how he could frame his persona within the wider industry and sell himself to Hollywood. But at the same time, we also see Kubrick announcing, indeed even setting the boundaries of his creative autonomy. Kubrick told Pryor about a new project he would direct and produce, an untitled fiction feature that would become *Fear and Desire*. Kubrick explained that even though he would be forced to hire a professional cinematographer (Kubrick was not a union photographer) the camera man would be required to "agree in advance to follow the blueprint" laid out by him.[66] In commencing the next transition of his career, from documentary shorts to fiction features, Kubrick was clear that he would maintain control of all aspects of production.

Conclusion

The year 1950 was pivotal in Kubrick's career. It was a transitional moment in which he made a gamble in leaving the stability of *Look* magazine to commence a career in filmmaking. And while the evidence suggests the move did not pay off financially in the way that he had perhaps hoped, he had gained something much more important in the process: cultural cachet and industrial contacts. The most important of these was Richard de Rochemont, who was as integral as Kirk Douglas and James B. Harris in terms of sponsoring Kubrick's career and who would play a vital role in the next two years, as discussed in chapter 2.

The industrial conditions that had allowed Kubrick to make the transition had largely been the continuing tradition of the documentary newsreel short. And while Kubrick may not have necessarily wanted to work in the medium, it was a way of displaying his range of filmmaking talents, directing, writing, editing, and producing. The latter was the most important, as it became clear that Kubrick was able to negotiate and to bring together talent to help develop his films. But he had a desire to work in fiction. This is evident not only in the interview with Thomas Pryor, in which he announced his first fiction feature, but also in the fact that he had been collaborating with the likes of Alex Singer on ways of producing a fiction film, including a potential adaptation of *The Iliad*, throughout the late 1940s.[67]

Within months of the release of *Flying Padre* and *Day of the Fight*, the documentary newsreel short was facing an existential crisis. De Rochemont's "The

March of Time" series was shut down in July 1951, followed by RKO Pathé's "This Is America" in the autumn of 1951. Kubrick had been fortunate to exploit the genre at the time that he did. By the end of 1951, documentary short producers like de Rochemont and Burton Benjamin were looking to work in the television documentary format. As we shall now see, this would be a realm that Kubrick would soon find himself being pushed to work in, despite his leanings toward fiction.

2

The Unknown Early Years, 1951-1953

● ● ● ● ● ● ● ● ● ● ● ● ● ● ● ● ● ● ● ●

In February 1951, Stanley Kubrick took to the San Gabriel Mountains in the north of Los Angeles County. He was producing his first feature film, what become known as *Fear and Desire*. The project was privately financed and involved Kubrick producing what has since been described as the first "entirely independent American art film in the decade after World War II."[1] This is a bold claim; Kubrick's film was certainly ambitious and displayed an art-house sensibility, largely a result of its low budget and guerilla production methods. But as will be examined in both this chapter and chapter 3, *Fear and Desire*, along with Kubrick's subsequent feature, *Killer's Kiss* (1955), can be seen within wider industrial, cultural, and production contexts and trends of the late 1940s and early 1950s.

I would suggest that we need to "de-center" Kubrick from these early films and view them on their own terms, rather than with any kind of reference to Kubrick's later work. Instead, *Fear and Desire* should be located within the broader narrative of Kubrick's continuing and precarious transition from his career at *Look* into the film industry. After all, little is really known about how Kubrick developed between the production of *Fear and Desire* in 1951 and the production of *Killer's Kiss* in the autumn of 1953. This approximately thirty-month period can be approached almost as the "dark ages" of Kubrick's career; there is limited archival evidence available related to the period, while Kubrick himself did everything he could to suppress the history of these years from being publicly available. This included a lack of enthusiasm in discussing *Fear and Desire* or the third short film he was hired to direct, *The Seafarers* (1953).

This chapter explores these unknown early years as Kubrick made the second and arguably more hazardous transition from short documentary filmmaker to feature film producer and director. The archival evidence that is available shows the extent of the complicated narrative of this period and how Kubrick was moving between projects with no obvious career plan. Focus is given to his relationship with producer Richard de Rochemont, the man who turned down *Day of the Fight*. De Rochemont provided Kubrick with several working opportunities during this period, including as an assistant director on *Mr. Lincoln* (1952) and in some capacity for an informational documentary, *World Youth Assembly* (1952). In addition, de Rochemont contributed financing to *Fear and Desire*.

The period between 1951 and 1953 is also crucial to understanding Kubrick's developing creativity and ambition in terms of the kind of material he wanted to produce and how he turned his hand to screenwriting. Kubrick was busy developing ideas, forming his understanding of what constituted a good story, and his approach to cinema as a business and profit-making industry. During this time, Kubrick filled notebooks with outlines and treatments as well as brief sketches of his thoughts on the film industry. He was also potentially making himself available to work for hire on the projects of other directors and producers. The chapter concludes on the release of *Fear and Desire* via the art-house distributor Joseph Burstyn. By the end of the chapter, we shall see the extent to which Kubrick had become creatively engaged during this two-and-a-half-year period, while also fully aware of his ontological status as a "filmmaker" three years after leaving his secure employment at *Look* magazine.

Producing Ambition: *Fear and Desire*

Whether Kubrick had always harbored an ambition to produce a feature-length picture or whether it grew out of his experience working on short films is unclear. Certainly, there were indications, perhaps even as early as the late 1940s, that Kubrick was interested in producing fiction films.[2] He was surrounded by creative individuals throughout his teenage and twentysomething years, with Taft High School seemingly a key site of cultural ambition, churning out a core group of friends who dreamed of success in the creative industries, particularly Hollywood. The group included, among others, Paul Mazursky, Alexander Singer, Howard Sackler, Gerald Fried, Toba Metz, and, of course, Kubrick. Metz and Kubrick would marry in 1947 and moved to Greenwich Village, along with the other members of the group. It was in the bohemian surroundings of the Village that they whiled away their days talking about their dreams and ambitions. Most of them were unemployed, except for Kubrick and Fried. As such, the group were in awe of Kubrick due to his substantial income and status as a staff photographer at *Look*. But Kubrick too indulged in the sharing of lofty dreams, including his conviction that he wanted to become a major Hollywood filmmaker someday.[3]

The circle in which Kubrick operated also brought him into contact with a wide variety of artists and intellectuals. This included Hans Richter, a German Dadaist, painter, and film theorist who, upon moving to the United States, took up a teaching position at the City College of New York (CCNY) and ran the Institute of Film Techniques. Kubrick had taken some evening classes at CCNY after leaving William Taft High that would have brought him into contact with Richter. Indeed, Kubrick makes a brief appearance in Richter's low-budget experimental feature film *Dreams That Money Can Buy* (1947), alongside Toba Metz. The film was a collaboration between Richter and other "leading twentieth century artists comprising: Max Ernst, Man Ray, Marcel Duchamp, Fernand Leger, and Alexander Calder."[4] The film was shot mostly on location in New York on a budget of $15,000 and utilized some of Richter's own property in order to save on costs. It explored psychological themes through a series of dream sequences. Such ideas were a core aspect of the way in which Richter and the film's producer, Kenneth Macpherson, approached filmmaking, both heavily influenced by Freud and psychoanalytic theory.[5] However, the primary importance of *Dreams That Money Can Buy* for Kubrick was as a potential "early introduction to contemporary, independent low-budget filmmaking outside of the studio system."[6]

The influence of *Dreams That Money Can Buy* and of the broader intellectual milieu of Greenwich Village on Kubrick is to some extent reflected in his notes from the period. By 1950, he was exhibiting a philosophy that placed him in opposition to the trends of mainstream Hollywood film producing, expressing plans to his friends about a desire to "revivify the motion picture medium."[7] Kubrick's plans seemed to include a desire to "antagonize" the established mode of production and to take full autonomy of his own work, producing films for mainstream studios but on his own terms. He was cautioned by some friends that he was being overly ambitious and that it would perhaps serve him well to contain his "bombastic energy" until he was established within the industry. Kubrick's prevailing attitude and ambition seems to have been one of criticizing Hollywood and the quality of filmmaking, believing he could do much better.[8]

Kubrick's plan was to produce a war film, *The Trap*, on a budget of $50,000, to be financed primarily by his uncle Martin Perveler. As he described it in an interview to the *New York Times*, the film was "about 4 soldiers in a battle who are trapped behind enemy lines. He describes his drama as 'a study of four men and their search for the meaning to life and the individual's responsibility to the group.'"[9] The eventual screenplay, renamed *Shape of Fear*, was credited to Howard Sackler (1929–1982), a New York–based poet. Sackler had attended William Taft High and, like Kubrick, had contributed to the school's literary magazine, the *Taft Review*. By the late 1940s, Sackler was contributing reviews and poetry to major periodicals, including *Commentary*, a magazine described by Nathan Abrams as "the premier post-war journal of Jewish affairs."[10] By November 1950,

Sackler was a confirmed published writer when his poem "E.A. Poe" appeared in *Commentary*.[11]

Fear and Desire was probably written sometime in 1950, maybe after the completion of the first version of *Day of the Fight*. Vincent LoBrutto recounts an anecdote that Kubrick had apparently offered Richard de Rochemont a copy of a lengthy screenplay that he worked on with Howard Sackler.[12] There is no date ascribed to this event, only that it took place in 1950. It could have been that, following de Rochemont's rejection of *Day of the Fight* but his promise that he hoped to soon have a project of interest for him, Kubrick finalized a draft of the screenplay. There is certainly a gap, as it were, in the narrative of Kubrick's career between August and October 1950, when RKO-Pathé bought *Day of the Fight* and commissioned *Flying Padre*. Kubrick could have feasibly worked on the screenplay during this period. Whatever the circumstances, it was clearly ready by the beginning of 1951 when Kubrick finally turned to his uncle for financing.

One further indication that the screenplay was being completed in the late summer of 1950 is the evidence that Kubrick was consuming a number of Joseph Conrad novels at the time, as shown in correspondence he was writing in June and August of that year.[13] He does not specify at this time if he read Conrad's *Heart of Darkness* (1899), a book that would heavily influence *Fear and Desire*, but it is plausible, particularly given that a friend urges Kubrick to "go into the street and gather up all the Conrad you have read and not read . . . read and reread . . . shudder and marvel and wonder."[14] *Fear and Desire* is replete with references to *Heart of Darkness*. The film is about a group of soldiers trapped behind enemy lines who must travel along a river in order to return to their own battalion, but in the process make a diversion to kill an enemy general. Along the journey, the soldiers gradually descend into barbaric behavior, including the apprehension of a young girl whom they tie to a tree. The film's allegorical themes are explicit in echoing those of *Heart of Darkness*, not least the absurdity of evil and what James Naremore terms "self-destructive human drives."[15]

Kubrick took the decision to relocate the production of *Fear and Desire* from New York to California. This was despite the fact that he received an offer to shoot the film on wooded land in New York belonging to John T. Gwynne, assistant to the executive secretary of the New York Chamber of Commerce.[16] Such an offer reflects the ongoing connections that Kubrick was forging among cultural, commercial, and industrial networks. But Kubrick turned down the offer. The decision was pragmatic in two ways: First, the film was being bankrolled primarily by his uncle, Martin Perveler, who lived in Burbank, not far from the San Gabriel Mountains. Such proximity between the location of the production and the film's source of financing ensured Kubrick would be able to keep in close contact with his uncle should more money be needed. And second, Perveler was given an associate producer credit and, while he was not involved in the film's creative decisions, presumably could have influenced Kubrick to shoot the film on his doorstep in California so that he in turn could keep an eye on his investment.

Kubrick's proximity to the spiritual home of the American film industry—Los Angeles—did not go unnoticed in the press. Presumably Kubrick had approached New York–based publications about his production in a bid to promote both the film and himself. The news stories about Kubrick from between 1950 and 1951 were suggesting that he was locating *Fear and Desire* "within the mainstream of America," while emphasizing his "desire to be in control of his films with the ambition to make it in Hollywood."[17] The most interesting of these press stories is one from the *New York Journal-American*, which compares Kubrick's persona, along with his decision to produce *Fear and Desire* in California, to independent Hollywood producer Sam Goldwyn.[18]

Kubrick seems to have been inhabiting two cultural worlds. The first involved him promoting his own image as a future Hollywood producer; it's not hard to imagine that Kubrick himself raised the comparison to Goldwyn. It was a comparison that probably proved irresistible: Goldwyn was a business and creative maverick, responsible for cofounding two of Hollywood's major studios, Paramount and MGM, and for exhibiting demonstrable levels of creative and business control as an independent producer from the 1920s onward. But Kubrick inhabited a second cultural world, producing work that exhibited the art-house aesthetic of the New York independents he was living and working with: *Fear and Desire* was indebted to the theoretical and stylistic approach of Hans Richter and the Institute of Film Techniques, not least the eventual Soviet montage editing Kubrick used on the film. By filming in California, on the periphery of Los Angeles, Kubrick was showing how he wanted to be close to the commercial center of the American film industry, but at the same time how he wanted to remain outside of the mainstream in order to do things his own way and to have control of how his films were produced.

This duality of producing personas arguably resulted in *Fear and Desire* possessing a crossover of styles, both exploitation and art house.[19] There are moments of high art and pretentious style in the film, particularly Kubrick's use of montage and lengthy scenes of philosophical dialogue. But Kubrick offers the viewer moments of extreme gratuitousness and violence, what Naremore has placed within the tradition of the "aesthetics of the grotesque,"[20] but which more probably belong to the notion of exploitation. I. Q. Hunter describes exploitation as "a film that is blatantly gratuitous, prurient and very definitely *not* art."[21] And certainly *Fear and Desire* contains many moments that are explicitly gratuitous, most obvious being the storyline of the girl (Virginia Leith) tied to the tree. The girl is taunted by Sidney (Paul Mazursky), who licks her hand in a moment of almost sexual sadism.

Even the film's title speaks to its exploitation potential, most likely renamed by its eventual distributor Joseph Burstyn. *Fear and Desire* evokes sexuality, male fantasy, and of course sexual "desire," similar to other exploitation films of the era: *So Young, So Bad* (Vorhaus, 1950), *Racket Girls* (Dertano, 1951), *Girls in Prison* (Cahn, 1956), *Girls on the Loose* (Henreid, 1958), and *The Flesh Merchant* (Connell, 1956). Kubrick may well have been aware of the commercial and production contexts in which he was working: a low-budget film production, but a desire to appeal to a more commercial audience than the narrowness of art-house. We know that Kubrick believed in cinema as a commercial medium more than anything, even at this early stage in his career. In notes Kubrick wrote sometime in 1951 or 1952, he argued that cinema was a mass medium that could reach more people globally than any other form, bar radio. He also complained of the snobbery of some filmmakers and their refusal to watch commercial films, arguing that those who only liked foreign films displayed an art-house patron smugness.[22] So while Kubrick was circulating in a climate of bohemian creativity in Greenwich Village that leaned toward experimental and avant-garde cinema, as espoused by Hans Richter, and which showed itself in some of the ways Kubrick produced *Fear and Desire*, he was also clearly drawn to producing films for more mainstream audiences and that had greater commercial potential.

Fear and Desire was initially budgeted at approximately $10,000, with Kubrick entering a contractual agreement with his uncle to obtain the financing.[23] But the costs would escalate, not least because the decision to film in California meant that Kubrick had to relocate the predominantly New York–based cast and crew to the state. Still, he could potentially rely on deferring the salary of the crew, many of whom were his friends, such as Steve Hahn (unit manager), Robert Dierks (assistant director), Chet Fabian (makeup), and Herbert Lebowitz (art direction), while his wife, Toba Metz, provided administrative support and acted as the dialogue director.[24] The cast, largely unknown, also included friends and collaborators from Greenwich Village, such as Paul Mazursky. For all of them, this was their first substantial feature-film acting experience.

The small scale of the crew, and the inexperience of the cast, meant that a lot of the production depended on Kubrick as the producer and director to guide his collaborators and to ensure the project was brought in on budget. Those who worked on the film described Kubrick's overpowering sense of ambition and determination, including Paul Mazursky, who recalls that when they needed more cash, Kubrick would visit his uncle in Los Angeles: "So we drove down from the mountains—Frank Silvera and myself, and Stanley driving. And on the way down Stanley was telling us he was going to get 5,000 bucks out of his uncle, and he was so determined that he spat at the windshield. I had never seen anything like it. I was 21 years old and Stanley was about 23, and I had never seen a guy that age with that kind of determination. And he got the 5,000 bucks out of his uncle."[25] Kubrick would later boast that the film was brought in *under* budget—to some extent, this was true as the production costs came to approximately $5,000—but the budget itself would balloon due to the cost of postproduction. Kubrick made the decision to postsynch the sound and dialogue, and while this initially lowered the production costs, it ultimately contributed to the overall budget expanding to over $50,000.[26] This included the need to loop the dialogue in a recording studio in New York a year after the film had finished shooting.[27] The exponential increase in the budget required Kubrick to seek completion funding and to try to find a distributor that would purchase the film and cover the remaining costs and, hopefully, ensure a profit. In addition, Kubrick approached Richard de Rochemont to request financial assistance in covering some aspects of the postproduction costs.[28] Kubrick most probably approached de Rochemont given that he was being hired by the producer to work on a number of projects between 1951 and 1952, as discussed below.

Kubrick was officially credited as *Fear and Desire*'s producer, as well as having directed, photographed, and edited the film. In a statement to accompany the promotion of the film, Kubrick wrote, "The entire crew . . . consisted of myself as director, lighting, cameraman, operator, administrator, make-up man, wardrobe, hairdresser, prop man, unit chauffeur, et cetera."[29] While the statement later briefly mentions the assistance of friends and his wife, Kubrick was clearly positioning himself as an all-controlling producer, in command of all creative and business aspects of his film. This was the point of *Fear and Desire* and the way Kubrick approached producing it: it was a means of self-promotion toward accessing the approval of mainstream Hollywood and to validate his status within the industry. At the same time, it was about projecting control, placing himself at the center of everything that occurred on his production, in order to further obtain and maintain control on future productions.

Such self-promotion was integral to Kubrick's producing approach if he was to sell *Fear and Desire*. It wasn't until 1952 that he began to reach out to major studios to try to interest them in the film, but all those he approached turned it down.[30] Kubrick probably knew how improbable it was that the major studios would buy *Fear and Desire*, but it showed his determination to break into Hollywood. He was also aware of the precarious financial situation he now found himself. He spoke of his anxieties about the situation in a letter he sent to Mark Van Doren, a professor of literature at Columbia University. He had obligations to a variety of financiers, including his uncle, and so he needed to sell the picture as soon as possible. Kubrick was requesting that Van Doren review the film and, in the process, admitted that "I would not be overstating matters if I said that upon the financial outcome at the box office rests my chance for ever again being in a position to make another film."[31] In writing to Van Doren, Kubrick confessed that he realized now that making a feature film was far too costly, particularly without the backing of a major Hollywood studio. While Kubrick's anxieties were not without cause, he may have been overstating the case to Van Doren in order to pressure him into writing a positive review of the film, which Kubrick had screened for him. At the same time, Kubrick was also candid in assessing the quality of the film; once Van Doren had supplied Kubrick with a review,[32] Kubrick, almost apologetically, told the professor that the film was poor in both content and style and that he hoped he would someday get another chance to "do another film a little better and with a bit more substance."[33] Kubrick seemed resigned to the possibility that his gamble in leaving *Look* to establish a career in the film industry had not paid off and that, at best, he would have to content himself working as a documentary filmmaker and maybe even rely on work from Richard de Rochemont.

But on July 21, 1952, Kubrick submitted *Fear and Desire*, still titled *Shape of Fear*, for entry in the Venice Film Festival.[34] The film screened at the Palazzo del Cinema on August 18, 1952, and as a result Kubrick received a certificate of participation from the festival director, Antonio Petrucci. It may well have been that Kubrick submitted to the festival on the advice of Joseph Burstyn (1899–1953), potentially as a means of increasing the film's market potential in Europe.[35] Burstyn was a distributor who operated two distribution companies, Mayer and Burstyn and Joseph Burstyn Inc. The former was a cofounded company with his business partner Arthur Mayer. Both of the companies specialized in the distribution of foreign-language films and independent productions in the United States since the early 1930s, responsible for the distribution of films like *Rome, Open City* (Rossellini, 1945), *Bicycle Thieves* (De Sica, 1948), and *Umberto D.* (De Sica, 1948) as well as low-budget productions by some of Kubrick's contemporary New York producers, including the Janice Loeb–produced *The Quiet One* (Meyers, 1948) and the Morris Engel–produced *Little Fugitive* (1953). The latter film demonstrated Burstyn's means of distributing low-budget independent films. The film became an art-house hit after Burstyn had secured European distribution; he had also arranged for it to be submitted to the 1953 Venice Film Festival, where it won the Silver Lion Prize. Burstyn's distribution deal, made on a cash basis, covered *Little Fugitive*'s budget, which was approximately $50,000.[36] In the United States it played extensively at New York City's Normandie Theatre, one of the city's first art-house cinemas that opened in the 1930s. Burstyn, however, did not want *Little Fugitive* to be categorized (and commercially hampered) as an art-house picture. He was convinced that the film had popular appeal and was "substantial fare for circuit bookings."[37] Burstyn's strategy for *Little Fugitive*, and films like it, was to eschew the usual method of trade showing the film to exhibitors, instead arranging sneak previews of the film in "large key houses in various cities so that film buyers can view the film with audience reaction."[38] The venues for the previews were the Mastbaum in Philadelphia, the Roger Sherman in New Haven, the Stanley in Pittsburgh, the Allen Cleveland and Adams in Detroit. Burstyn's strategy also included advertising the film in "mass audience newspapers which rarely receive arty product space. Aim is to attract a general audience as well as the followers of arty house pictures."[39] Burstyn projected that *Little Fugitive* could gross $500,000 on circuit showings, being coupled in 1954 with *The Man Between* (1953).[40] It had already grossed $40,000 in its first four weeks at the Normandie Theatre by November 1953.

Burstyn, in contact with this New York group of independent film producers of the early 1950s, would no doubt have been aware of Kubrick. Following attempts to promote *Fear and Desire* on the European film festival circuit, whether on the advice of Burstyn, Kubrick sent a copy of the film to him on November 16, 1952. In an accompanying letter, Kubrick promoted *Fear and Desire* as a poetic drama of "'man' lost in a hostile world-deprived of material and spiritual foundations-seeking his way to an understanding of himself, and of life around him. . . . It will, probably, mean many things to different people, and it ought to."[41] The over-the-top language may have served as Kubrick's attempt at providing Burstyn with publicity copy as well as to steer and control the way in which the film was to be marketed. Soon after, Burstyn purchased the film, and it was finally released through Joseph Burstyn Inc. in March 1953.

Reflecting the film's exploitation style, *Fear and Desire* was double billed with *Savage Triangle/Le garçon sauvage* (1951) on a limited release in New York and a handful of other cities, including at the Roxy Theatre in Detroit.[42] *Boxoffice* reviewed the film under the category of "exploitips," highlighting Kubrick's guerrilla credentials and calling him a "semiprofessional."[43] As for the film, the reviewers called it a "grim, moody and depressing war drama," which was "strictly adult fare, suited only to a few key city art houses."[44] It was reviewed alongside films such as *Bad Blonde* (Le Borg, 1953), a "rag-bone-'n'-hank-o'-hair murder story" that is "tragically grim";[45] *Guerrilla Girl* (Christian, 1953), "an intensely melodramatic foreign-made picture" that will "get by as a supporting dualer";[46] and *Raiders of the Seven Seas* (Salkow, 1953), a pirate picture that is a "bloody tale of a brave buccaneer and a beautiful babe," a film that isn't "top bracket," but "boasts sufficient gore and guts to satisfy seekers of fast-moving adventure stuff."[47]

In the end, this may have been the best that Kubrick could have hoped for. The film performed poorly at the box office, and the fees received from its sale to Joseph Burstyn did not recover the costs of the production. Still, *Fear and Desire* was an early example of a growing trend within the 1950s American film industry for exploitation cinema. Such films were ever more necessary to American theaters, many of which were still presenting double bills and therefore needed "inexpensive, attention-getting fare. The demand was met by independent companies that produced cheap 'exploitation' pictures. Having no major stars or creative personnel, these films cashed in on topical or sensational subjects which could be 'exploited.'"[48] These low-budget films often returned a greater profit yield for theaters than larger budget studio films.[49]

Fear and Desire had taken three years to move from development in 1950 to production in 1951, through to distribution in 1952 and 1953. It wasn't the breakout success that Kubrick had perhaps hoped for, largely as a result of some miscalculations in the producing of the film and the ambition of the story, and he would not produce another feature film until the autumn of 1953. But following the completion of *Fear and Desire* in mid-1951, Kubrick was once again faced with no obvious route of progression within the film industry.

Stanley Kubrick and Richard de Rochemont

The intervening months between the completion of the production of *Fear and Desire* in spring 1951 and its release in spring 1953 are perhaps the least well documented of Kubrick's entire career. The archival evidence that is available is scarce and spread across a variety of sites, from the Stanley Kubrick Archive at the University of the Arts London to the Richard de Rochemont Papers at the American Heritage Centre, and additionally in archives such as the Social Welfare History Archives at the University of Minnesota. Though there is a lack of clear archival documentation about this period of Kubrick's career, this is not to suggest that Kubrick was not active. Indeed, he was clearly needing to make money and, perhaps not sure how to follow up on *Fear and Desire*, particularly as it was still uncertain when and even if the film would ever be distributed in 1951 and 1952, he further allied himself to producer Richard de Rochemont, whom he had first approached in the summer of 1950 with a rough cut of *Day of the Fight*. De Rochemont was an established industry figure and had a consistent stream of work that would ensure Kubrick could continue to work in filmmaking in some capacity, if not quite as a producer, director, or writer. Therefore, through aligning himself with de Rochemont, Kubrick—in return for some form of income—was presumably giving up significant levels of creative and business autonomy. In other words, he was working for hire.

De Rochemont, born in 1903 in Chelsea, Massachusetts, a city north of Boston on the Mystic River, was a descendant of the French Huguenot family. His upbringing was relatively affluent, and after graduating from Harvard University, he commenced a career as a print journalist.[50] He first worked at the *Boston Advertiser* before moving to the *New York Sun* in the mid-1920s.[51] But he had a desire to move into the newsreel industry, and so in 1930 he joined Fox-Movietone News, a company formed in October 1927. Fox-Movietone became the United States' premier newsreel company and was the first to utilize sound, a process demonstrated in May 1927, when the company tested its sound-on-film camera and captured the sight and sound of Charles Lindbergh's *Spirit of St. Louis* taking off from Roosevelt Field, Long Island, at what was the start of his solo transatlantic flight. De Rochemont worked as the company's foreign editor, operating out of Paris. He left Movietone in 1934 to join his elder brother Louis, who was the producer of Time Inc.'s "The March of Time" film series. He remained with "The March of Time" for the next two decades, serving first as a European correspondent until 1940, then managing director of the series in New York until 1943, and taking over the series as executive producer from 1943.[52] He ran the series for eight years until the autumn of 1951, when the series was discontinued for theater exhibition by Time Inc.[53] As a result, de Rochemont left the series to focus on independent production for film and television.

De Rochemont was clearly interested in moving into fiction filmmaking, and this may well have been one of the reasons that he developed a working relationship with Kubrick, potentially sensing a future collaborator. Initially, he contemplated producing adaptations of literary novels, including Henry James's *The Ambassadors* (1903)[54] and Auguste Bailly's *La Danseuse a la Rose* (1929).[55] The latter production, a collaboration with producer Jean Benoît-Lévy, was left unmade. But de Rochemont's career after "The March of Time" was largely in television production and as a producer of information films for organizations across the globe. He signed a deal with Transfilm, a commercial television production company, in July 1952, signaling his intent to develop in the medium in the coming years as well as demonstrating its profitability;[56] the deal was worth over half a million dollars and committed de Rochemont to produce two "topical TV programs."[57] Television was a burgeoning market, and by the end of 1952 industry insiders were predicting an exponential growth in the number of available stations, upward of sixty across the country. This presented independent television producers like de Rochemont with an opportunity to make cheap and highly profitable content.[58]

It was these industrial conditions in which Kubrick was operating in the months after the completion of *Fear and Desire*; the very fact that the television market was lucrative and that there was a need for new product meant that Kubrick could, if he wanted, find work quite easily. And in the immediate months after the discontinuation of "The March of Time," de Rochemont was arranging deals for several television projects and commissions and therefore needed creative talent who could direct or help. To that end, Kubrick was an invaluable resource for de Rochemont between 1951 and 1952, possessing proven filmmaking and photographic talent. Without any obvious route into the film industry, Kubrick kept close to de Rochemont and the opportunities that television and documentary production offered.

One such opportunity was a commission that de Rochemont received from the World Assembly of Youth (WAY) to produce a short informational film. Established in 1948 by the Cultural Relations Department of the British Foreign Office, WAY was an international organization that brought together national youth leaders and, by the 1960s, had over fifty nation members.[59] The aim was for WAY to counteract the communist domination of the World Federation of Democratic Youth, founded in 1945, and to develop youth work across the globe, in the process promoting both democracy and human rights.[60] They financed youth seminars, youth leadership conferences, and international youth meetings. But more money was needed to fund the activities of WAY, and so it turned to "private" sources, donor organizations that later turned out to be Central Intelligence Agency (CIA) fronts. The CIA provided the vast majority of WAY's finances in the 1950s and 1960s, as it did for a number of other cultural organizations "in a punch for punch response to Soviet deviousness."[61] It wasn't until the 1960s that the source of WAY's funding was exposed by the *New York Times*, in the process revealing how the CIA funded "a whole series of 'screen' foundations, the overwhelming majority of youth & student organizations, not only in the US, but throughout the free world";[62] other youth organizations that were channels for CIA funds included the International Student Conference (based in the Netherlands), the Independent Research Service (based in the United States), and the United States Youth Council.[63] Those heading the various organizations, including WAY, were unaware that their funding came from the CIA or that the private donors were in fact "conduits for funds from the CIA."[64]

World Assembly of Youth (1953), subtitled *A Report on the First Triennial General Assembly of WAY at Cornell University, Ithaca, N.Y.*, was produced by de Rochemont, directed by D. Corbitt Curtis and Richard Millett, and distributed by the "News of the Day" newsreel series.[65] "News of the Day" was produced by the Hearst Corporation, with the newsreels distributed by MGM from 1934 to 1967. The film is a bland, matter-of-fact account of the WAY General Assembly that gathered at Cornell University between August 5 and 16, 1951.[66] The Ithaca conference brought together over five hundred WAY representatives from sixty-three nations, with the aim of developing an agenda for how young people of the world could "help in making human rights a universal reality."[67] The gathering in Ithaca was seen as a major global event, attracting extensive media attention along with messages of support from President Harry Truman.[68]

Lasting just over thirty minutes, and with a voice-over by Robert Wetzel and Richard de Rochemont, *World Assembly of Youth* follows the delegates as they arrive in New York City and travel to Ithaca and the activities they take part in during the two-week assembly. It also features debates and keynote speeches, including that given by Eleanor Roosevelt. But Kubrick is not credited in the film, nor is there any available surrounding documentation that contains reference to him (see Appendix A for full credits).

Despite long-standing speculation about Kubrick's involvement in the project, there is little evidence to support this. The first reference to *World Assembly of Youth* came in John Baxter's biography *Stanley Kubrick*, in which he suggests that Kubrick was connected to a documentary, "length uncertain, made in 1952 about the World Assembly of Youth, an early attempt by the US State Department, which sponsored the film, to mobilise college-aged kids to carry out socially worthy projects, an initiative that was to have its pay-off in John Kennedy's Peace Corps."[69] Baxter's source of information was a CV that Kubrick had sent film critic Theodore Huff in February 1953, in which he claimed to have worked on "misc. television and state dept. trivia."[70] The second source is the *New York Times*. In a short piece written by A. H. Weiler in June 1952, Kubrick is credited with having produced the "*Day of the Fight*, and *Flying Padre*, short subjects released by RKO, and a short on World Assembly of Youth made for the State Department."[71] Presumably it was Kubrick who supplied Weiler with this information as a means of self-promotion. It is wholly feasible that Kubrick had intended to participate in the production.

It may well have been that Kubrick was present at the WAY General Assembly in some other, nonproduction capacity. For example, he may have worked as a still photographer. Production photographs taken on location for *World Assembly of Youth* feature various members of the crew, including Robert Daly and Richard de Rochemont, but Kubrick is not present in any of them.[72] Kubrick could well have been, therefore, the person taking the photographs, hired by de Rochemont, who would have been aware of his experience as a staff photographer at *Look*. But it could be that Kubrick was involved in an alternative production. Was he, for example, connected to the production of a radio program about the WAY General Assembly for the Department of State? In a transcript of evidence given to Congress by officers of the DoS International Information and Educational Activities in 1953, it was revealed that the DoS had a special "events team" that was dispatched around the United States to make radio programs of various categories, including "news, commentary, interviews, features and little dramatic spots."[73] One such radio program included the DoS special events team covering "the World Assembly Youth meeting."[74] It is not out of the realm of possibility that Kubrick was somehow involved in the radio program, particularly given his developing sound production skills.

Whatever the circumstances of Kubrick's involvement in the *World Assembly of Youth* project, the full details of which will most probably never be known, we can determine that Kubrick had returned to the world of documentary production following *Fear and Desire*. In fact, by 1951 he had potentially accepted that he would be working as a documentary filmmaker for the foreseeable future. In the June 1952 interview with A. H. Weiler from June 1952, he indicated how he was resigned to such a fate: "'There's no point in talking about my next picture,' he said, 'until we see how "Shape of Fear" does both critically and financially.'"[75] Kubrick was being pragmatic: given the uncertainty of his own film career and his lack of power to operate within the mainstream, he was aligning himself ever closer with Richard de Rochemont and television and documentary video work in order to receive an income and to further develop his CV.

Producing for Television

Kubrick was probably contemplating his career options by the late summer of 1952. While he had aligned himself closely to Richard de Rochemont, he was still not guaranteed work. And his frustrations about how to develop an independent film producing career were becoming obvious. In August of that year, he somewhat ambitiously attempted to purchase the motion picture rights to several Joseph Conrad stories: his first novel *Almayer's Folly* (1895), set in the Borneo jungle; *The End of the Tether* (1902), a maritime tale; and the novella *Freya of the Seven Isles* (1911).[76] He also wanted the rights to *Chance* (1913) and *Nostromo* (1904), but these were not available.[77] Kubrick had contacted the stock and royalty department of J. M. Dent and Sons about purchasing the rights. The company agreed, but on the condition that Kubrick confirmed whether there was any prospect of the stories actually being produced.[78] Kubrick could have rights to the stories for a cost of $5,000, on the presumption that he would produce a feature-length film. But he kept his plans rather vague and left J. M. Dent and Sons guessing as to the kind of agreement required. By November 3, 1952, J. M. Dent and Sons withdrew the draft option for the stories due to a lack of a response from Kubrick.[79] Presumably, Kubrick realized that any adaptation of Conrad in the near future was impossible.

At the same time, Kubrick was corresponding with producer Peter Mayer (1914–1982), initiating contact sometime in late August or early September 1952. Whether the correspondence between the two had anything to do with Kubrick's speculative Conrad adaptations is unclear. The contact with Mayer was a further indication of Kubrick's cultural network. Mayer, who lived in Mexico, was the son of Arthur Mayer (1886–1981). The latter, who became a well-respected academic and film historian in his later years, serving as an adjunct professor at Dartmouth College, was the business partner of Joseph Burstyn, with whom he had imported foreign films such as *Bicycle Thieves* and *Rome, Open City*.[80] Arthur Mayer had started out his career working for Sam Goldwyn in New York as a salesman, before moving to work for Paramount and Adolph Zukor as a celebrity publicist and as the company's head of the advertising, publicity, and promotion department.[81] He later took over the management of Paramount's Rialto Theater located in Times Square. Kubrick most probably visited the Rialto on a regular basis and therefore became an acquaintance of Mayer. This could have been how Kubrick initiated contact with Joseph Burstyn.

As for Peter Mayer, he had worked as an associate producer throughout the 1940s on low-budget features mostly released by Monogram Pictures, one of the so-called Poverty Row studios. His films often featured a group of young actors referred to as the Dead-End Kids, later adapting reworked monikers such as the Little Tough Guys, the East Side Kids, and the Bowery Boys. With this group he produced *Pride of the Bowery* (Lewis, 1941) and *Flying Wild* (West, 1941) and later low-budget features directed by John Reinhardt in Mexico such as *For You I Die* (1947), *Open Secret* (1948), and *Sofia* (1948). The latter was shot on location in Mexico as well as at Mexico City's Estudios Churubusco studios. It was subsequently released by Film Classics, the low-budget distributor that Kubrick had previously encountered via a proposed production of *Enemy of the People* in 1950 (see chapter 1).

These were the industrial contexts that Kubrick was now contemplating and wanted to know more about. Specifically, he was interested in understanding more about the production conditions of Mexico and whether it was favorable to low-budget producers. Mayer answered a series of questions that Kubrick posed to him throughout September and October 1952. In reaching out to Mayer,

Kubrick demonstrated that he was not attached to any one geographical location in terms of where he would produce his films. He was clearly willing, even at this early stage of his career, to base his productions in countries other than the United States if it was logistically feasible and allowed for lowered production costs. At the time, Mexico was an increasingly popular location in which to base U.S. productions, not least for westerns. As Mayer explained, John Wayne was eager to start filming there in late 1951 for *The Alamo*, a film that he was set to direct.[82]

Kubrick does not seem to have provided Mayer with specifics about the production he had in mind. It may have been related to one of the Conrad stories, or even to an idea he was developing in September 1952 called *Jamaica Story*.[83] Either way, Mayer encouraged Kubrick to collaborate with Mexican producers, particularly Óscar Dancigers (producer of *The Young and the Damned / Los Olvidados* [Buñuel, 1950]), who was experienced in working with American filmmakers.[84] Mayer's correspondence hints that Kubrick was thinking of filming a television pilot; this would certainly fit with the career trajectory Kubrick was on in 1952, working with de Rochemont. Mayer explained to Kubrick that, should he collaborate with Dancigers, he would need to develop more than a single pilot, as Dancigers would consider only producing a television series of over twenty episodes. Whatever the project, it also seems that Kubrick was contemplating using Frank Silvera, with passing reference made to him (Mayer remarks that Dancigers "knows Frank, has used him in two or three of his pilots and thinks highly of him").[85]

If Kubrick was seriously contemplating making a television series, it was probably a result of his connection to de Rochemont, which had made him aware of the lucrative commercial potential of the medium. He would certainly have known about the television deals that de Rochemont was making. Mayer advised that the cost of a twenty-six-minute show, featuring dancing, music, and background locations (which required a day's travel from Mexico City), would be approximately $15,000, in contrast to an estimated $25,000 production cost in the United States.[86] Kubrick seems to have given serious consideration to the project, with Mayer even offering accommodation and help with production plans.[87] However, nothing seems to have come of Kubrick's planned television project, and the correspondence with Peter Mayer ended in October 1952. Instead, Kubrick accepted another television assignment from de Rochemont in the autumn of 1952: to work as an assistant director on an episode of a major five-part television series titled *Mr. Lincoln* (CBS, 1952–1953).

Mr. Lincoln

Mr. Lincoln, produced by Richard de Rochemont, written by James Agee, and largely directed by Norman Lloyd, was a docudrama commissioned for the newly conceived Omnibus series, which was financed by the Ford Foundation's

TV-Radio Workshop. The TV-Radio Workshop, which the Ford Foundation took over direct responsibility for in July 1952, was conceived as a means to improve the "educational use of television and radio within the normal practices of commercial broadcasting."[88] The Omnibus was to contribute to this aim by offering up a combination of programs of "literary, musical, artistic, historical and scientific material" that would advance the standards of television content as well as proving attractive to a national audience in an increasingly competitive market for television entertainment.[89] The series premiered on Sunday, November 9, 1952, on CBS, running for ninety minutes between four thirty and six in the evening. It reached a significant audience, broadcasting across a network of thirty-eight stations that covered approximately 75 percent of all television sets owned in the United States.[90] This could arguably have been Kubrick's biggest audience—certainly in terms of geographic spread—of his film career to date.

Mr. Lincoln initially focused on President Abraham Lincoln's assassination and funeral, before moving to look at his early childhood. The five episodes aired between November 1952 and February 1953 and were praised by critics for their poeticism, production values, and quality of writing.[91] As William Hughes has noted in his study of the series, "At the time, novelist Meyer Levin hailed the Lincoln series as the 'most original and important work so far created for video.' And even today Agee's treatment of the young Lincoln remains, in the words of film scholar Frank Thompson, 'among the finest—perhaps it is *the* finest—film about Abraham Lincoln ever made.'"[92]

The critical praise of *Mr. Lincoln* has remained focused on the primary authorial role of James Agee. Agee had been approached by the producer of Omnibus, Robert Saudek, to write the series, and in turn it was Agee who had requested that Richard de Rochemont's Vavin production company produce the series.[93] But one must arguably consider the authorial influence of the Ford Foundation. Afterall, the foundation, chaired by Henry Ford II, had a duty to ensure that its activities enhanced human welfare, including the stated aim of the support of activities that would "conserve and increase knowledge and enrich our culture."[94] The Ford Foundation's mission was not dissimilar to that of the World Assembly of Youth and can be seen against the backdrop of the "cultural" Cold War, in which an ideological battle was taking place between free-market liberalism and totalitarian communism. So concerned was the Ford Foundation with its mission that it received the advice of "influential Cold War thinkers" on the kind of content that should be produced for Omnibus. The Ford Foundation was of the belief that they could shape the public's opinion and view of the world—television as a mass medium capable of powerful effects. The foundation hired a range of influential opinion leaders, including government officials and academics who shared its liberal values, in order to devise a plan for socially responsible television. This blueprint involved the foundation attempting to "fortify the American social character by utilizing television to educate and enlighten viewers, while amplifying the liberal virtues that set the nation apart from totalitarian regimes."[95]

Against this context, it is interesting to consider that Abraham Lincoln was the figure chosen to be the focus of Omnibus's flagship docudrama. The foundation clearly felt that Lincoln represented the American ideal and was a key figure to portray freedom standing up to tyranny. While there is no evidence that the Ford Foundation interfered in Agee's writing of *Mr. Lincoln*, they had hired him because he shared the foundation's politics and ideals. As did, by all accounts, Richard de Rochemont.[96]

Kubrick's own connection to the project is complicated. He was already acquainted with James Agee through the mutual contact of photographer Helen Levitt and of course had an established working relationship with de Rochemont. But he also had an indirect connection to the Ford Foundation through one of its trustees, John Cowles. Cowles was the president of the Minneapolis Star and Tribune Company and co-owner of the Cowles Media Company along with his brother, Gardner "Mike" Cowles Jr. The company also owned *Look* magazine, which was founded by Gardner, who also acted as its editor in chief, including during Kubrick's years working there. Kubrick maintained a good relationship with Cowles even after leaving the magazine and invited him and his wife to view *Fear and Desire* in July 1952.[97] Even though it was de Rochemont who facilitated Kubrick's hiring to work on *Mr. Lincoln* (he asked director Norman Lloyd to find him a role), the cultural networks of power and influence that Kubrick had amassed was proving impressive. Vincent LoBrutto suggests that when de Rochemont had asked Lloyd to hire Kubrick he was seemingly hesitant; he viewed *Fear and Desire* at de Rochemont's insistence and found it of dubious quality, but did not want to cause "complications" and so agreed to hire Kubrick. Whether John Cowles, or his brother Gardner, was influential in any way in ensuring Kubrick was hired on the series is unclear. But it is interesting to note that Kubrick is listed as serving initially as the assistant to the producer, Richard de Rochemont, in addition to being hired by Lloyd as a second-unit director.[98]

Kubrick sensed an opportunity with *Mr. Lincoln*: he could further enhance his own profile and promote himself as a maverick talent working on a major television series. While working on location in Kentucky, Kubrick spoke to a local newspaper journalist, Paul Hughes of the *Courier Journal*. What emerged was a portrait of Kubrick as *the* director of *Mr. Lincoln*. The resultant article, "The Lincoln Story Breaks into TV," included a full-color picture of Kubrick on set and enhanced his role on the project, as is clear in the following quote: "With Agee's script in hand, director Kubrick and assistant director Tom Buscemi arrived at Hodgenville a couple of weeks ahead of the date set for the first shooting to seek out locations for various scenes in the Lincoln country.... At a shallow ford, Kubrick picked up a site for the moving scene in which the boy Lincoln saw his first wagonload of slaves on the way to an auction market."[99] Kubrick was positioning himself as possessing creative authority on *Mr. Lincoln*, using the series as a blatant means of self-promotion. In the process, he was contributing, even manipulating, a particular image about himself, what Filippo Ulivieri— an expert on Kubrick's art of self-promotion—has deemed Kubrick's emerging "wunderkind" image.[100] Norman Lloyd, when made aware of how Kubrick was telling the press that he was, in effect, the director of *Mr. Lincoln*, effectively dismissed Kubrick from the production, sending him back to New York once the second-unit directing was completed.[101]

Conclusion

Kubrick's primary talent as a producer was emerging more clearly by 1952: that of a self-publicist intent on utilizing his growing network of cultural and industrial contacts to develop a carefully crafted image about himself. He had the acumen to talk to journalists in order to generate a myth about himself. This myth, as Ulivieri has explored, would take form by 1953 with the release of *Fear and Desire* and establish Kubrick as the wunderkind of independent American filmmaking.[102] Producing such an image was vital to Kubrick's success and demonstrated his ambition and ability to use any given opportunity to leverage his own position and further his own aims. In many respects, the self-publicizing behavior Kubrick exhibited on *Mr. Lincoln* was the essence of whom he was as a producer.

At the same time, 1952 was a year of frustration for Kubrick. If in 1951 he had intended to become a fully fledged independent producer of feature films, the dream had not quite worked out. Instead, Kubrick was increasingly drifting toward the production of television and informational shorts. While no doubt still creatively engaged during this period, he was clearly aware of his precarious ontological status as a "filmmaker" and therefore aligned himself closely with the likes of Richard de Rochemont as a means of ensuring a safety net should his ambitions not work out.

3

The New York "Film School," 1953–1955

• • • • • • • • • • • • • • • • • • • •

Kubrick endured a busy year in 1953. Not only was *Fear and Desire* finally released, but he also directed another short film, *The Seafarers* (1953), was developing a number of script ideas, formed a professional production company, Minotaur Productions Inc., and in the autumn commenced work on his second feature, *Killer's Kiss* (1955). But despite this flurry of activity, Kubrick was still working for hire and making money wherever he could. He seems to have made the conscious decision to break away from production for television and doggedly pursue a career as an independent film producer, with the years 1953 to 1955 marking the final key transition of his early years, moving from the guerrilla producer of *Fear and Desire* to professional producer with the sale of *Killer's Kiss* to United Artists (UA) in early 1955. This chapter traces Kubrick's move from amateur to professional producer, placing him within the contexts of the 1950s New York filmmaking scene. It also considers Kubrick's developing ideas about cinema and his deliberate move to work within genre filmmaking.

Working for Hire

The release of *Fear and Desire* in March 1953 seems to have solidified Kubrick's ambition and drive to succeed as an independent film producer. While the film received a limited release and overall performed poorly at the theaters it played, it did provide Kubrick with a substantial amount of publicity. As Filippo Ulivieri has argued, with the release of *Fear and Desire* "Kubrick became a 'wunderkind,' a 'boy genius,'"[1] and indeed even began to develop a reputation as a local celebrity, even if it was only minor.[2]

With all the attention he was receiving in the spring of 1953, Kubrick made the decision to forge ahead with his next feature film. But while he may have become a New York celebrity of sorts, he still lacked the finances to make his films. It is in this context—the need to work for hire out of pragmatism—that we can view Kubrick's workload in the middle part of 1953. There is one file in the Stanley Kubrick Archive that indicates the extent to which Kubrick allowed himself to be hired out for roles other than directing, writing, or producing. Kubrick had acquired good editing, sound recording, and dubbing skills during the postproduction of *Fear and Desire* and seems to have attempted to use them to his own profit-gaining end. After all, he was living precariously during the 1950s, right until his years working with Kirk Douglas. Titled *Shark Safari*, the file contains nothing but receipts, invoices, and a brief handwritten form with expenses and postproduction costs.[3] There is also one brief telegram. Taken together, these materials do not amount to much. They are frustrating leftovers of a period in Kubrick's career in which he was furiously working to make a living and attempting to keep alive his hopes of working in the film industry.

The material indicates that Kubrick was involved in the postproduction of a project titled *Shark Safari*. However, it is not clear what the film (if that's what it was) was about. It was most likely a low-budget exploitation picture given the apparent involvement of writer James Atlee Phillips (1915–1991). There is a telegram from Phillips to Kubrick dated April 23, 1953, in which Phillips requests that *Shark Safari* be available for him to screen in New York on April 26. He explains that he understood the pressure and technical demands of his request but was anxious to have the film ready for release as soon as possible. He was aware of two rival films that could limit the market potential of *Shark Safari*. As such, he advised Kubrick to take short cuts on the music, sound effects, and narration that would not affect the quality of the film.[4]

Phillips was a noted author of pulp detective novels and short stories, including *The Inheritors* (1940), *The Case of the Shivering Chorus Girls* (1942), *Suitable for Framing* (1949), and *Pagoda* (1951).[5] He served in the U.S. Marine Corps and was later contracted as the operations manager for China National Airlines in Rangoon, Burma, and, following World War II, to run the Burmese National Airlines, under employment by the Burmese government.[6] There have been suggestions that Phillips worked for the CIA; his brother, David Atlee Phillips, was a key CIA agent for nearly thirty years and was implicated in the assassination of John F. Kennedy.[7] James Phillips's experiences in the military and his adventures across the globe served to inform his writing, what Lee Server has described as "colorful, sophisticated adventure fiction, exotic, authentically detailed foreign settings, and tough, inventive spy fiction."[8] He also wrote screenplays for television and film, including an uncredited contribution to the John Wayne western *Big Jim McLain* (Ludwig, 1952), *Thunder Road* (Ripley, 1958), and episodes for the anthology series *Fireside Theatre* (NBC, 1949–1955) and *Schlitz Playhouse of Stars* (CBS, 1951–1959).

Shark Safari may never have been released or potentially released under a different title (one invoice from May 25, 1953, refers to "Fishing Story").[9] Additional archival documentation suggests that Kubrick was working with actors such as Frank Silvera and Margaret O'Neill to record dialogue, with a substantial session of rerecording taking place on May 11, 1953, at RCA's Studio B in New York. Whatever the project entailed, Kubrick was hired in a technical capacity and, as a result, received a fee for his services.

Kubrick received a further commission shortly after *Shark Safari*, this time for an informational documentary short for the Seafarers International Union (SIU). The resultant film, *The Seafarers*, was written by Will Chasan and produced by Lester Irving Cooper. The commission for the film, which was intended to boost membership of the SIU, came from the Atlantic and Gulf Coast District branch of the union.[10] The SIU, along with other unions, had become aware of the potential for short films to promote its image and services; *Variety* went so far as to describe the SIU as "show biz minded."[11]

How Kubrick came to work on *The Seafarers* is less certain. It may well have been that the SIU had approached Richard de Rochemont, who in turn handed the commission to Kubrick. However, the most prominent name on the credits is that of Lester Cooper. His name is given precedent over that of Kubrick, while the name of his company, Lester Cooper Productions (LCP), is the final title card at the end of the film. LCP was a New York–based production company, while Cooper himself was a television documentary producer.[12] He had previously written the screenplay of *Meet the Navy* (Travers, 1946), a British musical comedy notable for the Technicolor cinematography of Geoffrey Unsworth (Unsworth would later work with Kubrick on *2001: A Space Odyssey*). But how Cooper became aware of Kubrick is less certain. Whatever the circumstances, *The Seafarers* made clear, as did *Shark Safari*, that Kubrick was prepared to work for hire in order to obtain funds for his personal circumstances and presumably toward future projects.

Killer's Kiss

By the summer of 1953 it had been over two years since Kubrick had been in production on one of his own films, *Fear and Desire*. The years of working as a hired hand, while useful, were surely frustrating. But Kubrick finally began to turn his thoughts to producing a second feature film. Sometime in mid-1953 Kubrick was drafting ideas for potential names for a new independent production company: Red Moun, Red Mountain, Molescule, Monitor, Mirador, Minot.[13] None of them were right, but he was working toward his final choice: Minotaur Productions Inc. The company was formed with the intention of using it to produce a script cowritten by Kubrick and Howard Sackler titled *Along Came a Spider*, a thriller about a boxer, Davy Gordon, who falls in love with the mistress of a violent club owner and gang boss.[14]

Kubrick had budgeted his new project at $60,000, but the conditions of production meant he would have to rely on private sources of income. As a means of obtaining funds, Kubrick set about making Minotaur a more professional outfit, even styling himself as the company's president. He designed and ordered professional letterheads for the company, and in all legal documentation it was referred to as a New York corporation that had its principal place of business in Midtown Manhattan, in an office close to Times Square.[15] The professionalism of Kubrick's producing on the project is clear through the series of contracts he developed, wrote, and signed throughout September 1953. This included a loan agreement and stockholder agreement between Minotaur Productions and Morris Bousel.[16] The agreements stated how *Along Came a Spider* was to be primarily funded through a loan provided by Bousel, and in return, Bousel was given 50 percent ownership of Minotaur Productions.[17] Bousel was "a wealthy pharmacist and acquaintance of the Kubrick family";[18] in return for financing the film, and for his 50 percent stake in Minotaur, Bousel received a producing credit. Once again, it was a pharmaceutical entrepreneur who was sponsoring Kubrick's venture, just like his uncle, Martin Perveler, had done with *Fear and Desire*. It may have been that Bousel had learned of Kubrick through Perveler. Why Bousel decided to take the risk in financing Kubrick is uncertain, though Kubrick most probably had a hand in convincing him to finance the project, perhaps even suggesting that he would make a profit by selling the film to a major distributor. The contractual arrangements with Minotaur suggest that Bousel was trying to prevent unnecessary investment risk to himself.[19]

The level of professionalism Kubrick was attempting with his new film extended to employing a more fully formed crew, perhaps as a result of the pressurized and somewhat inexperienced approach he had taken on *Fear and Desire*. Kubrick drew up a range of contracts with the primary crew he was to employ: Eugene Friedman (camera operator), Arthur Weld (apprentice technician), William Goodman (soundman), Nathan Boxer (boom operator), David Golden (electrician), Robert Farren (assistant cameraman), and Jesse Paley (operating cameraman).[20] He also finalized a contract with Howard Sackler that handed the rights of *Along Came A Spider* to Minotaur, with Sackler to receive a twelfth of any net profits the film made.[21] The various contracts suggest that Kubrick was already thinking ahead to the film's sale and distribution, most likely wanting agreements in place prior to the film being purchased by a major distributor. In the same vein, Kubrick was probably also thinking about the market for his film, changing the title to fit with low-budget, sensational exploitation trends of the era. By the end of September 1953 it had been retitled *The Nymph and the Maniac*, with a further change by late 1953 to *Kiss Me, Kill Me*.[22] The latter was close to the film's eventual alliterative release title, *Killer's Kiss*, most likely chosen by the distributor, UA.

Of all of Kubrick's early films, *Killer's Kiss* is the most well documented in the Stanley Kubrick Archive. The production files provide an insight into the perils of low-budget producing, but also reveal how Kubrick was displaying a level of confidence as a producer that was vital to ensure a variety of contractual agreements and deferrals to get his film made. While Bousel had invested a substantial amount of money in the production, Kubrick still needed to obtain further money and arranged loan agreements, deferments, mortgage pledges, and promissory notes with private companies across New York.[23]

One of the more significant deals Kubrick made was with the company Deluxe Laboratories, a film processing and development plant and a wholly owned subsidiary of Twentieth Century Fox.[24] Deluxe Laboratories was one of the biggest film developing firms in the United States in the early 1950s, at a time when Fox invested heavily in the company to allow it to convert to color processing.[25] Kubrick had previously worked with Deluxe on *Fear and Desire*, when an employee of the company, Alan Friedman, had granted him credit to process the film.[26] The agreement with Deluxe this time around, however, was not so relaxed. In return for advancing Minotaur Productions $5,000, loaned at 6 percent interest, along with supplying all necessary film stock and prints, Kubrick was required to meet the following stipulations:[27]

- Upon completion of postproduction, Minotaur had ninety days to sell the film to what was termed a "regular" motion picture distributor.
- The final cut of the film needed to be at least seven thousand feet; in other words, around eighty minutes in running time.
- Minotaur had to allow Deluxe the right to inspect its complete financial records at any time.
- Deluxe had to be the first company repaid from any profits that *Killer's Kiss* made from its sale and/or release.

Kubrick also agreed to a mortgage of chattels, in which, should he default on his contract, all rights to the eventual film, including any literary property it was based on, as well as all prints, would become the property of Deluxe in perpetuity.[28] Any default meant that all profit from the film would be paid to Deluxe.[29] And should Minotaur terminate or amend the agreement without the consent of Deluxe, again all profits of the film would be paid to them. Of course, it was entirely feasible that *Killer's Kiss* would make no profit; in such circumstances Deluxe made it clear that they would either sell off or destroy all prints of the film.[30]

Deluxe went even further in its legal arrangements with Minotaur, writing a "Notice of Irrevocable Authority" that had to be issued to any distributor of *Killer's Kiss*.[31] The document stipulated that Deluxe had advanced $5,000 to

Minotaur and authorized any distributor to repay Deluxe accordingly. The distributor would forward monthly copies of all financial statements to Deluxe, with details of the film's grosses.[32] Once Deluxe Laboratories' first lien on the income of the picture had been paid in full, then—and only then—could Minotaur receive its share of the profits according to any agreement with the distributor.[33]

The conditions of Kubrick's agreement with Deluxe were strict and reflected the precarious nature of low-budget producing outside of the Hollywood mainstream. As for Morris Bousel, who had invested his own money into Minotaur Productions, he would be the last to receive any repayments from the profits of *Killer's Kiss*. Still, Bousel agreed to the conditions laid out by Deluxe, maybe as a means of mitigating his own risk. The loan agreement and mortgage of chattels were ratified by the two stakeholders of Minotaur, Kubrick and Bousel, on September 17.[34]

Beyond loan agreements, Kubrick also negotiated a variety of fee and salary deferments both with his own crew and with production and postproduction companies in New York. This included with the Titra Sound Corporation, a subsidiary of the Paris-based Titra Films and a specialist in the subtitling and dubbing of foreign films.[35] On September 19, Titra agreed to provide equipment and all necessary services to Minotaur Productions until *Killer's Kiss* was complete. This included sound recording equipment and editing facilities.[36] The equipment was loaned on a fee deferment basis, with the cost to be paid out of the net receipts of any sale of *Killer's Kiss*. In agreeing to the deferment, Kubrick signed yet another mortgage of chattels, with the chain of repayments stacking up. The repayments to Titra would come second to those owed Deluxe.

However, Kubrick changed his mind about the use of sound recording on the film set and made the costly decision, as he had with *Fear and Desire*, to post-loop the dialogue. This meant that by May 1954, Minotaur owed Titra $5,000 just for the use of their dubbing facilities.[37] Kubrick's decision may have affected the aesthetic design of the film, with a lack of dialogue throughout. While this may have been a cost-saving measure, including using a voice-over narration, to avoid overly lengthy postsynchronization, it created a very visual film. This is particularly obvious in the opening twenty minutes, with much of the story conveyed visually rather than through dialogue.

One final key fee deferment was for the loan of camera rental equipment. Kubrick arranged a deal with the Camera Equipment Company (CEC) similar to that with Titra. But again, by February 1955 the debt Minotaur owed was significant: $20,361.42.[38] Frank Zucker, president of CEC, disputed the figure and claimed that Minotaur owed closer to $24,000.[39] However, Zucker was aware that by the spring of 1955 Kubrick was negotiating the sale of *Killer's Kiss* and came to an agreement that the repayments of the debt be deducted from any profits.

Killer's Kiss was shot on location in New York in early 1954, over a period of three months.[40] This allowed Kubrick to save on studio costs, which in the final budget came to under $1,000.[41] The film utilized locales such as "Manhattan's alleys, streets and rooftops, the Laurel Gardens Boxing Arena in New Jersey, a dance hall in Brooklyn, and a mannequin factory on Greene St, Downtown."[42] Laurel Gardens was a familiar location to Kubrick, having been the site of the boxing match featured in *Day of the Fight*. In fact, the high-angle wide shots used of the stadium are eerily similar. Could it be that Kubrick borrowed unused footage from *Day of the Fight* for establishing shots in *Killer's Kiss*? The fact that one of the key action centerpieces of the film is a boxing match shows Kubrick was drawing on his established contacts, most probably as a way of lowering costs. He was a known filmmaker to the owners of Laurel Gardens, and the fight scenes in the film were staged when the stadium was closed, with sound effects dubbed in afterward to suggest a large, raucous crowd. The boxing scenes are given a visceral quality via the handheld camera shots, extreme close-ups, and rapid cuts. It was precisely because the arena was empty that Kubrick was forced to film in such close-ups to disguise the fact. When composing the story, Kubrick and Sackler had purposely crafted it around several action sequences "that would carry the weight of film and [ensure it would] not be costly to shoot."[43]

Staging a lengthy boxing scene also made sense in terms of the marketability of the picture at that time. A cycle of boxing films had performed well at the box office during the late 1940s and early 1950s, most notably *Champion* (Kramer, 1949) starring Kirk Douglas. Other similar low-budget boxing films were also commercial successes, including *The Set-Up* (Wise, 1949). This cycle of boxing films was deemed by trade papers like *Boxoffice* to target a male audience, reflecting the increase in availability of boxing matches on television. Kubrick perhaps realized this and, needing an angle to sell his film, made his central character, Davy Gordon, a boxer. This in turn allowed for a good action sequence, along with having the resources to stage a boxing match at little cost.

Kubrick utilized the skills of his crew and friends as a means of saving on the budget. For example, the ballet sequence was choreographed by his friend David Vaughan and danced by Ruth Sobotka; Kubrick and Sobotka would marry in early 1955. Some of the other crewmembers also acted as extras or in minor roles, including Vaughan, who played a conventioneer. Talent costs (including all contracted actors, extras, and bit players) on the film equated to 5 percent of the final production budget, while the crew accounted for just 9 percent.[44] The cast totaled fifteen credited actors, and the crew amounted to thirteen, including Kubrick, Bousel and the composer Gerald Fried. Many of these individuals deferred fees or simply worked for free. Take Max Glenn, one of the film's two credited camera operators. Kubrick wrote to Glenn sometime in early 1955 stating that the $1,000 salary that was agreed with him "in consideration of services rendered by you" will be "paid from the net proceeds of the film . . . parri passu with the other salary deferments already incurred by us."[45] Kubrick himself received a paltry wage that equated to little more than expenses.

Kubrick's intent that *Killer's Kiss* be a professional production was shown by his acquisition of an MPAA seal, at a cost of $700. He also utilized the standard union agreement of the International Alliance of Theatrical Stage Employees and Moving Picture Machine Operators of the United States and Canada.[46] The agreement required Minotaur to display the insignia of the International Alliance on the film credits, while also obliging Minotaur to ensure "the wage scales... shall be those contained in the standard collective bargaining contracts now in effect in the N.Y. area."[47] It is not clear how closely Kubrick and Minotaur adhered to this agreement considering the number of salary deferments in place, though a dispute with the union resulted in Minotaur having to make a $5,000 settlement.[48]

Yet despite the professional intent and the effort to keep costs low, the anticipated budget of $60,000 had escalated to $90,000 by the end of postproduction. The costliest elements of the budget had been studio and equipment rental, while Kubrick's decision to postsynchronize all sound had led to inflated postproduction recording costs of $13,041.85, with over $11,000 of this being on the recording and synching of dialogue.[49] Kubrick continued to look for ways of cutting costs in postproduction, negotiating a deferment with Nat Sobel of Cineffects in June 1954. Explaining to Sobel that *Killer's Kiss* was still in no state for screening due to the lengthy postsynchronization process, Kubrick asked, "If without seeing the film, you would like to arrange a deferred agreement for the titles and opticals, I would be very pleased to oblige you."[50] Note the use of language by Kubrick—*you would like* and *I would be very pleased to oblige you*—as if Kubrick was providing Sobel and his business with a favor by arranging deferment of his own fees. This language was brazen, but it showed the level of determination and confidence needed to get an independent production made in the 1950s.

Kubrick and the New York "Film School"

Kubrick's producing of *Fear and Desire* and *Killer's Kiss* was part of a growing filmmaking scene in New York in the late 1940s and early 1950s. There was a cycle of independent film producers in the city who were making films outside of the traditional confines of Hollywood production.[51] As Kubrick noted some years later when he commenced a partnership with James B. Harris, the city was seen as a vital hub for independent film producers, in contrast to California, which was seen as not offering "much in the way of purposeful activity."[52] The New York filmmakers were maverick, enthusiastic individuals who would take their cameras to the streets of New York and film in a realist style, often without the permission of city authorities. They were a new wave of filmmakers that was one of just several new waves around the world—from the Italian Neo-Realists in the 1940s to the French New Wave in the late 1950s and early 1960s, with their low-budget techniques "redefining the notion of film" and creating a new modernist aesthetic in the process that "would enable the medium to create its own reality, its own way of speaking to and about the world."[53] Many of those in New York, Kubrick included, were using not corporate capital but money raised from a range of disparate and risky sources. As Blair Davis notes, "Their productions... were inherently more risky than those made by the major studios, entailing radically different production methods. With financial risk far greater than it had been in recent years, independent filmmakers often struggled to fund their films—a symptom of their maverick status within the industry."[54] This growing scene in New York was fueled by other arts, such as acting, dancing, and photography. The New York scene included filmmakers such as John Cassavetes, who would apply method acting in *Shadows* (1959), and Morris Engel, a photographer who would use pioneering methods on his realist film *Little Fugitive* (1953), such as the use of lightweight thirty-five-millimeter cameras that anticipated direct cinema documentary and postdubbed sound.[55]

Another key individual of this low-budget filmmaking scene was Terry B. Sanders, author of "The Financing of Independent Feature Films" (1955). Sanders would go on to produce more than seventy dramatic features over the course of his career, but it was a short film he produced in the early 1950s that gained him the attention of the Academy Awards. *A Time Out of War* (1954) won the Oscar for Best Short Subject (Two Reel) and led to Sanders, along with his brother Denis, being employed by Charles Laughton on *The Night of the Hunter* (1955) as second unit directors. Sanders proved that low-budget filmmaking acted as a calling card to larger budgets and to the big Hollywood distributors.

These New York low-budget producers were not affiliated to one another but operated with similar modes of production: Helen Levitt, who produced the documentary *In the Street*, shot on the streets of New York; producer-director Lionel Rogosin with *On the Bowery* (1956); Shirley Clarke's early short films set in New York; and Janice Loeb, who produced *The Quiet One*.[56] The latter film, produced by Loeb for the production company Film Documente, had been distributed by Mayer & Burstyn. The aesthetics of this emerging group, referred to by Jonas Mekas in the magazine *Film Culture* as the New York "film school," were not as important as the *way* they made their films on such low budgets.[57] Mekas argued that this new style of filmmaking and this new generation of filmmakers first emerged with *In the Street* and *The Quiet One* in the late 1940s and early 1950s, calling them "forerunners of the low-budget independent film."[58] Kubrick, emerging at the very same time, was very much a part of this "school" in terms of being a new breed of independent producer operating on a low budget with *Fear and Desire* and *Killer's Kiss*.

These filmmakers took their cameras out onto the streets of New York, filming immediate, direct narratives that challenged the notion of the need for costly budgets to make a commercial film. They were, in a way, precursors of the later

Hollywood Renaissance, some of them producing student films, such as Terry Sanders. This group of twentysomethings were forging not only a new independent cinema in America but also a new way of producing films. And it was what some within the mainstream industry believed was necessary to revitalize Hollywood. David O. Selznick was one of those calling for an injection of independent blood into the mainstream, saying that "young blood and young thinking is a prime pre-requisite if the picture business is to survive."[59]

The aim of these New York–based low-budget independent producers was primarily one of attracting the attention of Hollywood. This certainly was the case with Kubrick and *Killer's Kiss*, as it was with Kubrick's contemporary Morris Engel, who produced *Little Fugitive* around the same time. Though *Little Fugitive* and *Killer's Kiss*, both being distributed by Joseph Burstyn, were of different genres (the former a comedy about a boy who mistakenly thinks he has killed his older brother, the latter a crime thriller), they attracted the attention of Hollywood. This wave of New York independent producers proved that, in *Variety*'s words, "the amateur can enter the competitive film market on surprising film costs."[60] At the same time, the low budgets of *Killer's Kiss* and *Little Fugitive* dispelled the myth of the need for million-dollar production costs.[61]

Arguably, we need to revise our understanding of this growing independent filmmaking scene in New York in the 1950s. These were film producers bringing in their films on tight budgets not in an attempt to be flagrantly anti-Hollywood, or as any kind of film movement in opposition to Hollywood, but as "single individuals who were quietly trying to express their own cinematic truth, to make their own kind of cinema."[62] And in order to achieve this, their production methods required a guerrilla sensibility and experience, resulting in "low budgets, the small crews, and the visual and technical roughness imposed by the new and unpredictable shooting circumstances."[63] The production stills of *Killer's Kiss* reveal its low-budget nature, with very little crew and only a few actors, and filming taking place in grimy, empty locations.[64] In fact, Kubrick purposely shot the picture in the "shabbier sections of New York" to save money.[65] The effect was to give the film a realism and grit common to the urban crime thriller, a genre that was "part of a larger movement in the decade in which the low-budget gangster film provided a space for experimentation for both established and beginning filmmakers."[66] These low-budget crime films contributed to the "movement to the streets, to location filming, that permanently changed the *mise-en-scène* of American film. *Killer's Kiss* is in part a documentary of Manhattan in the early 1950s."[67] This documentary-like realism may have been influenced by Jules Dassin's *The Naked City* (1948), a film for which Kubrick took set photographs in 1947. It may be that Kubrick remembered *The Naked City* when filming *Killer's Kiss*, with the film's rooftop chase featuring "an early morning New York City skyline as background reminiscent of *The Naked City* and countless other urban crime films."[68]

The development of New York as the hub of American postwar independent cinema continued throughout the 1950s and into the 1960s, at which point it consciously developed as an anti-Hollywood movement, subverting the West Coast's mode of production and control through avant-garde and experimental filmmaking. Film artists such as Stan Brakhage, Andy Warhol, and Kenneth Anger and cooperatives such as Cinema 16 approached filmmaking with a commitment to "alternative points of view, democratic representation, and countercultural transformation."[69] A number of the New York independent filmmaking scene were eventually drawn toward the avant-garde group, while others, such as Kubrick and Engel, used their efforts in low-budget production as a means to obtain larger budgets and distribution with the Hollywood majors. Engel would go on to produce his next feature with a much larger budget of over $100,000, double that of *Little Fugitive*. Similarly, *Killer's Kiss* attracted the attention of UA, which purchased the film in the spring of 1955.

Trends

Killer's Kiss was purchased by UA for $75,000.[70] The sale was meant to allow Kubrick to pay back his investors and free him up to "join the UA indie producer ranks."[71] However, Minotaur was required to repay companies such as CEC and Deluxe and, as a result, made a net loss on its corporate operation of over $20,000.[72] If Kubrick had hoped to make any money from *Killer's Kiss* and independent producing, there was no immediate hope. However, UA did agree to finance another picture to be produced by Kubrick for $100,000.[73]

As for how UA had become aware of *Killer's Kiss* and Kubrick, it wouldn't have been out of character for Kubrick to have contacted its New York office directly. We know Kubrick had the ability and the confidence to reach out to establishment figures within the media, contacting high-profile journalists to promote both himself and his movies. In fact, that was a key approach for him as an emerging film producer. For example, in May 1954 he contacted A. H. Weiler at the *New York Times*, someone whom he had been in correspondence with many times previous.[74] He wrote to Weiler with a new story about *Killer's Kiss*, still titled *Kiss Me, Kill Me*, with his letter appearing verbatim in Weiler's piece on May 23, 1954. As Ulivieri has pointed out, much of the Kubrick "myth" was developed by Kubrick himself through extensive contact with the media from the very beginning of his career.[75] It's not improbable, as Ulivieri has demonstrated, that Kubrick supplied other journalists with embellished stories about himself to produce an industry image about himself. For example, in a piece for the *Sunday News* in September 1955, Kubrick was styled as the "newest and youngest producer in the business"—Kubrick was twenty-seven at the time—and as possessing numerous creative talents: "Not only is he a photographer of distinction, but he is a writer, producer, director, and editor as well. He performed all of these chores, he tells me, on his production *Killer's Kiss*."[76]

Kubrick was clearly aware that self-promotion was the main means by which to advance his career.

Kubrick's self-promotion and the development of his image as an independent producer may have been enticing to UA, along with the genre contexts of *Killer's Kiss*. Kubrick was promoting the film in a way that aligned with the low-budget trends of UA at that time. In 1954, he described *Killer's Kiss* as a "romantic drama which is largely action and very little dialogue" with themes of "jealousy" and "revenge."[77] Kubrick was surely aware of the low-budget trends in independent filmmaking of the era. In fact, he was busy developing ideas in 1954 and 1955, forming his understanding of what constituted a commercial story. During this time, he filled notebooks with outlines and treatments as well as brief sketches of his thoughts on the film industry. What seems to have appealed to Kubrick was to create films that were commercially viable, even going so far as to write that "creative talent of an individual may be accurately measured by examining the box office reports of the last film to which said talent was applied."[78] Kubrick knew that his progression and survival as an independent producer rested on his commercial success.

In his notebooks, Kubrick was engaged in a discourse with himself about the purpose of filmmaking and of what audiences might appreciate in terms of narrative and style. While he believed that cinema was a major art form equal to poetry, painting, theater, and the novel, he felt that those who only liked "foreign films" displayed an art-house patron smugness, akin to saying "I only like books bound in brown covers."[79] Kubrick was beginning to think about the kinds of films that were successful and what audiences enjoyed, concluding that "people like action—this mean visual."[80] His developing interest in box office trends led him to even conclude that beautiful cinematography was less important than visual action. His insistence on the visual is apparent in the film ideas he was starting to devise. Most were crude ideas, some merely sketches in notebooks, while others were much more substantially developed. Most of the stories Kubrick drafted were set in New York, with the city becoming almost a central character to his stories. He was drawing upon his experiences of living in the city, particularly Greenwich Village, regularly referring to cafés and restaurants he was familiar with, such as the Rienzi. And many of his ideas seemed to fit the crime genre that appealed to UA.

In September 1954 he wrote an outline for a crime film that focused on a character called the Duke. The idea—about a bank robbery—was highly visual, with no dialogue in the first six pages, depending on audience familiarity with cinematic language to understand what was happening. For example, when the Duke returns to his small apartment, he paces back and forth four steps at a time, with Kubrick concluding that "seasoned movie-goers will recognize the length of countless trips to and fro on the floor of a conventional prison cell."[81] The story outline is incomplete, but Kubrick continued to work on the heist film throughout late 1954, developing biographies for what would have been an ensemble piece featuring colorfully named characters such as Honest John, Don Juan, and the Hypochondriac Muscleman. The Duke was renamed the Colonel, who assembles a gang to help carry out the planned heist, but "after a preliminary success things begin to go completely wrong. The deaths of all the gang but for the Colonel."[82] The story has echoes of *The Killing* (1956) and shows that Kubrick was giving serious consideration to hard-boiled crime thrillers.

Kubrick developed a more substantial crime story by April 1955 called *The Cop Killer*.[83] The story reads like a pulp thriller in the vein of Ed McBain or Jim Thompson. The main character, Earl Slope, is forced to run away from his hometown of Lovelace, Texas, after he is discovered having an affair with the wife of another man, Preston Howard. Earl's father pays for him to move to New York, and upon arrival he moves around the city looking for a place to live. He discovers Greenwich Village and "liked it at once. He made a couple of friends at the San Remo bar, and they took him to a party on MacDougal Street where he met some very unusual girls. This, he decided, was the place to live."[84] The treatment consists of lengthy passages describing Earl Slope's experiences of Greenwich Village, reading like an autobiography of Kubrick's own life in the Village. Slope spends his evenings at coffee shops where "you could play chess and hear classical music, and the bars, where you might expect to meet a great variety of girls." Slope frequents the Rienzi Café and San Remo bar on MacDougal Street, the Limelight Café on Sheridan Square, and Julius's on Tenth Street, and spends his afternoons walking around Washington Square Park to stop at the chess tables. Perhaps reflecting on his own reputation in the Village (or his desired reputation), Kubrick describes Slope as having "quickly become a well-known figure around the Village and was regarded as 'the real thing' by the village characters."[85]

Kubrick was drawing on all aspects of his own life to inform the narrative and characters of *The Cop Killer*, including giving Slope a job as a postal clerk at the imaginary *Spot* magazine. Slope becomes fascinated by the photographer's lounge at the magazine, and Kubrick once more digresses from a discussion of the plot to focus on this element, perhaps giving us insight into his own time working at *Look* magazine: "Each photographer had his own locker and decked out on the extra-long table in the middle of the room was an assortment of 35mm cameras and lenses . . . another photographer was showing around his latest series of nudes posed in a hotel room."[86]

Following these lengthy descriptions of Slope's life in Greenwich Village the narrative resumes as a crime thriller. Slope receives news that his father has died and he wants to raise money to be able to fly out and pay for an extravagant funeral. Slope literally falls down a slippery slope into a world of crime in order to raise money. He steals a revolver from a gun shop and commits a series of robberies across the city. Kubrick was determined to keep these robbery scenes highly visual, describing them as "major visual sequences in the film," involving "suspense, force and excitement."[87]

Following a final botched robbery, Slope flees New York and returns to Texas with the money needed to pay for his father's funeral. The cyclical nature of the story becomes clear when, weeping at his father's grave, Slope notices a man approaching. It's Preston Howard, the man who had forced Slope to leave for New York in the first place. Howard is still desperate for revenge ("he had been drinking and was vengeance personified") and, despite the pleas of a sheriff who arrives on the scene, shoots Slope dead.

The Cop Killer is a crude pulp thriller, with shades of both *Killer's Kiss* and *The Killing*. It also shows that Kubrick was clearly inspired by the genre in his early years, probably out of a partial desire to make films on a practical budget and to ensure their commerciality. We know that he was looking for ideas about crime and murder, as shown by the fact he kept news clippings about real-life crime and macabre stories in New York. For example, he kept clippings about a Dr. Karl Tanzler, who was found to have kept the body of a dead woman in his apartment for eight years because he loved her so much, serenading her nightly with organ music.[88] Clearly, Kubrick was interested in mixing crime and thriller stories with themes of jealousy and obsession, perhaps with the aim of appealing to a young male audience.

The Cop Killer may also have been Kubrick's first substantial idea of what film he could next produce for UA following the sale of *Killer's Kiss* to the company. It is not a well-developed treatment, with poor structure and narrative, but it shows that Kubrick was actively developing and writing his own stories. This may have been out of a pragmatism that, given he was a low-budget producer, he didn't have the funds to hire a screenwriter or to purchase literary properties that he could adapt. In developing low-budget crime stories, Kubrick was showing how he fitted with UA's own priorities in the mid-1950s.

UA had developed a penchant for nurturing young independent producers like Kubrick by the mid-1950s, such as Edward Small (*Kansas City Confidential*, 1952), Alexander Gottlieb (*The Fighter*, 1952), and Clarence Green (*The Thief*, 1952). These were producers who filmed content on budgets of around $100,000 to $300,000 that was ideal for television distribution. *Killer's Kiss* proved Kubrick's credentials as an independent producer able to work on a tight budget, ideal for the kind of operation UA was running concurrent to its major funding stream with producers like Stanley Kramer and Burt Lancaster.[89] Its minor funding stream was nicknamed the abecedarian program (an apprentice or one who is learning the basic principles of a subject or craft), and UA required the young, independent producers who were part of it to "turn out product 'at a price.'"[90] As an abecedarian, Kubrick was allowed relative artistic freedom as long as he produced a film without an elaborate budget and that made a profit. In part, it was a way for UA to build "important producer alignments for the future."[91]

Producers placed on the abecedarian program tended not to have previous production experience. Instead, the aim was for low-budget films that made modest profits, while the producers were being "groomed for the big-time."[92] The films were usually cheap genre pictures: urban crime thrillers, westerns, or horror and science fiction. Many of the narratives were centered around the theme of revenge and were set in gritty and dark environments, dominated by urbanity and masculinity, and starring actors known for their roles in crime films, such as Edward G. Robinson, Robert Mitchum, Leo Gordon, and Sterling Hayden. They also proved to be highly successful at the box office, with the likes of *Vice Squad* (Levy, 1954) grossing over $1 million domestically.[93]

Unfortunately, *Killer's Kiss* wasn't so successful, with weak grosses and a limited release.[94] But it didn't necessarily matter. Instead, Kubrick had made significant advances in his career and had managed to secure the biggest sponsor of his career to date: a major Hollywood company, UA. Now he had to take full advantage of the opportunity presented to him.

Conclusion

The official narrative of Kubrick's early career assumes a continuous transitional path, from working as a photographer at *Look* magazine to producing three short documentaries and then progressing to privately financed independent features, before UA gave him his "big break." In truth, the early 1950s were a struggle for Kubrick and far from a smooth career progression, moving from photography to shorts and then features. Kubrick was an outsider from the very beginning and worked outside the mainstream. What he was attempting was to break through into the establishment, into the elite world of Hollywood filmmaking and the budgets that came with it. The industrial conditions of the American film industry were changing, but this did not necessarily help Kubrick as an independent producer.

There were three key reasons as to why Kubrick was able to make the various transitions in the early years of his career and to keep alive his ambition of becoming a film producer. The first was his use of self-promotion, developing an image through the media that positioned him as a multitalented producer working against Hollywood but producing highly original and daring work. This approach depended on Kubrick's own innate ambition and intuition to contact established journalists and his understanding of the "the value of promotion" and how the media worked.[95] Second, Kubrick was developing ideas and producing films that conformed to genre trends. By the mid-1950s he understood that the low-budget films he was producing needed to appeal to a young male audience and to make a profit. And third, and most important, Kubrick had a series of sponsors that allowed him to pursue his ambitions. These sponsors brought Kubrick both financing (for his projects and for his personal life) and the privileged access to a range of cultural networks that allowed him to advance his career and to make vital industrial contacts. The sponsors, from Martin Perveler and Morris Bousel to Richard de Rochemont, Joseph Burstyn, and Arthur Mayer, were vital to

Kubrick's transition in these early years. Without them, he most likely would never have progressed beyond making a few short films. But even as he stood on the crossroads between Hollywood and independence in 1955, Kubrick was still in need of further sponsors if he was to make the final transition to become a mainstream Hollywood producer.

Part 2

The Harris-Kubrick Pictures Corporation, 1955–1962

4

The New UA Team, 1955–1956

By the late 1950s Kubrick had progressed from privately financed film productions to producing films that were financed and distributed by major, mainstream Hollywood companies. Both *The Killing* and *Paths of Glory* (1957) were financed and distributed by UA (the former with additional investment from James B. Harris and his family), while *Lolita* (1962) was financed by Seven Arts Productions and distributed by MGM. More important, Kubrick directed a major Hollywood sword-and-sandal epic, *Spartacus* (1960), the most expensive film produced by Universal at that time. This rapid progression to become a significant Hollywood figure happened in the short space of four years, between 1955 and 1959. The most important changes came about between 1955 and 1957, during which time Kubrick moved from working on low-budget thrillers to collaborating with A-list Hollywood celebrities. But the key to this phase of Kubrick's career was the two most important cultural and industrial sponsors he would ever encounter: Kirk Douglas and James B. Harris. It is the latter, Harris, who is arguably the more significant, though Douglas (discussed in chapter 5) was also a chief player in Kubrick's final transition from producer outside the mainstream to Hollywood insider.

Kubrick commenced a business partnership with Harris in mid-1955. Together they incorporated the Harris-Kubrick Pictures Corporation, an independent production company with which they aimed to break through into the Hollywood mainstream. Harris provided the financial stability Kubrick sought to make his films, along with the requisite skills of an innovative producer. Together, Harris and Kubrick operated a company that developed a reputation for maverick, controversial productions and that diversified from low-budget crime thrillers (*The Killing*) to international productions (*Paths of Glory*) within the space of two years. This chapter focuses on the first two years of the company's existence to understand its management, organization, and production strategy as well as the development and release of its first production, *The Killing*.

James B. Harris, "The Boy Wonder"

Born in 1928 in Manhattan, James B. Harris was raised on the New Jersey Shore following a family relocation.[1] Aged fourteen, he moved back to Manhattan to attend the private Columbia Grammar School on West Ninety-Third Street.[2] Harris had ambitions of becoming a musician like his brother, but with limited musical abilities he instead began working for Essex Universal, a media company owned by his father Joseph that, among other things, financed and distributed theatrical films.[3]

In 1949, Harris, along with David L. Wolper, Sy Weintraub, and his father Joseph, incorporated Flamingo Films in New York to distribute films to the television market and to produce new content.[4] Harris was the company's president, with the company itself a subsidiary of Essex Universal.[5] Flamingo was incorporated after Harris became aware that, while domestic grosses for films were falling, television was becoming increasingly popular and that there was a growing demand for new programming.[6] Harris traveled around the United States to forge deals and sign contracts with production companies, developing skills in film business and deal making. He acquired the rights to a variety of feature films, cartoons, and serials to distribute to the television networks. In 1949, Flamingo had been capitalized at $6,000, but by 1955 it had a yearly gross of close to $3 million.[7] Harris distributed Flamingo's content to the major networks and attended major television conventions, such as the 1955 National Association of Radio and Television Broadcasters convention in Washington, DC, to screen shows the company owned; among them, the cartoon series *Telecomics* (NBC, 1950–1951), the Henry Donovan–produced adventure series *Cowboy G-Men* (1952–1953), and, between 1954 and 1964, one of America's most watched programs at the time, *The Adventures of Superman* (ABC, 1952–1958).[8] Harris's success as a pioneer of television feature film distribution in its earliest days led to him being titled the "boy wonder" of the industry.[9]

It was via television distribution that Harris came into contact with Kubrick in June 1955, though it's likely the pair had met before through the mutual contact of Alexander Singer, with whom Harris had served in the U.S. Navy. Kubrick was interested in selling his films for television distribution to Harris, starting with *Fear and Desire*. But the film was tied up in litigation following the death of Joseph Burstyn, the distributor, in a plane crash.[10] Still, a meeting went ahead between Harris and Kubrick at which they agreed to form a business partnership, sensing that they could be of use to one another in their attempts to make it big in Hollywood. Kubrick had a deal with UA to produce a feature film; Harris had the producing ability, the cultural and industrial contexts, and the money to be able to sponsor their venture. The aim was not to produce one picture but to establish their new company, Harris-Kubrick Pictures Corporation, as a prominent independent production company in Hollywood. Harris would serve as the producer of their films, Kubrick as the director. However, in effect both men served as a producer, particularly during the periods in which they were not in active production, with the pair agreeing that Harris-Kubrick Pictures would be an equal partnership with each having shared responsibility for all business decisions and production strategies.[11]

In truth, though, there was an unequal power balance in the relationship, weighted toward Harris. He brought with him substantial funds off the back of the success of Flamingo Films, funds that he would personally invest into Harris-Kubrick Pictures. But he also brought access to a range of cultural and industrial networks through the association with his father's Harris Group companies. Joseph Harris was in partnership with Joseph D. Blau, head of the National Telefilm Associates Company.[12] Joseph Blau and Joseph Harris were powerful industry players, who formed the Harris-Blau Group in order to buy a controlling stake of Republic Pictures from Herbert J. Yates in 1957 for $5 million.[13] A key contact to emerge from his father's network was Louis Blau, who would serve as a lawyer to Harris-Kubrick Pictures, and in later years to Kubrick. In addition, James Harris had contacts with future powerful Hollywood figures who had been school friends, including Kenneth Hyman, David L. Wolper, and Steve Ross.[14] Far from being an insignificant company, from its inception Harris-Kubrick Pictures had access to power within the media industry and was a close-knit network of family contacts and industrial ties. More important, it had two individuals operating the company who were ambitious and who would utilize these contacts to their advantage over the coming years.

According to Harris, Kubrick was at a loss as to what to produce for his next film,[15] though archival material shows this wasn't necessarily the case. It may be more appropriate to suggest that Kubrick was not happy with the original ideas he had developed, such as *The Cop Killer*, but he clearly had a sense of the *kind* of film he wanted to produce: a crime film, in keeping with the low-budget trends of UA in the mid-1950s. Following their June 1955 meeting, Harris visited a bookstore on Fifth Avenue, Scribner's, and browsed the crime section. He came away with several books, including Lionel White's thriller *Clean Break* (1955), a story about the robbery of a horse racetrack in New York. It was a story that conformed to some of Kubrick's ideas for a heist film developed in 1954 and early 1955. Both men agreed that the book would make a good story, and so using his own money and ability to negotiate a deal, Harris purchased the story rights to *Clean Break* for $10,000.[16] It was intended that this would be the first film produced by Harris-Kubrick Pictures as part of a three-picture arrangement with UA.[17]

Producing an Adaptation: *The Killing*

The acquisition of literary property would become the principal mode of development at Harris-Kubrick Pictures. This might have been a result of Kubrick's own awareness of his poor screenwriting skills as well as part of a wider industrial trend toward optioning and adapting literary work. We also know that Kubrick's ambitions in this period extended to potential adaptations. As early as 1952, he'd attempted to option the rights to several Joseph Conrad novels. In his ongoing reflections on filmmaking in his notebooks, he wrote that he believed the moment of "absolute success" for a director came when he was "allowed to film a great literary classic of over 600 pages . . . which is anyway impossible to film properly due to the complexity of the plot or the elusiveness of its form or content."[18] While *Clean Break* might not have been a literary classic, Kubrick had the opportunity with Harris-Kubrick Pictures and the sponsorship of James B. Harris to produce an adaptation.

The choice to adapt Lionel White's *Clean Break* showed that Harris-Kubrick Pictures consciously situated its production strategy within UA's abecedarian program. However, UA would not approve the adaptation until a screenplay had been completed, and so Harris hired author Jim Thompson to do just that. Thompson was known for his crime fiction, most notably by that point *The Killer Inside Me* (1952), *Savage Night* (1953), and *After Dark, My Sweet* (1955). His stories focused on outsiders—murderers, criminals, drifters, adulterers—and their sense of alienation. But by the mid-1950s, he had gained a reputation as being unreliable, with his hell-raising behavior compounded by his alcoholism. Many publishers were hesitant to work with him, and so he welcomed the employment offered to him by Harris-Kubrick Pictures.[19] He was paid $1,850 to write the screenplay, though he was given the credit only of writing the dialogue; Kubrick himself took the credit for the screenplay.[20] Still, Thompson would work for Harris-Kubrick Pictures on two further occasions: first as a writer on *Paths of Glory*, and second for an unmade project, *Lunatic at Large*.

With the script complete, Harris concluded negotiations with UA in September 1955 and secured a budget of $200,000. But the deal was a standard participation agreement, and Joseph Harris reproached his son for agreeing to such basic terms. UA did not even repay Harris-Kubrick Pictures for the cost of purchasing the rights to *Clean Break*, nor did they cover the costs of hiring Jim Thompson.[21] UA was a company without overheads, operating a subcontracting system of production. The company gave a minimal budget to untested producers and expected commercially viable, if somewhat low-budget product in return, which it would then distribute with no input from the independent producers. The only concession, following approval of the script and the major roles, was that

Harris-Kubrick Pictures had artistic autonomy of the production and control over the production budget.

The casting of the film was the first area in which UA attempted to assert control over Harris and Kubrick. This would have been an unnerving experience for Kubrick, who up to that point had cast his own choice of actors. The script for the film, given a working title of *Bed of Fear*, was sent to the Jaffe Agency, the talent agency established by Sam Jaffe in the 1930s that represented the likes of Humphrey Bogart, Lauren Bacall, Raoul Walsh, and Fritz Lang.[22] But it was largely ignored, something that Harris ascribed to the unknown status of Harris-Kubrick Pictures within the industry. The only caliber of actors that the agency offered up was Steve Cochran (*White Heat* [Walsh, 1949]) and Sterling Hayden (*The Asphalt Jungle* [Huston, 1950]). Harris and Kubrick agreed that Hayden would be ideal for the role, but UA's Max Youngstein—head of production and marketing—wanted a stronger male lead. He recommended Victor Mature, star of epic biblical tales such as *The Robe* (1953) and *Samson and Delilah* (1949), but he was tied up in other productions until late 1956. Youngstein advised Harris and Kubrick to wait for over a year until Mature became available, believing him to be a much stronger box office draw than Hayden.[23] Youngstein seemed to be basing his advice on the lackluster box office performance of other Hayden/UA products such as the Edward Small–produced western *Top Gun* (1955), and low-budget Republic westerns, such as *Timberjack* (1955) and *Shotgun* (1955). But Hayden's appearance in *The Last Command* (1955), a western that was originally meant to have John Wayne in the title role, undermined Youngstein's argument. As Harris argued, Hayden was in the lead role of a film that had a budget of over $1 million; he was more than strong enough for a film of the caliber that they were producing.[24]

Determined not to lose control of their production, Harris and Kubrick insisted on Hayden. As a result, Youngstein refused to allow the budget for the film to exceed the $200,000 set by UA. But when Harris hired a production manager, Clarence Eurist, to draw up a detailed budget for a twenty-three-day shoot, the cost came to $330,000.[25] With UA refusing to increase the budget following the fallout over Hayden, Harris and Kubrick were faced with a choice: either produce the film on a reduced budget or go against UA's terms and invest a further $130,000 into the production. UA warned that should Harris invest his own money in the project that it would reflect his poor judgment as a producer; he would not receive any return on his investment until UA had recouped their own $200,000.[26]

For Harris and Kubrick, the choice was not merely one of financial recompense but about their own future within the industry. They were determined to make the best film they could, one that stood out from the low-budget crime thrillers being produced as part of UA's abecedarian program. These were features that were often dismissed in the press as "mellers" (melodramas), competently produced but exploitative in nature and made to play as support on a double bill. Take a film like *The Big Bluff* (1955), directed by W. Lee Wilder; it was reviewed as having a routine narrative and being nothing more than a "modest melodrama ... tailored to the demands of the program market ... [it] will be an asset in twin bill bookings."[27] Similarly, *The Killer Is Loose* (Boetticher, 1956) was described as being in the suspense-thriller category but having "average b.o. prospects" and being a basic Hitchcockian meller.[28] Harris and Kubrick believed that if they produced their film on the $200,000 offered by UA alone it would result in a picture of *The Big Bluff* variety, that it would have to be produced on a much shorter shooting schedule, and that Kubrick's creativity would be hampered. Harris had savings of around $80,000 from his time at Flamingo Films and was able to negotiate a further $50,000 investment from his father. This allowed Harris to schedule a twenty-three-day shoot and a luxurious ten weeks of postproduction.[29]

It had been the original intention to base the production in New York, shooting at the Biograph Studio in the Bronx, and at a local racetrack.[30] But the decision was made to produce the film on location in California and at the Kling Studios (formerly the Charlie Chaplin Studios) on La Brea Avenue in Hollywood.[31] The stage rental costs of the Kling Studios were actually relatively cheap, at $13,000. This might have been, in part, because the Kling Studios were used from 1955 onward to film the *Adventures of Superman* series that Flamingo Films distributed to television via syndication. Harris could have been using his industrial contacts to negotiate the use of the studios.

A number of professional crew members were employed on the film, and Kubrick no longer had sole authorial control over the way the film was being photographed, having to work closely with cinematographer Lucien Ballard. Given that Ballard was an established figure within the industry and had commenced his career in pre-Code Hollywood, it was at times a tense collaboration. Ballard may have been a choice of UA rather than Harris and Kubrick; he had been the cinematographer on UA's *The Killer Is Loose*. But whatever the state of their working relationship, the results of Kubrick and Ballard working together were impressive.[32] From the use of dolly shots to a handheld shot of the dead bodies of the gang (personally operated by Kubrick), the film demonstrated an aesthetic quality that was far beyond its low-budget status. Kubrick asserted his directorial authority to develop a style that reflected a sense of "entrapment and isolation [that] is visually acute."[33]

As the production commenced, several stories were issued to the press. Harris was surely thinking ahead to how the film could be promoted and knew full well that once the film was handed over to UA, he would have no control over it. The stories showed that Harris and Kubrick were positioning the film as being innovative, original, and something that would appeal to young people. One such story promoted the fact that Ruth Sobotka, who was the film's art director, was apparently the first female to receive such a credit on a Hollywood feature. This story was surely provided by Kubrick, appearing initially in an A. H. Weiler column in the *New York Times*.[34] Another story played up the film's "dangerous" storyline: following a complaint from American Airlines, the film's ending had to be revised: "Original finale had Hayden being cut to pieces by a plane's propeller as he chased some $2,000,000 in wind-blown cash around an airport. Airline protested that it might lead the public to think airport safety regulations are laxly enforced, so the indie changed the ending to have Hayden shot down by cops."[35] It could well be that this story was put out as a means of generating interest in the film as well as a means of misdirecting the audience from the actual plot twist. Other stories appeared in the *Los Angeles Times*, no doubt as a result of press releases, including one that promoted actor Vince Edwards as the new Marlon Brando or James Dean.[36]

The production was mostly unproblematic, aside from a brief hiatus after Sterling Hayden suffered a back injury.[37] This did mean the need to hire a stunt man, Robert Morgan, to fill in for Hayden in some sequences.[38] However, UA was not pleased with the first cut of the film. Renamed *The Killing* (presumably at the behest of UA's publicity department), the film was edited in a nonlinear manner, with the narrative unfolding in a series of progressive flashbacks. Max Youngstein claimed this to be a serious problem that would affect the commercial potential of the film, along with the problem of Hayden in the lead role.[39] Youngstein was arguably being narrow-sighted given how popular the crime film was with audiences in 1956. Concurrent to *The Killing*, two other crime films—both set in New York—were released and performed well: *Patterns* (Cook, 1956) and *Crimes in the Street* (Siegel, 1956).

But perhaps as a means of punishing Harris and Kubrick for going against his advice, Youngstein barely gave *The Killing* any publicity, with limited advertising for the film. Even though they believed they had made an excellent picture, Harris and Kubrick appeared not to have made any advance in their status in the industry. As such, the pair devised their own ideas to promote the film, knowing full well that publicity and advertising were key to the success of the picture. Harris and Kubrick's ideas included a full-page ad that featured the pair in director's chairs under the headline "the new UA team."[40] The duo stare directly into the camera while beside them are two cases of film reels. Underneath is a diagram that introduces the three components of the advert: "1) the producer: James B Harris-Kubrick; 2) the director Stanley Kubrick; * the suspense picture of the year 'THE KILLING.'" The advert was hardly presumptuous; after all, UA had promised Harris-Kubrick Pictures a multipicture deal. Harris felt that the advert would promote both *The Killing* and also Harris-Kubrick Pictures. But when Youngstein saw the ad he dismissed it as inappropriate.[41] Harris published the advert regardless, and it appeared in *Variety* in March 1956. It further soured the relationship between Harris-Kubrick Pictures and UA, Youngstein describing it as being "near the bottom."[42] It now seemed that any immediate future project with UA was not forthcoming, particularly after Youngstein vented his fury in a telephone call to Harris, suggesting the advert had humiliated UA. Despite sending a written letter of apology to the company, the production partnership between UA and Harris-Kubrick Pictures was effectively over.[43]

In many respects, the deterioration in the relationship with UA freed Harris and Kubrick to pursue their own publicity for *The Killing*. They believed this to be necessary as they had no obvious route to a second feature. Harris began enlisting the services of a publicist, Kay Proctor, to generate Academy Award attention for the film. On October 29, 1956, Proctor sent a letter to Harris saying she had designed an advertising slogan for *The Killing*: "The Killing is tailor made for an Oscar."[44] She gave Harris permission to use the phrasing or the similar "Oscar calibre."[45] The ad was eventually published in *Variety* on November 14, 1956. But Harris's efforts did not prevent *The Killing*'s poor commercial performance, and he lost his $130,000 investment.[46]

The Killing did become somewhat of a minor hit on the U.S. art-house circuit, including in Minneapolis. The film had been an absolute box office failure in the major Minneapolis downtown theaters in the early summer of 1956, but by August of that year, *Variety* reported that the film was "doing sensational business at, of all places, a local neighborhood 'fine arts' theatre, the Campus."[47] There had been considerable growth in art-house cinemas in the 1950s and an increase in the screenings of European films.[48] These avant-garde and European films blurred the boundaries between exploitation and art, with their representation of sex on screen (what *Variety* called the "busty boom," in reference to stars such as Brigitte Bardot)[49] making it possible for them to be marketed equally in an art-house university theater and in an exploitation cinema on New York's Forty-Second Street.

The blurred boundaries of *The Killing* meant no theaters agreed to book the film in Minneapolis other than the Campus, an art cinema located next to the University of Minnesota. The Campus ran an ad campaign nicknamed the "double-your-money back guarantee": if theatergoers did not find the film the most suspenseful picture of the year, they got a refund—the theater received no refund requests.[50] The manager of the Campus had made the decision to book the film when his "attention was called to the film's merits and to the fact that its downtown stint had undoubtedly passed practically unnoticed and that few people probably were aware it had already played here (it hadn't even garnered a newspaper review)."[51] The largely student demographic made the film one of the Campus's highest grossers, despite the owner of the Campus being discouraged from booking the film, "with emphasis on the fact it isn't an 'art' attraction."[52] The success of *The Killing* at Minneapolis's Campus Theatre was replicated at other art-house venues, including Pittsburgh's Guild Theatre. The Guild's owners felt *The Killing* to be "late-summer filler before the top foreign fall product," but the film became one of the theater's highest grossing films of the year and its booking was extended long into the autumn.[53] The owners of the Guild explained that the film was "running way over and above takes for some of the outstanding overseas product... playing lately"; this included Jules Dassin's heist thriller *Rififi* (1955).[54] The Guild Theatre was located in Pittsburgh's Squirrel Hill district, which contained two private universities.

With a nonlinear narrative, voice-over, and existentialist themes, *The Killing* resonated with a growing youth demographic that was increasingly attracted to foreign and avant-garde films. Harris-Kubrick Pictures had attempted to diversify beyond the aesthetic and financial constraints of UA's low-budget abecedarian program by producing an ambitious art-exploitation film. Reviews of *The Killing* acknowledged both its "intellectual contemplation" and its "emotional engagement, corporeal thrills," while *Sight and Sound*'s Gavin Lambert described the film as a "shrewd, engrossing, complete-in-itself melodrama."[55] *Variety* described it as a "suspenseful melo" and as "sturdy fare for the action market, where it can be exploited for better than average returns."[56] At the same time, *Variety* identified one of the reasons for why the film would not perform well at the box office, describing the film as being "occasionally told in a documentary style, which at first tends to be somewhat confusing."[57] The *Manchester Guardian* proclaimed Kubrick the "new master of the thriller" and found it quite incomprehensible that the film was playing "as a humble 'second feature' at the Dominion" and other cinemas across London. The paper predicted that Kubrick was going to "leave his mark on the American cinema" and that he was already "the peer of John Huston."[58]

Lambert's comparison of Kubrick to Huston is not without basis. Huston largely adapted the films he made, either by himself or with a cowriter; they were often dominated by damaged male protagonists; they predominantly, but not exclusively, marginalized female roles; and he commenced his career working on pulp and urban crime thrillers (*The Maltese Falcon* [1941]; *The Asphalt Jungle* [1950]), before progressing to more literary and prestigious adaptations (his 1956 adaptation of Herman Melville's *Moby Dick* [1851] and 1979 adaptation of Flannery O'Connor's *Wise Blood* [1952], for example). Kubrick would do the same as he turned his attention to his future projects.

Overdevelopment

Kubrick no doubt recognized the irony that despite *The Killing* being the first feature that he was proud of producing, it received a limited release and limited publicity. He even started writing to his former colleagues at *Look* asking them to lobby UA to arrange screenings in their local cinema.[59] Kubrick was clearly keeping a close eye on the reviews of the film and the audience reaction. In stark contrast to *Fear and Desire* and *Killer's Kiss* where he witnessed audiences leaving with "slightly embarrassed expressions," he sensed that audiences found *The Killing* entertaining.[60]

Max Youngstein had perhaps been shortsighted in his approach with *The Killing* and in the working relationship with Harris-Kubrick Pictures. Internationally, the film was doing respectable business. UA's New Zealand office was particularly impressed with its performance and secured an extra week's screening for it as a single feature at the State Theatre in Auckland. The New Zealand office, so impressed with the reviews and performance of *The Killing*, also released *Killer's Kiss* and promoted it with a "Kubrick angle."[61] Meanwhile, the trade press and newspapers in the United States were writing numerous articles about Harris and Kubrick, profiling them as the "boy wonders," the industry's "most versatile young talents," and suggesting that the way they produced *The Killing* showed they had "more audacity with dialogue and camera than Hollywood has seen since the obstreperous Orson Welles."[62] The *Los Angeles Times* even suggested that, despite their youth, Harris and Kubrick were by now "veterans" of the film and television industry, and in many respects they were. Harris had been working as a producer for nearly a decade, while Kubrick had actively entered filmmaking seven years previous.[63]

The attention and critical praise Harris-Kubrick Pictures was receiving, along with the trade ad it had placed in *Variety*, attracted the attention of several studios, including RKO and Warner Bros. But it was Dore Schary, head of production at MGM, who enticed Harris-Kubrick Pictures, perhaps as a result of his desire to purchase *The Killing* from UA and provide it with a substantial publicity campaign. But UA refused to sell the film, Youngstein's grudge against Harris and Kubrick persisting.[64] In June 1956, Schary offered Harris-Kubrick Pictures a participation deal for their next project.[65] Harris and Kubrick wanted to adapt Humphrey Cobb's *Paths of Glory* (1935), but Schary refused; MGM's previous antiwar film, *The Red Badge of Courage* (1951), directed by John Huston, had failed spectacularly at the box office, with a loss of over $1 million. Instead, Schary was interested in a potential adaptation of Stefan Zweig's *Burning Secret* (1911), a story of an extramarital affair.[66]

By 1956, Harris-Kubrick Pictures initiated a deliberate production strategy that would become a defining feature of the company: overdevelopment. This was a process by which independent production companies would invest resources in more new projects than they could feasibly produce. This was done by acquiring literary properties, hiring writers to develop extended treatments, or registering potential titles. What resulted was a "surplus of unproduced films."[67] The strategy of overdevelopment adopted by Harris-Kubrick Pictures reflected wider industrial trends in the late 1950s, particularly of acquiring literary properties for adaptation. This was most likely as a result of the changing industrial conditions in Hollywood, moving from what head of production at Paramount Frank Freeman called "the old order to the new (participation agreements instead of contract performers and creative talent)."[68] The formation of independent production companies had become the norm by the mid-1950s, incorporated by producers, actors, writers, and directors. But this move to independent production companies packaging and producing films for distribution by the major Hollywood companies had a drawback: there was a rapid decline in the number of films being produced. In part this was because control of production had now moved from the major studios to independent producers like Harris-Kubrick Pictures, making it difficult for the majors to "plan a specified number of pictures annually."[69] But it was also because participation deals involved producers taking a share of the profits, leading to an overall increase in production costs.

Overdevelopment was a symptom of these changing industrial conditions. With independence came uncertainty that a project would ever be developed, produced, or even released. Therefore, independent producers developed a "constant flow of projects... because of the anticipated failure (or rejection) of most of them by the studios."[70] This was a belief that seemed to be at the heart of Harris-Kubrick Pictures' own business strategy by the spring of 1956. It had become clear that the three-picture arrangement with UA had ended, while the deal with MGM, though promising, might not have resulted in any actual production.

Harris's own role in overdevelopment was crucial. Though both he and Kubrick shared in the decision-making process, he was the one who negotiated deals and bought literary property. This commenced in earnest following the completion of *The Killing*. In March 1956, Harris-Kubrick Pictures hired Shelby Foote to write an original story, *The Down Slope*, about the Confederate Colonel John S. Mosby.[71] Foote was a novelist and American Civil War historian. He was to write a twelve-page outline, with the story focusing on Mosby's Partisan Rangers and the execution of six of his men by Union forces. In April 1956, the *New York Times* reported that Harris-Kubrick Pictures had purchased the rights to Foote's *Love in a Dry Season* (1951), a Civil War tale of love and infidelity in the American South that Kubrick would adapt.[72] It was unlike anything Kubrick had attempted to produce or direct up to that point and suggested both a personal artistic maturity and that Harris-Kubrick Pictures, through the process of overdevelopment, was attempting to diversify its product and brand.

Diversification was another side effect of the changing industrial conditions in Hollywood. Independent production companies needed to diversify their film output by the late 1950s to appeal, among other things, to a changing demographic in the United States.[73] Independent producers that limited themselves to a particular genre ran a significant financial risk given the inherent dangers of independent production, most significantly that of product differentiation. Throughout the 1950s, marketing and promoting the unique selling points of a film became crucial and relying on particular genre was not a guarantee of box office success. Producers such as Stanley Kramer and companies like Hecht-Hill-Lancaster "placed their eggs in single baskets: each produced essentially one kind of picture. Since these types only had limited appeal, the producers placed themselves at a disadvantage from the start by not diversifying."[74]

Harris-Kubrick Pictures instead diversified by moving from genre to genre with each new picture. It became more ambitious in scope and turned to literary adaptation, as demonstrated by the purchase of Foote's *Love in a Dry*

Season. But Harris-Kubrick Pictures' diversification was also linked to its strategy of overdevelopment. If a financier or major Hollywood studio did not like a particular genre of picture, say a Civil War romance, Harris-Kubrick could provide another package, say a World War I picture with a leading male star.

What occurred throughout 1956 was the purchase and development of a number of projects alongside the Civil War project (which would continue to interest Kubrick for the next two years). By July 1956, Harris-Kubrick Pictures had purchased the rights to Humphrey Cobb's World War I anti-military hierarchy novel *Paths of Glory* and hired Jim Thompson to write a screenplay;[75] Calder Willingham was hired to adapt with Kubrick Zweig's *Burning Secret* and later hired to work on *Paths of Glory*; the company developed a Hitchcockian thriller called *The Blind Mirror*; and it initiated the development of a series of original stories by Kubrick, including *Married Man*, *Jealousy*, *Perfect Marriage*, and fragments of many other ideas. But it seemed that only two projects were being given serious attention: *Burning Secret*, which was slated for production in the winter of 1956–1957, and *Paths of Glory*, which would be produced in Europe in the spring of 1957.[76]

But despite the ambitions, Harris-Kubrick Pictures was still at the mercy of industrial conditions and the fact its name was still not very well established. Between 1955 and 1959 MGM, with which Harris-Kubrick Pictures intended to produce *Burning Secret* and *Paths of Glory*, was undergoing "management turmoil... with the board of directors constantly fighting over who would control the company and what direction it would take."[77] MGM had suffered losses in the fourth quarter of 1955 and the first quarter of 1956. Dore Schary was thereby seeking ways to "bolster the company's output," perhaps why he had initially offered Harris-Kubrick Pictures a deal.[78] But by midsummer 1956, MGM was looking to make efficiency savings and to "reduce manpower in various departments."[79] MGM, along with Twentieth Century Fox, had been one of the slowest of the majors to adapt to the fast-changing industrial conditions in Hollywood. By 1956, MGM finally acknowledged a need to reevaluate its operational procedures, with Schary concluding that "in today's economy all studios 'must examine (their) economy and stop waste.'"[80] MGM began ending contracts with various personnel and hired an "efficiency expert," while shareholders forced Schary out of the company.[81] With Schary being paid off, MGM used it as an opportunity to "trim expenses" and remove from the payroll Harris-Kubrick Pictures.[82]

Existential Uncertainty

By the autumn of 1956, Harris and Kubrick were without any kind of deal or any immediate prospects of getting a film out of development and into production. Despite the critical esteem of *The Killing* and the numerous projects they had in development, they were in effect still outsiders in the American film industry. They faced an existential threat, with Harris-Kubrick Pictures needing to make a profit given the amount of money that had been invested by Harris and his father, while Kubrick himself was indebted to Harris.

The existential and financial uncertainty they faced, along with the outsider status, seems to have played on Kubrick's mind at the time. He developed a series of ideas for stories, most of which were probably never intended to be seriously produced, but which reflected his wider emotional state. They contain clear traces of autobiography and possess similar themes and tropes. *The Famished Monkey*, for example, tells the story of a poet living in Greenwich Village who indulges in numerous affairs and "lives off other people" but is desperate to end such dependency.[83] The story is incomplete, with only a few fragments left. But Kubrick pursued the idea repeatedly. In *New York Story*, the main character, Howard, is an unsuccessful painter who lives alone in a cold-water flat in Greenwich Village.[84] Howard is another libertine-type character who has never worked to support himself and is engaged in an affair with a fifty-year-old widow, mainly as a result of financial dependency. But just like *The Famished Monkey*, the theme was outgrowing such dependency.

Time and again the characters Kubrick created were failed artists trapped in doomed relationships. The latter was a theme that seemed to dominate his thinking in 1956, starting with the adaptation of *Love in a Dry Season* and *Burning Secret*. It may well have been that themes of love, marriage, and anxiety of new-found romance preoccupied Kubrick as a result of his own disintegrating relationship with Ruth Sobotka. In *Anxious Husband Prepares for His Bride*, Kubrick seemed to want to develop a scene that detailed the embarrassments of a newly married couple as they entered their "nuptial apartment."[85] In an untitled idea, Kubrick developed a scenario in which a man nervously prepares to confess to a longtime friend his undying love for her, but "when confronted with the reality of the situation loses all composure."[86]

Three significant stories that emerged in the mid-1950s were *Jealousy*, *Married Man*, and *The Perfect Marriage*. The three ideas reflected two key concerns for Kubrick. First was what he called his fascination in representing New York on screen, wanting to depict the city and its people "honestly and in realistic terms."[87] The second was his interest in love stories and to develop them in contrast to the typical Hollywood romance that had been "made over and over."[88] This seemed to mean developing stories that focused very much on the philosophy of love, dissected in a way that echoed novelists such as D. H. Lawrence. *Jealousy* tells the story of John Conrad, a wealthy business manager in New York who is suspicious that his wife is having an affair. He secretly follows his wife around Lower Manhattan, but finds nothing amiss. Still gripped with paranoia, he confronts his wife, who tries to reassure him. She suggests he visit a psychologist to talk through his anxiety. *Jealousy* then descends into an examination of psychoanalytical ideas, ideas that would have been prevalent in New York at that time and perhaps also reflected Kubrick's own ongoing psychoanalysis. Conrad begins to have visions of his wife's infidelity and so, after getting drunk in a New York bar, looks for a girl to sleep with. He returns to the girl's apartment but cannot bring himself to sleep with her. "I love my wife," he says.[89] *Jealousy* could very well have been Kubrick's attempt at loosely adapting Arthur Schnitzler's *Traumnovelle*, the book that would be adapted as *Eyes Wide Shut* (1999) some forty years later.

The Perfect Marriage and *Married Man* continued the themes of *Jealousy*. *The Perfect Marriage* was more a series of philosophical reflections on what Kubrick termed the "marriage story," rather than an actual plot outline. Some of the statements again echo themes from Schnitzler, particularly the claim of "the disappearing virtue of women and the lack of awareness of this fact by men" and what he said were the problems in a relationship caused by this.[90] *Married Man* is perhaps the most vicious and brutal of the marriage stories Kubrick developed at this time, incorporating all the themes he had been working on: present were the outsiders, the libertines, the failed artists, the financial dependents, the jealous lovers, and the failed lovers.

Married Man is largely told through dialogue and indeed reads almost like a stage play. The main characters are Howard (Kubrick's alter ego and a pornographer), Alice (Howard's wife), Peter (Howard's best friend), and Leslie (Howard's mistress). Howard confesses to Peter how much he hates being married to Alice, calling it a drag because she is obsessed with him. "Can you imagine the horrors of living with a woman who fastens herself on you like a rubber suction cup?" he asks. He doesn't understand how Alice can love him given he is the only man she has ever been with. Worse still, he isn't sure he can divorce her because of her fragile mental state. The tensions between Howard and Alice are on display later that evening when they invite Peter for dinner. Howard excuses himself from the dinner as a means of escaping Alice and to meet up with another friend, Lionel. He tells Lionel that he hopes Peter will make an advance on Alice, knowing full well that he is in love with her. Lionel is a despicable womanizer, and his dialogue filled with sexual innuendo. He turns to a young woman, Bambi, and invites her up to his apartment for a "chess lesson." Meanwhile, Howard pursues his affair with Leslie, meeting her at the Rienzi café. She admits that she wants to marry him and wishes he'd end his marriage to Alice. So Howard manufactures an argument with Alice, accusing her of cheating on him with Peter. A violent disagreement ensues in which Howard, hysterical with rage, hits Alice and calls her a "phoney, simpering, stupid, crummy little tramp." The scene has echoes of the arguments between Jack and Wendy in *The Shining*, right down to Howard mimicking Alice's voice in the way Jack mimics Wendy. Howard leaves Alice and marries Leslie, at which point the story abruptly ends.[91]

What these stories show is Kubrick's confidence in developing projects beyond the kind of genres he'd been working in throughout the early 1950s. His work was becoming motivated by his own intellectual interests and even his own life experiences living in Greenwich Village. The dubious quality, even viciousness of his "marriage stories" was perhaps too much for them to ever truly be considered for serious production, but it is clear that he was thinking about how to develop a story about love and marriage. This might have been an artistic development encouraged by Harris, or maybe even an exercise to write away his own inner turmoil and anxieties, particularly due to the existential crisis his career faced by the end of 1956.

But there is also another reason we know that Harris-Kubrick Pictures was intent on pursuing projects more seriously than the marriage stories. Along the margins of the outline for *Married Man* are handwritten notes about *Paths of Glory*, with a focus on the cast. Among other things, Kubrick scrawled the names of his desired choices for the role of General Broulard, including Spencer Tracy, Peter Ustinov, Clark Gable, Humphrey Bogart, James Mason, and Gregory Peck. Kubrick had written to Peck in November 1956 to ask him if he would be interested in the role and provided him with a copy of the Calder Willingham–revised script.[92] As for the role of Colonel Dax, Kubrick scrawled the names Richard Burton, Henry Fonda, Robert Mitchum, and Kirk Douglas. Kubrick's thoughts on potential stars show that Harris-Kubrick Pictures was considering a leading man for *Paths of Glory*. This fed into a document compiled by the company titled "Factors Influencing Movie Attendance," in which it was concluded that for a film to be a success, in terms of both being picked up by a studio and performing well at the box office, it needed the combination of a quality writer and a major star.[93] Harris-Kubrick Pictures was putting together a package that it hoped would bring to an end the outsider status from which it was suffering by the end of 1956. The package it was developing was intended to be irresistible to the major companies: an action picture starring Kirk Douglas, one of Hollywood's leading men.

Conclusion

In partnering with James B. Harris, Kubrick had found the sponsor he had needed to move him from the precarious circumstances of the privately financed pictures he was producing in the early 1950s. Together they had produced *The Killing*, which, notwithstanding its commercial failure, attracted the attention of Hollywood players like Dore Schary. Unfortunately, they were still outsiders, part of a new industrial situation in which independent production companies were vying for financing from the major studios. As a result, Harris-Kubrick Pictures implemented a business strategy of overdevelopment and diversification in order to demonstrate it could make more than just another low-budget crime thriller.

But the situation for Harris-Kubrick Pictures by the end of 1956 was fragile. The company needed a development deal and, more important, a sponsor to help it break through into the mainstream and to have access to the influential cultural networks of Hollywood. Despite Harris's own networks—which it must be noted included major players like David B. Stillman, a lawyer to film executives and who would serve as the president of Seven Arts Productions from 1960 to his death in 1963—was not enough. What was necessary instead was the sponsorship of a major star. Therefore, it seems that a conscious decision was made by Harris and Kubrick to package a picture with a major Hollywood actor who could elevate them and their company into the mainstream of Hollywood production culture. As discussed in chapter 5, Kirk Douglas would become that sponsor—arguably one of the most influential sponsors of Kubrick's entire career—but in aligning themselves with Douglas, Harris and Kubrick would run the risk of permanently losing their business and creative autonomy.

5
New Modes of Producing, 1957–1959

By the end of the 1950s, spaces of autonomy had opened within the American film industry. The rapid postwar increase in the incorporation of independent production companies meant that large swaths of creative control now rested with the actors, writers, directors, and producers who had once been contracted to the major studios. One former studio boss who understood the paradigm shift that had taken place in Hollywood was Darryl F. Zanuck of Twentieth Century Fox. Zanuck left the studio in 1956 to become an independent producer and later reflected on this decision: "The head of the studio was no longer in charge; he was becoming a negotiator, an executive, a peacemaker."[1] Yet the balance of power was still in favor of the major studios, with companies like Fox, Paramount, MGM, and UA in control of the product the producers were making due to being the distributors, promoters, and financiers of their films. UA, for example, retained control over the publicity strategies of the films it distributed, creating a "progressive promotion program" leading to an increase in promotion budgets and an increase in film revenue.[2] Publicity and distribution became a key battleground for control over the coming decade as independent producers like Kubrick attempted to obtain full creative and business autonomy, in the process marginalizing studios to the role of nothing more than a global distribution service. What was happening in Hollywood throughout the 1950s and 1960s was that independent producers, Kubrick prominent among them, were taking advantage of the spaces of autonomy that had been created by the shift in the mode of production as the Hollywood studio system transitioned to a form of semi-independent production.

By the start of 1957, Harris-Kubrick Pictures was presented with the opportunity to exploit these spaces of autonomy when it agreed a deal with Kirk Douglas's Bryna Productions. Bryna was Douglas's independent production company that he had incorporated in 1949 following the success of *Champion* (Robson, 1949), a boxing drama produced by Stanley Kramer. The agreement with Bryna and the working relationship with Douglas was, in many ways, the most significant point in Kubrick's career. By collaborating and even working for Douglas, Kubrick had entered the heart of Hollywood. But at the same time, he was at a transitional crossroads whereby he could easily lose the control of his productions, and his career that he desired.

This chapter traces the perilous "Kirk Douglas years," initially focusing on the period of 1957 to 1959, in which Harris and Kubrick produced *Paths of Glory* (1957), developed several unmade projects, and even threatened to part ways with each other. It was a chaotic period, but also one of Kubrick's most creatively fertile, despite the contractual bondage to Kirk Douglas. It was also a period in which Harris-Kubrick Pictures diversified to become an international production company, relocating to Europe to produce *Paths of Glory* and contemplating producing numerous other projects abroad. However, this chapter begins with a consideration of the deal Harris-Kubrick Pictures made with Bryna Productions.

Deal with Douglas

Harris and Kubrick met with Kirk Douglas in his Palm Springs mansion sometime at the beginning of 1957. It would be a "crossroads" moment for Harris and Kubrick, one in which they would potentially sell their autonomy in return for one of Hollywood's biggest stars to agree to help package *Paths of Glory*. But, as Harris recalls, despite being offered "the most outrageous deal," he and Kubrick were desperate and "anxious as hell" for his support and attachment to the project.[3] In return for Douglas appearing in the lead role of *Paths of Glory*, Harris-Kubrick Pictures would make three further films for Bryna on a nonexclusive contract. Harris and Kubrick agreed.

The details of the agreement were set out at a lunch at the Brown Derby restaurant in Beverly Hills in January 1957. Present were Harris, Kubrick, Douglas, their respective agents, and Stan Margulies, who ran Public Relations Ltd, the company that oversaw the publicity and merchandising of Bryna's films and had a specific remit to protect Douglas's star image.[4] A five-point memorandum of understanding resulted from the meeting, which set out the conditions of the four-picture deal between the two companies, which included *Paths of Glory*.[5] Bryna Productions would have no ownership interest in *Paths of Glory*, with Douglas serving merely as an employee of Harris-Kubrick Pictures. But the film would be branded as a Bryna Production, despite being produced by Harris-Kubrick Pictures. Presumably, this was because Kirk Douglas would be the one to approach UA, the company that financed and distributed the project, to make a deal; after all, as discussed in chapter 4 the relationship between Harris-Kubrick Pictures and UA had broken down during the production of *The Killing*. In contrast, Kirk Douglas and Bryna had an ongoing working relationship with UA, including a nonexclusive six-picture contract that had commenced in 1955.[6]

Harris and Kubrick agreed to Bryna taking the production credit for *Paths of Glory* only in return for the promise that Bryna and Public Relations' publicity campaign would build them "as individuals."[7] The motivation for Harris and Kubrick joining forces with Kirk Douglas was the hope that he would promote them and allow them to gain access to the mainstream of Hollywood. However, in the coming months, the deal did not work out quite as planned. Harris and Kubrick knew they'd made a mistake once they started to see the agreement written in legal form. Harris-Kubrick Pictures was required to use Bryna's "administrative and other facilities" in Los Angeles, including the services of Public Relations.[8] The primary function of Public Relations was to "create, execute and supervise all publicity, exploitation and advertising on motion pictures produced by Bryna," to "hire and supervise personnel needed," and to work with the "publicity-advertising department of the distributing company."[9] In effect, Harris-Kubrick was left with no control over the publicity of the films it produced for Bryna nor of the publicity of *Paths of Glory*.

The remaining three contractually bound projects after *Paths of Glory* required Harris and Kubrick to work as employees of Bryna. The first picture had to be made within fifteen months of the completion of postproduction on *Paths of Glory*. Bryna could designate a project of its choice, and Harris and Kubrick would write, produce, and direct the picture.[10] The financial terms of this project entitled Harris-Kubrick Pictures to receive "an amount equal to 15 percent of budget of picture not exceeding $75,000."[11] This would suggest the production budget was set at $500,000, half that of *Paths of Glory*. On top of this payment, Harris-Kubrick Pictures would receive a percentage of any profits, shared equally with Bryna. While the contractual agreement for the first two films was firm (*Paths of Glory* and a further picture to star Kirk Douglas),[12] Bryna could choose to exercise the option on the final two pictures "three months after the completion of the second picture and both pictures to be made within eighteen months after the exercise of option."[13] Harris-Kubrick would receive a much smaller producer's profit on these two option pictures, particularly on the final option where it would receive an amount "equal to 10 percent of the budget ... plus 10 percent of 100 percent of the net profits."[14]

The most alarming feature of the agreement was that Bryna could force Harris-Kubrick to sell any literary property it owned.[15] This included any original stories or creative property that the company had in development. Harris-Kubrick had entered a contractual arrangement that would leave it without any legal producing authority or creative control following the completion of *Paths of Glory*. This was a heavy price to pay in order to secure Douglas in the lead role and "was antithetical to what Kubrick aimed to achieve leading to an absolute loss of autonomy."[16] Even though this was a nonexclusive contract, it effectively bound Harris-Kubrick Pictures to Bryna for the foreseeable future and "put Bryna and Douglas in a position of ownership over its creative and business functions."[17] In their agreement to the deal, we can see just how desperate Harris and Kubrick believed the situation was for them and their company; it must have been a case that should they have turned down the agreement, Harris-Kubrick Pictures most likely would have ceased operations, in turn bringing to an end Harris and Kubrick's own careers in the industry. Harris recalls that he knew the deal was unfair, but it was an investment, in terms of not only the hoped-for commercial returns on *Paths of Glory* at the box office, but the cultural networks it would open up by producing a film with Kirk Douglas. The aim would be for Harris and Kubrick to produce *Paths of Glory* and then to get out of the deal with Bryna by whatever means necessary.

Runaway Productions

Paths of Glory is an adaptation of the bleak anti-military establishment novel written by Humphrey Cobb in 1935. Set on the Western Front trenches in World War I, it focuses on the hypocrisy of the French military High Command. An attack is ordered on an impenetrable German fortress, but when the attack fails a court-martial is convened, with three soldiers selected at random to face charges of cowardice. Their commanding officer, Colonel Dax, attempts to defend them but realizes the trial is nothing more than a sham designed as a means for those in command to receive promotions. The soldiers are found guilty and executed by firing squad.

Harris-Kubrick hired Jim Thompson and Calder Willingham to adapt the script throughout 1956 and early 1957, with Kubrick also working on a version of the script in 1957. Kubrick first approached Willingham in June 1956 to work on the adaptation of *Burning Secret*.[18] Willingham was a prolific author who had written a best seller by the age of twenty-five, *End as a Man* (1947), a controversial work that attacked the machismo culture of military life. It is set in a military academy in the southern United States, where the cadets are subjected to a "rigid aristocratic discipline," overseen by the "sadist, Jocko de Paris," a corporal known for his "excessive brutality to his squad."[19] The book was noted for its realism, satiric humor, and critical view of U.S. military life. As such, Kubrick probably viewed Willingham as the ideal writer to adapt *Paths of Glory* given its anti–military hierarchy theme.

Kirk Douglas was also keen to provide his own suggestions on the development of the script. Shortly after the agreement between Harris-Kubrick Pictures and Bryna in January 1957, Douglas commenced researching *Paths of Glory*, reading the book and comparing it to a January 1957 draft script. He sent his notes to Kubrick in February of that year and, while noting the project was Kubrick's "baby," genuinely felt that the script could be improved.[20] Douglas focused his changes on the character he was to play, Colonel Dax, calling for the role to have greater prominence and more characterization.[21] Kubrick acknowledged Douglas's letter, but the changes in characterization were largely unheeded. And while Douglas had said he was not "wedded" to any of the criticism he had made, he did protest a revised ending to the script in which the condemned soldiers were saved from execution.[22] The proposed change had come about as a means of commercializing the film, but Douglas vetoed the decision. After all, a key reason he had agreed to make *Paths of Glory* was because he felt strongly about its antiwar themes;[23] they resonated with his liberal instincts, which became an increasing feature of the films he starred in and produced by the end of the 1950s.

The change in *Paths of Glory*'s ending may also have been a result of the controversial nature of the plot and the potential for problems with national censors, particularly in Europe. The MPAA warned Harris-Kubrick Pictures that the overall theme of the film and its representation of the French military would inevitably lead to protests about its release in France. As such, the MPAA recommended that "UA and Harris-Kubrick needed to work closely together in their approach to publicising the film in Europe to avoid any potential political fallout."[24] However, despite the caution issued by the MPAA, Kubrick reverted the script to its original ending, retaining its powerful anti-military hierarchy theme.

The film was shot on location in Germany, including at the Schleissheim Castle north of Munich and at Munich's Geiselgasteig film studios. The decision to base the production overseas conformed to a growing trend of internationalization within the film industry. American productions increasingly took to filming outside of the United States throughout the 1950s, taking advantage of, among other things, European government subsidies as well as perceived lower costs of production. These "runaway productions," as they came to be known, caused consternation within the American film industry, particularly among unions, which feared that it was leading to specialized roles being given to overseas workers.[25] But Frank Freeman, a former Paramount executive and chairman of the Association of Motion Picture Producers, issued a stark warning to those with such fears: without foreign market revenue most of the Hollywood majors would be out of business and so "companies must produce pictures with an international appeal."[26] As Peter Krämer has argued, Kubrick's own work "in terms of both subject matter and production circumstances, . . . became ever more international" from the late 1950s onward.[27] In many respects, Kubrick had always been focused toward producing his films wherever the production circumstances were best suited: whether that be shooting a film or television series in Mexico or in Turkey (as he considered in April 1958), the motivating factors were always "the possibilities of co-financing... the production facilities and the costs."[28]

Paths of Glory was not the only UA-backed production to move overseas in 1957, with the company earmarking approximately $20 million for overseas productions, more than any other U.S. film company at that time.[29] But industrial contexts might have had less to do with the relocation of *Paths of Glory* overseas than the fact that *The Vikings*, a Bryna Production for UA with Douglas in the starring role, was to be shot in Europe immediately after, and therefore it suited Douglas, and UA, to have the production based overseas.[30]

Press releases throughout the production emphasized *Paths of Glory*'s German production, with Stan Margulies directing the film's unit publicist, Syd Stogel, to document Kirk Douglas traveling around the region. A press release joked that Douglas, upon arriving in Munich, had developed German language skills due to a book "he carried under his arm. The title? 'Learn to Speak German in 20 Easy lessons.'"[31] Another press release showed that Douglas was settling in to local life, visiting regional Bavarian ale houses.[32] When Margulies and UA learned that Harris was creating a documentary to record the production, they directed him to develop a travelogue, with Douglas visiting local tourist spots.[33]

Paths of Glory was the most ambitious film that Harris and Kubrick had produced, re-creating an authentic World War I battlefield and employing the services of a military adviser, Baron von Waldenfels. The production ran from March 20 until June 3, 1957, with a total of fifty-nine shooting days. Such a long shoot was necessary given the complicated exterior scenes in the trenches that take place in the first half of the film. The main exterior location used for the battle sequence was Puccheim, a small city twenty-five miles west of Munich. Despite the filming of the sequences in Puccheim not taking place until May, the production was already organizing the logistics to achieve the necessary realism in March. Much of Harris's time was devoted to the complicated administration of these sequences, including liaising with the U.S. Army about the use of troops in the film.[34]

The film came in at just over $1 million, $350,000 of which was the salary paid to Kirk Douglas. But despite the scale of the project and the quality of the final film, Douglas still reproached Harris-Kubrick Pictures for what he believed poor budgetary management, claiming that the company needed to be more economical in its production methods. His own review of the budget "found many ways where money could be saved."[35] Douglas was right that the production had run over budget, but it was minimal and was largely a result of the numerous extras employed for the battle scenes.[36] Douglas would have been aware that UA adopted a rather relaxed attitude toward budget management, leaving the production budget in the control of the independent producer. This was in line with UA's mode of operation in the 1950s, wanting to create an atmosphere of creativity that allowed producers "to work autonomously once a project is agreed upon."[37] Underlying this was the company attitude that every picture had to be considered a failure from the start, "then if it's a success, well, that means the hard work has paid off and we're agreeably surprised."[38] Certainly there was an inherent risk in UA's policy of granting autonomy of the budget to independent producers, but Arthur Krim, the company's president, claimed that independent producers who were financed or released through the company "very rarely run seriously over budget," with the expectation that all budgets would go over by approximately 10 percent.[39] Producers stood to lose out if the production budget went over, and therefore it was their responsibility to ensure it didn't, with fiscal controls ensuring that the producer "lived up to his part of the bargain once shooting began."[40]

UA's casual attitude to budget overspend was probably due to the fact that they made their profits from film rentals and distribution fees, something they wished to maximize through control of the publicity and distribution of all films. UA, along with other major Hollywood companies, wanted to maintain control over these two key areas. As Krim made clear, "We try to be partners in sales with our producers. . . . That's despite the fact that, under our contract, we do have a right to overrule the producer. We believe in cooperation, both in sales and in advertising-publicity, and we listen eagerly when the independent has ideas for campaigns to sell what, after all, is his picture."[41]

There was a three-way power struggle over the ad campaign and publicity for *Paths of Glory*, fought between UA, Harris-Kubrick Pictures, and Public Relations. It was the director of the latter, Stan Margulies, who oversaw the liaison of publicity with UA on behalf of Bryna, with assistance from Myer P. Beck. Both men, though, had a conflict of interest: their overriding need to report back to Kirk Douglas and to protect his and Bryna's other ongoing productions. In theory, they sought authorization from James B. Harris as the film's producer. But Margulies had appointed a unit publicity director to the production, Syd Stogel, against the wishes of Harris.[42] Stogel's duties were to comply with UA's Publicity Manual and to ensure all necessary publicity material was obtained during production, including photographs, synopses, press releases, and cast and crew biographies. But he was caught in the middle of the struggle for control of publicity and, confused by the hierarchical structure of the production, sought clarity from Margulies as to whom he should report to; on-set authority came from Harris, but Stogel also had to report to Margulies and Beck.[43] They in turn sent regular daily memos to give Stogel new tasks, such as telling him to gather and write "home town stories and art" about the hired American army personnel in minor roles.[44] But Stogel stressed that, given his freelance contract to specifically work on *Paths of Glory*, he was hesitant to attend to any of Kirk Douglas's or Bryna's other publicity needs.[45]

Kirk Douglas's time was increasingly being consumed by prepublicity for *The Vikings*, which was due to commence shooting on June 1. Harris was fully aware that Public Relations put the interests of Bryna and Kirk Douglas ahead of *Paths of Glory* and neglected to keep either him or Syd Stogel involved in ongoing matters. He detailed his concerns in a letter to Stan Margulies in March 1957 and suggested that Bryna and Public Relations may be in breach of their agreement with Harris-Kubrick Pictures. His language revealed his frustration at the situation, feeling that Harris-Kubrick Pictures was being undermined: "I get the feeling that you are not working for Harris-Kubrick Pictures and United Artists.... The function of your office is to service Harris-Kubrick and United Artists. What I am trying to say is that I am getting the feeling many times of being put on notice what is happening instead of being counselled with or asked for my opinion."[46] Harris argued that Margulies would make decisions in coordination with UA's publicity executives and then tell Harris-Kubrick Pictures what was being done. Such behavior would, in Harris's words, "absolutely destroy our working relationship."[47]

Harris's accusations were not wholly unfounded. For example, Harris and Kubrick wanted to hire Saul Bass to design the film's adverts. But Saul Bass's fee of $15,000 caused hesitation, and Harris concluded that UA would not approve the cost.[48] Myers Beck suggested to Margulies that Douglas himself should intervene and contact Max Youngstein at UA. Margulies resisted Beck on the issue, stating that Douglas was "saving his ammunition for 'The Vikings.'"[49] Margulies's attitude also revealed who continued to retain power over publicity: UA. He'd already been reminded of this when UA had admonished him for not seeking approval for adverts he had placed in regional magazines. Roger Lewis, UA's head of advertising, told him, "There is one thing that I would like to make clear. It isn't merely a matter of your submitting your ads to me.... I not only want to see proofs but I would like to know what your schedule plans are."[50] The national ad campaign was taken over by UA's head of production, Max Youngstein, who "wanted to have a real all-out action campaign with no projection whatsoever of unusualness."[51] This was again counter to what Margulies himself had suggested, arguing that tying *Paths of Glory* too closely to its World War I setting would endanger the potential of convincing audiences that it was "a modern hard-hitting, up-to-date film about men at war."[52]

The three-way struggle for control of publicity resulted in a confused promotion campaign, a process that began with Stogel on the set of the film. His press releases concentrated, as Richard Daniels has argued, "very much on the war and violence. Much of it emphasises action sequences. The press releases never even mention the court martial."[53] The only action sequence in the film was the attack on the Anthill, with most of the story centered on the drama and politics of the court-martial. However, we can understand the promotion of the film if we place it within the wider context of UA's releases at the time, particularly *Attack* (Aldrich, 1956), an antiwar film set in World War II. Both films shared thematic and narrative similarities, with tales of antiheroes and less than positive portrayals of the military. But the similarities extend to the way the films were promoted with strikingly similar posters. Despite the character-driven aspects of the narratives of each of the films, with action almost secondary to their stories, the posters both play up the generic contexts of the films: these are action pictures first and foremost.

UA, following Youngstein's direction, created ad copy for *Paths of Glory* that, according to Margulies, used "clichéd and tired adjectives" that made it "sound like 'Time Limit.'"[54] *Time Limit* (1957), the only film directed by actor Karl Malden, was also a UA release and depicted the court-martial of a soldier accused of treason. Again, the film poster was similar to those of *Paths of Glory* and *Attack* and described the film as showing "the face of war you've never seen before." The ad copy for *Paths of Glory* drew on simple, alliterative devices, and crafted an image of a generic war picture that dwelled upon the scenes of the attack on the Anthill, with phrases such as "the boldest bayonets-charge that ever hacked its way through hell," "there were 8,000 of them . . . mud splattered, shell-shattered 'heroes,'" and "the bombshell story of a colonel who led his regiment into hell."[55]

As for Kubrick himself, he wanted to personally oversee the publicity strategy for *Paths of Glory* but was aware that he had little influence with UA. Instead, he lobbied Public Relations in the hope that the company would intervene on his behalf. Kubrick believed that the focus on the film as a war picture was in fact detrimental to his core appeal among college audiences, particularly in areas such as New York with its young liberal demographic. He wrote to Myers Beck and asked that adverts for the film include a headshot of Susanne Christian (stage name for Christiane Kubrick, whom he married several years later), the only significant female character in the film. His motive was to "imply that there is a love interest in the film."[56] Kubrick's reasoning came down to the fact that *Darby's Rangers* (Wellman, 1958), a World War II film starring James Garner in the lead role, had taken a similar approach and had achieved huge success. He felt this indicated that "the emphasis of 'Darby's Rangers' advertising campaign, namely four romances as well as its obvious action sales appeal, may have been more appealing than the straight action plus class review approach of 'Paths of Glory.'"[57] Kubrick even went so far as to suggest new copy to accompany a photograph of Christiane that read, "one girl amidst two thousand men."[58] The suggestions were not heeded, however, and *Paths of Glory* failed to achieve its anticipated grosses. Even the national trailer, which Kubrick had personally overseen, had a waltz scene cut in January 1958 that featured, in Kubrick's words, "lots of pretty girls dancing."[59]

What we see in his interventions is how Kubrick was approaching the producing of his films with a commercial mind-set, aware of his own audience and market appeal. It was perhaps also a recognition of how he understood the contexts of some of UA's other releases at that time. After all, there is an overriding thematic link of existentialism and pessimism in UA films such as *Paths of Glory*, *Attack*, *The Night of the Hunter*, and *The Man with the Golden Arm*. These films feature characters who are attempting to survive in an indifferent and even hostile universe, and their storylines are controversial and unusual. Such films, not always resounding successes at the box office given their niche appeal and bleak vision, would have appealed to the growing art-house audience to which Kubrick referred. These films could be seen as part of UA's "Europeanised" program, films that were inherent commercial risks but appealed to the liberal critical circle and drew heavily on the themes of European cinema. Kubrick was sophisticated enough as a producer to understand that a section of the American cinema audience was responding to films with a more serious and at times pessimistic tone, which offered new visions of America, alongside innovative and even challenging narratives.

Kubrick was also in tune with how controversy could be stoked to create publicity and was an advocate for fanning the flames of the film's contentious storyline in France, in complete opposition to the strategy UA had imposed. From the outset, UA refused to engage in any discussion of the potential controversy the film's representation of the French military could instigate. As Arnold Picker, vice president for publicity at UA, reiterated, in response to a publicity strategy document compiled by Public Relations,[60] it would be a "mistake" to even discuss the film's controversial plot line until after it had been released.[61] Conceding to UA's demands, Public Relations put together a revised publicity strategy in which it was now the edict that "it is essential that we avoid at all costs stirring up a premature and unplanned fight during production."[62] This move to suppress the controversy was, in Kubrick's view, a failure of strategy. He sensed that the controversy would allow *Paths of Glory* to thrive at the box office, both in America and in Europe, particularly appealing to younger audiences. By giving up control of the way the film was reported in France and other European nations, it allowed the media to control the narrative. Events soon got of hand, with protests across France and other countries such as Belgium. The film was deemed to be subversive propaganda and offensive to the French nation, with President Charles de Gaulle threatening a ban on all UA releases in the country if *Paths of Glory* was released there and demanding that his European counterparts take the same course of action.[63] UA relented to the pressure and the film was not released in France until 1975.

It is probable that UA was not merely giving in to political pressure exerted against one film but rather protecting its wider commercial interests. Arnold Picker conceded as much to Stan Margulies when he told him that UA "will want cooperation and help" from European nations in 1957 and 1958 for the production of Kirk Douglas's *The Vikings*.[64] *Paths of Glory* was being sacrificed in favor of a picture in which UA had a much greater financial stake. Kubrick was dismayed at the course of events, clearly sensing that UA was favoring the Kirk Douglas star machine at the expense of his own film, so he took it upon himself to see if he could secretly negotiate for the film to be released in France. He contacted a French distributor to try to convince it to buy *Paths of Glory* from UA, in the belief that a native distribution company "could convince the [French] press to view the film as anti-war, not anti-French."[65] He was perhaps being overly optimistic in his claims that the film would become one of the biggest grossing films ever released in the country, but genuinely believed that as much controversy as possible was necessary to ensure commercial success: "The controversy over it would undoubtedly cause front page headlines and public demonstrations. At the risk of sounding cynical, one could hardly hope for a better kind of movie publicity and promotion."[66] Such opinions allow us an insight into how Kubrick had a clear understanding of how to develop a reputation as a filmmaker, with controversy being at the center of his approach.

Dissolving Harris-Kubrick Pictures

Between the end of production of *Paths of Glory* in the summer of 1957 and Kubrick being hired to direct *Spartacus* in the spring of 1959, Harris-Kubrick Pictures entered a period of heavy overdevelopment, with two key bursts of literary property acquisition taking place in the spring and autumn of 1958. But the strategy this time, in comparison to the flurry of acquisitions in 1956, was driven by a multiplicity of factors, including the desire to leave the contract with Bryna Productions and to protect the creative and business autonomy of Harris and Kubrick as producer and director. It was also likely that this overdevelopment came with the added motivation of searching for a commercial hit, something that still eluded Kubrick. Still, while trying to extricate themselves from the Bryna deal, Harris and Kubrick took advantage of Kirk Douglas's cultural network, gaining access to A-list celebrities and initiating collaborations with the likes of Marlon Brando and Gregory Peck.

However, the deal with Bryna was the overriding concern of Harris and Kubrick during this period and even drove them to consider the dissolution of Harris-Kubrick Pictures in May 1957, an idea that they relayed to Kirk Douglas on the set of *Paths of Glory*. Douglas immediately contacted his lawyer, Sam Norton: "I talked to Jimmy and Stanley the other day. They have told me that after this picture they are splitting up. How would this affect my contract with them?"[67] Douglas's letter to Norton reveals his motivations in working with Harris and Kubrick, stating that his "primary interest" was in making a deal with Kubrick, believing he was talented but that he needed "a lot of help, much more help than he cares to admit."[68] It may well have been that Douglas already had Kubrick in mind to direct *Spartacus*, a project to which he was beginning to give serious consideration. As for Harris, Douglas concluded, somewhat dismissively, that "I will see what I can do with Harris, although I certainly don't want to insult him."[69] He had no use for an independent producer, with Bryna already having producers like Jerry Bresler (*The Vikings*) and Edward Lewis (*Spartacus*) on the payroll.

Prior to the suggestion that Harris-Kubrick Pictures could be dissolved, there had been persistent contractual negotiations and confrontations with Bryna over the original January 1957 agreement. Several revised deals emerged as a result, starting on February 6, 1957. This new agreement set out in detail what Douglas wanted from Harris and Kubrick as well as the roles and responsibilities they would carry out as employees of Bryna.[70] Realizing that he would have restricted creative and business control of his own career, Kubrick initially refused to sign this revised agreement. His opposition was a result of the wording of the contract—in fact, just one word: "Stanley wants the word 'including,' appearing in the next to the last line of this paragraph on page 7, changed to 'excluding.' In other words, Stanley wants artistic control of each picture in which he works."[71]

The line in question legally obliged Kubrick to relinquish all artistic authority to Douglas, "in all matters including those involving artistic taste and judgment."[72] Changing this was something that Douglas could not allow as he saw all power on a production as residing with him as the producer and executive of Bryna Productions. As Bryna's vice president Edward Lewis made clear, "Douglas is on every single facet of filming. . . . He is consulted about wardrobe, lighting, casting, background, historical data . . . everything. . . . Kirk's the driving force of every picture he does . . . Kirk calls all the shots."[73] What had emerged between Kubrick and Douglas was a battle for control of legal authority on the pictures they were producing. As such, Harris explained that further contractual revisions were necessary. This was essential by May 1957, when Harris and Kubrick announced their plans to dissolve Harris-Kubrick Pictures. Harris explained to Douglas, "The original concept of the agreement was for Bryna to acquire the services of Harris and Kubrick as a team. This is definitely impossible at this time regardless of whether or not a contract exists. So as long as we all know that such a situation is not workable, why try to force it."[74]

But it was clear that Harris and Kubrick were deliberately frustrating the contractual obligations they had with Bryna and even trying to avoid producing any more pictures for the company. This, after all, had been the aim as soon as they had agreed to the Bryna deal: to "get out of this deal, somehow, someway."[75] Because of this overriding motivation, it is probable that the threat to dissolve Harris-Kubrick Pictures was merely a tactic to bring about the end of the Bryna deal. But in a letter to Kirk Douglas in July 1957, Sam Norton laid out the situation, explaining that Harris and Kubrick had apparently "disassociated themselves" from each other.[76] But Bryna Productions called Harris and Kubrick's bluff as well as threatening legal action, and by the summer of 1957 Kubrick signed the revised contract, the wording unchanged. And Harris-Kubrick Pictures remained a functioning production company until 1962.[77]

Production Strategies Post–*Paths of Glory*

The failed attempt to end the Bryna deal in the spring of 1957 pushed Harris-Kubrick Pictures into a period of fertile creativity and overdevelopment. The company's strategy of overdevelopment, with a number of unmade projects to its name by 1959, was more than likely a new way to end the Bryna deal as quickly as possible. The first serious project that emerged after *Paths of Glory* was *I Stole*

$16,000,000, an adaptation of Herbert Emerson Wilson's 1955 autobiography. Wilson was a pastor turned criminal who committed a series of bank robberies in Canada and the United States throughout the 1920s. Harris-Kubrick Pictures and Bryna seemed to genuinely put aside the contractual disagreements and collaborate on a new film; at least, on the surface this seemed to be the case, with Bryna honoring its deal by promoting Harris and Kubrick individually in press releases it issued. The choice of *I Stole $16,000,000* was made by Harris-Kubrick, though Bryna purchased the motion picture rights.[78] The choice of the book reflected Harris and Kubrick's long-standing interest in the crime genre and their ongoing working relationship with crime authors like Jim Thompson. The project may also have been a bid to create a commercial hit, with Wilson's book a best seller and therefore having a presold audience, while Harris and Kubrick believed the setting of the 1920s created an added atmosphere of "interest and excitement."[79]

But there may also have been an ulterior motive in Harris and Kubrick seemingly collaborating with Bryna. Douglas was to play the lead role in the film but would not be available for production until April 1958.[80] Kubrick was paid by Bryna to work on the script through February 1958, when a draft had to be submitted to Douglas. This included expenses-paid trips to visit Wilson in Tijuana, Mexico.[81] In the meantime, Stan Margulies set in motion the Kirk Douglas publicity machine, issuing various press releases about the film via Public Relations. For Harris-Kubrick Pictures, the free publicity was ideal to promote the company within Hollywood and the wider international film industry; Harris and Kubrick were using the agreement to their advantage, "allowing their names to be further established via Douglas's power network and through the close association with the Douglas star brand."[82] And while Public Relations continued to promote them, Harris and Kubrick set about working on other non-Bryna projects.

It is doubtful as to whether Bryna or Harris-Kubrick Pictures ever intended to produce *I Stole $16,000,000*, at least in 1958. First, Douglas was tied up with other production commitments, including *The Vikings* and a potential western for producer Hal Wallis.[83] In fact, Douglas often overcommitted himself to acting roles for other producers, impacting the number of films he could produce for Bryna.[84] As Harris concluded, "We are at the mercy of the stars due to their crowded schedules."[85] Second, the project faced serious issues with American union as Harris and Kubrick wanted to produce the film in Germany, given the lower production costs. However, Harris believed that the unions would take issue with an American-financed picture about an American criminal being filmed in Germany.[86] And third, Harris and Kubrick were actively developing other projects, including seeking out the rights to books in February and March 1958, including *The Raw Edge* (1958), a New York–set crime novel that was marketed as being "a behind-the-scenes novel of the New York waterfront"; an unpublished manuscript of *The Vanishing Evangelist* (1959), recommended by

Herbert Wilson and which told the story of the apparently staged kidnapped of the Christian evangelist Aimee McPherson; *Ashes and Diamonds* (1948), a Polish-set World War II novel by Jerzy Andrzejewski that focused on the underground anticommunist Polish army resistance, and eventually adapted by Andrzej Wajda in 1958; *Original Sin* (1954) by Giose Rimanelli, set in southern Italy in the immediate aftermath of World War II; *The Last Parallel* (1957), a semiautobiographical account by the U.S. marine Martin Russ of the Korean War; and, most intriguing of all, the Arthur C. Clarke novel *The Deep Range* (1957). The story is set underwater in the future, with the world's oceans being farmed. One of these farmers sets about capturing a giant sea monster. Far from being an interstellar science fiction novel in the vein of Kubrick's eventual collaboration with Clarke, *The Deep Range* is more in keeping with the production contexts of the era, most specifically the Walt Disney family adventure *20,000 Leagues under the Sea* (Fleischer, 1954), starring Kirk Douglas. The film had been a phenomenal success at the box office, and it may well have been that Harris-Kubrick Pictures was considering ways of emulating it.[87]

By February 1958, Harris concluded that Harris-Kubrick Pictures would focus on another project instead of *I Stole $16,000,000* given the doubts it would ever be produced. Harris and Kubrick were looking to produce their next picture in Munich, in a potential coproduction deal with producer George von Block; von Block had served as the production manager on *Paths of Glory*. Kubrick confided to von Block that *I Stole $16,000,000* would not go into production until at least early 1959.[88] Instead, Harris-Kubrick Pictures would begin development and preproduction for *Mosby's Rangers*, the project first initiated with Shelby Foote in 1956 and what Kubrick now termed as being a lavish Civil War epic.[89] And just as with *I Stole $16,000,000*, Harris-Kubrick Pictures wanted to produce *Mosby's Rangers* overseas, utilizing a German crew to shoot in Germany or Yugoslavia.[90]

There was an ongoing political furor within Hollywood about the increase in runaway productions. Unions in Hollywood were actively protesting those producers who relocated their films abroad, believing it threatened their jobs. Kubrick was keenly aware of this fact and wanted to keep Harris-Kubrick Pictures' strategy of overseas production as discreet as possible, as he outlined in a letter to Hollis Alpert. Alpert had published a news story that claimed the only reason *Paths of Glory* had been produced in Germany was because of cheaper production costs and the lower wages paid to production staff. Kubrick explained that publishing such a claim endangered the future production strategy of Harris-Kubrick Pictures by tossing it "right into the boiling union pot out here now stewing about runaway productions."[91] Kubrick sensed that the unions were looking to make an example of an independent production company and that such a story as the one published by Alpert would provide them with an excuse to target Harris-Kubrick Pictures.

The research for *Mosby's Rangers* was becoming sizeable, with Kubrick compiling hundreds of index cards that detailed research, key dates, and snatches of dialogue from Mosby's own memoirs.[92] Kubrick also compiled photocopies of Civil War military documents and battle plans. The research was utilized for a draft script, which Kubrick completed by April 1958. He was clearly excited about the project, raising it regularly in correspondence with a range of individuals. A coproduction deal with Gregory Peck's Melville Productions was announced in February 1958, with Peck himself to play the lead role in the film. But he would not be available until the end of the year, thereby delaying the production.

But even if *Mosby's Rangers* went ahead, it would mean that Harris-Kubrick Pictures would be unavailable to Bryna Productions until sometime in mid-1959.[93] By developing projects without the knowledge or approval of Bryna, Harris-Kubrick Pictures was in effect in breach of its contractual obligations.[94] The combination of contractual dispute and the ways in which Harris and Kubrick were obfuscating their obligations to Bryna culminated with a termination agreement in May 1958.[95] The termination agreement, which was promptly signed by Harris and Kubrick, enforced a series of fees that Harris-Kubrick Pictures would have to pay to Bryna on all of its future feature film releases as well as requiring repayments for the development of *I Stole $16,000,000*. The termination agreement also brought an effective end to *Mosby's Rangers*, with Harris-Kubrick Pictures required to pay a 66 percent share of net profits if it produced and released any film based on the material developed for *Mosby's Rangers*. Anticipating that Harris and Kubrick would attempt to negate the termination release by dissolving Harris-Kubrick Pictures, the agreement extended to cover Harris and Kubrick individually.

Despite the release from the three-picture deal with Bryna, Harris-Kubrick Pictures was still legally bound to the company in any future productions. The termination agreement included an appendix of stars that they could not use without incurring further punitive net profit fees of 20 percent; the list read like a roll call of clients of MCA (the talent agency run by Lew Wasserman, Kirk Douglas's agent), including John Wayne, Marilyn Monroe, James Stewart, Rock Hudson, and Gregory Peck.[96] In 1957, Kirk Douglas had provided Harris-Kubrick Pictures with access to his cultural network. A year later, he was closing the gates firmly shut.

Alternative Production Strategies

By shutting off access to the roll call of MCA stars, Bryna Productions was forcing Harris-Kubrick Pictures down alternative production routes. Peck was now out of the question for *Mosby's Rangers*, while *I Stole $16,000,000* would not be produced either. At the same time, the company had to navigate the precarious contexts of the termination release with Bryna to find a way of avoiding paying the various fees set out in the agreement. Harris-Kubrick Pictures was in debt, in need of a deal, and in need of a box office hit. And this needed to happen soon.

As Kubrick concluded by the spring of 1958, "It would take more than just a lightly sketched idea to get us into motion on a project at this point."[97]

What followed in the coming months was a series of frantic, even chaotic production moves to try to get a project out of development and into active production. Harris set out about undertaking an aggressive literary property acquisition strategy, commencing in April 1958, with further "gluts" of acquisition in the summer and autumn of 1958. Motion picture rights were purchased in April for, among things, *Eldorado Jane* (1956) by Phyllis Bottome; *The Fancher Train* (1958) by Amelia Bean; *. . . and Save Them for Pallbearers* (1958) by James Garrett; *Private* (1958) by Lester Atwell; *Night March* (1958) by Bruce Lancaster; *The Crack of Doom* (1958) by Willi Heinrich; *The Mission* (1958) by Dean Brelis; and *The Phantom Major: The Story of David Sterling and His Desert Command* (1958) by Virginia Cowles. This glut of literary acquisition displayed key narrative trends that Harris-Kubrick Pictures was interested in: the American Civil War, stories about teenage sexuality, and stories of World War II, including from the perspective of the German army.

Of course there were also properties that Harris-Kubrick expressed interest in that did not fit any of these categories; *Anatomy of a Murder* (1958), the courtroom drama written by John D. Voelker and adapted for the screen by Otto Preminger in 1959, was one such example. But most of the novels were contemporary and mostly released in 1958, demonstrating that Harris—he was the one acquiring the properties—was keeping an ever-watchful eye on the latest releases and attempting to purchase them ahead of other independent producers. He wasn't successful with *Anatomy of a Murder*, a book for which a bidding war soon broke out, despite offering to pay more than any other producer.[98] In fact, Harris seems to have been purchasing the motion picture rights to novels almost as soon as they came out. Shortly after the release of Langston Hughes's *Tambourines to Glory* (1958), a novel that had initially been written as a stage play and told the story of Harlem Gospel singers, Harris wrote to publisher John Day to express his interest. Similarly, no sooner had Samuel Hopkins Adams's novel *Tenderloin* (1958), a book about a Christian social reformer working in New York's red-light district, been released than Harris had contacted the publisher to purchase the rights.

Harris-Kubrick Pictures also registered a number of film titles with the MPAA at this time, including *The Fool, the Fatman, and the Hunchback*, *The Girl from Beneath the Sea*, *The Electric Chair*, *The Things That Come in the Night*, *Sick, Sick, Sick*, and *Hannibal*. Some of these may have been related to the literary properties that had been acquired; maybe *The Girl from Beneath the Sea* was related to the sea-monster adventures of Clarke's *The Deep Range*? But the registration of film titles was a long-standing Hollywood practice, with the aim of preventing a potentially marketable title from being taken by a rival producer or studio. Film titles were registered with the MPAA's Title Registration Bureau, regardless of whether the producer or production company intended to use them.

But independent producers could find themselves in conflict with the larger Hollywood studios when it came to the similarity of film titles. Harris-Kubrick Pictures experienced exactly that when, after registering the title *Hannibal*—presumably in case the company ever made a biopic of the Ancient Carthaginian general, which was highly unlikely by 1958 but maybe demonstrated the company's awareness of the trend for sword and sandal epics—Columbia protested that it was too similar to its *The Legions of Hannibal*. Legal action was thereby threatened to prevent Harris-Kubrick Pictures from ever using the title.[99]

But out of all the stories that Harris-Kubrick Pictures was exploring, it was the category of World War II stories that now seemed to dominate the company's attention, increasingly so as 1958 progressed. It may have been that Harris and Kubrick, in persistent contact with George von Block, wanted to build upon their preexisting working relationship with the Geiselgasteig film studios, particularly given their experience in producing *Paths of Glory* there and in successfully achieving an authentic and realistic depiction of war. Kubrick admitted that he was eager to develop a combat film that mixed fiction and documentary vignettes.[100] Further motion picture rights were bought to World War II novels, including *Cross of Iron* (1956), another Willi Heinrich novel about a German platoon trapped behind Russian lines on the Eastern Front and that was adapted in 1977 by Sam Peckinpah. By the summer of 1958, Richard Adams, a former paratrooper, had been hired by Harris-Kubrick Pictures to work on a World War II story that would depict the German army point of view, tentatively titled *Nazi Paratrooper*; the title was purposely chosen to arouse controversy.[101]

Nazi Paratrooper evolved over the coming months as Kubrick worked on the screenplay with Adams, retitling it *The German Lieutenant*.[102] Among those Kubrick considered for the cast was Orson Welles as a German colonel and Alan Ladd in the lead role.[103] Extensive research was also conducted, including locating combat stock footage from the U.S. government, with Kubrick intent on incorporating documentary film.[104] Kubrick was also interested in utilizing songs from the Nazi era, contacting Audio Rarities about the potential of utilizing their record *Hitler's Inferno—In Words, in Music 1932–1945—Marching Songs of Nazi Germany*.[105] George von Block was heavily involved in the development of the project, devising a production schedule (forty-eight days shooting were required) and looking into using American soldiers as extras in the film.[106]

The film never entered preproduction, but there were extensive logistical investigations as to what would be involved in producing the film. Draft budgets were drawn up and Harris-Kubrick Pictures entered negotiations with George von Block for a coproduction deal.[107] It was never entirely certain where the production would actually be based, with consideration given to Germany, Austria, Yugoslavia, and Turkey; where to base the production was based on weighing up the lowest possible production costs against the quality of the technical talent available.[108] While production costs in Yugoslavia were approximately 20 percent lower than in Germany (one production manager quoted Kubrick

$160,000 for below-the-line costs, something he couldn't quite believe), the low standard of technical facilities would require a longer production schedule.[109] But the project was left unmade, Kubrick's attention by the spring of 1959 turning to *Spartacus*, a film for which he was hired to direct by Kirk Douglas (see chapter 6).

It might also have been that the number of unmade Harris-Kubrick projects during 1958 and 1959 was a result of the company's ambitions getting ahead of practicalities. The company was indebted to Douglas still, while the costs of Harris's literary acquisitions were mounting up. The company had received no income from *Paths of Glory*, which by the start of 1959 had made no profit, while the money Kubrick had earned for the development of *I Stole $16,000,000* was now owed Douglas as per the terms of the termination agreement. In mid-1958, Harris-Kubrick Pictures had looked at the possibility of liquidation of Kubrick's outstanding personal loans. The company was in constant need of financing in order to fund its production strategy of overdevelopment, which in itself did not seem to be working. By the autumn of 1958, the company was no closer to moving any of its projects out of development and into production, largely a result of the restriction of the termination agreement.

Seen in this context, it becomes clear why in early 1958 Harris-Kubrick Pictures accepted a loan agreement deal with Pennebaker Inc., the production company of actor Marlon Brando. The deal allowed Pennebaker to loan the services of Stanley Kubrick as a director for six months for the fee of $100,000. It was for a project being developed by Brando tentatively titled *Guns Up*, with a script by Calder Willingham based on the novel *The Authentic Death of Henry Jones* (1956) and produced for Paramount Pictures.[110] The arrangement, however, did not work, and by November 1958 Kubrick had quit the project, now retitled *One-Eyed Jacks* (1961).[111] Harris suspected that Brando merely wanted Kubrick to provide technical services—the setting up of shots—while he would direct the picture himself.[112]

By the start of 1959, Harris-Kubrick Pictures was once again faced with an existential threat to its survival, with an uncertain financial future. And worse, in order to cover their costs of operation, Harris and Kubrick had to obtain a new sponsor: Joseph Harris. He loaned Harris-Kubrick Pictures sizeable funds, and in return, Harris-Kubrick Pictures gave up all rights to *The Killing*, including any future income, assigning the property outright to the Harris Group.[113]

Conclusion

The strategy of overdevelopment pursued by Harris-Kubrick Pictures reflected the company's precarious situation, and in all likelihood, most of the properties acquired and films being developed would never have been produced. Harris and Kubrick were acutely aware of this fact. But the process of project development and loaning out the services of Kubrick for this purpose meant that, even if a project was more than likely left unmade, Harris-Kubrick Pictures could still generate a profit. This was certainly the case with *Guns Up!*, a film that did not get produced for several years, finally released only in 1961, but which provided Kubrick with a sizeable fee for his services.

But while 1957 to 1959 were chaotic and uncertain for Harris-Kubrick Pictures, clear trends of artistic interest did emerge for Harris and Kubrick, with a fascination in developing either a combat film or a story of sexual obsession. What also developed was an understanding of the logistics of film producing and how they needed to fully internationalize their company. As a result, they were both constantly looking at how they could produce their next film outside of the United States, with no commitment to any one country but rather the most *competitive* country in terms of production costs and facilities. This would become an overriding factor in the evolution of Harris-Kubrick Pictures in the coming years. But for now the company needed financial support, which came mostly from Joseph Harris, and a commercial hit. And while antagonism had grown in the working relationship with Bryna, its executive, Kirk Douglas, would come to the rescue and free Harris-Kubrick Pictures from its woes: Stanley Kubrick would direct *Spartacus*.

6

Swords, Sandals, Sex, and Soviets, 1959–1962

● ●

Spartacus came to dominate the functions of Bryna Productions by the end of the 1950s. An epic tale of ancient Rome, it brought together an international cast of some of the most renowned acting talent in the industry at that time, while the budget escalated to make it the most expensive picture Universal had ever financed by 1960. But the film was not without problems. Kirk Douglas was known throughout Hollywood for his careful deliberations and desire to collaborate, talking through issues at length and reworking stories thoroughly until they matched his own belief system. His liberal ideology was increasingly playing a role in the kinds of films he produced and the messages he wanted them to convey. But the scale of *Spartacus* and the egos involved in its creation, all the while answerable to demanding executives at Universal who were more concerned about the cost, meant that Douglas was met with a range of competing voices who all wanted their say on just how the film should be made. This included Stanley Kubrick, brought in at the last minute to direct the picture and who sensed an opportunity to finally work on a blockbuster Hollywood feature that would establish him as a major player within the industry.

This chapter explores the final stages of the working relationship between Douglas and Kubrick and how the contractual arrangements between Bryna Productions and Harris-Kubrick Pictures came to an end. Desperate for Kubrick's creative help on *Spartacus*, Douglas conceded to certain demands put to him by James B. Harris. But in agreeing to them, Douglas arguably pushed Harris-Kubrick Pictures into developing *Lolita*. While Kubrick worked on *Spartacus*,

Harris set out about looking at how to produce an adaptation of Vladimir Nabokov's scandalous novel and how to fully internationalize the operations of Harris-Kubrick Pictures. At the same time, the company still needed to clear its debts owed to Joseph Harris. To do so, the company took on hired work for Joseph Harris, notably the dubbing of Soviet historical epics for U.S. distribution. Taken together, the period between 1959 and 1962 was the most important for Harris-Kubrick Pictures in finally establishing itself as a maverick, commercial, and international production company and for Kubrick's career as a film producer individually. If the 1950s had been a period of struggle and uncertainty for Kubrick, 1960 changed all that, and the ensuing decade was a period of immense box office success. From 1959 to 1962 Kubrick worked for hire in the heart of the Hollywood mainstream, in the process learning just exactly who had control and legal authority in the film industry.

Sword and Sandals

By the beginning of 1959, Harris-Kubrick Pictures formally terminated the loan agreement it had with Pennebaker Inc., bringing to an end the collaboration with Marlon Brando.[1] But this did not stop Brando from persisting in asking Kubrick to direct his project, contacting him again in February 1959 to consider taking on *One-Eyed Jacks*.[2] Kubrick was noncommittal though, explaining that he had a couple of his own ideas that interested him more; this would become a stock line throughout his career when passing on projects that people wanted him to develop. But Brando's persistence in asking Kubrick to direct *One-Eyed Jacks* shows how Kubrick, by 1959, had gained a reputation as a prestigious director capable of working with the biggest stars in Hollywood. This was perhaps a key selling point when it came to convincing Universal that Kubrick should direct *Spartacus*.

Spartacus was an adaptation of the 1951 Howard Fast novel of the same name, telling the story of a slave uprising in the Roman Republic, led by Spartacus. The film was adapted by Dalton Trumbo, then a blacklisted screenwriter, and produced by Bryna Productions (a combined effort of Stan Margulies, Edward Lewis, and Kirk Douglas). In fact, Douglas was heavily involved in producing the picture from its inception, advising Trumbo on the script, negotiating with Hollywood studios to obtain financing, and contacting a host of A-list celebrities to try to interest them in working on the project. He was also exploring options for directors, initially approaching actor Laurence Olivier in the summer of 1958.[3] Olivier had experience directing and producing Shakespearian epics for the screen, including *Henry V* (1944), *Hamlet* (1948), and *Richard III* (1955), the latter costing $6 million but failing spectacularly at the box office. If that reason alone did not disqualify Olivier, the fact that he turned down the role did; he had prior theater commitments, contracted to play at Stratford-upon-Avon in *Coriolanus*, with rehearsals commencing in the summer of 1959.

But he was interested in playing the character of Crassus, as long as the role was "improved" in relation to the three roles of Gracchus (Charles Laughton), Batiatus (Peter Ustinov), and Spartacus (Kirk Douglas).[4] Olivier's intervention made clear the power struggles that would take place on the film, with the cast all vying to use *Spartacus* to emphasize their own reputation within Hollywood.

Douglas reached a financing and distribution agreement with Universal-International in May 1958, with an initial budget of $4 million.[5] Universal had undergone seismic changes in the 1950s, first being taken over by Decca Records in 1952 and then selling its backlot property in Los Angeles to Music Corp of America (MCA) in 1958.[6] The deal between Milton R. Rackmil (president of Universal Pictures) and Lew Wasserman (president of MCA) involved the buyout by MCA of the 370-acre Universal backlot, including a hundred fifty buildings and sixteen soundstages at a cost of $11.250 million.[7] Wasserman and MCA had radically altered Hollywood in the 1950s, becoming a talent agency that maximized the power of the actors. One of Wasserman's clients was Kirk Douglas, while Harris and Kubrick had joined the agency in 1958. Prior to the deal with MCA, Universal had been in the process of implementing budget cuts, reducing its production output from around forty pictures per year to twenty.[8] This might contradict the sizeable investment in *Spartacus*, but the film represented a new production strategy at Universal that focused on "productions of the highest magnitude."[9] In effect, this meant historical epics. Universal wanted to exploit the historical epic cycle of the 1950s, with *Spartacus* "an example of U's entry into the big budget field."[10]

The historical epics of the 1950s and 1960s usually had a biblical theme (*The Ten Commandments*, 1956) or classical setting (*Ben-Hur*, 1959; *Cleopatra*, 1963). Many of the films broke records with the size of their budgets and their box office grosses and "can be counted as some of the most commercially successful Hollywood films ever released."[11] Universal was keen to highlight the fact that *Spartacus* was the most expensive film produced in the studio's half-a-century history.[12] The investment in *Spartacus* was meant to demonstrate the scale of ambition at Universal and to represent confidence, in contrast to how in fact it had struggled to adapt to the rapidly changing industrial contexts in Hollywood.

Following MCA's purchase of the Universal backlot, Wasserman had increasing influence over the business operations of Universal and its product. MCA rented the backlot to Universal as well as allowing access to its list of clients.[13] It was Wasserman—Douglas's agent—who had suggested that he pitch *Spartacus* to Universal following its rejection by UA and other studios and that he attach a big name director to the project, such as Olivier.[14] Universal, encouraged behind the scenes by Wasserman, agreed to a multiple-picture financing deal with Bryna in 1958.[15]

To what extent Wasserman or Universal influenced and even pressured Douglas over the choice of director for *Spartacus* is an issue that is unclear. Anthony

Mann, the first director of the film, had most likely been hired at the insistence of Wasserman; Mann was a client of MCA, and Wasserman had packaged Mann as the director of a series of successful westerns starring James Stewart in the 1950s.[16] But it's likely that Douglas was bending to the wishes of Wasserman to some degree, particularly following the buyout of Universal by MCA. As Douglas noted some years later, "At the beginning of *Spartacus*, Lew Wasserman at MCA was my agent; he worked for me. In the middle of shooting [*Spartacus*], MCA bought Universal; I worked for him."[17] But whatever had led to the decision to initially hire Mann in October 1958,[18] by February 1959, just four days into the shoot, he had left the picture under unclear circumstances.[19] Kubrick replaced Mann three days later, on February 16, after a hurried phone call from Douglas requesting his help.[20] It is more than likely Douglas now had his preferred choice directing *Spartacus*.

Douglas's desire to hire Kubrick presented Harris-Kubrick Pictures the opportunity to revise the May 1958 termination agreement with Bryna. The termination had, in effect, pushed Harris-Kubrick to consider producing alternative projects in a bid to avoid the punitive measures of the agreement. This included Vladimir Nabokov's *Lolita* (1955) (discussed below), purchased by Harris in September 1958.[21] Its purchase came during another cycle of popular or best-selling literary acquisitions by Harris for the company in mid-1958, making it hard to determine just how serious the project was being considered for development at that time; after all, it was a period during which Harris-Kubrick Pictures was suffering serious questions about its future. However, the March 1959 loan-out agreement between Harris-Kubrick Pictures and Bryna Productions for the services of Kubrick led to a conversation about Bryna giving up interest in literary property owned by the company. Douglas confirmed there was one picture he certainly did not want to be associated with nor for Bryna to be connected with: *Lolita*. Douglas believed, like a number of other leading Hollywood stars at the time, that the book's scandalous reputation as pornography—it had been published by Olympia Press in Paris, a well-known pornography press—would damage his reputation and star branding. Therefore, a deal was reached: Douglas and Bryna would not be associated with *Lolita* in any way, and it was excluded from all of the conditions of the 1958 Termination Agreement in return for Kubrick directing *Spartacus* on a temporary contract.[22] In effect, the deal with Douglas pushed Harris-Kubrick Pictures into producing *Lolita*.[23] It was probably the best deal either company would ever make: "What resulted were the two most successful pictures of each company's respective histories, as well as two of the most commercially successful films in Hollywood history. Therefore, there was a further side-benefit to Kubrick directing *Spartacus*: it provided him with the necessary credentials to rightly claim that he had successfully directed a multi-million dollar epic (the most expensive film ever financed by Universal) with a stellar cast of some of Hollywood's biggest names. The cultural capital that this brought him, and Harris-Kubrick, cannot be overstated."[24]

Harris-Kubrick Pictures had signed up to the loan-out agreement with Bryna out of self-interest. The company was in need of income, and in return for his services, Kubrick received a fee of $5,000 per week, paid directly into the company account.[25] In addition, the company needed to extricate itself from the restrictive terms of the May 1958 Termination Agreement. It managed to revise the deal, ensuring that *Lolita* was exempt from the 20 percent fee imposed by Bryna on all Harris-Kubrick Pictures.[26] Were it not for *Spartacus*, it may well have been that Harris-Kubrick Pictures would never have produced *Lolita*.

As for issues of creative control on *Spartacus*, the loan-out agreement did not make any explicit references, despite this being the undoing of the original three-picture contract between Bryna and Harris-Kubrick Pictures. Far from being under the control of Bryna, Kubrick remained an employee of Harris-Kubrick Pictures while working on *Spartacus*, with few obligations to Bryna beyond ensuring the film was competently directed. The deal went as far as to absolve Harris-Kubrick Pictures from any responsibility should Kubrick's work on *Spartacus* not satisfy Douglas and Bryna.[27]

Absolved of any legal authority or responsibility to Universal or Bryna, Kubrick seemingly went about directing the picture in his own indomitable way, looking for artistic shots and having a high shooting ratio.[28] Kubrick was able to make a definite artistic contribution to *Spartacus* including (limited) script suggestions.[29] This in part came about because of the collegiate atmosphere on set, in which Douglas welcomed opinions and discussions of the film and script.[30] Douglas was certainly open to persuasion and, even though the final decision remained his, was willing to facilitate Kubrick's suggestions and working methods. For instance, Kubrick showed a tendency to direct the smallest of details during scenes featuring hundreds of extras, to the exasperation of the crew.[31] Douglas accommodated this behavior by sending a memo to the assistant director, Marshall Green, asking him to "instruct one of your assistants to keep a careful eye on all the extras ... a careful observation by one of your assistants can help Kubrick quite a bit in concentrating on other areas."[32] Douglas also admitted to producer Ed Lewis that he had been "weaned off" certain scenes in the script, including the mass wedding scene, because of the "subtle influence of twenty-nine year old Kubrick."[33]

Kubrick took full advantage of the opportunity to direct *Spartacus*. After all, the scale of the film, with a budget increasing to over $10 million by February 1960, was immense.[34] Harris and Kubrick saw no disadvantages, particularly with no contractual responsibilities beyond merely providing directorial services. In interviews with the press at the film's premiere in autumn 1960, Kubrick emphasized the importance of his own role. Quoted by Eugene Archer in the *New York Times*—in a piece that was entirely dedicated to Kubrick's work on *Spartacus* at the exclusion of everyone else, perhaps indicating that he had, once again, approached the *New York Times* with the story—he stated that *Spartacus* was "just as good as *Paths of Glory* and certainly there's as much of myself in it."³⁵ He was equating the scale, vision, and ambition of *Spartacus* with the work of Harris-Kubrick Pictures. The article went on, "'I don't mean to minimize the contributions of the others involved, but the director is the only one who can authentically impose his personality onto a picture, and the result is his responsibility—partly because he's the only one who's always there.' In assuming the responsibility for 'Spartacus,' the self-confident Mr. Kubrick was undeterred by either his occasional disagreements with the producer-star, Kirk Douglas, or by the fact, at 31, he is the youngest director ever placed in charge of a $12,000,000 film."³⁶ Kubrick used the article in the *New York Times* to advance his own agenda, including an image of uncompromising artistic control. Indeed, Kubrick told Philip Scheuer of the *Los Angeles Times*, "I was given complete freedom."³⁷ The image presented in the *Los Angeles Times* piece, as well as that in the *New York Times*, was of a director at complete ease in controlling actors of the caliber of Douglas, Olivier, Laughton, and Ustinov as well as a director able to impose all of his own artistic decisions. Kubrick was even quoted as saying, "I always cut my pictures."³⁸ The latter was a point that aggravated the Motion Picture Film Editors (MPFE) union, which contested Kubrick's claim. The MPFE provided a correction to the *Los Angeles Times*, stating that "approximately 25 members of the (editors) Local 776, IATSE headed up by Robert Lawrence actually edited the picture. . . . Producer Kirk Douglas gave them screen credit . . . and none to Mr. Kubrick for film editing."³⁹

As had been the case in the early 1950s, Kubrick was asserting his own authorial presence on the films on which he worked by talking to the press, what was in effect brand management. This allowed him to produce an image of control and power that could then be utilized in developing his own sphere of influence moving forward. The aim was to also use the articles in the *New York Times* and *Los Angeles Times* as a means of launching the publicity process for *Lolita* off the back of *Spartacus*, announcing that *Lolita* would be a film "taken seriously" in contrast to the "usual costume epic" extravaganza of *Spartacus*.⁴⁰ The articles show how Kubrick generated controversy about the films in which he was involved; with *Spartacus*, he gossiped about conflict on set, including between himself and Douglas ("I had a lot of arguments with Kirk"),⁴¹ between himself and the cast ("I had a couple of arguments with Laughton and intermittently with Ustinov"),⁴² and about his own artistic interventions in changing the script ("We fought about that one," he added wryly, "but I won").⁴³ Controversy was a means by which to produce publicity and it became a central tenet to the way Kubrick would develop his own image and sense of control in the coming years.

Kubrick later reflected on the issue of control on *Spartacus*, saying of the relationship between the film's producers and him as director that "if I ever needed any convincing of the limits of persuasion a director can have on a film where . . . he is merely the highest-paid member of the crew, *Spartacus* provided proof to last a lifetime."⁴⁴ The limits of persuasion Kubrick referred to can be interpreted as legal and contractual obligations or restrictions: the power of the producer or the director was in their respective contracts with the production companies. For Kubrick, when he was working on *Spartacus*, this meant the ever-present threat of his immediate dismissal by Kirk Douglas. Though the hastily arranged deal did not expressly state issues around artistic control, it did have a clause that stated Kubrick could be dismissed at any time if he "fails, refuses or neglects to perform his required services."[45] If this had occurred, Harris-Kubrick Pictures would have been obliged to financially compensate Bryna Productions for the termination.

Still, whatever his eventual opinions of *Spartacus*, the film was Kubrick's first commercial hit. By February 1961, just four months after its premiere, *Spartacus* had garnered a worldwide theater gross of over $5 million. But more important, the film had established Kubrick as one of the brightest talents working in Hollywood.

The Soviet Connection

Harris-Kubrick Pictures was involved in a curious aside production context during this period: a brief flirtation with the Soviet Union. In fact, it is a context that first emerged in December 1958 when Harris was in negotiations to purchase the motion picture rights to *Doctor Zhivago* (1957), the Boris Pasternak novel about the life of a physician in the years after the Russian Revolution.[46] Harris found it difficult to obtain the rights to the novel and even contacted Pasternak directly to see if the author could help.[47]

An adaptation of *Doctor Zhivago* seems to have emerged as a potential collaboration between Harris-Kubrick Pictures and Bryna Productions; Douglas had previously professed a desire to film in Russia. This followed an invitation from a cultural attaché at the Soviet embassy in Washington for Kirk Douglas to produce an adaptation of Jules Verne's *Michael Strogoff* (1876) in the Soviet Union.[48] A cultural exchange program had been developed between the U.S. government and the Soviet Union in January 1958 in order to foster potential feature film coproductions. Any potential coproduction on *Michael Strogoff* soon dissipated though, with Verne's book being deemed as containing "false elements."[49] It may well have been that *Doctor Zhivago* emerged as an adaptation to take the place of the abandoned *Michael Strogoff*, with Harris-Kubrick Pictures eager to exploit the U.S.–Soviet Union cultural exchange program and any potential lucrative coproduction deal. But whereas *Michael Strogoff* was an adventure story with "no political connotations," *Doctor Zhivago* was much more controversial, and the book was banned in all Soviet states for its supposed attack against the Soviet Union.[50]

However, Harris-Kubrick Pictures had a further, much more substantial connection to the Russian film industry in the 1950s via Joseph Harris. In 1957, Joseph Harris incorporated a new company, Art Theatre of the Air (ATA), with producer Sig Shore. The company was formed as a successor to Flamingo Films, the company that James B. Harris had worked with until 1955. The aim of ATA was to import the "finest" foreign films and distribute them to television, with some notable deals including *Rififi* (Dassin, 1955), *Mr. Hulot's Holiday* (Tati, 1953), and *The Wages of Fear* (Clouzot, 1953).[51] Joseph Harris set out his thinking in an article for *Variety* in July 1959, arguing that "the foreign or art film is no longer the seldom-seen curio appealing only to the avant-garde, but rather an increasingly popular entertainment purchase.... Outstanding foreign product that we have sold to television indicates that there is a mass audience for fine dubbed foreign films."[52] Joseph Harris saw himself as a disruptor to the often stale methods of conducting business within Hollywood, not too dissimilar to the maverick status his son had adopted at Harris-Kubrick Pictures. As Joseph Harris noted, "It took the motion picture people too many years to revise their policies and product to offset the changes in taste of the movie going public."[53]

Joseph Harris rightly noted that there was a change in audience taste that allowed for imports of foreign films on a mass scale, with the potential for substantial profit. ATA was an example of the way in which Harris had long diversified his business portfolio, which allowed him to become, as one profile piece described him, "a millionaire industrialist."[54] His business strategies no doubt influenced Harris-Kubrick Pictures. ATA began to diversify by 1959, investing heavily in the import of Russian-filmed ballets that had been shot in studios in Moscow, including a fifty-two-picture deal with Artkino Pictures for films like the Bolshoi Ballet's *Swan Lake*.[55] Realizing the potential theatrical appeal of Russian imports, Harris formed a new company with Sig Shore and fellow Flamingo Films partner Sy Weintraub, Vitalite Film Corporation, which had bought out the Distributors Corp of America (DCA); whereas ATA would import and sell for syndication foreign films, Vitalite would import and dub Russian and other foreign films specifically for the theatrical market.[56] By July 1959 Harris and Shore had acquired a range of films for Vitalite, including *Tamango* (Berry, 1958), a film that could be released only in New York at first due to its controversial depiction of a biracial relationship, and *The Executioners* (Podmaniczky, 1959) (renamed *Hitler's Executioners*), a documentary about the Nuremburg Trials. Vitalite also purchased erotic thrillers and stories of lust, including *A Question of Adultery* (Chaffey, 1958), *The Flesh Is Weak* (Chaffey, 1958), and *Back to the Wall* (Molinaro, 1958).

But it was an acquisition from a business trip that Harris and Shore made to Moscow in the summer of 1959 that soon involved Harris-Kubrick Pictures: *Ilya Muromets* (Ptushko, 1959). The film was a $10 million Russian epic based on a folk legend about the invasion of the country by the Mongols and the Tartars in the thirteenth century, featuring armies of dragons. In return for the purchase of *Ilya Muromets*, Vitalite sold the Russians a picture of its own; what this picture was is not certain. Could it have been a Harris-Kubrick picture? What is certain is that Joseph Harris believed that the spectacle of *Ilya Muromets* played into Hollywood's cycle of sword and sandal epics, including *Spartacus*, but also fantasy adventure epics like *Hercules* (Francisci, 1958). The latter was an Italian-produced film that had been purchased by producer Joseph Levine for U.S. distribution; it was dubbed into English and released by Warner Bros. and proved a significant box office hit, largely a result of Levine's intense publicity campaign.[57]

Harris believed Vitalite could replicate the success of foreign exploitation imports like *Hercules*.[58] He eventually prepared a publicity campaign for the film similar to that of *Hercules*, with his plans including "a national department stores tour of the costumes" and a Dell "movie classic" comic book tie-in, as well as a "$1 story treatment for early distribution."[59] He also hired Harris-Kubrick Pictures to oversee the reediting and dubbing of *Ilya Muromets*, retitled for the U.S. market as *The Sword and the Dragon*.[60] Harris-Kubrick Pictures undertook the dubbing at Ryder Sound Services and the film processing at Consolidated Film Industries (CFI), both located in Los Angeles, in the autumn of 1959. The work was for a fee, and all costs of the dubbing and editing were to be covered by Vitalite.[61] This did not immediately occur though, and Harris-Kubrick Pictures was instead receiving invoices from Ryder and CFI for the outstanding payments. *The Sword and the Dragon* assignment was, Kubrick believed, affecting the reputation of Harris-Kubrick Pictures, as he explained to Joseph Harris: "Jimmy and I are becoming known in this very small town as bad credit, dishonest. Both companies accepted the Sword and Dragon account on the strengths of our names and assume us responsible."[62] Kubrick was concerned that the work that he and James Harris had done to establish themselves as reliable producers in Hollywood would soon be undone if Vitalite did not pay the debts immediately. But more important, Kubrick was probably thinking ahead to any future Harris-Kubrick Pictures productions in which the services of the respective labs might be needed.

Kubrick was also worried that Harris-Kubrick Pictures could be tainted by its Soviet connection. He outlined his concerns to Sig Shore, referring to the Russian situation and the pressures he felt in undertaking the supervision of *The Sword and the Dragon*. Joseph Harris attempted to assuage Kubrick's concerns about his reputation, in terms of both the Russian and Los Angeles situations. He sympathized that "it must be a terrible world we live in if a young man like yourself can become alarmed over the pressure that may be used by some fanatical group," in reference to Kubrick's concerns about the potential impact of any kind of connection to communism.[63] In a bid to assuage Kubrick's concerns, Harris explained that he had discovered that the Russians were great admirers of his, seeing him as a "great talent" and seeing it as a "compliment" that Kubrick had agreed to work on *The Sword and the Dragon*.[64] Harris learned of Kubrick's reputation in Russia after attending the 1959 Moscow International Film Festival (MIFF) and more than likely instigated an invitation from the MIFF committee to Kubrick in the summer of 1959 to serve as a festival jury member. Kubrick declined.[65]

This brief overview of the Soviet connection shows the contexts in which Harris-Kubrick Pictures was working. The company was still indebted to Joseph Harris and so worked on *The Sword and the Dragon* as a way of repaying that debt. It may also have been a way of further securing funds for Harris-Kubrick Pictures toward its future production plans. At the same time, Joseph Harris sensed that audiences wanted more controversial, risk-taking product, the kind being made overseas. He realized that money could be made in exploiting the international cultural relationships that were on offer: specifically, taking advantage of a cultural pact between the U.S. and Soviet governments. But this also reflected the wider internationalist approaches being taken in film production and distribution more widely and the need to look beyond purely domestic American audiences. This was very much the case when it came to Harris-Kubrick Pictures' next production, *Lolita*.

"How Did They Ever Make a Movie of *Lolita*?"

Harris-Kubrick Pictures had a long-standing interest in developing controversial stories around the themes of obsessive, even transgressive love and sexual desire. From the earliest days of its operation, the company had invested in purchasing literary property centered on such themes, including *Burning Secret* and *Natural Child* (1952); the latter was a Calder Willingham novel that the company considered adapting but which the PCA deemed unacceptable due to its "extremely light and casual approach to the subject of illicit sex" and the topic of abortion.[66]

By June 1958, Harris-Kubrick briefly considered adaptations of Henry Miller's novels *Tropic of Cancer* (1934) and *Tropic of Capricorn* (1939), both of which had been banned in the United States for their candid portrayal of sex. The company believed it could adapt both novels into a single film that would overcome any censorship issues by excluding the most sexually explicit material to ensure a "tasteful" movie.[67] It may have been that Harris-Kubrick was exploring options as to how to produce a controversial film about sex and how a screenplay could even be written based on such material. After all, the first stage in overcoming any problems with the PCA was in the script. This is exactly the approach taken with the potential Miller adaptation: Harris-Kubrick purchased the motion picture rights as a means of exploring whether a screenplay could even be written that would still possess the "atmosphere" of Miller's books.[68]

Sex and infidelity also informed a series of ideas developed by Kubrick throughout the mid-1950s, some of which could have been early attempts at a project that was tentatively titled *The Unfaithful Wife*.[69] It is certainly the case that the themes that informed ideas like *Married Man* and *The Perfect Marriage* continued to be reworked by Harris and Kubrick individually throughout the late 1950s (see chapter 4). This culminated with a significant attempt at adapting author Vladimir Nabokov's *Laughter in the Dark / Camera Obscura* (1932) between 1959 and 1960. The project was developed by Harris-Kubrick Pictures in collaboration with actor Carlo Fiore (a close friend of Marlon Brando) at a cost of $2,000.[70] *Laughter in the Dark* in many respects foreshadows *Lolita*, telling the story of a middle-aged art critic, Albinus, and his growing infatuation and eventual affair with a seventeen-year-old girl, Margot.[71] Two treatments of *Laughter in the Dark* are now housed in the Stanley Kubrick Archive. The first relocates the story from Germany to France, very much like the actual 1969 adaptation directed by Tony Richardson. But a second treatment moves the story to New York, giving it a much more contemporary feel and early traces of *Eyes Wide Shut*.

But it was *Lolita*, a story of a middle-aged university professor's obsession for a twelve-year-old girl—a "nymphet"—called Dolores Haze, which Harris-Kubrick Pictures pursued as its first official project since *Paths of Glory*. And while the book was written by a literary master, already considered one of the greatest novelists of the twentieth century, the story did possess an atmosphere of exploitation, made clear in one short synopsis by *Variety*: "A man who has a passion for 'nymphets'—meaning girls from 10 to 14. The male marries a woman for the purpose of being with her daughter of the 'nymphet' age. The woman dies and he carries on with the girl."[72] *Lolita* was a book with a scandalous reputation, meaning controversy was inevitable for any potential motion picture adaptation. To this end, it was in keeping for Harris-Kubrick Pictures to pursue such a project. Harris seems to have been the key figure in purchasing the motion picture rights to *Lolita* for $150,000 in mid-1958. He set about looking at how to produce a film based on Nabokov's book throughout late 1958 and early 1959.[73] Harris had great enthusiasm for an adaptation of the book, calling it the "greatest property in existence," and predicted that it would return a substantial profit for Harris-Kubrick Pictures because of its controversial nature.[74]

But it was the very reputation of *Lolita* that posed the initial problems in producing an adaptation. After all, the book's reputation had seen it labeled as pornographic. This was because the Paris-based Olympia Press had originally published it after it failed to find mainstream publication.[75] Olympia, run by the publisher Maurice Girodias, launched a series of erotic, pornographic books as part of its Traveller's Companion series: *The Enormous Bed*, *Tender Was My Flesh*, *The Chariot of Flesh*, *The Loins of Amon*, *White Thighs*, *Until She Screams*, *Roman Orgy*, *The Sexual Life of Robinson Crusoe*, and *A Bedside Odyssey*. In addition, the series also published more "literary" work, including Henry Miller's so-called *Rosy Crucifixion* trilogy (*Sexus* [1949], *Plexus* [1953], and *Nexus* [1959]) and erotic literature like *The 120 Days of Sodom, or the School of Libertinage* (Marquis de Sade, 1904) and *The Carnal Days of Helen Seferis* (Alexander Trocchi, 1954). *Lolita* was number 66 in the Traveller's Companion series, and as the series became a publishing success and a global phenomenon by the mid-1950s, governments around the world tried to ban them and prevent their import from

France. This included the UK government, which banned the publication of *Lolita* in the country or the reselling of the Olympia version in 1956.[76]

Any film adaptation of *Lolita* was automatically associated with its pornographic reputation. This posed problems for Harris-Kubrick as it attempted to package a film based on the book and obtain financing. Harris had come close to finalizing a deal with Warner Bros. for $1 million, along with a 50 percent producers share of the profits. But the deal was turned down on the basis that "Harris-Kubrick refused to allow WB any say-so in story treatment, which latter demanded."[77] Kubrick was causing, in *Variety*'s words, "hassle over 'artistic control.'"[78] The trade press also reported that another unnamed film company "flatly refused to finance 'Lolita' when [Harris-Kubrick Pictures] . . . allegedly demanded 'impossible' terms, including 'no look' at the screenplay."[79] This was probably UA, which had expressed an interest in funding the development of a screenplay but eventually rejected the idea. UA explained that it rejected Harris-Kubrick because it had made "one of the most presumptuous and arrogant demands for a deal that we have ever had, particularly when it comes from a couple of youngsters like these."[80] The control that Kubrick was specifically requesting on any future production deal was not possible, and in 1959 Harris-Kubrick still did not have the reputation or standing to demand such terms, particularly on a project as controversial as *Lolita*.

Just as the major Hollywood studios were wary of financing *Lolita*, stars were wary of appearing in any adaptation. Laurence Olivier had been approached while Kubrick worked with him on *Spartacus*, and he provisionally agreed to play the lead role of Humbert in 1959.[81] But less than a month after indicating his commitment, Olivier wrote to Harris-Kubrick to backtrack: "[I do] not feel my mind grasping a film conception of the subject, and I therefore don't feel that I can very well bear the onus of the responsibility of partnership in the script of a subject concerning which strong doubts are so uppermost in my mind. . . . I fear that told in terms of dialogue the subject would be reduced to the level of pornography, to which I am afraid quite a few people already consign it."[82] Harris believed that the MCA, the agency that represented Olivier, had talked him out of the project, concluding that they would have told him that "Sir Laurence Olivier can't walk into a project like this with these two kids and, God knows what they're going to do . . . you're Laurence Olivier, you can't run the risk of telling the story of a paedophile."[83] Harris also approached David Niven for the role of Humbert but was told that he was already committed to a series with Four Star Television and that, should he agree to the role, the sponsors would withdraw their support for the program. Association with the subject material was causing jitters in the industry.

A conflation of factors was mounting against *Lolita*, at least in the United States. This was exacerbated by a writer's strike called by the Writers Guild of America (WGA) in the winter of 1959. The WGA had authorized strike action against the major Hollywood studios and associated independent producers in response to stalled negotiations for a new guild contract for all writers. The strike called for all writers not to work for the major studios or independent production companies, including Harris-Kubrick Pictures and all its related subsidiaries (which included Kubrick's Minotaur Productions).[84] By February 1960, the strike was effectively over and had led to Harris-Kubrick Pictures signing up to a new WGA contract with associated clauses, which included the entitlement of writers to 4 percent of the producers' share of any profits on the sale of a film for television distribution.[85] The success of the writer's strike led to increasing calls for the Screen Actors Guild for a similar strike to improve the terms and conditions of its members.

The production conditions in the United States were increasingly unfavorable to Harris-Kubrick Pictures, and so Harris set about looking to produce *Lolita* overseas. In 1959, the UK government allowed the publication of *Lolita* by Weidenfeld & Nicholson. The anticipation of the book's publication by other major publishing houses in Europe led to disproportionately high sales across Europe. Keeping abreast of the business context of the book, Harris told Kubrick that this would mean "a comparable ready-made audience in those countries."[86] And based on the book's presale figures, Harris considered preselling the film to European distributors. Harris outlined his thinking to Kubrick, saying that the publishing world was "buzzing" due to the anticipated success of the republication of *Lolita* in Europe.[87] This was shaping up to be not an American film but an international project. The aim was to package the film with a script by Nabokov along with an A-list cast to increase its commercial viability and convince distributors in Europe of the audience potential before the film had even been produced. Harris concluded, "Not only will we have multiple millions exposed to the book all over again but can work out a separate movie edition when the picture is released."[88]

Harris believed that the reputation of Harris-Kubrick Pictures outside of the United States would play to its advantage in producing *Lolita*: "It's my guess that Paris, London and Rome are the places to be. We have big reputations and films seem to mean more over there."[89] Utilizing his cultural network, Harris approached Kenneth Hyman, a school friend and now a producer at his father's production company Seven Arts. Hyman was producing a film in Europe with Brigitte Bardot and told Harris that Bardot would soon be available for another project, maybe even *Lolita*. The prospect of relocating Harris-Kubrick Pictures to a European country became real, with Harris telling Kubrick, "I bet there are many other European starlets that we could find if we were there. Try and get to these cities while you're in Europe."[90]

Harris was attempting to persuade Kubrick of a European move, baiting him with the allure of stars like Bardot. But he was also investigating the industrial contexts of the British film industry. He sent Kubrick a copy of a document titled "British Lion Films—Standard Arrangements in the UK for Financing First

Feature Films by Independent Producers."[91] The document reflected the scope of the research being conducted, which also included investigating state subsidies being offered by the UK government.[92] On offer was what had become known as the Eady Levy, a government subsidy paid out by the British Film Fund Agency to productions that suitably qualified as British.[93] In order to qualify, producers needed to ensure the film was produced in a British territory and "at least 75 percent of labor costs to have been paid to British persons."[94] The qualifying criteria for the Eady Levy thereby influenced the production choices on *Lolita*, including the casting of Peter Sellers and James Mason, two British actors, in lead roles.

The decision to relocate Harris-Kubrick Pictures to the United Kingdom may also have been prompted by the fact that Kenneth Hyman was also moving to London at that time. Hyman had been appointed the head of UK operations for Seven Arts.[95] Upon hearing this, Harris initiated a meeting with Hyman that led to a deal in which Seven Arts would finance the production of *Lolita*. By 1959 Seven Arts had expanded its interests in other entertainment media, including the record industry, Broadway plays, and the development of leisure resorts in the Bahamas.[96] As Seven Arts enacted its diversification strategy, its main company officers, Eliot Hyman and Lou Chesler, pursued a business strategy of creating a "family" of producers to create a constant stream of packaged feature productions.[97] They offered "stock inducements to top rated actors, producers and directors to become members" of this family, with the added enticement of not just having their pictures financed but also participating "in the overall success of the company and not merely in individual pictures."[98] Seven Arts offered producers either complete or partial financing or arranged financing through a distributor on behalf of the producer for a fee. Similar to UA, Seven Arts allowed independent producers considerable creative control of the actual production process but was heavily involved in the way films were promoted and distributed. By September 1960, Seven Arts had approximately fifteen pictures in production and had contributed $17.5 million to their financing, including *The Misfits* (1961), *West Side Story* (1961), *By Love Possessed* (1961), and *Two for the Seesaw* (1962).[99] Harris-Kubrick Pictures was included in the Seven Arts "family" as part of Hyman's diversification strategy, and *Lolita*, their first picture together, would be a fifty-fifty partnership.[100] The deal also included putting under contract whoever was cast in the title role of Lolita, a contract to be shared between Seven Arts and Harris-Kubrick. The role was given to Sue Lyon.

With Seven Arts financing the film, Harris and Kubrick could turn their attention to the adaptation itself. The absolute creative freedom on the script that Kubrick desired would prove impossible, despite his brazen confidence when discussing the issue of censorship with potential stars of the picture, such as Peter Ustinov: "The censorship thing does not concern me very much.... I don't think the MPAA will give us a seal, but if you've been following the grosses of similar films, it doesn't make a difference."[101] His confidence on the censorship issue was twofold: first, Seven Arts intended to road show *Lolita* for the first year of its release, and, second, the film would be "fairly innocent as far as ... the eye will see," leading Kubrick to conclude that "the MPAA thing becomes merely academic."[102] Films that had previously been released without a seal had gone on to become box office hits, including two films by Otto Preminger, *The Moon Is Blue* (1953) and *The Man with the Golden Arm* (1955), and Elia Kazan's *Baby Doll* (1956); the Legion of Decency condemned them all.

Harris and Kubrick wrote the final screenplay based on their own ideas and drafts that had been prepared by Calder Willingham and Vladimir Nabokov and on Nabokov's original book, though they departed quite substantially from the source text. There had been a number of disputes in the writing of the screenplay, starting with Willingham, who was fired from the project due to departing from the creative vision relayed to him by Harris and Kubrick.[103] The fallout was substantial, with Willingham accusing Kubrick of being a controlling producer with a dislike for collaboration. He was also incensed by the fact that he felt "screwed" by Kubrick, claiming he had introduced Harris-Kubrick Pictures to *Lolita* and therefore required a "finder's fee" as a means of expressing "moral gratitude," particularly because Willingham believed the adaptation of *Lolita* would prove lucrative.[104]

Harris-Kubrick Pictures subsequently hired Vladimir Nabokov to write the screenplay. He had initially turned the company down, believing he had little creative control.[105] But shortly after the firing of Willingham, Harris-Kubrick attempted to reopen contractual negotiations with Nabokov in December 1959. This time Nabokov was more responsive, with his wife Vera stating that he was more in the mood to adapt the book and could have it ready by as early as May 1, 1960.[106] However, Nabokov would agree to writing the screenplay only in return for a substantial fee and "a considerable amount of freedom and noninterference."[107] Harris-Kubrick agreed to Nabokov's demands and allowed him to write the first draft in isolation, renting a lodge for him in Mandeville Canyon. Why Harris-Kubrick allowed Nabokov such freedom when it had demanded creative freedom from major studios is questionable. It is likely that the script being developed by Nabokov was never going to be utilized but rather would allow the company to use the Nabokov brand name as a shield from attacks that the project was nothing more than exploitation and pornography. The script that Nabokov presented to Harris-Kubrick Pictures was over four hundred pages long and unfilmable. But it did mean the company could credit him with writing the screenplay, even if Harris and Kubrick themselves substantially reworked it.

It was also clear that the creative freedom Nabokov wanted was unworkable in terms of the production contexts in which Harris-Kubrick Pictures was operating. Seven Arts looked to mitigate the risk involved in its financing of *Lolita* and to ensure it would be passed by the various censorship bodies by hiring a script technical adviser, Martin Quigley, coauthor of the Motion Picture

Production Code in 1930. It was a pragmatic decision that Seven Arts and Harris-Kubrick Pictures mutually agreed to, with the hope that Quigley would steer *Lolita* away from any potential censorship issues. Quigley even led the postproduction negotiations with Geoffrey Shurlock, the head of the PCA. Quigley found a number of problems in the script prepared by Harris and Kubrick, and all of the changes he recommended to the first eighty-two pages were incorporated by the start of the shoot on November 28, 1960.[108] Further problems were identified in the final eighty-three pages of the script, but due to shooting having commenced and it being impractical for either Harris or Kubrick to meet with Quigley to discuss them—they were both in the United Kingdom—Hyman requested that they "avoid any shooting of what would be included in these last eighty-three pages, until such time as this has been settled."[109] Hyman asked that Harris inform him of any scenes that were scheduled to be imminently shot from the last eighty-three pages so Quigley could be consulted to see if he had any issues with them. Hyman's requests amounted, in a sense, to legal control over what kind of material Harris and Kubrick could film on the instruction of Quigley. In a letter of November 28 to the pair, Hyman asked them to fully recognize Quigley's suggestions and thinking because he felt there was increasing societal demand for the "elimination of subject matter onerous to the public at large" and that failure to cooperate with Quigley would lead to a "most unhappy situation."[110] It would seem that Quigley had a direct line to Hyman, bypassing James B. Harris, who was absent from issues of censorship, seemingly stripped of the power to control this by Seven Arts.

In producing *Lolita*, Harris-Kubrick Pictures was repeatedly forced into relinquishing control over aspects of production as a result of the underlying tension about the film's subject matter. But an area that Harris-Kubrick Pictures wanted to ensure it had control over, or at least some kind of strategic input, was publicity. The company was keen to promote the film's new star, Sue Lyon, as a means of maximizing publicity for both *Lolita* and any future productions in which Lyon appeared; she was now contracted to Harris-Kubrick Pictures. Harris-Kubrick intended to control the publicity of Lyon through a photography campaign that emphasized the "Lolita image."[111] The campaign looked to ensure that Lyon was presented as being similar in real life to the character she portrayed in the film.[112] One such photographic profile appeared in *Life* magazine and discussed how Lyon had to portray Dolores Haze as possessing "both girlish innocence and far too much experience."[113] The media campaign presented Lyon as a confident woman who was carefree and lighthearted and possessed experience beyond her teenage years. Such images played up to the official film poster, showing Lolita provocatively sucking on a lollypop as her eyes peek suggestively over the brim of her heart-shaped sunglasses. A bold headline across the poster asks, "How did they ever make a movie of Lolita?" and plays up the fact that the film was only "for persons over 18 years of age."[114] Critical quotes on one version of the poster provocatively suggested, "Sue Lyon makes you believe that she is

Lolita!" The *Lolita* image Harris-Kubrick crafted was one of the tantalizing prospect of sex. It suggested that the audience would see Sue Lyon / Lolita act out the book's most notorious passages, all the while playing on its pornographic association to Olympia Press. Kubrick himself acknowledged in a 1970 interview with Joseph Gelmis that the narrative interest of both the book and film "boils down to the question, 'Will Humbert get Lolita into bed?'"[115] The *Lolita* image drew upon the exploitation aesthetics of sex and violence of the low-budget genre pictures that Harris-Kubrick Pictures had started out production in as part of UA's abecedarian program. But just as *The Killing* blurred the boundaries between exploitation and art film, the promotion of *Lolita* aimed toward such confused categorization through the exploitation of Sue Lyon's *Lolita* image and the use of Nabokov's literary credentials.

The insinuation of an "adults only" movie became a key part of TV spots for the film and led one NBC affiliate to refuse to show the advert, even though it had been deemed acceptable by both NBC executives and censors.[116] The promotion of *Lolita* drew upon the various aesthetic associations to sexploitation and pornography, while at the same time moving toward a European art-house complexity, developing a story with psychological depth and auteur credentials. This is a process that Elena Gorfinkel calls cultural distinction, of the merging of sexual and cinephile taste, bringing art-house legitimacy to sexual representations on screen, increasingly seen in European movies such as *The Fourth Sex* (1961), *The Twilight Girls* (1957), and *The Libertine* (1969).[117] These pictures expanded the "sphere of acceptable consumption in a period of re-stratifying public taste."[118]

The issue of Lyon's publicity stemmed from not only the fact that Harris-Kubrick Pictures signed a multiple-picture contract with her but also the aim to pry control of publicity away from Seven Arts and MGM, the company to which *Lolita* had been sold for distribution. Both Harris and Kubrick had come to realize that publicity was one of the most vital components of a producer's job, and without control of it a film's prospects at the box office could be ruined. The issue came to a head with Seven Arts in August 1961, when Harris-Kubrick attempted to select its own publicist for *Lolita*. Its choice was Sig Shore, who prior to entering the film industry had worked as an advertising director for *Dance* magazine and established his own ad agencies in New York and San Francisco. Seven Arts did not want Harris-Kubrick selecting its own publicist and forced the company to drop the suggestion of Shore.[119]

But Kubrick argued with the logic of Seven Arts in giving over control of publicity to MGM: "It would appear that you believe if we get a sizeable advance or guaranty from a major company, we must therefore forfeit all the usual rights of publicity and advertising approvals and suggestions that any producer would normally have on a picture of this nature."[120] Kubrick was addressing the fundamental issue of who had control of a film; for him, being an independent producer relying on the money of others also meant having absolute control and legal authority. His view was based on the belief that the producer of the film had an investment that was not merely financial but also creative; the film was being made out of a passion for the story, and he did not trust a corporate entity to take over the responsibilities of the picture at the last stage. This had been the case on *The Killing*, a project destroyed at the box office by the lack of publicity from UA. Kubrick was explicit in this belief to Seven Arts: "Jim and I simply cannot believe that you have so much faith in the wisdom . . . of any of the major studio sales departments that you would be willing to entrust them entirely to do the best possible job. . . . Seven Arts and ourselves would be asking for the most gratuitous chances of things being messed up."[121] The issue of control over publicity would become the central tenet of Kubrick's battles with Hollywood throughout the remainder of the 1960s.

But the controversial nature of *Lolita* generated sizeable audience interest. By the end of 1963, the film had taken $4.5 million in domestic rentals, placing it in *Variety*'s "All-Time Top Grossers" list.[122] The film's success demonstrated the growth of Harris-Kubrick Pictures and how its strategy to internationalize its productions and to take advantage of the blurring of transgressive topics and arthouse aesthetics had created a product of cultural distinction that resonated with audiences.

Conclusion

Following the completion of production on *Lolita*, Harris-Kubrick Pictures came to a mutual agreement with Bryna Productions to bring a final end to all contractual obligations. Signed on December 15, 1961, the agreement allowed Harris-Kubrick to sever all links with Bryna and Kirk Douglas. The only repercussions of this final deal were three payments totaling $40,000, which had to be paid by installments through December 1963. Failure to pay these fees on time would result in further punitive measures, legal action, and even potentially the reinstatement of the 1958 deal.[123] But Harris-Kubrick Pictures, and Harris and Kubrick individually, was now free of the nearly five years' worth of legal authority Bryna and Kirk Douglas had possessed over the company. What the deal also demonstrated was that Harris-Kubrick was finally in a position that it did not require the cultural sponsorship of a major star like Kirk Douglas. The very fact that it had produced a picture as controversial as *Lolita* showed that the company now had the confidence and international reputation to hold its own in Hollywood. Here was a company that had evolved and emerged to become a significant industrial player within the American, indeed the global film industry.

Harris-Kubrick Pictures had reached such a powerful position by the start of 1962 by taking advantage of the spaces of autonomy that the industrial transitions in Hollywood offered. With *Paths of Glory*, the company was given relative creative autonomy on both the development and shooting of the script, allowing it to craft a bold anti-military hierarchy film that firmly established Harris and Kubrick's position within the industry as visionary producers. The film suffered, however, from a lack of control over its publicity. With *Spartacus*, Kubrick could take the credit of director of a multimillion-dollar picture that was a huge box office success, regardless of the level of his autonomy on set. The commercial success of *Spartacus* combined with the artistic prestige of *Paths of Glory* gave Harris-Kubrick Pictures the necessary combination of esteem and financial clout to advance their future projects. Harris himself noticed the difference in his attempts to package *Lolita* post-*Spartacus*: "They knew about *Paths of Glory* and *The Killing* and they knew that Stanley was doing *Spartacus* with Olivier and Laughton and Ustinov and Kirk. And, you know, we had this tremendous prestige going for us that we were able to get the actors to agree to do the screenplay."[124] The limits of control of a producer came to dominate Kubrick in the coming decade. He would analyze his contracts in fine detail, highlighting single words (just as he had done with the original Bryna / Harris-Kubrick Pictures contract) that might affect the limits of his power. But the one area in which studios and distributors were retaining control was over publicity and promotion of a film, the very thing used to create a brand. If Kubrick was going to gain full legal authority over his pictures, he needed to create his own corporations and his own sphere of influence.

Part 3
Polaris Productions and Hawk Films, 1962–1969

7

The Establishment of a Producing Powerhouse, 1962–1964

•••••••••••••••••••

By the final full year of its existence in 1962, Harris-Kubrick Pictures Corporation had become an established independent production company with an international focus and subsidiary companies based (for tax purposes) in Switzerland. It frequently based its productions overseas and even loaned out its principal director, Kubrick, to work on a historical epic with a multimillion-dollar budget. The company expanded its affiliations to include independents like Seven Arts and to several major Hollywood companies such as Columbia, MGM, and UA. The company had also increased in size to the point of having ten individuals on its payroll who received monthly salaries and expenses by March 1962.[1] This included Harris and Kubrick; a publicist, Benn F. Reyes (hired from Public Relations), who was paid $500 a week; a reader, Kit Bernard, who provided reports on potential literary material, a role Kubrick would consistently attribute to an individual on his staff (it was later allocated to Anthony Frewin and, in the late 1980s, to an entire team of readers at Kubrick's Empyrean Films [see chapter 10]); and an up-and-coming actress, Sue Lyon. Most important, and perhaps purposely, Harris-Kubrick Pictures courted controversy, pursuing subject matter that gained it attention in the media.

But despite this success the time had come for the company to dissolve and its two partners, Harris and Kubrick, to go their own ways in October 1962. Together they had entered the heart of Hollywood and established themselves as important players within the film industry. All the while they had mentored each other in the respective roles of producer and director. But Harris was eager to begin directing his own films, while Kubrick wanted to pursue his quest for full legal control of his productions and to begin working as his own producer. To do so, he established two new production companies, Hawk Films and Polaris Productions, and continued to base himself in the United Kingdom following the production of *Lolita* there. As for his filmmaking brand, it remained controversial, with plans announced in May 1962 "for a potentially explosive screen subject," what would become *Dr. Strangelove*. This chapter, along with chapter 8, explores how Kubrick established himself as one of the most powerful producers operating within the Hollywood mainstream, with a focus on the battle for control of publicity.

Old and New Production Companies

Harris-Kubrick Pictures Corporation was liquidated over a course of several months, commencing in the autumn of 1962 and continuing throughout the preproduction and shooting of *Dr. Strangelove*. The company was indebted to Harris personally, who had invested heavily over the years to ensure its survival. Not only that, there were subsidiary companies to dissolve, including Anya Productions in Switzerland, stocks to be sold (primarily Universal Controls, Gluckin, and Seven Arts Stock), expenses and loans to clear, and other assets to sell, including a restaurant deal that Harris-Kubrick had invested in at the advice of Joseph Harris. The company also had ongoing contracts, not least with Sue Lyon, a contract shared with Seven Arts. This meant that, as Harris and Kubrick commenced on new career paths separate to one another, they remained in almost daily contact between November 1962 and the spring of 1963, sharing advice and concerns, but also occasionally disagreeing about how to dismantle Harris-Kubrick.

The correspondence relating to the liquidation of Harris-Kubrick reveals a portrait of two young producers with acute business skills, with Kubrick demonstrating a level of caution as a producer and businessman. It is likely that this stemmed from the fact that Kubrick was, in effect, going it alone for the first time in his film career. He no longer had a sponsor to fall back on, with the financial security that Harris had brought since 1955 now gone. By going it alone, Kubrick knew he would have to be, in the short term at least, extraordinarily careful in how he managed the budgets of his own independent production companies going forward.

The liquidation of Harris-Kubrick meant a variety of expenses and debts had to be cleared. This included deferred fees owed to the staff who had been on the company's payroll and to individuals who had performed temporary services, such as lawyers and agents. But Kubrick queried any charges or expenses that were unexplained, such as "cash for travel" and "telephone bills," expense claims that had been submitted by lawyer Jack Schwartzman.² Kubrick wanted Harris to challenge Schwartzman over these expenses, arguing, "Why should we have to shyly and tactfully accept the thing on this basis?"³ Far from being unreasonable, Kubrick was conducting his affairs in a professional manner and expected those who worked for his companies to provide clear explanations for the expenses they were generating, right down to submitting appropriate invoices and receipts, what Kubrick described as being a "routine" process.⁴ Kubrick's attitude also extended to the choices being made by staff when claiming expenses, such as favoring cheaper modes of transport. As Kubrick explained to Nat Weiss in December 1962, "I am not a major company and I think the principal involved in all expenses, local or foreign travel, should be that they be kept modest (within reason) as possible. A good guide would be what would you spend personally."⁵

Kubrick knew that what he was asking, while fiscally responsible, could gain him a reputation as being frugal and mean within the industry, something he was keen to avoid. He told Harris to be discreet in all matters relating to the querying of expenses and to avoid making him seem "a bastard."⁶ He also advised, somewhat tongue in cheek, but partly reflecting an understanding of how the building and shattering of reputations worked within Hollywood, to "burn" all his letters regarding expense claims.⁷ Kubrick was relying heavily on Harris for advice during this early period of going it alone as a producer, displaying just how much he had been dependent on the business and administrative functions of his producer for seven years. But now that he had left Harris-Kubrick Pictures, Kubrick had the opportunity to develop his own power base and sphere of influence in Hollywood, and to do so meant he had to craft an image of control.

The first move to achieve this came on October 10, 1962, when Kubrick's lawyer, Louis C. Blau, incorporated the first of two new production companies, Polaris Productions, in Los Angeles.⁸ Blau acted as the agent of Polaris and put together an agreement between the company and Kubrick as a director-producer, despite Kubrick being the company president. This was quite possibly to enshrine in contract the legal authority that he sought when "loaning" himself out from Polaris to his independent productions, which were to be produced by Hawk Films. Hawk was incorporated on October 23, 1962, fifteen days after Polaris, and was based in London. The agreement stated that Polaris exclusively employed Kubrick's services as a producer and director and that he was not to render his services to "any person, firm or corporation other than ourselves."⁹ The Polaris contract also assigned the rights of all literary work and original material that Kubrick owned to Polaris and prevented any "person, firm or corporation to infringe upon such right."¹⁰ The contract also included a clause that prohibited Kubrick from being employed by any motion picture producer or production company other than Polaris. However, with Kubrick's agreement Polaris could loan out his services to producers or production companies of his choosing.¹¹ Subsequently, Polaris would loan Kubrick's services as a producer and director to his other production company, Hawk Films.

Hawk Films was set up as a means of establishing a semipermanent producing base for Kubrick in the United Kingdom, with the aim of taking advantage of the British Film Fund. Moreover, the company was used to leverage power for Kubrick as a producer in the British film industry more widely. By the beginning of January 1963, Hawk Films had opted into membership of both the Federation of British Filmmakers (FBFM) and, later, the British Film Producers Association (BFPA).[12] The FBFM and BFPA were the principal unions for independent producers in the United Kingdom and lobbied the government, the UK Board of Trade, and international organizations to procure better terms and conditions for the British film industry as a whole. This included regular consultation about changes to the Eady Levy,[13] as well as a central priority of obtaining greater control for film producers in an increasingly internationalized film industry.[14]

The relationship between Polaris and Hawk was as follows: Polaris would provide Hawk with above-the-line services, including story rights and the loan out of Stanley Kubrick as a producer, director, and writer. Polaris would also contract out any above-the-line cast, that is, those actors in a leading role, as well as non-UK-based personnel. And most important, Polaris would arrange financing with major studios and in turn provide Hawk with any and all production costs. Hawk was the operation unit of a Stanley Kubrick production, tasked with the actual creation of a film. Hawk had the much larger payroll, employing all the necessary technicians and other crew as well as most of the cast and extras. Polaris, on the other hand, had a much smaller payroll, though it could come to an equal or even greater cost than Hawk as it included Kubrick and the leading actors. Polaris also received numerous expenses and participatory profits for Kubrick.[15] Once Hawk had completed production of a film it would then assign the rights to Polaris, which in turn liaised with the relevant distributor.[16]

Polaris served as Kubrick's publicity and merchandising company, in a similar way in which Public Relations had served Kirk Douglas. Other independent producers also established their own in-house publicity units as part of a wider industrial trend. These in-house units were siphoning off publicity talent from the major studios, such as Columbia, MGM, and Twentieth Century Fox. Polaris was initially based in Midtown Manhattan, close to Park Avenue and Fifty-Sixth Street, before relocating to an apartment that had belonged to Kubrick on Central Park West by 1964. Kubrick was the company's president, with a vice president who ran the day-to-day operations. Nat Weiss was the first to perform this role, joining the company in December 1962 after he left Twentieth Century Fox, where he had served as a publicity manager.[17]

The primary function of the Polaris vice president was to liaise between Kubrick and the distributor financing his films, along with ensuring that Kubrick was at the center of all publicity campaigns. The vice president had to ensure that distributors regarded a Stanley Kubrick production as the most important picture on its payroll and therefore deserving of the best publicity campaign

Table 1
Polaris Productions Vice President and Publicity Director, 1962–1973

Name	Years Occupied Role
Nat Weiss	1962–1963
Roger Caras	1965–1967
Benn Reyes	1967–1968
Mike Kaplan	1971–1973

possible. Nat Weiss claimed he would achieve this aim by making Polaris a sphere of influence, releasing news breaks that distributors would not act on, in the process taking ownership of how Kubrick and his films were being sold to the media and cinema audiences.[18]

Publicity had become central to Kubrick's view of filmmaking, in terms of both how his films were sold to audiences and how he could craft his own image. By having control of publicity, he could steer the strategy to ensure the best possible box office returns for his films, but also place himself at the heart of their creation. He would become a brand. To signify how Polaris was a producing power base, Kubrick even devised a corporate logo for the company that he envisaged being used as a trademark in future adverts.[19] As early as 1951, Kubrick had attempted to control the way he was portrayed in the media by contacting journalists at the *New York Times*. But he had not had control over the publicity and distribution of his earliest features, something he believed had directly led to a deleterious effect on their box office performance.

Kubrick effectively saw the role of vice president of Polaris as a de facto executive producer on his films.[20] But none of those who took up the role of vice president of Polaris lasted long in the position (see table 1). This was partially a result of the fact that, despite promising that he would decentralize a number of strategic and operational responsibilities to the vice president, Kubrick maintained a hold over many of the role's functions. He was a micromanager, to the frustration of each of Polaris's vice presidents.

The first vice president, Nat Weiss, was fired by Kubrick in July 1963, just eight months into the role. Weiss had coauthored *The Cleopatra Papers* (1963) with a Twentieth Century Fox colleague, Jack Brodsky. It was an exposé of the affair between Richard Burton and Elizabeth Taylor during the troubled filming of *Cleopatra*, told through the letters and phone calls between Weiss and Brodsky, with the book creating "a stir in the entertainment industry with its revelations about the Burton-Taylor affair, as well as the administrative power wars at Fox."[21] The book annoyed industry insiders for making public "the behind-the-scenes business transactions of one of the major film production companies going through financial difficulties."[22] Many in Hollywood condemned the book, including Ken Clark, vice president of the MPAA, who described it as vilifying the film industry: "You besmirch an entire medium of communications with slander. You have accomplished one thing. You've exposed to all what it is really like inside the Inner Sanctum."[23] The adverse publicity as well as Kubrick's desire to keep his own productions confidential were the probable causes of Weiss's dismissal.[24]

Roger Caras took up the role during the preproduction for *2001: A Space Odyssey*. He lasted longer in the position but found he was often working at cross-purposes to Kubrick. When an offer came along to produce his own films, he resigned, with *2001: A Space Odyssey* still over a year from release. Caras was swiftly replaced by Benn Reyes, who had previously worked as a publicist for Harris-Kubrick Pictures. Reyes was an excellent administrator and more liable to follow Kubrick's orders than assert his own authority. Tragically, he died of a heart attack on December 8, 1968, eighteen months into the role, aged just fifty-three. Reyes was in Stockholm at the time publicizing *2001*.[25]

With Polaris, Kubrick was creating a company from which to exert influence and control over his role as a producer within the film industry. Kubrick's intention was to grow his sphere of influence as an independent producer, and the contract with Polaris—with himself—would affect his thinking in any future deals with major distributors. This is seen in contract negotiations with Columbia in June 1964 for a new project following *Dr. Strangelove*. Kubrick minutely analyzed the contract and wrote a twenty-three-page critique of it.[26] One point in the contract stated that negative costs needed to be compared to other pictures of a similar cost being produced by Columbia at that time. But Kubrick believed there were no comparable "independent producer with great influence producing a picture," placing his own stature as an independent producer against the likes of Sam Spiegel and Otto Preminger.[27] Kubrick now envisioned himself as a significant independent producer who required "complete total final annihilating artistic control" and urged the distributors to reduce their own power to merely one of approval over the budget, the two principal stars, and issues over censorship approval.[28] Everything else should be a matter for *his* approval as the film's producer.

Dr. Strangelove

In some respects, *Dr. Strangelove* can be viewed as the last Harris-Kubrick Pictures project. It was a film that had its origins while the company was still in operation, with Kubrick working out of its New York office. James B. Harris had been involved in early iterations of the screenplay, even devising satirical scenarios with Kubrick (though Harris never believed that Kubrick would give the ideas serious consideration). And it was Harris who had helped oversee the project's initial financing through a deal with Seven Arts. To promote the deal, Harris-Kubrick Pictures placed a one-page ad in *Variety* in May 1962, with two large photographs of Kubrick and Harris above the headline "Kubrick, Harris and Seven Arts."[29] The ad signaled how *Dr. Strangelove* would be a continuation of the company's controversial productions, stating "from the challenge of *Lolita*, director Stanley Kubrick and producer James Harris again join with Seven Arts."[30] It was a direct connection to the company's previous project and the reputation that it had developed. *Dr. Strangelove* was a legacy of Harris-Kubrick Pictures, and as discussed above, Kubrick still turned to Harris for advice throughout the film's preproduction and shooting period.

But Kubrick had to go it alone as a producer when, in his words, Seven Arts pulled a "dirty trick" on him and sold the package for *Dr. Strangelove* outright to Columbia in the autumn of 1962.[31] *Variety* reported that the Seven Arts deal had fallen apart by the beginning of October and replaced by a deal with Columbia.[32] But Kubrick had to negotiate a new deal between Polaris and Columbia, which resulted in a two-picture contract.[33] Columbia's vice president, Mike Frankovich, was looking to develop new contracts with independent producers.[34] He announced an "ambitious programme" of new, largely British-based productions in late October 1962, to include *The Victors* (Foreman, 1963), *The Running Man* (Reed, 1963), *The Long Ships* (Cardiff, 1964), and *Dr. Strangelove*.[35]

Because Kubrick was still in the process of setting up Hawk Films and Polaris Productions in October 1962, the initial deal was between Kubrick, Columbia, and Trooper Films Ltd, the latter presumably a temporary company of one of Kubrick's lawyers, another affiliate, or even just the provisional name of Polaris Productions.[36] The deal was lucrative for Kubrick, who received $200,000 for his services as a producer-director, additional living expenses, and a producer's share of the profits.[37] The deal was eventually transferred to Kubrick's Polaris, which contracted the production to Hawk. But the contract arranged with Columbia shows how *Dr. Strangelove* had to fit with Frankovich's strategy of British-based productions; the film was required to qualify for the Eady Fund and had to be produced by a British corporation (Hawk). But Polaris had hired an American, Lee Minoff, to take over the functions that had been performed by Nat Weiss. Kubrick had agreed to give Minoff the credit of executive producer and production associate, but this posed a problem with the British Board of Trade and with the ACTT union.[38] Minoff did not have a foreign labor permit (he was based in New York) nor membership of the ACTT, but the credit required him to possess one of these. To protect his reputation in the industry, to ensure smooth relations with the British trade unions, and to guarantee *Dr. Strangelove* met the Eady criteria, Kubrick did not give Minoff the credit.[39]

Dr. Strangelove qualified as a British film because of the largely British crew, most notably Victor Lyndon, who was the associate producer. Kubrick also cast Peter Sellers in multiple roles (Mandrake, Muffley, and Strangelove), a suggestion that had been part of the deal with Columbia. Sellers had previously been cast in three roles in *The Mouse That Roared* (Foreman, 1959), a film produced in Britain and distributed by Columbia. The film had striking similarities with

Dr. Strangelove besides the presence of Sellers. It was a satirical farce about the fictional country Grand Fenwick, which declares war on the United States. The leaders of the country obtain a prototype Q-bomb, created by a German scientist and capable of destroying an entire continent. Just like *Dr. Strangelove*, *The Mouse That Roared* made fun of political and military power and the arms race and arguably paved the way for *Dr. Strangelove* to be produced. By 1960, the film had grossed over $1.25 million in domestic rentals in the United States and reflected the increasing success of "British" films at the U.S. box office.[40] Indeed, by the early 1960s the United Kingdom had come to be seen as a "production centre of international importance," with a number of box office hits produced in the country, qualifying to be registered as British films and awarded Eady Levy funds.[41] Within this context, it is clear to see why Columbia had taken on *Dr. Strangelove* and made it a condition of their deal with Kubrick that the film qualify as British and that it feature Sellers in multiple roles. According to Terry Southern, a cowriter of the *Dr. Strangelove* screenplay, Kubrick told him, "'I have come to realize ... that such crass and grotesque stipulations are the *sine qua non* of the motion-picture business.' And it was in this spirit that he accepted the studio's condition that this film, as yet untitled, 'would star Peter Sellers in at least four major roles.'"[42]

Kubrick more than likely agreed with Columbia's requirements about casting Peter Sellers. After all, his career to date showed how he was attuned to the commercial necessities of the American film industry, even conforming with industrial trends where necessary, whether through producing genre pictures that met box office demands (*Killer's Kiss*, *Spartacus*) or films that conformed to the production conditions of a particular studio (*The Killing*). Kubrick also probably recognized the box office appeal of Peter Sellers following on from his success in multiple roles in *The Mouse That Roared* as well as his success in *Lolita*, another film in which he appeared as several different characters. The producer instinct in Kubrick would have additionally sensed the financial logic in casting Sellers in multiple roles: in return for his fee, Kubrick was cutting down the need to cast any more actors.

Cost reduction was clearly on Kubrick's mind throughout the production of *Dr. Strangelove*. For example, he had briefly given thought to casting Gene Kelly in the role of General Ripper, but this was dependent on Kelly's stated fee. Kubrick coordinated contact with Kelly via James B. Harris, telling Harris to be vague on the terms of any deal to avoid "embarrassment ... if asking price too high."[43] Any negotiations with Kelly had to "create the impression in his mind that we're very tight on money (we are)."[44] But the deal never came to anything, and instead Harris-Kubrick Pictures arranged a deal with Sterling Hayden on behalf of Hawk Films, at a cost of $10,000.[45] Similarly, Kubrick tried to negotiate reduced fees for the use of music, including reusing songs from *Lolita*. He corresponded with Harris about the possibility of the *Lolita* "Ya Ya" theme being used as music played on Mandrake's radio as he enters Ripper's office. As he explained, "I can buy very cheap stock music here for about £20 already recorded which has, as you might imagine, a slight sound of nothing to it. There isn't any room in the budget for paying very much more."[46] But there was a mandatory charge of $350 to use the music and the need for Seven Arts' permission;[47] Kubrick opted for the cheap stock music.

Kubrick's concerns over the costs of the film suggested that he was being both cautious on this first venture as a producer post–Harris-Kubrick Pictures as well as keen to ensure that he developed a reputation as a fiscally responsible producer. If he allowed his budget to balloon to excessive levels, he could have easily found future deals more restrictive in terms of control. He also endeavored to bring the project in on time, but the shooting schedule was delayed by a month (production was meant to begin in January 1963) due to the Mirisch Corporation still requiring the services of Peter Sellers, who was filming *The Pink Panther* (Edwards, 1963). In return for agreeing to delay the start of production on *Dr. Strangelove*, Mirisch paid Hawk Films a delay fee of nearly $50,000.[48]

Reputation was a key objective of the entire *Dr. Strangelove* project. Kubrick's future as a film producer largely rested on the success of the film, how it was marketed, and how the media portrayed the production and Kubrick as a filmmaker. It was therefore Polaris's role to try to control these issues and to take ownership of the narrative of *Dr. Strangelove* ahead of the film's actual release.

Polaris and the Kubrick Reputation

Kubrick believed he had excellent strategic marketing skills and understood his audience and how to brand himself and his productions. He made it expressly clear to James B. Harris that he thought *he* had been largely responsible for the successful *Lolita* ad campaign, managing to pressure Seven Arts and MGM in the choice of copy and how the trailers were cut. He claimed that without his interventions the box office performance of *Lolita* would have been "unsatisfactory."[49] Kubrick was perhaps overselling his influence, given that the marketing on *Lolita* had also depended upon word of mouth and the hype surrounding the controversial nature of the film.

Kubrick's films appealed to "metropolitan tastes," with the likes of *Dr. Strangelove* performing well in cities such as New York but struggling outside of major urban areas.[50] *Dr. Strangelove* became a cult hit in university towns and demonstrated how Kubrick's films attracted "urbane, sophisticated audiences."[51] This appeal informed the marketing approach of Polaris, which largely pushed the initial publicity of the film in the first half of 1963. Nat Weiss had developed a publicity unit for *Dr. Strangelove*, the sole purpose of which was to deliver major news breaks throughout the production of the film. The team included a publicity writer, Lee Minoff, who contributed articles about the film to the *New York*

Times. One such piece from April 1963, titled "Nerve Center for a Nuclear Nightmare," presented the film as a "nightmare comedy," but with a heavy emphasis on the film's intellectual concerns about nuclear warfare.[52]

As Peter Krämer has stressed, these early attempts at marketing the film portrayed it more as a nuclear thriller than as satire or comedy, with Kubrick more prominent in the profile pieces than the film's main star, Peter Sellers.[53] Kubrick seems to have wanted to play up the controversial nature of the film: here was a production that was making *fun* of nuclear war at a time when the Cold War was at its hottest, with the production of *Dr. Strangelove* coming just several months after the Cuban Missile Crisis. Could audiences be allowed to laugh at such a horrifying prospect as nuclear war? The publicity emphasized how the subject was of grave importance to Kubrick, with Minoff stressing in news stories the scale of the research Kubrick had conducted into the topic, including consulting over seventy books and meeting with prominent strategists like Herman Kahn.[54] Kubrick was not treating the subject lightly but could see no alternative other than laughing at the grim reality, telling the *Los Angeles Times*, "Comedy can be more realistic than straight drama because it takes into account the bizarre."[55] But the topic of the film and its controversial treatment as a comedy were purposely highlighted in news breaks and how it had generated debate in the United Kingdom. As one news columnist reported, "Stanley Kubrick has been accused of filming a mammoth sick joke, of turning horror into black comedy and of producing the slickest piece of anti-American propaganda in years. On the other side, people are asking what the fuss is all about. The film is a comedy they say, so why take it so seriously?"[56] The controversy of the film's grim humor was directly linked to Kubrick as a film producer and the kinds of stories he liked to tell, with one news piece quoting him as saying, "All storytellers tell different stories and this reflects their personalities. I suppose the films I've made reflect mine." The article sardonically listed the topics of Kubrick's stories: death, war, famine, pestilence, and atomic annihilation, what it called the five horsemen that made up Kubrick's filmmaking personality.[57] This supposed controversial debate that was taking place in the United Kingdom was picked up by other news outlets, suggesting that the story was a Polaris plant. In an apparent exclusive for the *New York Times*, the paper reported that the political debate raging in the country "seems to increase the length of box-office queues."[58] It was a manufactured debate as a means of generating further publicity and interest in *Dr. Strangelove*.

Kubrick's authorial control and reputation on *Dr. Strangelove* were also stressed in the publicity put out by Polaris. As Nat Weiss outlined, Polaris had to be more than a "Strangelove affiliated" company, with an overall corporate mission of future proofing the Kubrick production brand and reputation.[59] Kubrick was placed at the heart of the creation of *Dr. Strangelove* in news breaks that were issued in early 1963, while Polaris made it clear to Columbia that Kubrick did not want *Dr. Strangelove* promoted as a Peter Sellers film because this would restrict it to the comedy genre. It was the function of Polaris to put the Kubrick producing name front and center of the companies distributing his films. As Weiss made clear, this meant making Polaris "a force to move a *Lawrence [of Arabia]* dominated Columbia."[60] But this wasn't necessarily an approach that Columbia favored. By late 1963, Kubrick's centrality to *Dr. Strangelove* had been diminished in publicity material, while the theme of sex was foregrounded.[61] This was more than likely a result of Columbia's own strategy, not Polaris's. Columbia's publicity department had expressed deep reservations about Kubrick's preference for marketing himself over his primary stars, such as Peter Sellers. In fact, Columbia was adamant that Kubrick's intrusion into areas of publicity ultimately had an adverse effect on the box office potential of *Dr. Strangelove*, due to his "insistence on a number of ill-advised points in the advertising style."[62]

Columbia preferred a showcase release for *Dr. Strangelove*, with concentrated advertising in metropolitan areas like New York, an approach it had first taken in early 1964 with *The Victors*.[63] This reflected a wider industrial trend, in which films were released in a limited number of first-run theaters with higher ticket prices, with the aim of generating faster box office revenue. For *Dr. Strangelove*, Columbia assigned field staff to work in specialized areas, such as on university and college campuses. In addition, an extensive merchandising campaign was supervised by Roger Caras, including tie-ins with candy stores, an album of music from the film, and a "novelization" by Peter George published by Bantam Books.[64] The latter, a paperback, was published without any mention of Kubrick on the front cover, while the image design very much played up the sexual innuendo of the film; it was a black-and-white image of General Turgidson's (George C. Scott) secretary from her bust down to her legs, with no sight of her face.

In the end, it may well have been that, regardless of the various marketing approaches, *Dr. Strangelove* merely struck a chord with audiences of the era. After all, the film allowed them relief from the anxiety they felt at the very real and dangerous threat of nuclear war. And while Kubrick himself was not adverse to the fear of nuclear war (he gave serious consideration to moving to Australia to avoid any such fallout),[65] with *Dr. Strangelove* he was "blithely daring his audiences to laugh at the prospect of the end of the world."[66]

Conclusion

The early 1960s represented a fundamental shift in Kubrick's career. By leaving Harris-Kubrick Pictures he was making the final transition in his career, from that of an independent producer relying on sponsorship for access to cultural, industrial, and financial networks to an independent producer controlling his own affairs. In forming Polaris Productions and Hawk Films, he was creating a power base that signaled the levels of independence and control he expected from the major Hollywood distributors. But Polaris demonstrated that Kubrick also wanted full control over the way his films were promoted and distributed as well as how his own image was represented in the media. It was a company that was tasked with placing Kubrick at the center of his film's publicity strategy: the Kubrick name—the producing brand—came first.

Polaris certainly allowed Kubrick to establish an image of control and authorial agency with *Dr. Strangelove*, at least in the initial stages of publicity in early 1963. However, it may be that, because of the unfortunate need to fire Nat Weiss by July 1963, Polaris's strategy was somewhat diluted, giving precedence to Columbia's campaign approach. But even so, Kubrick continued in trying to wrestle control of publicity from Columbia, ultimately to the detriment of his working relationship with the company. And so Kubrick pursued his own means of publicizing the Kubrick producing brand without Columbia, even hiring the services of a publicity company dedicated to devising Academy Award campaigns.[67] If there was one thing Kubrick wanted to seal his reputation and his producing brand, and to establish himself fully within the Hollywood establishment via what he called the "institutional effect," it was an Oscar.[68] Maybe his next film could net him this coveted prize.

8
Kubrick versus MGM, 1964–1969

●●●●●●●●●●●●●●●●●●●●

In the weeks and months following the release of *Dr. Strangelove*, Kubrick's producing brand was the strongest it had ever been. The commercial success of *Dr. Strangelove*, earning domestic box office rentals of $4.1 million by the end of 1964,[1] combined with the fact that three of his feature films (*Spartacus, Lolita*, and *Dr. Strangelove*) were listed in *Variety*'s "All Time Top Grossers" by January 1965 with North American domestic rentals of over $23 million,[2] placed Kubrick in a powerful position within Hollywood. He was now a force to be reckoned with, no longer merely a prodigious boy wonder making privately financed low-budget thrillers but a producer who had established a power base for himself. The 1960s were proving to be a lucrative decade for Kubrick, in terms of both garnering ever greater control of his productions and winning commercial and critical success.

But Kubrick was still at the mercy of the studios that financed his productions when it came to publicity and distribution. It was the one key area that he wanted control over. Incorporating Polaris Productions had been the first step in achieving this control, but he now wanted to go further in establishing his producing company as a significant sphere of influence within the industry. The 1960s was a complex decade for Hollywood. The transition in mode of production, from the studio system to the postwar independent producing system, had led to studios divesting elements of creative control to independent producers. But as the major Hollywood studios were keen to protect the property they were financing and distributing, the best way to do so was to retain control over publicity and distribution. It was this issue that would bring Kubrick into direct conflict with one of Hollywood's grandest and oldest studios: MGM.

For Kubrick, the majority of the 1960s was dominated by the development and production of *2001: A Space Odyssey*, produced for MGM. From the outset *2001* made extensive use of Kubrick's American-based company, Polaris Productions, in order to create one of the largest merchandising campaigns in Hollywood history up to that point. Roger Caras, the company's new vice president by 1965, envisioned an ambitious publicity and merchandising campaign for *2001*. This chapter expands on the analysis of Polaris to understand how it contributed to Kubrick's rise as an independent producer obtaining ever greater business and creative control of his productions. It shows how Kubrick's power as a producer grew exponentially as he wrestled for control of publicity, merchandising, and exploitation of *2001* from MGM. But at the same time as he seized ever more control of his productions, the first signs began to emerge of his own undoing as a producer: he was acquiring more control than he could feasibly manage.

Success

Dr. Strangelove proved that Kubrick was a producer with audience appeal who made a distinct kind of movie product: films that were controversial and cutting-edge. Now Kubrick needed to preserve that image and protect his producing reputation. When London's *Evening News* published a news story claiming that Kubrick based his productions in the United Kingdom only because he was convinced the country offered greater freedom to make "controversial films," he refuted the suggestion. He made clear to the editors that "the freedom that any filmmaker has is wholly dependent on his reputation and status with film distributors rather than any geographical climate of opinion."[3] It also depended on his ongoing success at the box office. And with ever greater success came the prospect of ever greater failure in the future.

For Kubrick, his status and reputation with film distributors flowed from his image of control produced by Polaris Productions. Simultaneously, they depended on his working relationships with the most powerful executives within Hollywood. Going forward, these executives and corporations would be his new sponsors, the people he needed to persuade to part with their money and control in order to allow him to produce his films in his own way, from development to distribution. Over the next twenty years, from 1965 onward, Kubrick cultivated relationships with some of the most powerful men in Hollywood: from Robert O'Brien at MGM to a swath of executives at Warner Bros., including Steve Ross, John Calley, and Terry Semel. Kubrick had reached the position by the mid-1960s where he could now communicate with the industry at the executive level. And the respect he commanded meant that distributors, writers, actors, directors, and other producers all wanted to work with him and to be associated with the Kubrick producing name.

By late 1964, Kubrick began to use this newfound influence to try to help the careers of those producers less successful than him. This included forwarding scripts to his own contacts, as he did for the writer Richard Hudson in October 1964. Hudson had sent Kubrick a script titled *Drizzle Island*, but as Kubrick explained, "I have no personal interest in it myself to do it as a film and I wonder if there is anything that you want me to do for you in sending it around to anyone else."[4] Similarly, he forward a script from an anonymous writer to a Broadway producer, believing it would make a "smash Broadway or London play," offering to negotiate a deal on behalf of the writer.[5] It could well be that Kubrick was acting in the capacity of an executive producer—someone in Hollywood who deals in stories and literary property and often secures deals with studios and distributors. This certainly was the case with Kubrick's involvement in director and producer Bryan Forbes's *Séance on a Wet Afternoon* (1964). The film had been released in the United Kingdom by the Rank Organisation in June 1964, but Forbes was looking for an American distributor. Kubrick offered to help Forbes "to make a deal," saying that "nothing would be more enjoyable."[6] Forbes welcomed Kubrick's intervention and forwarded the relevant information to support any potential deal, including quotes from British critics. The film was eventually distributed in the United States by Artixo Productions. What Kubrick's contribution was in securing the distribution deal is not clear.

Also following on from the success of *Dr. Strangelove*, Kubrick started to receive an influx of requests to direct or produce a range of original projects or adaptations. Among the offers were *Little Big Man* (1964), Thomas Berger's western that was eventually directed by Arthur Penn in 1970; Kubrick turned down the book as not being "substantial enough."[7] He also received offers of collaboration from major Hollywood figures, including actor Steve McQueen, fresh from the box office success of *The Great Escape* (Sturges, 1963) and looking to produce a picture based on his love of motor racing. He wanted Kubrick to direct an adaptation of Robert Daley's *The Cruel Sport* (1963), a history of the earliest years of Formula One racing. But the subject just did not entice Kubrick, despite a desire to work with McQueen.[8]

Kubrick did come close to securing a deal with producer David O'Selznick in the summer of 1964, for a film adaptation of James Baldwin's play *Blues for Mister Charlie* (1964), based on the murder of Emmett Till in 1955.[9] The plan was for Kubrick to direct and produce the adaptation, with O'Selznick as an executive producer, presumably because O'Selznick owned the motion picture rights to the book. A requirement of the potential deal was for Kubrick to secure "top box office stars" and a distribution deal. But by the autumn the project had fallen through, with the motion picture rights instead purchased by producer Jack Jordan's Melissa Productions.[10]

But what were Kubrick's motivations in selecting or rejecting potential new projects? The process of overdevelopment, at least overdevelopment as operated by Harris-Kubrick Pictures—a company that had been in perpetual instability—no longer seems to have been the driving force. Instead, Kubrick was responding to projects first at an intellectual level—the project had to sustain his interest as an artist, hence his rejection of *The Cruel Sport*—but also at the commercial level, looking to the current industrial trends. The latter perhaps explains his interest in *Blues for Mister Charlie*, a play that performed well on its Broadway debut but spoke to current news events, with Lyndon B. Johnson signing into law the Civil Rights Act of 1964. Any film adaptation would be controversial given it would be produced at a time of inflamed racial tension in the United States. As we have seen, Kubrick was not adverse to the film treatment of controversial, even explosive subject matter. The number of offers that Kubrick rejected during 1964 was substantial. They included, among others,

- An adaptation of *Winged Victory* (1934), a novel by Victor Maslin Yeates about the foundation of the Royal Air Force set during the final months of World War I. Kubrick wanted to be kept up to date on the project and how it would be produced. He was interested in the production cost of any adaptation because in his words "it is barely worth doing without a tremendous recreation of atmosphere."[11]
- An offer from the writer-director Herbert Biberman to produce a project titled *The Slaves*.[12] This could have been an adaptation of the 1962 novel by Isaac Bashevis Singer, rather than Biberman's own adaptation, *Slaves* (1969), of Harriet Beecher Stowe's book *Uncle Tom's Cabin* (1852).
- A biopic of the life of Oliver Cromwell, loosely based on John Buchan's *Oliver Cromwell* (1934), written by director John Hughes.[13] Hughes had tried for several years to get the project off the ground, finally directed it in 1970, released as *Cromwell*.
- An adaptation of "Ride with Terror," an episode of the television show *The DuPont Show of the Week*, executive produced by David Suskind.[14]
- A project titled *The Spy in G-Flat*, a comedy that Kubrick suggested he could forward to Peter Sellers, commenting that "it seems just the sort of thing he'd like."[15]
- Several projects suggested by his former agent, Ronnie Lubin, including a proposed Spanish Civil War epic (Kubrick wanted to see the treatment first, which was being developed in collaboration with Hugh Thomas, a British historian),[16] an adaptation of *Mila 18* (Leon Uris, 1961), a novel about the Jewish ghettos of Warsaw in World War II,[17] and an adaptation of *The Four Seasons of Manuela* (von Hagen, 1952), a biography of Simón Bolívar and his relationship with Manuela Sáenz.

These projects were largely historical epics (with the exception of the B-movie territory of "Ride with Terror"), with locales ranging from medieval Russia and Civil War–era England to World War II Poland. Kubrick's rejection was often based on similar motivations: a lack of interest in the stories, the conviction that they would be too expensive, and the need for him to conduct extensive historical research. This was very much the case with the proposed biopic of Bolívar, with Kubrick stating that "the complexity of Bolivar's political and military adventures and schemes would present anyone with a difficult problem doing a script, but I should say that unless whoever did the script became somewhat of an expert from a historical point of view, the script would inevitably become just so much hogwash."[18]

Kubrick was constantly searching for new projects, and it was a key task of Polaris Productions to find "prospective film material."[19] But Kubrick, in contrast to the rapid acquisitions of Harris-Kubrick Pictures, was being much more selective. The way Polaris approached the search for new projects was often by acting on recommendations about potential adaptations. This was the case, for example, when Polaris requested galley proofs of the as then unpublished *Hitler Moves East, 1941–1943* (1964), an account of the German Army's advance on Eastern Europe written by Paul Carell;[20] Carell was a former SS officer and later a spokesman for Joachim von Ribbentrop. It could well have been that the interest in *Hitler Moves East* was an extension of the previous development undertaken by Harris-Kubrick Pictures on *Nazi Paratroopers* and *The German Lieutenant*.

But Kubrick also seemed interested in developing another comedy, one with more explicit sexual themes, again extending a thematic interest of Harris-Kubrick Pictures and of his own reputation for controversial, even adult-orientated films. Kubrick was in correspondence with the author and journalist Michael Leigh throughout the summer of 1964. His primary interest was in Leigh's book *The Velvet Underground* (1963), an account of underground sexual behavior, including sadomasochism, group sex, wife swapping, and paraphilic fetishes. Kubrick was fascinated by the subject and the way that Leigh had interviewed people from the United States involved in these sexual practices, believing there was "an incredible comedy lurking somewhere in this subject: the contrast of folksy squareness and way out behavior."[21] But even though *The Velvet Underground* was left unmade, Kubrick continued to explore the prospect of producing a film that explicitly dealt with sexual fantasy over the next three decades.

So what was Kubrick looking to produce in the immediate aftermath of *Dr. Strangelove*? Simone Odino has argued that probably as early as February 1964 Kubrick was considering a science fiction project. But he was also committed to a series of other projects between 1963 and 1964, including a TV series that would celebrate the twenty-fifth anniversary of the founding of the United Nations. The series was to be supervised by Edgar Rosenberg on behalf of the

Telsun Foundation, while Xerox, the office equipment supplier, was to underwrite the production, at a cost of approximately $4 million.[22] The series brought together a roster of Hollywood talent, from Marlon Brando and Paul Newman to Sam Spiegel and Fred Zinnemann;[23] even Peter Sellers appeared in an episode of the series, titled "Carol for Another Christmas."[24] The six-part series was intended to dramatize the full scope of the United Nations' activities, but Rosenberg was having difficulties in securing a broadcaster. By April 1964, CBS-TV had turned down the opportunity to broadcast the series, proclaiming it to be "propagandistic in nature."[25] CBS-TV made the decision based on the fact that Xerox had announced the series was meant to portray the United Nations in a "favourable way," which the broadcaster believed would amount to sanctioning subjective journalism.[26] Instead, ABC agreed to broadcast the series. It was around this time that Kubrick decided to withdraw from the project, potentially on the grounds of protecting his reputation from the accusations leveled by CBS-TV.[27]

But it was more likely that Kubrick left the UN project due to his growing prioritization to produce a science fiction film. He had considered an adaptation of the BBC radio science fiction drama *Shadow on the Sun* (1961) in October 1964, proposing it as the basis for a science fiction film in collaboration with Arthur C. Clarke.[28] While *Shadow on the Sun* was not developed into a film, Kubrick did return to the series again in 1989.[29] Kubrick also explored the possibility of purchasing the rights to the "Shaver Mystery" stories in 1964, first published in the pulp magazine *Amazing Stories* edited by Ray Palmer, and later published in the *Hidden World* magazine.[30] Written by Richard Sharpe Shaver, the stories told of an underground cavern deep in the earth inhabited by evil aliens. Shaver claimed that the stories were true and based on his own firsthand experiences and that the underground cavern was being kept secret by the U.S. government.

Kubrick clearly wanted to make a film about outer space more than any other project.[31] He approached science fiction author Arthur C. Clarke, via the mutual contact of Roger Caras, about a collaboration in March 1964.[32] But even this did not necessarily commit Kubrick to producing a science fiction film. It was merely a means of exploring the *possibility* of producing a science fiction film, armed with the knowledge that both he and Clarke would be in New York that spring. The project picked up momentum by May 1964, when a deal was signed between Kubrick and Clarke for the development of a treatment, along with the purchase of several of Clarke's short stories and novels, among them *The Sentinel* (1951). It was this book that would serve as the basis for the story that had been titled *Journey Beyond the Stars*. Kubrick's producing style was becoming one of exploration, considering the feasibility and logistics of a production before commencing. In the summer, Kubrick compiled a draft budget for *Journey Beyond the Stars* in comparison with the budget of *Dr. Strangelove*. He knew that if he was to make a science fiction film he needed a sizeable budget, particularly when it came to the special effects, which he estimated at $900,000, treble that of *Dr. Strangelove*. Kubrick's budget estimate came to just under $4 million.[33]

Kubrick also gave serious consideration as early as 1964 about where to base the production. He requested his staff at Polaris Productions to conduct research into the filming facilities in Japan, with Ray Lovejoy contacting producers at Toho, the film company behind *Godzilla* (1954). The intention was clear: Kubrick needed expert special effect technicians if he was to make a successful science fiction film.[34] But his preference was to once more return to the United Kingdom, a country in which he had established key working relationships, telling Peter Sellers that he was working on a new script and was thinking of a way of "swindling it over to England."[35]

But there was a slight problem in Kubrick's desire to produce a science fiction film: the genre was just not seen as being commercial within Hollywood. There had been a decrease in the number of science fiction films produced in the early 1960s in comparison to the genre's "golden" era in the 1950s.[36] Hollywood producers considered the genre juvenile and not suitable to achieve mainstream box office success.[37] So in order to produce a science fiction film, Kubrick would have to pitch his project within the industrial and production contexts of the era. When he finally completed a lengthy treatment with Clarke in December 1964 of *Journey Beyond the Stars*,[38] he pitched it to MGM as an epic in space, deeming it "How the Solar System Was Won," a nod to the MGM epic western *How the West Was Won* (1963), a film made on a budget of $14 million but grossing over $50 million at the box office and made for Cinerama projection.[39] MGM was looking for further Cinerama movies to be road showed in the mid-1960s, particularly following on from the industry successes of *Lawrence of Arabia* (Lean, 1962) and *The Sound of Music* (Wise, 1965). Cinerama had been developed as a way of competing with television and to encourage audiences to attend the cinema following a decline in audience figures.[40] One of the key motivations behind MGM's decision to finance Kubrick and *2001* was the Cinerama format,[41] a justifiable position given that the film would eventually gross $1 million from eight Cinerama theaters in the United States on its opening run, while in Tokyo the Cinerama theaters had advance bookings in the thousands and in London the opening weekend was a record breaker for the Casino Cinerama.[42]

Journey Beyond the Stars also spoke to wider public interest in the Space Race, with the Apollo program escalating throughout the decade, toward the goal of landing a man on the moon. Such a context made the film an even more tantalizing prospect, given Kubrick's commitment to an epic production that would make full use of the Cinerama technology. This all appealed to the direction of MGM, a studio that had made nearly $18 million in profit in 1964 (in contrast to a $30 million loss in 1963) and was looking to build on its future earnings.[43] The company's president, Robert O'Brien, confirmed that this would be achieved by investing in three road show films shot for Cinerama release.[44] Kubrick and his science fiction epic looked to O'Brien and the MGM shareholders as a potential box office success. And so, in February 1965, it was announced that Kubrick would produce, direct, and write *Journey Beyond the Stars* for MGM.[45] As Peter Krämer has suggested, more than anything MGM was investing in Kubrick, "whose track record could be seen as a promise of future success."[46] As Robert O'Brien concluded in a letter to Kubrick, "I am sure that we are going to have a very pleasant and profitable experience together."[47]

"The Day of the Merchandiser Has Come": Industrial Contexts

O'Brien's confidence in Kubrick was apparently predicated on his record of possessing an "unusual combination of qualities: artistic ability, management ability, and a sense of coherence. And, not least, a splendid sense of economy."[48] It was believed that Kubrick was a producer that did not take undue risks with the money given to him. The confidence was also borne of Kubrick's working relationship with O'Brien, who in effect became Kubrick's latest sponsor: if *2001: A Space Odyssey*, as it had been renamed by April 1965, was to be a success, Kubrick required the confidence of O'Brien to protect him from the MGM shareholders. Therefore, he developed a close rapport with the MGM president, even praising him and the way he was running the company: "I am pleased at how things have progressed between myself and MGM. I am impressed by the intelligent, thorough and efficient way things seem to happen. These qualities are rare anywhere, most especially in the film business."[49]

But behind the friendly façade, Kubrick was attempting to drive a hard bargain in the ongoing contractual negotiations taking place between Polaris Productions (led by Kubrick's lawyer, Louis C. Blau) and MGM. Kubrick annotated the draft contracts presented by MGM, questioning every clause to understand what it meant for him as a producer and the control he had over every facet of his production. Kubrick was to contract his services as a producer-director to Hawk Films and would supervise all of the creative functions of the production, pending an additional contract between Polaris and Hawk being approved by MGM.[50] But MGM could intervene in certain creative decisions, including approval rights for the casting of the three main roles of Bowman, Poole, and Floyd. When Kubrick wanted to cast Sterling Hayden in the latter role, MGM vetoed the decision, based on audience reaction to the actor in an MGM-run focus group.[51] Kubrick had tried to convince MGM that an inexpensive deal could be reached with Hayden that would also provide a "much healthier Eady position"; a stipulation of the contract was that *2001* had to qualify for Eady money.[52] But MGM refused and instead sent Kubrick a list of alternative actors from which to cast the role of Floyd.[53]

Kubrick's annotations on the draft contract also signaled that he already knew *2001* would not be ready by autumn 1966, as originally pitched to MGM and announced in press releases. Next to a clause that required the film to be completed by October 30, 1966, Kubrick writes "likely?" Other points of the contract caused Kubrick confusion and consternation. MGM apparently had the right to approve all the contracts Hawk agreed with cast and crew, leading Kubrick to scrawl "!!!" It was something that went against his very nature as a producer in control of his own productions and selecting the individuals he thought best qualified. He questioned similar clauses that gave control to MGM. For example, he wanted to know who in MGM would make decisions about any changes to Kubrick's final cut of the film, writing "who decides?" Similarly, he questioned a clause that required him to consult "with us" in the editing of the picture (even though he was allowed the "sole right" to cut and edit the film). Kubrick scrawled "with who?" The answer, it seemed, was Robert O'Brien.

Kubrick was probably aware of O'Brien's reputation. Elected as president and CEO of MGM in 1963, O'Brien was credited with turning around the company's fortunes (the previous president, Joseph Vogel, was blamed for allowing *Mutiny on the Bounty* to run over budget)[54] and, by 1965, was named the "Motion Picture Pioneer" of the year.[55] The upturn in MGM's success was seen to be a result of how O'Brien represented a "new breed" of motion picture executive, one that believed that artistic quality and commercialism were symbiotic.[56]

But O'Brien was also seen as possessing too much power and making too many centralized decisions; if producers wanted something, then they needed O'Brien on their side.[57] O'Brien's business strategy was one of synergy, in that MGM's subsidiary interests (music, records, television production, licensing of features to TV and merchandising), when combined, would lead to greater overall earnings than just relying on film distribution. It was an acknowledgment that the traditional core operation of MGM, film production, was no longer the key to generating profit. Producers had to consider how to link their productions with MGM's other media interests and allow the company's publicity department to devise an appropriate strategy that would maximize profits across all these disparate income streams.[58]

O'Brien's approached reflected a wider industrial trend in the early 1960s, as the former studios, now acting primarily as distributors, looked to consolidate control over publicity, exploitation, and merchandising to the concern of some independent producers. Companies like MGM, and others such as Paramount, Columbia, and UA, substantially expanded these departments in the early part of the decade. In part this was due to how independent producers had created what UA's Roger Lewis termed "spheres of influence" for themselves within the industry and were trying to infringe upon areas beyond the production, including how films were advertised and distributed.[59] Lewis perceived changes ahead in the way films were to be promoted, with the industry "beginning to experiment with a more progressive concept of film advertising,"[60] claiming that "the day of the 'merchandiser,' and I mean the term in the total sense, is yet to come."[61]

Many of the studio's ad departments were run by executives seen as the "old guard," men who held conservative attitudes to experimentation and new methods of advertising and exploitation. But the 1960s brought substantial reorganization and the sweeping away of this old guard. Along with the growing spheres of influence of independent producers, the industry itself was transforming, and the studios sensed they had to modernize their advertising departments to "conform with the 'new' motion picture industry that is presently emerging."[62] The studios recognized that they had to market more toward a growing under-thirty demographic, based on projections of population statistics.[63] For example, Twentieth Century Fox believed it had to diversify its advertising, focusing drive-ins on the family audience through a process of "de-sexing" its ad campaigns.[64] This had to be done "subtly so that the younger generation won't catch on."[65] The changes in advertising were summed up by Twentieth Century Fox's vice president for publicity and advertising, Charles Eingeld: "A major change that has taken place in film advertising concepts is that exhibitors are no longer buying pictures but the publicity and advertising campaigns. 'They don't even have to see the picture,' he says. 'It's like selling soap. A supermarket will stock a brand of soap if it's convinced the manufacturer is backing his product with a big ad campaign. That's what is happening with pictures. It's a tremendous development.'"[66] These conditions led to the rapid growth of publicity and merchandising departments in the 1960s. For instance, Paramount expanded its operations in 1966 with the creation of three new executive posts to work under Joseph Friedman, vice president and director of advertising and public relations.[67] The aim was to create a new "top level creative and operational team . . . designed to serve Paramount's long and short-term merchandising and marketing needs."[68]

Prior to the 1960s, most studios would not begin promotion and publicity until the film was complete, or "more likely they began after the advertising department had taken its first look at the finished production."[69] However, by the late 1950s this was beginning to change. Columbia, for instance, revitalized its merchandising operations based on what they called their "Campaign-in-Depth" strategy.[70] It intensified its merchandising campaigns in order "to reach a massive pre-sold audience."[71] This may have been an influence of the exploitation practices of independent companies such as American International Pictures and Allied Artists in the mid-1950s. Teenagers were targeted in marketing campaigns that sought to tie in a movie with its soundtrack, particularly with rock and roll films such as *Blackboard Jungle* (1955). With *The Cardinal* (1963), *The Victors* (1963), *The Quick Gun* (1964), *Psyche 59* (1964), the 1964 rerelease of *The Bridge on the River Kwai* (1957), and *Dr. Strangelove*, Columbia put together its most ambitious and far-reaching merchandising campaigns ever, many of them overseen by Roger Caras. *The Victors* was the company's biggest ever campaign, with multiple tie-ins, such as with a women's fashion line, heavy promotion of the soundtrack album, and a deal with Dell Publishing for a paperback novelization.[72] Columbia's promotion of *The Devil at 4 O'clock* (1961) began before the film had even entered production, with advertising layouts being designed and "ideas for the trailer blueprinted."[73] Columbia's publicity department "lived with the picture throughout its production and even its preparation so that every avenue of merchandising would get the individual attention of the department's personnel."[74] *Gidget* (1959) had its "promotion angles" created before the script had even been completed.[75] Studio strategies involved audiences being presold a picture a long time in advance of its release, as much as three years in the case of *The Guns of Navarone* (1961), a film with which Columbia set the "pace" for future film merchandising.[76]

These long-term publicity strategies invariably required some level of involvement and cooperation of the independent production company and producer. The major distributors allowed producers to appoint a representative that could liaise with the respective advertising department. But this led to tension over control between the independent producers and the distributors. UA's Roger Lewis believed the sphere of influence that producers had obtained was leading to an attitude that led them try to intrude upon publicity, commenting to *Variety* that "a large group" of independent producers unwisely regarded themselves as experts on publicity, exploitation, and merchandising.[77] Producers, Lewis argued, believed that they were more of an authority on domestic and international publicity and advertising than the distributors.[78] This was compounded by the fact that the publicity representatives hired by the independent production companies to liaise with the majors "take a 'narrow' view i.e. to worry primarily about the producer's personal ego and his status on the Hollywood circuit. That means getting column breaks etc.... Their tendency is to keep their clients happy and to overlook the big, wide world that exists beyond them."[79]

Surprisingly, Lewis's view was supported by James B. Harris, who, in an interview with *Variety* in 1965 that appeared to be a thinly veiled attack on Kubrick, suggested that producers were motivated by ego when trying to take control of publicity and distribution.[80] Harris believed that producers and distributors should concentrate on the making of a film and "leave the decisions re advertising, promotion and distribution to the people whose business is just that, namely the distibs."[81] In reference to Harris-Kubrick Pictures, Harris felt that the company had unwisely attempted to obtain control over publicity and distribution, with little actual industrial knowledge or expertise, therefore affecting the performance of films like *Paths of Glory* and *Lolita*. In fact, Harris was explicit in his criticism of Kubrick, particularly in the way he had advised on how *Lolita* should be distributed, which led to a poor performance of the film in the New York area.[82] What had led to these attempts to control publicity and distribution was producing "ego," and it was ultimately detrimental to both a producer's role and a film's performance.[83]

Kubrick was still insistent on having control of publicity and distribution though, but his contract with MGM restricted his involvement in these areas. His control amounted to "the right, but not the obligation, to consult with [MGM] in the formulation of the final policy to be used.... It is expressly agreed that [MGM's] decision with respect to the formulation and development of such advertising and publicity policy shall be final and binding upon you [Kubrick/Polaris]."[84] The contract was specifying that MGM required Kubrick's cooperation and access to the production of *2001* in order to undertake a successful long-range publicity campaign. As Robert O'Brien explained to Kubrick, MGM had a "vigorous propaganda machine" that would be geared toward working for *2001*.[85] But Kubrick was intent on centralizing control of publicity and merchandising within Polaris Productions.

Spheres of Influence

In June 1965, Kubrick appointed Roger Caras as the vice president of Polaris Productions, as well as appointing him to the board of directors of Hawk Films.[86] Kubrick had become acquainted with Caras during the postproduction of *Dr. Strangelove*, when Caras was Columbia's national director of merchandising and had been heavily involved in putting together the film's merchandising and exploitation campaign. Caras was born in 1928 in Methuen, Massachusetts. He'd graduated from the University of Southern California in 1954, majoring in cinema, prior to which he'd served in the army, where he had studied filmmaking during his tours of East Asia.[87] By the mid-1950s, Caras was working for Columbia, initially in the company's exploitation department, before moving to its radio and television division.[88] His rise through the ranks at Columbia was meteoric. In 1960 he became a general executive for the company, in 1961 he worked as an assistant to Paul N. Lazarus, Columbia vice president,[89] and in 1962 he was an assistant director to Joyce Selznick, head of the talent and story department.[90] By 1963 he was the company's exploitation manager, supervising twenty-nine field promotion staff.[91] The experiences and skills he built up at Columbia would prove invaluable during his time working for Polaris.

Caras had been central to the growth in publicity and merchandising campaigns at Columbia, organizing two-day brainstorming sessions with his field staff and theater circuit executives in a bid to "cover every possible promotional detail."[92] Caras made these meetings a key part of his exploitation strategy, conducting them on *The Bridge on the River Kwai*, *Good Neighbor Sam* (Swift, 1963), *First Men in the Moon* (Juran, 1964), and *Dr. Strangelove*.[93] He also developed what became known as the "flying squad," a crack force of exploitation specialists. The squad consisted of specialized publicity staff briefed on a film's local publicity and merchandising campaign. Exhibitors could make a call to the squad and swiftly receive intense "personal on-the-scene consultation from as many exploitation specialists as necessary to insure success of a local-level campaign."[94] Caras's strategy was part of Columbia's wider policy direction, in which "the era of the two-week 'all out' campaign at release time is over" and "exploitation at the local level begins not two weeks but two years in advance—the day a property is mounted for production."[95] A core component of this strategy was the establishment of a "communications network" whereby constant communication would be kept between the studio, production, and field staff via a network of well-informed assistants.[96] Caras believed that a publicity campaign could be successful only if all stakeholders involved—the producer, distributor, field staff, and exhibitor—maintained a constant and consistent dialogue. Control of publicity could not be centralized in one figure—i.e., the producer—but needed to be decentralized among a national, even international network of publicists.

Caras attempted to construct his own power and sphere of influence at Polaris shortly after his appointment, recruiting assistants in order to build his own communication network. This included Ivor Powell, who became the Publicity and Art Department liaison on *2001* and a key colleague for Caras.[97] But Polaris had limited resources; despite being a California registered business, it operated out of a New York address. Following the establishment of the New York office in 1962, Nat Weiss had joked to Kubrick that he had "spent a quarter and bought that primer about running a one man, one girl office in New York."[98] Kubrick was concerned about setting up a Polaris bank account in New York, given its status as a California corporation. Instead, all of Kubrick's major accounts were directed to the United Kingdom, and a limited cash expense account was run for the Polaris office, with weekly expenses to be sent to Ray Lovejoy, who now worked for Kubrick's Hawk Films.[99] Kubrick kept a watchful eye over this expense account and would query the slightest financial irregularity. Caras found the situation dissatisfactory, complaining that Kubrick knew full well "how extremely difficult this will make things . . . this represents a hardship and an inconvenience."[100]

Despite Caras's supposed devolved control of Polaris and the four thousand miles between him and Kubrick, he was persistently micromanaged and had to seek permission from Kubrick on most matters.[101] When Caras did not first check with Kubrick about an issue, he would find himself reprimanded. For instance, in July 1966, Caras, in conversation with Mort Segal of MGM discussing the release date of *2001* and whether it would be delayed, had said that he had "not heard of any delay nor did [he] see why there would be one."[102] Kubrick, on hearing of what Caras had said, responded by telling him not to ever "take any responsibility for discussing what, why, when and where on my behalf."[103]

Caras's main working contact at MGM was Dan Terrell, MGM's executive director for worldwide advertising, publicity, and promotion. Terrell had been an instrumental figure in fashioning the modernization of publicity and merchandising at MGM. He had joined the company in 1940, working as the regional director of publicity in the Washington, DC, area.[104] He was promoted to the role of national director of exploitation in February 1950 and by 1952 had developed an internal power base, merging MGM's publicity and exploitation departments,[105] a move Terrell saw necessary to extract the "salient features" of the two respective departments.[106] Shortly after the election of Robert O'Brien as MGM's new CEO, Terrell oversaw a further merger in 1963 and was appointed the executive director of advertising, publicity, and promotion.[107] The aim was for the department to act as a counter sphere of influence to the increasing power of independent producers and came about as part of a wider organizational restructure implemented by O'Brien. This included promoting Clark Ramsay to executive assistant to O'Brien and placing him in charge of a new "marketing group," in which "all future creative advertising promotion, selling and research activities" were integrated under him.[108] The restructure brought the entire production process under the coordination of the triumvirate of O'Brien, Clark, and Terrell, "from selection of a property through to release."[109]

The triumvirate intended to create films that were designed for a mass audience, what they termed "the mass segments," and it was Terrell who was tasked with finding "every possible method of reaching them more effectively and efficiently."[110] Terrell aggressively took this new strategic approach forward, saying, "This policy of pre-planning advertising, publicity and promotion in advance of the completion of a particular product . . . allows us great freedom in determining which approach is best for that particular product."[111] He strengthened the approach with the appointment of Mort Segal. Segal worked as Terrell's special assistant, assisting him "in all areas of advertising, publicity and promotion."[112] Segal's appointment was part of a "further move designed to strengthen the growing MGM publicity, promotion and advertising departments in relation to the increased line-up of important films about to be released and going into production," including *2001*.[113]

Terrell had grown accustomed to controlling the strategic approaches to publicity on MGM product. For *The V.I.P.s* (1963), he had mapped a two-month step-by-step promotion plan for the film, taking it up to the initial release of the picture.[114] He devised step-by-step activities for exhibition managers, with promotion activities mapped out in sequential order. The remarkable press kit for the film included lobby cards and posters and prepared publicity stories to be planted in the local press on exact dates as instructed by Terrell. The publicity campaign was unprecedented, with the day-by-day scheduled predicted to become an industrial norm.[115] Terrell had overhauled MGM's publicity department by 1965, creating his own sphere of influence that would come into conflict with independent producers.

Terrell attempted to assert control over Polaris and *2001* once contractual agreements with MGM had concluded. Terrell contacted Caras to inform him that he had commissioned his team to prepare artwork for a "special letter head to be used here for all releases on the picture."[116] In response to Terrell's influence, Polaris put in place various measures to assert its own control, such as a complete breakdown of the rates for adverts in national newspapers. Kubrick had instructed Caras to develop the resource so that it would be "instantly available for reference as a way of creating ideas for exploitation and responding quickly and with apparent knowledge to any suggestions which come from the motherland."[117] Kubrick was attempting to prove his own expertise in publicity over those of Terrell and MGM. In October 1965, Caras explained to Terrell that "it was mandatory [Kubrick] be given the opportunity either directly or at least through me to approve all ads, all designs, all artwork, all copy."[118]

Terrell was, on the surface, understanding of Kubrick's desire for control of publicity, but still directed his own team to devise a marketing strategy and exploitation plan that could be presented to Kubrick.[119] The aim of the plan was to encourage and excite what MGM referred to as the "larger mass of people, the infrequent ticket buyer" by selling *2001* as an "enormous social epic."[120] Central to this idea was the film's grand philosophical and religious themes, what MGM saw as its thoughtful Christianity, and importantly the visual spectacle of Cinerama, all of which would "lead to the most profound promotion that has ever been designed for a picture."[121] Indeed there seems to have been an initial consensus between MGM and Polaris, with Kubrick agreeing that the adverts for the film should subtly convey that the film would appeal to young children. Children would become a key demographic in the initial publicity campaign,[122] including through merchandising tie-ins for three jigsaws by the publisher Springbok, coloring books "and other children's activity devices" with Western Publishing, and a planned children's comic book (this did not emerge due to Kubrick's reluctance to release the script to the publisher's illustrator). Kubrick commissioned Saul Bass to design adverts that were then forwarded to Terrell and O'Brien. Kubrick believed Bass's designs removed the "onus of past sci-fi films as they are associated in people's minds," instead presenting the film as "fun."[123] But such a cordial working relationship would not last long and tensions would soon emerge about Kubrick's overbearing producing style.

Exploiting the Future

Roger Caras set out in detail to Kubrick how he saw Polaris and his own role functioning as production on *2001* commenced.[124] Polaris would act as a factory that turned out daily promotional copy—what Caras termed "a regular supply of column news bits"[125]—all of which were to be sent to Dick Winters at MGM New York to be planted in the press.[126] Caras also wanted to devise a Polaris newsletter that would be sent to MGM field representatives and other key contacts on a regular basis. He described the newsletter as being a "news chatty type thing to keep people posted on the progress of the production."[127] This never went ahead because of Kubrick's need for absolute control and secrecy over what was occurring on the set at Borehamwood.

Caras was in daily contact with Kubrick, to whom he would send multiple letters and faxes, including what he headed his "Carasgrams"—bulleted updates on ongoing issues. But the power base that Kubrick and Caras were attempting to construct at Polaris soon began to cause consternation and resentment within MGM's publicity department. There was a sense that Kubrick was driving a publicity strategy that made no sense and would not benefit *2001*'s box office potential in the United States. When Kubrick proposed that $25,000 be sent on an advert in *Le Figaro*, two years ahead of the newly revised release date of spring 1967, Caras explained that MGM was "not very happy."[128] The conclusion was that Kubrick's publicity strategy was simply wrong, but MGM went ahead with the advert in order to demonstrate its confidence in *2001* to the wider industry (and, presumably, to MGM shareholders).[129] This was probably in the hope of hiding any tensions (or mounting delays) that were occurring given that much of MGM's future financial health was predicated on the success or failure of *2001*.

Terrell decided to begin commissioning adverts without consulting Kubrick as a way of avoiding conflicts over control. Caras learned of one such advert to be placed in the *Sunday Observer* in December 1965 and argued that this contravened Kubrick's request for a coordinated advertising schedule.[130] Caras argued that MGM needed to respect Kubrick's wishes to discuss all publicity strategy and plans rather than to ignore him. Caras was also shielding Kubrick from insults coming from senior executives at MGM, including the suggestion that Kubrick was "not serving the picture, that he was not serving MGM, that he was, in fact, doing absolutely nothing but serving his own ego."[131]

Caras became a conduit through which MGM believed they could control Kubrick. But it also worked vice versa, with Kubrick using Caras to attack MGM in a bid to gain control over the publicity process. The letters that Caras sent to MGM were often annotated by Kubrick, suggesting they were going through several drafts. One such draft stated that *2001* had enormous earning potential, but collaboration was essential between MGM and Polaris, with both companies needing to "officiate at the conversion point between investment and earnings."[132] This was a direct challenge from Kubrick to MGM. In effect, he was stating that the producer—himself—had to have authority over every area of production, including publicity, merchandising, and distribution, despite the financial investment by MGM.

Merchandising was key to *2001*'s promotion and was built into the very fabric of the film's aesthetic, with the logos of major American corporations prominent in the set design, including IBM, Pan Am, Hilton, and Howard Johnson. Caras's role was to develop "the most comprehensive merchandising program ever put together in the history of our industry,"[133] approaching numerous businesses to supply props and develop tie-in products, though not all of the ventures were successful. This was because some of the ideas were simply too ambitious, such as a global reservation system that would allow audiences to book tickets for a screening anywhere in the world.[134] But it was also because Caras's ideas were met with growing indifference from Kubrick, such as his plan to approach Hertz to use its logo on a storefront during the eventually abandoned Lunar Park sequence—nothing came of it.[135] Kubrick had suggested that the film would feature a credit card used by Floyd on the Moon Base. When Caras had a firm offer from American Express to furnish the film with a credit card, Kubrick was noncommittal, to Caras's obvious frustration: "Why wouldn't it be an American Express card? You said you wanted a bank on the Moon. Why wouldn't it be an American Express bank? American Express is very much in the banking business."[136]

Caras grasped the merchandising potential of *2001* and how there was the scope for long-range publicity by arranging tie-ups, particularly for youth- or family-orientated products.[137] Caras's approach to merchandising reflected wider consumerist trends on films being produced for the Cinerama format. As Caras explained to General Mills, the branded consumer food company, *2001* would allow audiences to revel in consumer products of the twenty-first century.[138] Many other Cinerama features similarly used the scope of the format's size as a means to advertise consumer desire: the scale of the screen was an opportunity to sell modern consumerism and the desire for luxury items, and *2001* had the added bonus of selling the future.[139] Some of Caras's ideas were successful, not least a tie-in with Hamilton watches, which designed a wristwatch for the film, and that appeared in adverts in *Vogue* titled "*2001*—the watch of the future, for men, for women."[140]

But the managerial organization of Polaris meant that Caras needed Kubrick's approval for all decisions, something that became increasingly difficult to obtain given that Kubrick's attention was focused ever more on production of the film, which was running over schedule and over budget.[141] As a result, many of the potential merchandising opportunities were abandoned. There was no loop of information, only what Kubrick thought on any given day, which led on more than one occasion to what Caras referred to as "confusion, confusion, confusion,"[142] and on another occasion to declare that "I am beginning to feel like the fifth leg on a horse."[143] And not only was Caras being kept uninformed about the decision-making process, but much was also being kept hidden from MGM. Caras was instructed by Ray Lovejoy of a secret communication system in which "all cables of a non-confidential category . . . e.g. non-eyebrow raising, be sent by direct cable . . . confidential cables e.g. eyebrow raising, panics or general chaos, be sent individually to either Stanley's home address . . . or my home address."[144]

The decisive optimism and energy that Caras espoused in the early days of his appointment to Polaris had dissipated after several weeks working at the company and the realization that every decision—*every* minute detail—had to pass through Kubrick, which inevitably resulted in a blockage. Caras emphasized that he knew creative control resided exclusively with Kubrick, but he attempted to assure him of his own administrative and business expertise.[145] At other times, Kubrick's centralizing of power slowed the production of the film drastically, and Caras complained of working at "cross purposes."[146] His decisions were also mysteriously undone at times, such as when two companies, Seabrook Farms and General Mills, that were being used for merchandising tie-ins for the food eaten by the astronauts were dropped and replaced by Bird's Eye. Caras had agreed to a merchandising opportunity with General Mills to create a food product called

"2001" that was to be launched in 1967 to coincide with the film's release. In canceling the tie-in, Polaris was giving up the opportunity of General Mills "spending several million dollars at the time of the picture's release, pushing their product, all of it tied in together with point of sale display in every supermarket and food store in the USA."[147]

Kubrick's indecisiveness also had unintended but serious consequences. Tom Buck, who worked as an advertising agent for *Look* magazine, had spent several months working on a *2001* advertising supplement for the magazine in liaison with Caras. But Kubrick would not give the final go-ahead and the project fell through. Buck was fired by *Look* due to having gone "so far out on a limb for this project and then had it crumble beneath him because he could not guarantee dates."[148] Kubrick sent apologies and asked Caras, "Can I write to anyone at *Look* and explain it is my fault?"[149] As a compromise, Buck was appointed on a short-term contract to MGM by Dan Terrell, tasked with working on various marketing strategies, and was later briefly employed by Hawk Films.

By withholding information, Kubrick also destroyed potential merchandising agreements with the likes of Macy's department store, because he would not tell Caras his envisioned release date for the film.[150] Throughout 1966, Caras requested that Kubrick give him something, even if it was only an approximate target given in good faith.[151] There was an ongoing protracted battle between Kubrick and O'Brien about the release date of the film.[152] Kubrick's response to Caras was, "What if the date I give you is incorrect, either too early or too late? Unless I know this I can't answer your question."[153] Without a release date, Caras could not secure merchandising opportunities with Macy's.

The impression had also started to emerge in the industry that *2001* was in fact a documentary. Kubrick expressed concern to O'Brien that a demonstration reel, which contained no story elements or dialogue, had left some people with the impression that *2001* was a documentary about space travel.[154] Kubrick blamed Dan Terrell for creating a publicity campaign that led people to think the film was a documentary.[155] But Kubrick himself had been withholding much of the information that would have helped in the creation of the demonstration reel, while a trade ad that he himself had approved possessed ambiguous copy: "Stanley Kubrick has created a film which is a major breakthrough in motion picture techniques. It is an epic of mankind, its pre-history and its future. It is an astonishingly beautiful visual experience seen in the breathtaking sweep of Cinerama. You will be projected into an adventure of exploration from earth to moon, through the solar system, out to Jupiter and then on to the stars."[156] Robert O'Brien intervened to say he agreed with Dan Terrell that the above copy was responsible for creating the feel of a documentary. He had instructed Terrell and his team to revise the copy and move the publicity of the film more toward entertainment.[157] But Kubrick was obstinate, refusing to accept that the copy had created an impression of a documentary and that MGM had to refrain from making "irrational" publicity choices to "offset an illusory problem," even though he had been the one to raise the issue.[158] Kubrick argued that focusing the copy more on entertainment, using phrases such as "Stanley Kubrick uses the Cinerama screen to sweep you into the drama and adventure of a voyage through time and space," would cheapen *2001* and consign it to the category of genre and science fiction.[159] Kubrick argued that he would do all he could to prevent such an "impediment" from being placed in the way of the film's success.[160]

Kubrick's moves to prevent MGM's publicity department from devising an entertainment-focused campaign caused considerable frustration for Dan Terrell. He had been in contact with publicity executives at Columbia, who had warned him that Kubrick would attempt to take control of publicity. Caras relayed Terrell's concerns to Kubrick, explaining he was being unrealistic "in matters of advertising and that decisions [Terrell] should be making you are now making, although you don't have the time to evaluate the long range needs that MGM must be aware of in order to protect their investment."[161] Terrell was convinced that Kubrick's attempts to control publicity were harming the potential of *2001* and leading to a confused campaign and that this could be avoided only if Kubrick "surrendered the right to people equipped to make decisions."[162] In relaying Terrell's message, Caras confessed that he was in agreement with the accusations: "Many of the things they say are very difficult to argue against. They want to see film, they want to read a script, they want the right to judge for themselves what is good publicity, what is good exploitation, what is good art and what is good advertising."[163] Some at MGM, including Clark Ramsey, were critical of their own company for allowing Kubrick and Polaris "complete latitude in everything" and that it had resulted in a mode of production and producing style of a "six hundred thousand dollar art film."[164]

Kubrick's moves to control publicity by withholding information and decisions led to one of the most unusual publicity campaigns for a film with a multimillion-dollar budget. Very few press releases were issued compared to other films of its type, such as *Spartacus*, and Caras repeatedly urged Kubrick to authorize the release of stories to the press, saying, "I think it is time now for us to start getting exposure. The air of mystery that now exists is working for us but I do think we have to start making an impression."[165] Such was the air of mystery that Keir Dullea reported that "no one knew he was the star of [the] film."[166] There was a notable lack of what *Variety* termed "course-of-production publicity on the film, and the absence of color-spreads in the weekly magazines."[167] The few major stories that did emerge, such as a forty-page spread in the *New Yorker*, were heavily controlled profile pieces arranged by Polaris and focused on Kubrick. Arthur C. Clarke said that the virtual embargo on news breaks was nothing more than a publicity stunt.[168] But even his novel had been delayed by Kubrick, despite its potential to presell the film to audiences, with bids for its publication commencing only in April 1968, concurrent to the film's release.[169]

Kubrick's micromanagement certainly had an impact in terms of the organization of Polaris Productions. When Caras resigned in March 1967 to pursue his own producing career, there was a need for a handover to the newly appointed vice president of Polaris, Benn Reyes. Kubrick felt that a two-week transition would be enough, allowing Reyes to take full control of Polaris by April 1967.[170] But Kubrick's prediction was a gross underestimate, and by April 26 Reyes and Caras were still in the process of transitioning, with a request that Caras be kept on for an additional week "to complete transitions and indoctrination."[171] Caras was still working for Polaris in May 1967, and the trades did not announce Reyes's appointment until the beginning of July 1967.[172] But even following Caras's formal resignation from the company, the complex nature and scope of the project meant that Reyes and Caras remained in contact over the coming months, with Caras guiding Reyes on merchandising and publicity issues. Caras's input was perhaps necessary given Kubrick's lack of decisiveness on a variety of issues, leading Reyes to plead with Kubrick in a cable at the beginning of May 1967, "These matters and many others need your specific intervention and direction."[173] The list of matters Reyes was referring to was extensive, including at least twenty-two outstanding merchandising and promotional opportunities at the time of Caras's resignation.[174]

The publicity campaign for *2001* was unique in the era of long-range publicity and merchandising campaigns. MGM launched its "major mail-order campaign" for *2001* just five weeks in advance of its world première.[175] The campaign included a four-page advert in the *New York Times*, *Los Angeles Times*, and *Washington Star*, followed by "one-a-week one-page ads in seven other papers."[176] And due to resistant cooperation from Kubrick, MGM was forced into using paintings by the artist Bob McCall because of the late arrival of photographic art from the production.[177] Terrell confirmed that the paintings would "for the moment" form the basis of the publicity campaign, pending new still photographs to be approved by Kubrick.[178] Terrell was also forced to deny rumors that the use of McCall's artwork was in fact because the publicity campaign was delayed by Kubrick's refusal to cooperate with MGM's publicity department.[179]

The film posters did reflect a compromise, with the tagline "An epic drama of adventure and exploration" blending together the two approaches (fact and entertainment) desired by Polaris and MGM, respectively. But the four-page adverts in the major newspapers were much vaguer, with no credits beyond labeling *2001* as a "Stanley Kubrick Production."[180] This reflected what Kubrick had really wanted to be the central promotional element of the film: himself. Polaris acted as a sphere of influence by which Kubrick sought not only to wrestle control of publicity from MGM but also to allow him to have control over his own image. Indeed, the lack of press stories about the production led to what Caras described as a "mystique" developing about Kubrick in Hollywood.[181] Caras, who was visiting Los Angeles, told Kubrick that "everywhere I went in Hollywood, they asked about you and the picture. They are terribly curious about the picture and hold you in a kind of reverential awe. The legend is definitely building."[182] The projection of power within the industry was just as important as actually possessing it, and this was at the heart of Polaris's publicity strategy, as outlined in correspondence between Caras, Tom Buck, and Mort Segal: "The editorial focal point must be Kubrick and his involvement in '2001—A Space Odyssey.' Everything else is subservient."[183]

Conclusion

In a bid to gain ever greater control of his productions, Kubrick had used Polaris Productions as a means of withholding information to frustrate the publicity strategy of MGM. He even withheld his cooperation, which was necessary to ensure that there was a coordinated long-range publicity and merchandising campaign. But arguably there was very little that MGM could do, having invested so much in *2001*: the budget tripled from $4 million to over $11 million, while MGM's future profits depended on its timely release and commercial success. But Kubrick had micromanaged *2001* to the point that it was greatly overschedule and over budget, ultimately contributing to MGM's perilous financial state by the end of the 1960s. Robert O'Brien confessed to this in 1967, saying, "The reason Metro-Goldwyn-Mayer failed to pay off any of its outstanding debt during the course of the past fiscal year . . . is that the company has experienced 'a growth in inventory without a corresponding playoff of inventory.' Or, putting it more specifically, O'Brien conceded that his debt reduction prediction about a year and a half ago had been 'based on the premise that 'Space Odyssey' would be in release.'"[184] O'Brien's personal investment and trust in Kubrick had not paid off.

But *2001* was, despite everything, a commercial success. In part, this was probably down to word of mouth, critical attention (which was far more positive than is often portrayed),[185] debate about "what the film means" (what *Variety* called the "coffee cup debate"),[186] and the way it resonated with the fifteen to twenty-five demographic.[187] All of this was an "unintended promotion that quickly outstripped the more conventional advertising campaign plotted by MGM."[188] Polaris's activities in setting up merchandising tie-ins, often targeted at children, may also have initially steered the publicity for *2001*, given this was at times the only information MGM had to go on. By the end of the decade, Kubrick had fashioned himself considerable power as an independent producer with a film that eventually expanded beyond this family demographic to become a major hit with the growing youth audience. Kubrick received an Academy Award for Special Visual Effects in 1969 and was the only named recipient of the award (see chapter 9 for more on this decision). It was the prize he hoped would lead to an "institutional effect,"[189] firmly establishing his reputation as Hollywood's preeminent producer. With the film having made over $20 million by 1973,[190] Kubrick had seemingly established the Kubrick producing brand as a commercially viable and prestigious label heading into the 1970s and a period of economic uncertainty for Hollywood.

Part 4

The Decline of a Film Producer, 1970–1999

9
Kubrick and Warner Bros., 1970–1980

Just what caused the decline and fall of Stanley Kubrick? This is not a question commonly asked when it comes to Kubrick's association with Warner Bros., which commenced in 1970. The typical assumption is that Kubrick, in producing films for Warner Bros., was at the zenith of his powers as a producer. But while this might be the case in terms of the controls he had over his productions, archival and anecdotal sources suggest, along with the obvious evidence of the increasingly long gaps between the releases of his films, that he was finding it ever more difficult to move a project out of development and into production. In short, he had too much control. It was a situation that was exacerbated by the production strategies of Warner Bros. in the early 1970s that granted Kubrick ever more control. As a result, he produced fewer films in the latter half of his career compared to the first half.[1]

Filippo Ulivieri has identified how it was during the 1970s that stories began to emerge in the media, most likely at the instigation of Kubrick himself, that presented him as a maniacal, all-controlling, eccentric producer.[2] For Ulivieri, this was Kubrick's aim, to establish himself "as a one-of-a-kind filmmaker: hermetic and hermitic."[3] But even if this was a carefully crafted media image, the stories of a "mad" filmmaker perhaps signaled a deeper problem with Kubrick's managerial structure as a producer. After all, following the success of *2001*, Kubrick failed on more than one occasion to get his long-planned *Napoleon* into production, while other projects were mooted, including an adaptation of Arthur

Schnitzler's *Traumnovelle* (1926). Kubrick's production output became increasingly protracted due to a combination of his own working processes (the need to produce high quality and completely controlled product; sacrificing large crews in order to allow for a longer shooting schedule) and industrial factors (rival projects; a box office becoming dominated by high-concept blockbusters). But it is also arguable that his inability to get projects into production in the immediate wake of *2001* may have been a result of his producing methods and insistence on absolute control. His reputation within the industry now preceded him. With *2001*, he had been vastly over budget and greatly overschedule and had contributed significantly to the financial crisis that MGM found itself in by 1968. He therefore needed to regain control of his image and reputation, in the process creating an alter ego of sorts.

This chapter considers the industrial and production contexts that Kubrick operated in within the early 1970s and how it was that he came to produce films for Warner Bros. for the remainder of his career. What were the conditions that led to his contract with Warner Bros., and just why did the company grant him so much control? And more important, what was the impact of that control on Kubrick's career trajectory? It was during this period that Jan Harlan, Kubrick's brother-in-law, became his permanent executive producer, overseeing the logistical operations and administration of each Kubrick production from the 1970s onward. The chapter also looks to understand how Kubrick perceived his power in relation to the wider global film industry.

Industrial Trends

On July 22, 1966, Roger Caras informed Kubrick of a seismic industrial change he had heard was about to take place in Hollywood: United Artists was to be taken over by the conglomerate Consolidated Food.[4] While the deal with Consolidated fell through and UA instead merged with Transamerica Corporation in 1967, Caras was aware of the industrial significance of the takeover: the conglomeration of Hollywood's major studios. Caras argued that this would lead to creative indifference from companies "whose principal concerns are ball bearings and not art."[5] By the end of the 1960s, many of Hollywood's studios had been taken over by vast global conglomerates, becoming subsidiaries within growing media empires. It represented a major revolution in Hollywood that opened up new spaces of autonomy to be taken advantage of by powerful independent producers like Kubrick.

Perhaps reacting to the industrial changes, Kubrick made a bold move in February 1968 by purchasing five thousand shares of MGM stock, at an investment of $205,000.[6] He had previously owned company stock while at Harris-Kubrick Pictures, including with Universal. But MGM was a struggling company by 1968 and Kubrick's investment must be seen in this context, with share prices having fallen steeply throughout the first quarter of that year by over $25 a share.[7] MGM was not without other celebrity stockholders, including Carlo Ponti, producer of the likes of *Doctor Zhivago* (1965). But Kubrick's motivation in buying the shares was probably a combination of factors. Financial strategy was key, with Kubrick perhaps anticipating a profit and keeping abreast of the developing power struggle at the top of MGM (see below). But it was also an investment based on reputation. Kubrick wanted to project confidence and power. His purchase was noticeable for the amount he bought, equating to approximately $1.5 million at today's prices. *Variety* reported one source saying that it was, in effect, a vote of confidence ten times over by Kubrick in his own picture.[8] The purchase of the MGM stock may have been an attempt to signal confidence in *2001* and his own producing brand, maybe even a way of calming industrial nerves.[9]

Prior to the purchase of the shares, Kubrick had been an initiator of a series of adverts supporting MGM's management, specifically Robert O'Brien, who was involved in a power struggle with Philip Levin, an MGM majority stakeholder since February 1965.[10] Levin wanted to remove O'Brien as CEO. This led Kubrick to persuade sixty-three other producers and directors, including John Frankenheimer and David Lean, to sign an advert that was placed in *Variety*, *New York Times*, and the *Wall Street Journal* in January 1967. The adverts stated that O'Brien was "orientated toward as much quality in film-making as is consistent with commercialism."[11] Kubrick was motivated to take out the advert of support for O'Brien because he believed "something should be done in the current situation to demonstrate the esteem in which O'Brien is held by creative people who have worked with him."[12] However, it was likely that Kubrick was also motivated by a desire to protect his interests, including his control as a producer and the ongoing production of *2001*. After all, MGM retained a 50 percent share in *2001*, along with perpetual distribution rights.[13] There would be uncertainty as to what would happen to Kubrick and *2001* should the company be taken over and O'Brien removed as CEO. Levin was infuriated by Kubrick's advert and made a complaint to the Securities & Exchange Commission.[14] Though Levin was ultimately not granted the injunction he wanted on the adverts, nor successful in his efforts to usurp O'Brien (O'Brien was later forced to resign in January 1969),[15] he was victorious in his efforts in the shareholder vote and elected his desired candidates to the Board of Directors.[16] By July 1968, Kirk Kerkorian, a private investor, had initiated an aggressive takeover of MGM.[17]

Kubrick's strategy may also have been in respect to his own future production plans. By the summer of 1968 he was planning a new project, a biopic of the life of Napoleon, an epic that he wanted to produce for MGM. But Kubrick's producing reputation with the company was not favorable and the takeover by Kerkorian cast doubts over any future production plans. MGM's drastic financial downturn and its eventual takeover by Kerkorian had been a result of its earning status, which, as discussed in chapter 8, was predicated for three years on the timely release of *2001*. MGM management were probably not inclined to immediately fund another Kubrick production, certainly not one as ambitious as *Napoleon*. Despite the success of *2001*, Kubrick was struggling by the end of the 1960s to obtain financial backing.

Kubrick announced his *Napoleon* project to the media in July 1968, generating considerable hype. This is what Kubrick needed if he was to interest a company in financing the project. The plan was to commence shooting in 1969, with Kubrick producing and directing his own original script.[18] European countries wanted to encourage Kubrick to produce the picture overseas, leading to a deal with the Bucuresti Studios in Romania.[19] The deal would allow Kubrick to utilize the Romanian cavalry to depict Napoleon's first Italian and Russian campaign. Kubrick commenced research for the film by contracting professor Felix Markham as the principal historical advisor on the project in autumn 1968.[20] And Jan Harlan was hired in his first official role for a Kubrick production, conducting research on picture material in Switzerland and Germany and being recruited as a production assistant for a year in Romania.[21]

The planned production of *Napoleon* came at a time of renewed interest in Napoleonic-era war films. This included considerable international success for Sergei Bondarchuk's *War and Peace* (1966–1967), a quartet of films that won the Academy Award for Best Foreign Language Film in 1969. But despite the success of Bondarchuk's *War and Peace*, MGM turned down a deal to finance Kubrick's *Napoleon* by 1969, citing that they were involved in "too many ultra-high budget previous commitments."[22] Other studios, including UA, also turned down the project.[23] There was likely a confluence of factors at play in the inability to find support for *Napoleon*. Some companies were no doubt fearful of funding a bloated epic, while several rival Napoleon projects had already been announced. This included one by Warner Bros. to be directed by Bryan Forbes and another to be produced by Dino De Laurentiis and directed by Sergei Bondarchuk for Paramount.[24]

But Kubrick's *Napoleon*, indeed whatever film he chose to pursue after *2001*, was at the mercy of industrial conditions. The U.S. economy had entered a recession in 1969, lasting until 1970, from which Hollywood was not immune.[25] Major cuts to projects and staff were made across most of the principal Hollywood companies, including Warner Bros., Paramount, Twentieth Century Fox, and MGM. Kerkorian and MGM's new head of production, James Aubrey, implemented drastic financial cutbacks to combat the company's $15 million deficit.[26] This included making redundant over 35 percent of the company's domestic payroll, including key executives like Dan Terrell.[27] By the end of 1969, MGM had canceled over twenty big-budget films.[28] Instead, MGM pursued a new production strategy focused on low-budget films targeted at the eighteen- to twenty-five-year-old demographic.[29] This was part of a wider trend in Hollywood toward low-budget movies on the back of the success of the likes of *Easy Rider* (Hopper, 1969), made on a budget of $400,000 but grossing over $60 million.[30] The film had led to a conviction among Hollywood executives that low-budget, youth-orientated films were what audiences wanted.[31] In this industrial climate, Kubrick's *Napoleon*, budgeted at $11 million, was commercially unviable.

Warner Bros. was undergoing changes similar to those at MGM. The company had undergone two takeovers in two years, first by Seven Arts in 1967, followed by a further takeover in 1969 by Steve Ross's Kinney National Company, aided by Ted Ashley. Ashley was appointed as the CEO of Warner Bros. and was instrumental in "greenlighting controversial and socially relevant projects."[32] Ashley, along with head of production John Calley, implemented a series of new policies, including budget cuts of $5 million and a move toward smaller-budgeted films that were often of a controversial nature and generally targeted at a younger demographic. Of the slate of projects that Warner Bros. announced in 1970, the average budget was $1.7 million.[33] Ashley's intent in lowering budgets was to mitigate against the tendency for projects to be abandoned or remain unreleased; by 1969, the Warner Bros. annual report showed the company to have a $2 million backlog of unmade projects, property, and scenarios.[34] The new policy regime also involved strict cost restrictions on story development.[35] This was again a means of trying to combat losses for films that were abandoned.[36]

The youth-oriented market interested Warner Bros. after *Woodstock* (Wadleigh, 1970) achieved a domestic gross of $14 million by January 1971, leading Steve Ross to announce in an annual Kinney report that *Woodstock* was an example of the "kind of broad-based product that WB will concentrate upon in future."[37] In line with Ashley's new policy direction, new Warner Bros. productions were to be filmed primarily on location, usually in Europe. Calley had outlined this approach in an interview with *Variety* in September 1970, saying, "I think feature films, since they are being made one time only, are best made off the lot on the actual locations. It seems to work out better creatively."[38] It also worked out better for Warner Bros., which was arranging stage rental deals for television production.[39]

It is within these wider industrial trends that we can begin to locate Kubrick's eventual deal with Warner Bros., which was announced in February 1970.[40] The initial three-picture deal was to commence with Kubrick producing, directing, and writing *A Clockwork Orange* (1971) in place of *Napoleon*, though Kubrick informed A. H. Weiler at the *New York Times* that he still intended to produce *Napoleon* after *A Clockwork Orange*.[41] However, it's clear that *Napoleon* did not fit with the strategic direction of Ashley and Calley. Instead, the announcement of Kubrick's deal with Warner Bros. stressed that *A Clockwork Orange* would be a "foreign production."[42] Concurrent to Kubrick's deal, a flurry of other British or European productions was announced, including a deal for Ken Russell to direct and coproduce *The Devils* (1971), Jack Clayton to direct and David Susskind to produce an adaptation of *Casualties of War* (Daniel Lang, 1969),[43] and Luchino Visconti to produce, direct, and write *Death in Venice* (1971).[44] Warner Bros. was also keen to emphasize the quality of the producers, directors, writers, and actors who had been signed for their 1970 production and release slate, including George Lucas, with *THX 1138* (1971) to be released ahead of his second planned feature for the company, *Apocalypse Now*, which was abandoned; Clint Eastwood to star in *Dirty Harry* (1971); Alan Pakula to produce and direct *Klute* (1971); Jon Voight to appear in *Deliverance* (Boorman, 1972) and *The All American Boy* (Eastman, 1973); and Italian-language features *The Voyeur* (Indovina, 1970) and *The Priest's Wife* (Risi, 1971), both starring Marcello Mastroianni.[45] Many other projects were announced by Warner Bros. as part of this wave of new productions and releases, with an outlay of over $50 million, but many were ultimately abandoned or bought by other companies, including *The Lonely Passion of Judith Hearne*, distributed by Island Pictures in 1987; *Siddhartha* (Rooks 1972), distributed by Columbia; and the Sam Peckinpah–directed *Summer Soldiers* and the Stuart Rosenberg–produced *Diary of a Rapist*, both of which were abandoned.

A number of these features received X ratings in the United States, including *Stop* and *The Devils*, due to the portrayal of violence, sex, and taboo subjects. *The Devils* had initially been contracted to UA, but the company turned down the project upon seeing the script and deeming it too controversial.[46] Warner Bros. subsequently picked up the project and allowed it be released with an X rating, though following the imposition of cuts on Russell's original edit.[47] There were some producers and executives in the American film industry who believed the new ratings system, introduced in 1968, presented a marketing opportunity and that the X rating appealed to a younger audience. Some producers even went so far as to put an X rating on their film posters as a marketing device. This went against the more common view that the X rating would hurt a film's commercial potential and had to be avoided at all costs.[48]

A Clockwork Orange clearly met the criteria of Ashley and Calley's production strategy. It was a low-budget, youth-oriented, controversial feature. And given the speed with which the project was produced by Kubrick, it was clear he was trying to establish a reputation and good standing with Warner Bros. in order to allow him to direct *Napoleon*. It may well have been that the deal to produce *Clockwork* came about at Warner Bros.'s suggestion, a mutual pact of sorts that would see Warner Bros. allow Kubrick to continue to develop *Napoleon* in return for a quick turnaround on *A Clockwork Orange*. Raab-Litvinoff, the British production company, owned the rights to Anthony Burgess's novel and was reportedly putting together a package for an adaptation in December 1969.[49] By February 1970, Si Litvinoff was corresponding with Kubrick, providing him with both U.S. and UK versions of Burgess's novel.[50]

Kubrick's approach to *A Clockwork Orange*, which he developed throughout 1970, was one of efficiency. He determined to keep to schedule and bring the film in under budget. He even wrote the screenplay himself rather than hiring a writer, maybe as a way of saving on development costs in line with Warner Bros. policy. In early 1970, he put together a production analysis in which he contemplated filming *A Clockwork Orange* in black-and-white to save on laboratory costs.[51] He reasoned that "atmosphere" was not vital to enjoying the story, therefore money could be saved by shooting entirely on location and, if the budget was tight, then to "cheat on décor and clothes."[52] The entire aim of the production was to develop a standing with Warner Bros. executives that would allow for a conducive working relationship going forward and the potential that they would finance *Napoleon* as part of his three-picture contract.

The Deal

Kubrick's deal with Warner Bros. was viewed internally as being exceptional in that he was awarded almost total creative and business freedom over all stages of production, from development through publicity and distribution. As one interoffice memo from 1970 stated, "Key creative and business decisions are made by Kubrick," the only caveat being that he had to consult Ashley or Calley about his thought processes and production strategy.[53] His contract with Warner Bros. required him to give at least "reasonable" access to his productions and to liaise with a Warner Bros. representative to give updates on progress and decisions being made. The memo concluded that "the Kubrick contract is very different from our normal production/distribution arrangement."[54] Some Warner Bros. staff even joked that they had to take an aspirin in order to even approach reading Kubrick's agreement, given its unprecedented nature and the way in which it handed so much control to Kubrick.

Other archival documents begin to shed light on the kind of arrangement Kubrick had secured with Warner Bros. In a memo between two Warner Bros. executives, Frank Wells and Sidney Kiwitt, anxiety was shared about the control Kubrick had been given over the areas of postproduction, publicity, and distribution. Warner Bros. would be covering the costs of Kubrick's publicist—his vice president of Polaris—throughout the production of any of his films for a "reasonable period of time," with Kubrick having strategic oversight of how his films were publicized and distributed.[55] In addition, Kubrick had the absolute right of approval on the final cut of all trailers produced, which led Kiwitt to conclude, "If he wanted to be a 'bitch' we could have no trailer!"[56] Kubrick could also choose the laboratories that would process his film stock, based on his expert knowledge of the facilities available.

The contract empowered Kubrick as a producer, providing him with strategic control over not only creative decisions but business decisions that would normally have been carried out by executives at Warner Bros.

All of this raises the questions of just *why* Warner Bros. divested such powers to Kubrick and just *how* different Kubrick's deal was compared to others made at that time. John Boorman, who produced and directed three films for Warner Bros. between 1971 and 1981 (*Deliverance*, *Exorcist II: The Heretic* [1977], and

Excalibur [1981]), described working at Warner Bros. under the leadership of Ashley and Calley as being a "tremendously innovative and exciting period, when the prevailing policy at the studio was to support the film directors' visions, and Warner Bros. was clearly leading the way."[57] Ashley was a key figure in supporting Warner Bros.'s producers, providing them with the space in which to develop their projects, all the while being "plugged into every production decision."[58] That was a stipulation of Kubrick's arrangement; he always had to maintain communication with Ashley and keep him abreast of his decisions and strategic thinking. This included Kubrick always having to "pitch" his projects to Ashley and Calley, providing them with a budget and a provisional cast, before they would officially approve it.[59]

Even though Kubrick's arrangement caused disquiet among some Warner Bros. executives, he was not the only producer or talent to be granted significant levels of creative and business freedom. Clint Eastwood, following his success in *Dirty Harry*, signed a nonexclusive contract with Warner Bros. to produce less commercially driven films, which the company was not averse to financing. Eastwood believed this was because of prestige: the company wanted a library of films that it was proud of and that it could rerelease due to their quality.[60] Kubrick believed that this was partially the case with his own arrangement, though he ascribed the control he had been given more to the fact that his films were within "reasonable limits" and performed well at the box office.[61] Kubrick perhaps more accurately described the arrangement as being a "mutual relationship";[62] in return for control, Kubrick would provide Warner Bros. with quality films and commercial potential.

But more than anything, the control that Kubrick garnered at Warner Bros. was probably due not to an explicit tablet of commands laid out in a contract but rather the vague spaces of autonomy that his contract afforded. Archival documentation, including correspondence held at the Stanley Kubrick Archive, suggests that Warner Bros. executives and staff were unclear about just where the limits of Kubrick's control ended and what he could or could not make a decision about. As Frank Wells admitted to Sidney Kiwitt, they would just have to "work it out as we go along,"[63] while Frank Parsons advised Warner Bros. staff that they might want "to check with me about any specific points which come up."[64] Other producers may well have had spaces of autonomy in their own contract with Warner Bros., but it was Kubrick's desire that was arguably different. He wanted control over *all* aspects of production, whereas others might not. And in that difference, in those spaces within his arrangement, were the seeds of his own downfall as a producer. As the 1970s and 1980s progressed, he became ever more bogged down in every decision, however minute, because he realized he could request ever more information and data. There was no limit on how long he could be involved in areas of business strategy. If he wanted to dedicate his time to the finer points of distribution and regional promotion in, say, Peru, then he could and he would.

The Deal in Action

Kubrick's initial three-picture deal with Warner Bros. was, in many respects, fulfilled quickly. The three pictures were produced and released over a ten-year period, from 1970 to 1980, starting with *A Clockwork Orange* and followed by *Barry Lyndon* (1975) and *The Shining*. All three were produced, directed, and written by Kubrick, apart from the latter, which was a screenplay cowritten with Diane Johnson. All three films also continued Kubrick's preference for adapting novels, two of which were known contemporary works: Burgess's *A Clockwork Orange* and Stephen King's *The Shining*.

But while these three pictures were produced relatively quickly, at least in contrast to the films produced as part of his second deal with Warner Bros. in the 1980s, Kubrick's pace overall was decreasing. In the 1950s and 1960s he had produced and/or directed four films per decade. But the contract with Warner Bros. now allowed Kubrick in the 1970s to focus on all elements of the production, with his time increasingly taken up by administration and coordination of his film's publicity and distribution strategies. He also became heavily involved in the VHS releases of his films by the end of the decade, while focusing his attention to the release of *Paths of Glory* in France in 1975 and 1976. And Kubrick's level of involvement cannot be overstated. He would keep informed of all aspects of publicity and distribution across the world, requesting research and information about local campaigns, while also overseeing the dubbing of his films in most countries. Serenella Zanotti, in her work on Kubrick and dubbing, concludes that Kubrick was a rare example of a producer-director who "took an active role in the creation of foreign-language versions" of his films.[65] And in taking such an active role in dubbing, Kubrick was extending his producing control and, in the process, his authorial imprint. As Zanotti argues, the dubbed foreign language versions of Kubrick's films that he oversaw equated to official authorized versions that had been given the Kubrick seal of approval.[66]

Kubrick's involvement in all areas of production was not usual, with his control of the dubbing process reflecting this more than anything else. Standard industrial practice was for a film distributor to "purchase the distribution rights to a local market, usually a branch of the major American distributors or a smaller company, select the dubbing and/or subtitling company and the whole process [was] managed locally."[67] By bypassing such industrial conventions though and taking personal control, Kubrick generated considerable tension. Take his involvement in the dubbing of *Barry Lyndon* for Iranian release in January 1977. The local agent, Robert Timms, who was meant to be overseeing the dubbing, was instead subjected to what he referred to as "the same time consuming controls as other territories."[68] Kubrick had clearly gained a reputation for his controlling style. Timms wanted to complete the dubbing process by himself and then forward the completed tapes to Warner Bros. Kubrick did not appreciate Timms's tone and replied that he, and executives at Warner Bros., should appreciate the final quality result that he was aiming to achieve.[69] In contrast to the disbelief shown by Timms, and others like him, at Kubrick's control, Kubrick was himself in disbelief at why they did not understand that he had such control, commenting, "You guys still think the routine job done by hacks is the way to do it—don't you?"[70]

At the heart of Kubrick's approach though seemed to be a level of micromanagement brought about by a fear of failure. Just as Gerald Fried, Kubrick's high school friend and composer in the 1950s, commented, Kubrick was in constant fear of failure.[71] Just like how HAL 9000 fails on *2001: A Space Odyssey*, Kubrick was on the lookout for such failures on his own productions. He monitored his staff, the decisions being made, and the systems in place to catch the failure before it occurred. And his approach to combat such failure was to increasingly centralize all decisions within his power as a producer, even if it was not realistic to supervise every function of his productions. The logic seems to have been that if Kubrick possessed control, then it eliminated the risk of failure. This, believes Fried, is why Kubrick moved to using mostly preselected music by the end of the 1960s: it eliminated the risk that he might not like the music that was being created and avoided the costly decision to not use the score after several months of investment.[72]

The example of Kubrick's control of the dubbing on *Barry Lyndon*, and the tensions it led to, was representative of Kubrick as a producer in the 1970s and 1980s as a whole. There is ample archival evidence that shows Kubrick's level of micromanagement and the conflict it caused both with local Warner Bros. units and with some Warner Bros. executives. There was a clear mood among some Warner Bros. staff that Kubrick should not have had such levels of control and that the highest echelons of Warner Bros.—Ashley and Calley—should have intervened to restrict his involvement. To have done so may also have allowed Warner Bros. to hasten Kubrick's contractual obligations to the company. But the caution and hesitation of Warner Bros. executives to limit Kubrick's control probably stemmed from his work on *A Clockwork Orange*, a film with which he was determined to prove that he could strategize and successfully develop publicity and distribution campaigns. In many respects, Kubrick had to prove his producing ability in these areas in order to cement his control and develop a power base within Warner Bros. In doing so, it led to a power struggle among Warner Bros. executives, in which Kubrick was involved, as is discussed below.

A Clockwork Orange

From *A Clockwork Orange* onward Kubrick would regularly employ close family members in senior positions on his productions as well as working with the same crew members, meaning that "many of the relationships and organisational hierarchies were already established."[73] Operationally, Kubrick's productions were led by Jan Harlan. Pragmatic in his approach, Harlan was to transform ideas that had been expressed to him by Kubrick into logistical reality. He also arranged contracts and permissions for location shooting and for the rental of props and other equipment. Harlan was appointed as a director of Hawk Films and took care of the day-to-day running of Kubrick's production companies, along with the likes of accountant John Trehy. Harlan would sign off on requisition orders and other expenses as well as negotiate deals with below-the-line crew and actors.[74]

Kubrick's shooting schedules were longer than average for films produced at Warner Bros. *A Clockwork Orange* was sixty-two days overschedule by the completion of principal photography in February 1971. In contrast, other similar budgeted films, such as *Deliverance* (a production of just under $2 million), had much faster turnarounds. John Boorman commenced shooting of *Deliverance* on location on May 17, 1971, and had wrapped by the beginning of September, just under four months, compared to *Clockwork*'s nearly seven months, and this in spite of filming on difficult rural locations in Georgia throughout.[75] And yet, despite their differing shooting schedules, both films came in at roughly the same budget. In fact, Kubrick was hailed as a "hero" by executives at a Warner Communication's annual meeting in New York in 1972 for "combining aesthetics with fiscal responsibility" on *A Clockwork Orange*.[76] Kubrick ensured that costs on the film were kept to a minimum, allowing him the luxury of time, a method stressed by Harlan; in return for having a lengthier shooting schedule, the crew size had to be reduced. The total crew employed at various stages on *A Clockwork Orange* totaled approximately fifty, in contrast to *Deliverance*, which had just over seventy, roughly the average for small-budgeted Warner Bros. productions, including *Dirty Harry* and *The Exorcist II: The Heretic* (1977).[77]

Kubrick's need to minimize costs was also in response to potential "severe penalties" from Warner Bros. should he go over budget.[78] The excesses of *2001* seem to have been eliminated during the Warner Bros. years, in part perhaps because of Harlan's own administrative oversight. What the severe penalties would have been is not certain; they may have been a restriction on Kubrick's producing control. So a strict procurement process was implemented by Harlan and production manager Bernard Williams, in which "no purchases or orders of any kind [could] be made without the approval of Stanley Kubrick."[79] By centralizing the approval process in Kubrick, he was taking full responsibility and, again, looking to avoid failure. Approvals pertained not just to large cost items, but also to petty cash. Kubrick did not allow Hawk Films to cover the mileage costs of crew members using their own cars, while taxi fares would only be covered if it had been ordered by the central Hawk Films' office for an explicit purpose. Kubrick even refused to acknowledge New Year's Day 1971 as a bank holiday, with any crewmember wanting to take the day off receiving a one-fifth reduction in their salary.[80]

Cost reduction was at the heart of Kubrick's producing method in the 1970s. Take how Hawk Films commissioned a company called Abacus to inspect the

A Clockwork Orange print following issues with Kodak. Upon receiving an invoice for the work, priced at £1,450, Kubrick immediately queried the cost and labor involved. The invoice stipulated that the inspection of the *A Clockwork Orange* print had totaled 101 hours, with a further 44 hours operating a film printer, at an hourly rate of £10. But this was not acceptable to Kubrick, who demanded a breakdown of the 101 hours, even after Abacus had offered a reduced bill of £1,015.[81] Kubrick's logic was that the cost represented a budget the size of *2001: A Space Odyssey*, not *A Clockwork Orange*.[82] Kubrick was negotiating with Abacus to achieve as low a fee as possible but was also demonstrating how he was concerned about the budget of the film, telling Abacus that he would have "great trouble in trying to explain this [the invoice price] to Warner Bros."[83] Kubrick was not the only producer feeling such fiscal pressure from Ashley and Calley. John Boorman felt it acutely on *Deliverance*, having to sacrifice any use of a score because "Warners said they wouldn't make the film unless I cut the budget."[84] Kubrick perhaps sensed the unusual privilege he had been gifted by Warner Bros. and therefore wanted to avoid unnecessary expense and an out-of-control budget that could lead to the loss of control he had long sought. Fiscal responsibility was utmost. And as *A Clockwork Orange* moved intro postproduction, so was its commercial potential.

Mike Kaplan, a former national publicity coordinator at MGM, had been appointed as vice president of Polaris Productions in May 1971.[85] Kaplan had been responsible for a revised publicity campaign of *2001: A Space Odyssey* in 1970. Despite the film's success, Kaplan was of the belief that the original campaign put together by Dan Terrell failed to target a growing youth demographic in the United States. Kaplan argued that the original campaign, with its Bob McCall artwork, presented the film as a "modern *Flash Gordon*. Instead, Kubrick had created a metaphysical drama encompassing evolution, reincarnation, the beauty of space, the terror of science, and the mystery of mankind. The campaign had to be reconceived."[86] Even though the film *did* appeal to a broad family audience,[87] MGM wanted to reorient the publicity campaign, with Kaplan giving it a "hip" youth appeal focus.[88] The new marketing campaign exploited the previous use of the phrase "the ultimate trip," which had featured in MGM Records' adverts in summer 1968 for the *2001: A Space Odyssey* soundtrack. Under a red-tinted close-up of Bowman from the Star Gate sequence and the bold heading of "The Ultimate Trip," the advert claimed, "That's what they're calling it on 'underground' FM. And they're playing it like Progressive Rock. Above ground, they're calling it the sound track album of the year. And it's selling like there's no tomorrow."[89]

The new campaign, including a redesigned "Star Child" poster, looked to draw upon this underground, youth audience. The poster, a grainy close-up of the enigmatic figure from the closing sequence of the film, featured the same tagline—"the ultimate trip"—along with only one name: Kubrick's. On seeing the relaunched campaign, Kubrick concluded that Kaplan was the only person he knew of who had the knowledge to handle his films and requested he leave MGM to work solely for him as vice president of Polaris.[90] Over the next four years, Kubrick and Kaplan were in almost daily contact, planning and strategizing publicity, promotion, and distribution of his films.[91]

With *A Clockwork Orange*, Kaplan believed that Polaris conducted "a perfectly choreographed advertising-publicity-exhibition campaign that broke house records in every major city."[92] Kaplan devised several promotional approaches, including a tie-in graphic novelization of the film, a distinct poster design, a *Newsweek* cover story, a newspaper for the film—the *Orange Times*—a soundtrack album, and a bold press brochure. A number of these promotional items sought to exploit the controversial nature and reception of the film and play up its youth appeal. Kaplan and Kubrick also devised a unique distribution campaign, making decisions on the "crucial selection of cinemas, which were usually decided by a studio's sales executives."[93]

Kubrick tasked one of his secretaries to collate box office data from back issues of *Variety* into his own personal distribution database. *Variety* recorded weekly grosses for key cities and their cinemas across the United States. By May 7, 1969, the trade journal introduced a weekly "50 Top-Grossing Films" chart, showing the highest grossing pictures nationally based on key theaters in the major cities.[94] Kubrick's database broke down gross data for films similar to *A Clockwork Orange*, including *Midnight Cowboy* (Schlesinger, 1969) and *The Wild Bunch* (Peckinpah, 1969), showing in which cities and cinemas they performed best. The ledgers were organized by the name of the city, ticket prices, name of the films screened, and number of tickets sold from 1970 to 1972.[95]

Kubrick and Kaplan used the database to target where they wanted *A Clockwork Orange* released and the relevant local publicity budget required. These data were used for a distribution plan devised in collaboration with Leo Greenfield, the head of distribution at Warner Bros., in the summer of 1971. Kubrick wanted *A Clockwork Orange* to open in only four cities: New York, Los Angeles, Toronto, and Denver.[96] This was a much narrower distribution strategy than the average Warner Bros. release at the time and caused Greenfield concern, telling Kubrick, "I do not believe you are doing justice to the picture going as narrowly as you propose."[97] But Kubrick's approach ultimately paid off, with *A Clockwork Orange* maintaining a longer than average presence in *Variety*'s top-fifty box office chart of forty-three weeks. By the end of its initial run in the top fifty, *A Clockwork Orange* had grossed domestic rentals of $8,187,595, in comparison to the Warner Bros. average of $4,904,901.

Alongside his control of distribution strategy, Kubrick, in collaboration with Kaplan, devised a publicity strategy targeted at what was described as the "strongest Kubrick followers ... the youth media-college underground."[98] The aim was to reach this target audience prior to U.S. colleges breaking up for the 1971 Christmas vacation period. Kubrick requested that Warner Bros. compile information for him on college publications and their publication dates to allow for a coordinated publicity campaign.[99] The strategy also called for Kubrick to be interviewed on the community college series *The Sound on Film*, while adverts were to be placed in music publications such as the *Los Angeles Free Press*, *Village Voice*, *East Village Other*, *Good Times*, *Organ*, *Rolling Stone*, and *Crawdaddy*. A second wave of ads was to be placed in smaller underground music publications in January and February 1972, including in *Creem*, *Changes*, *Interview*, *University Review*, *Fusion*, *Rock*, *Zygote*, *Ramparts*, *Other Scenes*, and *Screw*. This was to be complemented with airtime on underground radio stations prior to the release of the film and for the two weeks following. It was agreed that audiences "would respond heavily, and additional expenditures here could wait until sixth to eighth week or when sustaining push needed."[100]

Kaplan placed Kubrick at the center of the publicity campaign for *A Clockwork Orange*, which allowed Kubrick to project an image of absolute authorial control. For example, Kubrick supervised what he called a graphic novelization of the film, a book that presented a frame of each cut of the film, accompanied by dialogue and action text approximating where this took place in any given scene. It was published by Ballantine Books in 1972 and titled *Stanley Kubrick's Clockwork Orange, Based on the Novel by Anthony Burgess*. Kubrick had envisaged the book as an innovative method of rendering the visual experience of film into a graphic record.[101] But the book was primarily a publicity device for the film and for Kubrick himself. In promotional material, Ballantine talked up the fact that it had been Kubrick who had both "conceived" and "put together" the book.[102] The way it was devised and marketed suggested a strategic branding exercise of Kubrick himself. Profit motivation was also undoubtedly a reason for the book's publication. Warner Bros. instigated novelizations of other films it was financing, such as *Summer of 42* (1971) and *Dirty Harry*, part of a trend from the 1970s onward that, as Deborah Allison has argued, was a result of Hollywood's conglomerates recognizing the "financial advantages of exploiting their most popular properties."[103] Kubrick clearly understood the profit potential of novelizations and recommended that Sig Shore, his close friend, follow his lead in publishing a novelization of *Super Fly* (Parks, 1972) with Ballantine.[104]

Two further publications emerged from Polaris that cemented Kubrick's authorial brand and image of control. The first was a publicity item devised by Mike Kaplan called the *Orange Times*. It was a compilation of reviews, quotes, and essays that promoted *A Clockwork Orange* and served as a "comprehensive editorial handout that would become both the production notes and the solution to the advertising ban in markets where X-rated films had limited media access."[105] The editorial of the *Oranges Times* discussed Kubrick's control, claiming that "in addition to producing, directing and adapting *A Clockwork Orange*, he operated the camera, lit the sets, was involved in every decision regarding casting, art direction, scoring and mixing."[106] This startling claim was not unprecedented. In fact, it was part of a pattern by which Kubrick asserted the image of absolute control in the press. Three years previous, in 1969, Kubrick had disputed an advert by Hewlett-Packard that stated the special effects in *2001: A Space Odyssey* had been overseen by Douglas Trumbull. In response, an open letter was published to the media by Kubrick in which stated that the Hewlett-Packard advert was wrong and that it gave the impression Trumbull "was in charge," and that the official credits of the film listed those involved by their comparative importance, with Kubrick being listed first. *He* was in charge, no one else.[107]

The editorial in the *Orange Times*, the open letter to Hewlett-Packard, and other instances like it were all part of a carefully orchestrated media image that had begun some two decades previous. Kubrick had been asserting his own importance in the creation of his films, indeed placing himself at their center, since 1950 through the interviews he had given to journalists like Thomas Pryor of the *New York Times*. By the 1970s, this involved Kubrick insisting on seeing the copy of interviews he had given so he could edit them. Kubrick clearly recognized the means by which interviews communicated an identity for himself and therefore were key to the brand he was fashioning.

The second publication to emerge that emphasized Kubrick's authorial brand was in the form of an interview he granted *Newsweek* in January 1972. Kubrick was to be the cover story, and *Newsweek* was set to dispatch a photographer from its art department in New York to Kubrick's British home to take his picture. But Kubrick took the unprecedented step of insisting that *he* would take the photograph, to the annoyance of *Newsweek*. Kubrick took the photograph with the assistance of his wife, Christiane, and Harlan, in his wife's studio.[108] The final image showed a relaxed Kubrick in a casual sports jacket and holding a small film camera while pointing decisively into the near distance, with the heading "The Startling Vision of Stanley Kubrick."[109] It was an image of a confident, authoritative filmmaker. The image was communicated in words in the press book for *A Clockwork Orange*, which described Kubrick as "exhilarating and exhausting" and "enigmatic," as having an "unpampered self-sufficiency."[110] What was being suggested was that Kubrick was a Hollywood outsider who simply had a movie camera and a vision.

After *Clockwork*

The two projects that emerged after *A Clockwork Orange* and that fulfilled Kubrick's three-picture contract with Warner Bros., *Barry Lyndon* and *The Shining*, were less commercially successful in the United States. Partially, this was because of their increased budgets. *Barry Lyndon* had cost around $11 million, but Steve Ross, at an annual meeting of Warner Communications shareholders, declared the film to have been a "flop."[111] *The Shining* was declared as being a success by Kubrick, who was keen to stress its domestic rentals in a trade press advert he approved in January 1981. The advert announced *The Shining* had earned domestic film rentals of $31 million, making it "the 5th biggest film in the history of Warner Bros!"[112] In reality, the film barely broke even as a result of its significantly high publicity budget of $12 million that Warner Bros. was contractually obliged to spend, combined with a budget of around $18 million.[113] And while the film opened to high ticket sales in its first week of release, sales dropped steeply by the third week.[114] A closer look at the film's week-by-week sales would suggest a high volume of audience interest, but in fact Warner Bros. had imposed high, nonfundable guarantees on exhibitors that booked the film, requiring them to pay $50,000 to play the film.[115] *The Shining* was outperformed by the low-budget horror *Friday the 13th* (Cunningham, 1980)—made for $600,000 and purchased for release in the United States by Paramount for $1.5 million—which grossed domestic rentals of close to $17 million.[116] In all, *The Shining* was not as commercially successful, at least on its initial release, as Kubrick tried to portray it. In that context, the trade press advert was most likely a means of reassuring how commercially integral Kubrick was to Warner Bros. and how he remained a viable financial prospect at the international box office following the disappointment of *Barry Lyndon*. The gestation of the two films and how Warner Bros. came to agree to them are not entirely certain, though we can propose some general assumptions.

Barry Lyndon was a film that was at a remove from the production contexts of Warner Bros. in the mid-1970s, indeed at a remove from Kubrick's own filmography. Prior to *Barry Lyndon*, Kubrick's productions had generally conformed to industrial or production contexts of the time. Even *2001* can be viewed as a product of the mid-1960s move toward technological wide-screen trends, being pitched and produced in 1965 as a Cinerama feature. But *Barry Lyndon* appears to have been more a product of Kubrick's own intellectual and artistic motivations. It was an adaptation of William Makepeace Thackeray's *The Luck of Barry Lyndon* (1844) and had been touted in the press as a *Gone with the Wind*–style epic.[117] It's not clear how Kubrick had pitched the project to Ashley and Calley, though one would presume it was presented as a sort of compromise *Napoleon*, with the film set during the Seven Years' War (1756–1763) and featuring battle sequences between European armies. But the film largely focuses on the intrigue and politics of seventeenth-century European aristocracy.

Between the announcement of *Barry Lyndon*'s production in 1973 through to its release in December 1975, the majority of pictures released by Warner Bros. were comedies (*The Thief Who Came to Dinner* [Yorkin, 1973]), buddy-cop comedy films (*Freebie and the Bean* [Rush, 1974]), action thrillers, westerns (*The Deadly Trackers* [Shear, 1973]; *Zandy's Bride* [Troell, 1974]), or crime (*Mean Streets* [Scorsese, 1973]; *Night Moves* [Penn, 1975]), horror (*The Exorcist* [Friedkin, 1973]; *Craze* [Francis, 1974]; *It's Alive* [Cohen, 1974]), martial arts (Warner Bros. distributed Shaw Bros. films such as *King Boxer* [Chang-hwa, 1973]), or Blaxploitation films (*Cleopatra Jones* [Starrett, 1973]; *Black Samson* [Bail, 1974]); the latter two genres would often be combined following on from the success of *Enter the Dragon* (Clouse, 1973), with an element of comedy, such as the Jim Kelly feature *Black Belt Jones* (Clouse, 1974). There were exceptions: Anthony Harvey, who had served as the editor on *Lolita* and *Dr. Strangelove*, directed the historical drama *The Abdication* (1974), but even this came in under the average 106 minutes running time of Warner Bros. releases during the period. And overall, there were few very actual period dramas, making *Barry Lyndon* exceptional in the production contexts of Warner Bros. at that time, particularly given its running time of over three hours.

Ashley and Calley were anxious to see the film Kubrick had produced and by April 1975 were pressuring him to present a preview of *Barry Lyndon*. But Kubrick resisted, explaining he didn't know when the film would be ready (he was still in the process of adding a narrator's voice-over and finalizing the music) and said that to show Ashley and Calley the film in its present state "would provide all the satisfaction of a premature ejaculation."[118] Kubrick was displaying the same producing tendencies he had on *2001*, frustrating the ability of Warner Bros. to protect its investment and for its senior executives to assess the product they needed to sell. But Ashley and Calley seem to have given Kubrick remarkable freedom on *Barry Lyndon*, with no draft budget even available by June 1973, despite the project being due to enter production in September of that year.[119]

Once Ashley and Calley had seen *Barry Lyndon* it was decided that, given it was very different from Warner Bros. films at the time, it needed a large publicity budget to ensure its success, with even Kubrick describing the budget as "unusually large."[120] Kubrick had been closely supervising the design of a logo for the film—a red rose underneath a pistol—but Warner Bros. was unsure what kind of audience to target the film toward, describing it as having "broad appeal."[121] As such, the market was defined as being the totality of all U.S. television owners, estimated by the Nielsen ratings audience measurement as sixty-nine million households, and a national network television advertising campaign launched in February 1976. But the media plan was comparing *Barry Lyndon* to the disaster and horror films *The Towering Inferno* (Guillermin, 1974) and *Jaws* (Spielberg, 1975), buying broadcast packages from ABC, CBS, and NBC to screen adverts during programs such as *The Rockford Files* (NBC, 1974–1980), *Police Woman* (NBC, 1974–1978), *Six Million Dollar Man* (ABC, 1973–1978), *Hawaii Five-O* (CBS, 1968–1980), *M*A*S*H* (CBS, 1972–1983), and *Petrocelli* (NBC, 1974–1976); these were police procedurals, action adventure series, and legal dramas. The media plan even put together proposals for a package to air adverts during the 1976 Winter Olympics, broadcast on ABC.[122]

In comparison to how *A Clockwork Orange* had sought to target a clear youth audience, *Barry Lyndon*'s publicity was much more ill-defined. Strange proposals were agreed for a radio promotion campaign, with a competition for couples to win tickets to a special Valentine's Day screening of the film.[123] The surrounding promotion presented *Barry Lyndon* as a romance, with the radio spot including the film's "love theme"—the song "Women of Ireland"—as background music.[124] An invitation was sent to the winners of the competition, reading, "This Valentine will admit you and someone you love to see...." The wording was placed inside a love heart, with Cupid's arrow pointing to the *Barry Lyndon* logo.[125]

Warner Bros. also believed that the source novel could put off audiences from seeing the film. Company publicity executives agreed that the book was challenging and that "most people will probably have trouble reading it"; if they attempted to read it, they would have a negative reaction.[126] As such, the company disassociated itself from any tie-in publication of Thackeray's novel and imposed a publicity strategy that discouraged any reference "to the fact that the book is 'now a major motion picture' and do not supply bookstores with posters or any merchandising aids which they might use to promote the connection between book and film."[127] By adapting a supposedly dense and challenging nineteenth-century book, Kubrick had left Warner Bros. without an exploitable literary material and shut down a potential avenue of publicity.

Uncertain of its target audience, even its genre, Warner Bros. was on the back foot in its publicity campaign. Demographic data were gathered by Warner Bros. in the week after the film's general release in the United States, along with audience reactions, which ranged from mixed and indifferent to outright negative. While the cinematography of the film was generally praised, the feeling from the sample audience members was that it was "a colossal bore," that it dragged and its running time was too long, that they lacked enthusiasm for the story, and that they wanted more sex scenes.[128] The most negative comments came from male members of the audience, with women more generally favorable to the film, though with limited praise. As for who were attending the film, it was a broad mixture ranging from teenagers to senior citizens, with the majority being couples, perhaps suggesting that the marketing of *Barry Lyndon* as a Valentine's romance had an initial effect on audience engagement with the film.

As a way of salvaging the commercial returns of *Barry Lyndon*, Kubrick focused his attention on its release in Europe, where it was performing much better, particularly in countries like France. Kubrick even requested a policy whereby exhibitors in the country could not book *Barry Lyndon* without also booking a reissue of *A Clockwork Orange*. In effect, he was tying *Barry Lyndon* to the overall Kubrick brand and the success of *Clockwork*, perhaps as a means to further entice audiences. However, by 1977, Warner Bros. executives concluded that the film had realistically failed and that the company had relinquished to too many of Kubrick's demands, spending over $2 million more in advertising in the United States than was normal; the spending was a result of the special relationship with Kubrick. Frank Wells estimated that Warner Bros. had made a loss of over $4 million on *Barry Lyndon*.[129]

In contrast to *Barry Lyndon*, *The Shining* had a much more clearly defined publicity campaign and target audience, along with being highly exploitable. The project had been suggested to Kubrick by John Calley, who provided Kubrick with a galley copy of King's novel in 1977 while it was still unpublished, perhaps indicating a degree of involvement by Ashley and Calley in Kubrick's project choices following *Barry Lyndon*. This time, Warner Bros. could presell Kubrick's film based on King's book, with marketing copy as early as 1976 tying the book to a motion picture adaptation by Warner Bros. and describing the book as a "presold prefab blockbuster."[130] The company had purchased the rights to King's *Salem's Lot* in 1975, along with *The Shining*; *Salem's Lot* was purchased as part of a three-picture deal with producer Stirling Silliphant and was to be directed by Larry Cohen. King was a best-selling sensation following the publication of *Carrie* (1974), adapted by Brian De Palma (1976) in what became one of the most successful films of 1976. Following the success of *Carrie*, there was an industrial cycle of horror films, with Warner Bros. financing and releasing a wave of horror and supernatural thrillers and dramas between 1976 and 1980, including *The Pack* (Clouse, 1977), *The Medusa Touch* (Gold, 1978), *It Lives Again* (Cohen, 1978), *The Swarm* (Allen, 1978), and *Friday the 13th*.

It is likely that Warner Bros., while not infringing on his creative freedom, was pushing Kubrick toward a more commercially orientated project and one they could begin promoting as a blockbuster event with immediate effect. Soon after it was announced that Kubrick would be adapting *The Shining*, with Jack Nicholson in the lead role, the media were calling the film Kubrick's "occult movie"[131] and that it was an attempt at "cashing in on the horror genre."[132] Certainly, the film was an attempt by Warner Bros. to "cash in" on the genre, with a more concerted effort to make *The Shining* a blockbuster success; it had a wide first-run release and an advertising budget of $11.2 million.[133] Warner Bros. also implemented a strict exhibition booking policy, in which exhibitors were required to run the film for eight weeks minimum and exclusively advertise *The Shining* in theater lobbies; trailers for other films would be permitted prior to any screenings of the film.[134]

But it was not only the commercial success of *The Shining* that was being stressed. The film was the final installment in Kubrick's first three-picture contract with Warner Bros., and it seems he was keen to stress his overall value to the company, both financially and culturally. In a press release that Kubrick approved, it was noted that his films, "more than the films of almost any other filmmaker, have a residual value that continues long after their first release."[135] Kubrick was making it clear that his films were exploitable long after their release, bringing in "highly profitable dollars," and claiming that *A Clockwork Orange* had earned Warner Bros. nearly $2 million and *Barry Lyndon* $600,000 in film rentals in 1980. *The Shining* in many ways was a way of convincing Warner Bros. that Kubrick was worth the investment and deserving of the levels of control he possessed.

Obstruction

Kubrick's growing power and control became ever more pronounced throughout his time producing films for Warner Bros. He was infringing on areas of business strategy that directly implicated Warner Bros. while even challenging the power of the company itself. Take for example how with *Barry Lyndon* Kubrick tried to prevent Warner Bros. from including its logo at the start of the film's credits. Frank Wells was forced to intervene, requesting Kubrick back down in his demands because the logo was about establishing "the identity of the company."[136] But Kubrick's concern was predicated on the fact that the Warner Bros. logo would contain a 1974 copyright label on a film that was primarily to be seen in 1976.[137] Warner Bros. resorted to involving the lawyer Peter Knecht, who reminded Kubrick that he was legally bound to allow the company to display the relevant copyright notice and the phrase "distributed by Warner Bros." in the appropriate place in the film credits.[138]

Kubrick was, somewhat remarkably, attempting to now control even the way copyright notices were displayed on the credits of his film, speaking to the power he felt he had by the mid-1970s. Such overt challenges were becoming ever more apparent in his relationships with the wider film industry and beyond and reveal how Kubrick viewed himself as a producer working in the United Kingdom: he had influence and could use it to protect his own interests. Kubrick would test the limits of this control over the coming years, including through contact with politicians.

Kubrick lobbied the UK government in the mid-1970s to try to halt the introduction of new tax laws. He was concerned about the election of a Labour government in March 1974, led by Harold Wilson, with Denis Healey appointed chancellor of the Exchequer. Healey had been instrumental in the fight to include a so-called annual wealth tax, among a proposed package of economic redistribution reforms, in the Labour Party's 1974 election manifesto.[139] Following Healey's March 1974 budget, the reforms were sent to a Parliamentary Select Committee for further scrutiny, with a proposed introduction date of April 1976.[140] The tax reforms would include foreign residents who had been in the United Kingdom for over nine years. Kubrick, who had relocated there permanently in the mid-1960s, knew that his personal tax and corporation tax contributions would increase substantially as a result. He began to compose draft letters to lobby the relevant unions, industrial figures, and politicians, putting together a draft statement in February 1975 to claim that "a mass exit of the American film colony in Britain has begun." He crossed out the word "exit" and replaced it with the much more melodramatic "exodus."[141] Kubrick raised his concerns with John Woolf, the British film and television producer, who was involved in bringing together a group of prominent industrial figures to meet with Harold Wilson at Downing Street in June 1975. Woolf promised that it would be made clear to the government that Kubrick was threatening to leave the country if the wealth tax was introduced.[142] Kubrick was joined by other expat producer-directors in the United Kingdom, including Norman Jewison, in announcing that they would leave.[143] But Kubrick made it clear why he was a special exception: his power. His argument was that he was responsible for the spending of nearly $30 million in the country since the 1960s and the new taxes would drive him away, robbing the United Kingdom "of all the financial benefits of me making a film here."[144] The issue continued to concern Kubrick throughout the 1970s, and he initiated a meeting with Conservative Party shadow ministers, most notably Geoffrey Howe, the shadow chancellor, in 1977.[145]

Kubrick was using his status and reputation as a means of self-preservation. But he was also clearly signaling that his power and control, and ultimately his success, were integral to wider systems of power, including the British film industry and even Warner Bros. This power, and the extent to which Kubrick had become a significant sphere of influence in the British film industry, was demonstrated in 1977. There were increasing calls from the two main British exhibitors, EMI and Rank, for the reissue of *A Clockwork Orange*. It had not been shown in the United Kingdom since its first-run release ended in 1973. Kubrick had come to a confidential arrangement with Warner Bros., one based on personal circumstances, that meant Kubrick did not want the film being reissued in the country while he was alive. He had apparently received numerous death threats following the furor over the film's purported role in influencing a spate of so-called "copycat crimes" in the UK, in which gangs of youths were said to be imitating the onscreen violence of Alex and his *droogs*.[146] But EMI was pressuring Warner Bros. in September 1977, based on the fact that *A Clockwork Orange* was a British-made film (it had qualified for Eady money) and that its reissue would prove financially beneficial to both companies.[147] The pressure to reissue *A Clockwork Orange* also seemed to stem from wider resentment British exhibitors had with Kubrick over persistent special concessions they had to make to him, such as how his films were screened in cinemas. As a result EMI posed an ultimatum: in return for years of granting Kubrick what he wanted, the company now wanted Warner Bros. to grant EMI the favor of reissuing *A Clockwork Orange*.[148] Kubrick was outraged and made clear that the reissue of the film in the United Kingdom was not negotiable. He would release his films when *he* thought the time was right.[149] Kubrick's response indicated the power balance between himself, Warner Bros., and exhibitors like EMI, commenting that, even though he did not have the contractual right to say when his films should be reissued, it was "the first time that I have heard of an exhibitor dictating to a distributor, or to a producer, when there will be a reissue of a film."[150] EMI did not get its way and *A Clockwork Orange* remained out of general release in the United Kingdom until 2000.

Kubrick was contributing to the potential breakdown in key industrial relationships, challenging established business conventions, and looking to utilize his power and influence to effect change at the highest levels of government policy making. He clearly was now in a position of influence that meant he could control and impact decisions beyond those made on his film sets or within his own companies. And more than that, he didn't necessarily have to account for his thought process and the actions that he took. In one draft note from sometime in the late 1970s, Kubrick set out thoughts in a way that encapsulated his power and his own view of the control he had: "I release my films when I think the time is right for them. I'm not sure I have to account for my judgement in these matters. It is for no one to tell me when that time is."[151] Presumably this note was in connection with the reissue of *A Clockwork Orange* in the United Kingdom. But it shows how Kubrick had reached the point at which he had centralized creative and business decisions for his films within his own power as a producer. And it was the overriding conditions at Warner Bros. and the executives who worked there that had enabled Kubrick to obtain such levels of control. As Julian Senior, director of European publicity and advertising for Warner Bros., explained to a bemused official in the Warner Bros. Brazil office, "It really is simpler to give Mr. Kubrick what he wants, when he wants it."[152]

Conclusion

It was Warner Bros. that ultimately facilitated Kubrick's decline as a film producer, with a contractual agreement, however vague in its wording, that allowed him to greatly enhance his power and control over all creative and business functions. Presumably, Warner Bros. executives did not expect Kubrick to infringe on as many areas of business control as he did nor to take control to the minute degree that he did of areas such as dubbing and regional advertising. Warner Bros. had operated, under the stewardship of Ted Ashley and John Calley, a wider strategy of providing major film producers with creative autonomy, but with the implicit understanding that it was Warner Bros. that possessed the industrial expertise in areas of publicity and distribution. But Kubrick was a producer who wanted control, partly out of a fear of failure of those around him. And so the business contexts of Warner Bros. were ultimately responsible for Kubrick becoming the producer that he did by the end of the 1970s: he expected to be involved in every decision; he requested ever more voluminous research; he wanted to know the outcome to every plausible course of action, both business and creative, before making a decision; he viewed dubbing editing as a key role that he should have direct control over; and he supervised the release, advertising, and even exhibition of his films in every region of the world.

It may be suggested that this represented Kubrick as the total artist. But it was having an adverse effect because by the end of the 1970s Kubrick was overwhelmed with work. He was ceaselessly producing, operating as a businessman, and devising new strategies in consultation with Warner Bros. and his own staff in how films should be released in theaters, on television, and on home video. This was restricting the time he could actually dedicate to being an artist and to move projects out of development and into production. Indeed, Kubrick had centralized control in his role as a producer to the extent that it was causing extensive delays in future projects because those around him had to wait for him, and him alone, to make a decision. As is discussed in the next chapter, the seeds of Kubrick's decline had been sown by Warner Bros. and its executives, yet they were now eager to motivate him to produce more films at a quicker pace. But Kubrick just had too much control.

10

The End, 1980-1999

In January 1984, it was announced that Kubrick had signed a new three-picture deal with Warner Bros.[1] But it would take him fifteen years to fulfill only two pictures on the contract: *Full Metal Jacket* (1987) and *Eyes Wide Shut* (1999). The period from 1980 to 1999 was the most dormant of Kubrick's entire career in terms of releases of films he had produced. The deal represented the last phase of Kubrick's producing life, and he likely knew that he would not fulfill the contract. Kubrick was beginning to doubt his own abilities as a filmmaker able to produce, direct, and write his own films; by the mid-1980s he even considered abdicating his role as a director to focus solely on producing. Though Kubrick never did take the drastic action of giving up directing, his thinking does suggest that he was aware of his own decline and how the control he had acquired over the years was crippling his abilities to function as a filmmaker. The new Warner Bros. deal represented the beginning of the end of Kubrick's career.

The decline of Kubrick suggests not a decrease in the artistic quality of his work but rather a decline in the efficiency of output and a struggle to successfully move a film from development into production. Kubrick had become an impotent producer, overwhelmed by his own centralized management style and the information and research that he sought. This overcentralized producing power structure is a tangible reality; I have had the privilege of entering the so-called archive strong room at the Stanley Kubrick Archive at the University of the Arts London. This is the secure, temperature-controlled repository where Kubrick's archive is now stored, shelved on a series of electronic rolling stacks that reach from floor to ceiling and are several meters in length. What struck me about the strong room was the scale of the material held there, described by

Richard Daniels as "filling over 800 linear metres of archive shelving and consisting of millions of individual documents."[2] I walked down one of the aisles that was stacked with row upon row of books. I assumed that this was Kubrick's personal library given the vast amount of books but was corrected by the archivist that in fact the books pertained to just one film that was never produced: *Aryan Papers*. It was at that moment I realized I was looking firsthand at what Kubrick had become by the 1980s: an artist gripped with an insatiable curiosity and vision but a producer with no limits on his control anymore. Stacked on those shelves was the physical embodiment of Kubrick's decline.

This chapter charts the final years of Kubrick's producing life to understand how his decline came about and how this resulted in several major projects being left unmade, including *A.I. Artificial Intelligence* and *Aryan Papers*. The aim is to try to understand why Warner Bros. allowed Kubrick's decline and whether there were any attempts to prevent it. The chapter also looks to understand the production contexts of his final two films, *Full Metal Jacket* and *Eyes Wide Shut*. Kubrick realized that he was working in an altered industrial landscape by the 1980s, competing against vibrant, powerful producers like Steven Spielberg and George Lucas, figures whom he became fascinated with and the commercial success of whom he wanted to replicate; between 1975 and 1993, Lucas and Spielberg dominated the global box office with blockbuster releases like *Jaws* (Spielberg, 1975), *Star Wars* (Lucas, 1977), *E.T. the Extra-Terrestrial* (Spielberg, 1982), and *Jurassic Park* (Spielberg, 1993). But in attempting to compete with these new producers—he never came close to achieving the grosses that Lucas and Spielberg did—Kubrick entered a period of extended development hell, with his output stalling. First, there was a seven-year hiatus between the release of *The Shining* and *Full Metal Jacket*, followed by a longer twelve-year hiatus between *Full Metal Jacket* and *Eyes Wide Shut*. But Kubrick was not inactive during these years. In fact, he was often occupied with matters of publicity pertaining to home video releases or theatrical reissues of his films. But I begin by first considering what kind of projects Kubrick was interested in producing in these final years.

Development Hell

Along with an artistic and intellectual interest in a story, Kubrick considered three other key factors when choosing to develop a project: logistics, budget, and commercial viability. He also had to submit a synopsis of any project he wanted to pursue, beyond merely exploratory development, to Warner Bros. There are archival examples of Kubrick submitting story ideas, the majority of which were adaptations of novels, to Warner Bros., including an outline of an adaptation of Joseph Roth's *Job* (1930) in May 1971;[3] the book told the story of one man's loss of faith in God following a series of personal tragedies. Submitting outlines was one of the conditions of Kubrick's arrangement with Warner Bros., in which he had to run his ideas past Ted Ashley and John Calley, and from 1980 Terry Semel, who took over Ashley's role of chief operating officer and vice president of the company. In doing so, Kubrick was also obtaining feedback and advice on the projects he was contemplating. He was in effect using the Warner Bros. executives as a high-level reading service.

By the mid-1970s, he delegated this reading role to his lawyer, Louis C. Blau, and to his close assistant, Anthony Frewin. It became a key function of the role of Frewin, who described himself as Kubrick's "in-house reader of novels, screenplays, and such."[4] Rather than acquire the rights to vast swaths of literary property, as had been the case during the Harris-Kubrick Pictures years, Kubrick instead had Frewin read through and write reports of as many novels and screenplays as he could. But the number of novels that Kubrick was giving Frewin overwhelmed him by the mid-1980s, so a new company was incorporated sometime around 1986–1987. Called Empyrean Films, the company was supervised on a day-to-day basis by Frewin. He employed a host of readers after placing an advert in the *Times Literary Supplement*, but the readers were not told that they were working for Kubrick, with it being paramount to Kubrick that the press and wider industry not learn "what novels etc he was considering."[5] Frewin administered the company, signing off payments to the readers, but it was Kubrick who selected the majority of novels or other literary material for the readers. Their role was to read the material and then provide a reader's report, which included a synopsis, strengths and weaknesses of the story, and a judgment on commercial viability. Some of the readers were even tasked to conduct research at places like the British Library. Empyrean Film invoices show the kind of research being requested, including "golem research" in 1990, in connection with *The Golem* (Megrink 1914);[6] "literary robot research" and research into "the year's best science fiction" between 1988 and 1990, most likely in connection with the development of *A.I.*;[7] and "Polish research" in 1991, presumably in connection with *Aryan Papers*.[8]

There were clear patterns of interest in the books that Kubrick gave the readers, particularly science fiction, the "literary" novel, and postmodern authors: Isaac Asimov, Philip K. Dick, and Thomas Pynchon were particularly prevalent authors given to the readers. Pynchon's *The Crying of Lot 49* (1965) was given particular attention, and Frewin was tasked with outlining the novel in more detail, looking at issues of logistics and wider industrial trends for "blackly funny humour."[9] Frewin's development report pointed out that "Pynchon has a great following in both the States and over here [United Kingdom]" with *The Crying of Lot 49* "easily being the most popular ... it has been continually in print in both countries since it was published."[10] But Frewin noted that Hollywood narrative trends had changed and that films like *Star Wars* and *E.T.*—the latter a film that fascinated Kubrick—had initiated a cycle of action-adventure, fantasy, and science fiction films.

These box office trends were reflected in the kind of material that Kubrick increasingly sent to the Empyrean readers, such as John Crowley's *Engine*

Summer (1979), a postapocalyptic novel; Evelyn Waugh's *Love Among the Ruins* (1953), a satirical dystopian novel set in the near-future United Kingdom; Ursula K. Le Guin's *The Dispossessed* (1974), a science fiction story laced with political overtones about the state of capitalism; William Gibson's cyberpunk science fiction *Mona Lisa Overdrive* (1988); and Bob Shaw science fiction short story collections such as *A Better Mantrap* (1982) and *Tomorrow Lies in Ambush* (1973). But while Kubrick's direction of Empyrean was in some ways tied to Hollywood trends, he still showed an interest in literary novels concerned with sex, marriage, and extramarital relationships, requesting reader reports on the likes of Dostoevsky's *The Eternal Husband* (1870) and Ian McEwan's collection of short stories *First Love, Last Rites* (1975). Kubrick was clearly looking for a way to adapt a story about marriage and infidelity, namely Schnitzler's *Traumnovelle*, discussed further below.

How serious Kubrick was about the novels he submitted to Empyrean is unclear, but it seems the company was a first step in sifting out material that might be worthy of further development. It's more likely Kubrick was taking a project seriously if option rights to a novel were purchased. In 1989, Jan Harlan was negotiating in perpetuity option rights to Robert Marshall's *All the King's Men* (1988).[11] The book was the real-life story of Henri Déricourt, a World War II French agent for the British espionage service, Special Operations Executive, who was reputedly a double agent in the pay of the Nazis' intelligence agency, the Sicherheitsdienst. Even though Kubrick did not pursue an adaptation of *All the King's Men* it came at a time when he was thinking of developing a World War II project, what became *Aryan Papers*, and shows how he would conduct extensive research into stories related to a particular theme in which he was interested.

Kubrick also explored projects via considerations of financial implications and logistical feasibility. Following how *Barry Lyndon* had predominantly been filmed on location, which had left Kubrick unable to control a range of variables such as the weather and time, he was more inclined to film on studio lots where he could retain control. In the early 1980s he became interested in an adaptation of Henry Rider Haggard's *The Saga of Eric Brighteyes* (1890), sensing it could be filmed as a children's action adventure story. The idea was explored shortly after the release of *E.T.*, demonstrating how Kubrick wanted to produce a film with broad family appeal like Spielberg's films. Frewin prepared a synopsis of the project in August 1982, which in itself was based on a treatment of Haggard's novel by Jan Harlan.[12] Kubrick was endeared to the book, which told the story of Viking explorers in Iceland in the tenth century.[13] But however much Kubrick loved the book as an artist, the producer in him realized the practicalities of filming it would be difficult, involving location shooting in the Arctic Circle, Iceland, or the northernmost reaches of Scotland. The project did not go ahead based on the logistics involved in any production.

The most substantial project that Kubrick developed an interest for in the 1980s was a science fiction story he had been developing called *A.I. Artificial*

Intelligence. The project stemmed from his growing fascination with the blockbuster movies of Spielberg and Lucas; he regularly requested box office figures for the films of the two producer-directors.[14] *A.I.* emerged from correspondence between Kubrick and science fiction author Brian Aldiss that commenced in November 1975.[15] Aldiss was in the midst of reviving the Science Fiction Luncheon Club, a society committed to public engagement work on science fiction literature, and wanted Kubrick to attend as a special guest. Aldiss held Kubrick in high regard, saying that he had "futurity in the palm of your hand" due to directing *Dr. Strangelove*, *2001*, and *A Clockwork Orange*, all of which made him one of the greatest science fiction storytellers of the era.[16] The invite precipitated Kubrick's interest in Aldiss's work, and by the summer of 1976, following phone conversations, Aldiss sent Kubrick several of his novels, including the manuscript for his then forthcoming *The Malacia Tapestry* (1976).[17] The aim was to try to interest Kubrick in a science fiction adaptation; at that time, he was also looking at the work of Barry Malzberg, including his *Beyond Apollo* (1972), a book he didn't think would be successful at the box office.[18]

Kubrick's interest was piqued by Aldiss's *Supertoys Last All Summer Long* (1969), a short story about artificial intelligence.[19] Set in a dystopian future, where Earth is overpopulated, strict birth controls have been put in place that require couples to ask for permission to bear children. As a result, many families own artificial children. But the protagonist of the story, David, is concerned his mother, Monica, does not really love him. The story ends with Monica relieved to discover she has been granted permission to give birth, and so she tells her husband that David must be sent back to a robot factory. Aldiss described Kubrick as being obsessed with the story, attracted by its themes of technology and human selfishness.[20] Work on developing the project commenced post-1977 as a result of what Aldiss described as Kubrick's professional jealousy at the success of *Star Wars*; Kubrick wanted to produce the project in a similar style, with Aldiss recalling that Kubrick began developing the film as "another big space opera."[21] The initial collaboration came to nothing, though the pair remained in correspondence over the ensuing years.

It wasn't until the release and subsequent box office success of Spielberg's *E.T. the Extra-Terrestrial* in 1982 that Kubrick returned to an adaptation of *Supertoys*, intent on creating a film to "rival" *E.T.*[22] But Aldiss believed that such an approach was detrimental and would result in a banal treatment, one that would conform to more conventional Hollywood narrative styles. Aldiss felt the story being developed with Kubrick was disappointing because of his continuing fascination with *E.T.*, what he called Kubrick's "E.T. syndrome."[23] Worse still, Aldiss felt he had lost his creative autonomy in working with Kubrick and that the project was destined to remain unmade because of the developing obsession with *E.T.*'s commercial success.[24] Kubrick was apparently insistent on the film having a "happy ending" and referred Aldiss constantly to *Pinocchio*.[25] Throughout December 1982, Kubrick engaged in ten-hour phone calls with Aldiss, culminating in the creation of numerous story outlines. It was at this point in January 1983 that Aldiss took to a writing retreat to work on an expanded thirty-thousand-word treatment for Kubrick. But according to Aldiss, Kubrick was disappointed with the eventual treatment.[26] By February 1983 Kubrick had become less enthusiastic about *Supertoys*—his attention was becoming ever more focused on *Full Metal Jacket*—and was growing concerned about the costs of development. Kubrick had not paid Aldiss for his work but wanted the author to forfeit the rights to two further short stories, *Who Can Replace a Man?* (1965) and *All the World's Tears* (1957).[27] Aldiss concluded that the project had "run into the rocks," and he was sorry that the collaboration had finished on "a dead-end argument over small sums of money."[28]

There were further attempts to develop the project, by then retitled *A.I.*, in the late 1980s and early 1990s. Kubrick further reworked the story, collaborating with writers Iain Watson, Sara Maitland, and Bob Shaw and a brief reprise in collaboration with Aldiss and even Arthur C. Clarke.[29] A graphic illustrator, Chris "Fangorn" Baker, was also approached to design storyboards for the film, which captured the scale and vision of what was being created.[30] Upon seeing the computer generated imagery (CGI) of *Jurassic Park*, Kubrick was convinced that the world of *A.I.* could be brought to life. Deals were negotiated with Industrial Light & Magic (ILM), the special effects company behind the CGI of *Jurassic Park*, though the company was experiencing an upsurge in demand and its services would not be available until around 1995 or 1996.[31] But by 1993 Kubrick was in email correspondence with Steven Spielberg about the project, sending him all of the material he had to date on *A.I.*,[32] and by 1996 the pair had arranged a "deal";[33] Kubrick was to serve only as a producer on the film, with Spielberg to direct.[34] This was a seismic moment in Kubrick's career and perhaps reflected a realization on his behalf that he was struggling to develop the project on his own. The contemplation of abdicating directorial responsibility, besides even agreeing a deal with Spielberg, went against everything Kubrick had worked toward, but it shows he was himself aware of his own decline. Aldiss, reflecting on his time working with Kubrick, says he was witnessing a filmmaker "reaching the end of his creative career" by the 1980s.[35]

Aryan Papers

One project that nearly did enter production, and in many respects was a rival project to *A.I.*, was *Aryan Papers*. It was an adaptation of Louis Begley's *Wartime Lies* (1991), with Kubrick working on the screenplay by himself. The project underwent significant preproduction between 1991 and 1993, utilizing the efforts of key personnel at Hawk Films, including Jan Harlan and Philip Hobbs. What follows is a brief reconstruction of the development and preproduction of *Aryan Papers* to better understand the efforts involved in getting a Kubrick film into production and the wider contexts as to why it was left unmade.

Begley's novel was based on his own life story and follows the protagonist, a young boy named Maciek, as he grows up in a Jewish family in Nazi-occupied Poland. Maciek, along with his aunt Tania, assume Catholic identities in order to obtain their Aryan papers and allude Nazi persecution. The story was a continuation of Kubrick's longtime interest in World War II and, more specifically, the Holocaust. These narrative interests, what Geoffrey Cocks has labeled Kubrick's "German subjects,"[36] had consumed Kubrick's attention at various points throughout his career, commencing with the World War II–related projects explored with Harris-Kubrick Pictures, including *The German Lieutenant*. Kubrick was even briefly interested in producing a film about Otto Skorzeny, the SS lieutenant colonel who was reputedly involved in the Nazis' Operation Long Jump, an apparent plan, led by Skorzeny, to assassinate Winston Churchill, Franklin Roosevelt, and Joseph Stalin at the 1943 Tehran Conference, but was canceled due to being uncovered by Soviet intelligence agencies.[37] Skorzeny was later instrumental in helping the highest echelons of Nazi leadership, and those most intimately involved in the administration of the Holocaust, escape from war crime trials in the 1950s, supposedly leading a ratline organization called Die Spinne, part of the wider ODESSA Nazi underground escape organization. Die Spinne may have been responsible for allowing the likes of Josef Mengele and Adolf Eichmann to reach South America.

It was following contact with a Spanish-based talent agent, Niels Larsen—presumably when he was directing *Spartacus*—that Kubrick expressed an interest in Skorzeny's life and an adaptation of his memoirs, published in 1950.[38] Skorzeny had become something of a popular media figure, receiving numerous offers from Hollywood producers to make films based on his memoirs. Larsen was keen to make a deal with Kubrick and even invited him to meet the former Nazi in Spain in 1960. Skorzeny had fled to Madrid following his escape from the Darmstadt internment camp in 1948. Kubrick declined the offer to meet Skorzeny and turned down the deal offered by Larsen.[39]

Kubrick was clearly interested in the subject of World War II and of the crimes perpetrated by the Nazis and continued to return to the subject throughout his career. For example, he considered an adaptation of *Swing under the Nazis: Jazz as a Metaphor for Freedom* (1985), Mike Zwerin's (a trombonist who played with Miles Davis) account of jazz musicians in Nazi-occupied Europe. And when in correspondence with Harold Pinter in the 1970s,[40] Kubrick admitted to wanting to produce a film about the Holocaust and that *The Destruction of the European Jews* (Hilberg, 1961) was "constantly illuminated by the kind of vivid detail which can be the spark of narrative ideas. Indeed, there are so many ideas, situations and characters set forth, the problem is more one of selection than anything else."[41] Around 1976, Kubrick considered making a film about the UFA studios in Berlin during the 1930s and 1940s.[42] UFA had been purchased by Alfred Hugenberg, who gifted it to the Nazis in the early 1930s. Soon after, it became a key component of Joseph Goebbels's Ministry of Propaganda and was used by directors like Veit Harlan, the uncle of Jan Harlan.[43] Sometime after considering the UFA project, Kubrick requested Jan Harlan to explore the possibility of a deal to collaborate with Nobel laureate Isaac Bashevis Singer. Singer's fiction explored Jewish themes, with some of his books set during the Holocaust, including *Enemies, A Love Story* (1972) and *Shosha* (1978). Unfortunately, Singer turned down the offer of collaborating with Kubrick.[44]

Kubrick's Jewish heritage and the Holocaust pervaded his work, even the films he did produce, and remained an overriding obsession for him.[45] As Cocks notes, paraphrasing Kubrick, "what he most wanted to make was a film about the Holocaust, but good luck in putting all that into a two-hour movie."[46] Instead, Cocks argues that Kubrick indirectly alluded to the Holocaust—or "sublimated his feelings"—through a number of his works, most prominently in *The Shining*.[47] But the desire to make a film about the Holocaust persisted well into the 1990s, with a focus on producing a fiction film, rather than a documentary, in order to be able to tell a story that had drama (his comments to Pinter, above, hint at this). By 1991, Kubrick seemed to have found the ideal story to produce following the publication of Begley's *Wartime Lies* and so set about entering preproduction.

It was in July 1991 that Kubrick began to assemble the necessary components in order to pitch *Aryan Papers* as his next project and to obtain the necessary financing. He still had no script and so intended to make a deal based on a treatment, production schedule, budget, and production plan.[48] His notes from the time reveal a series of tasks that he needed to complete in order to produce the film, including, most importantly, the need to make a deal. The deal seemed to involve Kubrick contemplating an offer from Michael Ovitz, president of the Creative Artists Agency (CAA), with his notes detailing how he needed "to decide on Ovitz."[49] Ovitz had become one of the most powerful figures in Hollywood via his CAA talent agency, which negotiated package deals for actors, writers, producers, and directors. A *New York Times* profile from 1989 emphasized the power and influence Ovitz had, particularly over the major studios, due to the caliber of talent that was on the CAA payroll, including Steven Spielberg, Tom Cruise, and Martin Scorsese. As the *New York Times* profile noted, "'Money runs this town.' True enough. But Michael Ovitz controls access to a very great deal of potential money."[50] The packages that Ovitz negotiated often resulted in substantial profits for his clients.

Ovitz suggests in his autobiography that Kubrick had contacted him in relation to *Aryan Papers* in the early 1990s, mainly to find out the status of Martin Scorsese's rival Holocaust-themed project.[51] *Variety* was reporting in 1989 that Scorsese was to direct an adaptation of Thomas Keneally's novel *Schindler's Ark* (1982), produced by Steven Spielberg and slated for release in 1990 as *Schindler's List*.[52] Spielberg had been developing *Schindler's List* since the early 1980s and, after Scorsese withdrew from the project, directed it himself in 1993. Kubrick would no doubt have been aware of Spielberg's interest in *Schindler's List* given the two had initiated a friendship in the late 1970s and shared frequent phone calls. So what was the purpose of Kubrick's contact with Ovitz?

While Ovitz's own account doesn't seem to fit available archival evidence, it is probable to assume that he was in contact with Kubrick; after all, Kubrick was making notes that directly referred to Ovitz. Author Michael Herr, in his memoir *Kubrick* (2000), suggests that Kubrick and Ovitz were in correspondence as early as the mid-1980s, with Ovitz providing Kubrick with a copy of *The Art of War*. There were even reports that Ovitz may have become Kubrick's agent sometime in the early 1990s, something Ovitz has also previously suggested.[53] Ovitz was also close to Terry Semel, the vice president of Warner Bros., and in his memoir talks of how he and Semel would travel to Kubrick's home to listen to his pitches for projects like *A.I.* and *Aryan Papers*.[54] So there certainly was some kind of preexisting relationship that precipitated the contact between Kubrick and Ovitz on *Aryan Papers*, and it may well be that Kubrick used him to negotiate a better package deal with Warner Bros.

Kubrick commenced work on the *Aryan Papers* script amid the uncertainty of whether *Schindler's List* would ever go into production; by November 1991 the project had once more come to a halt.[55] In contrast, by February 1992 Kubrick had broken down *Wartime Lies* in order to consider how to construct the script,[56] concluding that he had to move away from how the novel told the story from Maciek's point of view. Instead, Kubrick wanted greater drama and to reveal aspects of the story that were not witnessed by Maciek firsthand. These included scenes of a sexual nature that Kubrick wanted to develop dramatically. By June and October, Kubrick had developed draft outlines, complete with camera annotations, as he began to think about moving into production.[57] The October 1992 treatment ran to 126 pages and included 208 scenes, along with a prologue and epilogue. The prologue was headed as "The Final Solution . . ." and scrawled next to it in Kubrick's hand was the word "stock"—he was to use documentary stock footage for this sequence and would feature such footage throughout the picture.[58] The writing of the outline had been aided by correspondence with Louis Begley to confirm story points and areas of historical accuracy.[59]

With a completed treatment (though, it would continue to be adapted and reworked over the next year) and with *Schindler's List* in development hell, preproduction for *Aryan Papers* was initiated, with Jan Harlan leading the logistics, supported by Philip Hobbs. Kubrick had already been thinking about a potential cast in July 1991, including whom to use in the lead role of Tania, listing a mixture of Hollywood, British, and Eastern European actors: Ellen Barkin (*Sea of Love* [Becker, 1989]), Anica Dobra (*The Fall of Rock and Roll* [Gajić, 1989]), Donna Dixon (*Wayne's World* [Spheeris, 1992]), Andie MacDowell (*Sex, Lies, and Videotape* [Soderberg, 1989]), Mia Farrow, Ellen Greene (*Little Shop of Horrors* [Oz, 1986]), Cheri Lunghi (*Excalibur* [Boorman, 1981]), Helen Mirren (*The Comfort of Strangers* [Schrader, 1990]), Rebecca De Mornay (*Risky*

Business [Brickman, 1983]), Julia Roberts (*Pretty Woman* [Marshall, 1990]), and Winona Ryder (*Edward Scissorhands* [Burton, 1990]).[60]

Many of Kubrick's casting decisions seem to have been informed by Spielberg. Kubrick's preference seemed to be Julia Roberts, who was in the process of completing filming on Spielberg's *Hook* (1991). Her agent, Jeff Berg, suggested a meeting in London between Kubrick and Roberts, which would give Kubrick the opportunity to pitch *Aryan Papers* to her.[61] For the role of Maciek Kubrick wanted Joseph Mazzello, who was playing Tim Murphy in *Jurassic Park*. Kubrick seemed set on casting Mazzello to the point of impacting on the actor's appearance in Richard Attenborough's *Shadowlands* (1993). Attenborough required Mazzello for a period of twenty-one days between April and July 1993, but Kubrick was insisting he needed Mazzello for forty days from June 1993 (despite having no actual firm production plans). Attenborough was desperate and pleaded with Kubrick to help him in the matter.[62] Kubrick, however, was adamant in his position: "Please believe me I would like to help. But I have some major problems with this."[63] The problem was that Kubrick required Mazzello for a longer period of time than was allowed for child actors by unions in the United Kingdom. As a result, *Aryan Papers* needed to be filmed abroad.[64]

The issue of location and where to base the production had dominated Kubrick's attention since 1991. The film was most likely to be shot in Europe during the winter months, and Kubrick had initially instructed Hobbs to gather research on Dutch film studios.[65] But in early 1993, following Spielberg's decision to shoot *Schindler's List* in Central and Eastern Europe, Kubrick dispatched Harlan and Hobbs to scout for locations and studios in the region. Harlan was focusing his preproduction efforts in the city of Brno in the Czech Republic and was arranging deals with local authorities to be able to undertake location shooting. This included a deal with the Brno city council to close the town center for one weekend and re-create Nazi-occupied Warsaw. Nazi flags were to be placed on buildings and authentic 1940s trams were to be borrowed from a local museum. The deal was extensive and costly.[66] But as preproduction of *Aryan Papers* progressed, it became apparent that Kubrick had doubts, with his need to have every outcome available to his decision making frustrating the production process.

Warner Bros. had issued press releases saying the film would enter production in the summer of 1993, with a 1994 release date.[67] But deals that had been made, or proposals put forward, were starting to unravel. Kubrick had changed his mind on the casting of Julia Roberts and canceled a meeting with her. He explained to her agent that he was embarrassed at having to cancel but that he was "no longer confident she is absolutely right for the part. This is of course one of those intangible assessments that drive people crazy, but until I can eliminate some of my doubts, I don't think it would be good to meet."[68] Even the casting of Mazzello was now somewhat vague, with his agent Scott Henderson saying only that there was a "commitment to his client and that they had been told to keep his summer schedule clear. However, neither he nor his client had seen a script."[69]

Despite the growing ambiguities surrounding *Aryan Papers*, not least the fact that Kubrick was struggling to turn the outline into a full working script, Harlan continued with preproduction in Eastern Europe, concurrent to Spielberg shooting *Schindler's List*. And as Harlan's work progressed, the scale of *Aryan Papers* was becoming apparent. He tasked Hobbs to find one thousand Mauser rifles as well as Schmeisser submachine guns, MG 34s and MG 42s, and numerous pieces of Russian, German, and Polish artillery. The film was even to feature epic scenes of the Jewish ghettos in Warsaw being cleared, with Kubrick to use aerial filming.

Harlan persevered in finding an alternative production base to Brno, focusing on Bratislava in the newly formed Slovakia. Harlan outlined the intentions of the production to the Czech and Slovak American Enterprise Fund (CSAEF) based in the city. The CSAEF was established by the American Congress in 1989, one of several funds that were part of the U.S. government's Assistance to Eastern Europe under the Support for East European Democracy (SEED) Act (1989). The Kubrick production team was keen to make use of the services of CSAEF and the contacts they had within the Slovak Ministry of Culture. Pressure was applied to the Slovak government to allow the production to take place, describing *Aryan Papers* as an important film.[70] Rick Senat, Warner Bros.'s vice president of European Affairs, contacted the Slovak government to suggest that, should they allow Kubrick to set up the "necessary company structure with satisfactory arrangements for VAT and exchange control" quickly, Bratislava would become their production base (alternatives included Prague).[71]

The fledgling capitalist economies of former Eastern Bloc countries, such as the Czech Republic, Slovakia, and Poland, were now looking to entice private business, including American film productions. *Variety* reported in August 1993 that there had been an increase in Hollywood productions in Eastern European countries and that "since the Iron Curtain came tumbling down, local production and service outfits have been aggressively marketing their countries wares," as a source both of hard currency to plough back into local productions and of work to keep the newly privatized film studios turning over.[72] Basing an American production in Central or Eastern Europe had the potential to cost 40 percent less than in the West, and the likes of Poland (the best actors), the Czech Republic and Slovakia (the best locations), and Hungary (the best technical services) were vying for foreign film shoots.[73] Spielberg was filming *Schindler's List* in Poland with "all on-location services provided by . . . Heritage Films" and $9 million of the film's $25 million budget spent in the country.[74] The governments of some of these countries were willing to "contribute up to 50% of a film's costs, depending on the size of the budget," with money accrued from big-budget Hollywood productions being reinvested into their respective national film studios.[75] There were also distinct tax advantages to filming in a country such as Slovakia, hence the Kubrick production team's pressure on the Slovak government. Price Waterhouse advised Jan Harlan that Kubrick's new production company, Hobby Films, incorporated in 1989, "would not be required to register for commercial or tax purposes in the country and will accordingly not be subject to direct tax on any profits."[76]

But these incentives did not overcome Kubrick's own indecision, which was holding up the entire production. Even though Harlan and Warner Bros. had started to negotiate deals for *Aryan Papers* to be filmed in Slovakia, it became obvious to Harlan that Kubrick was not prepared to commit himself to the country. The key problems in the way of an autumn 1993 shoot, in readiness for a 1994 release, were highlighted in a production document in May 1993.[77] And the key problem was Kubrick himself. The document stressed that Kubrick had to decide where to base the film no later than May 28 in order to start filming in early September. If no decision had been made by then, it would affect the hiring of a crew, any studio contracts, and visa applications.[78] The document was stark in its assessment and made it clear to Kubrick that major investment deals were at stake. This included a new production company, Albatross, which was to be incorporated to take advantage of European tax arrangements. The filing of the incorporation papers was put on hold though due to a "fundamental problem."[79]

The fundamental problem was that Kubrick was once again, in Harlan's words, "more interested in Brno than Bratislava."[80] It is not entirely clear why Kubrick had returned to the thought of basing the production in the Czech Republic; after all, it was reported that production costs in the country were much higher in comparison to other Eastern European countries, with prices for location work in the country "rapidly rising."[81] The contradictions in Kubrick's decision making were mounting, including asking Harlan to look at other European studios, such as the Rosenhugel Studios in Vienna and, to Harlan's clear annoyance, Bratislava. Harlan vented his frustrations to Kubrick on May 30, demanding explanations for what amounted to a wild goose chase.[82] But the only logic behind Kubrick's decision making seemed to be a need for ever more information—including daily weather forecasts for cities across Eastern Europe—but as he became ever more burdened by this information overload, he was unable to make a decision.[83]

By the end of 1993, preproduction, and *Aryan Papers* as a whole, was put on indefinite hold. Harlan contacted Tamara Holoubkova, his contact in Bratislava, to explain there had been a change of plan: "The film will still be made but at this stage I can't say where and when."[84] He attached a press release to the letter that detailed how Kubrick was instead to produce and direct *A.I.* and would reduce himself to a producer only for *Aryan Papers* in the coming years.[85] Kubrick had a commitment to complete two more films for Warner Bros., and the company executives were keen to see a new project released soon. It is probable that the company, particularly under the leadership of Terry Semel, was pressuring Kubrick toward projects they believed to be more commercially viable. Harlan has suggested that it was Semel who told Kubrick to abandon *Aryan Papers*, perhaps aware of the problems of preproduction, and pursue *A.I.*[86] There may also have been increasing pressure from Michael Ovitz for Kubrick to work with his clients. Ovitz had apparently promised Tom Cruise, one of the most sought-after actors of the time, that he would arrange deals for him to work with Hollywood's leading directors, including Kubrick. And by August 1994, Cruise was in contact with Kubrick. The actor was, in his words, counting the days until he could finally work with Kubrick.[87]

Why *Full Metal Jacket* and *Eyes Wide Shut*?

The question that emerges most strongly in this final phase of Kubrick's career in the 1980s and 1990s is, amid so many unmade projects, why did he produce just *Full Metal Jacket* and *Eyes Wide Shut*? What were the conditions that led to their successful production? And were there wider industrial, artistic, or maybe even financial factors that allowed Kubrick to bring them to the screen successfully? If the logic is that Kubrick's failure rate was attributable to his overriding desire for control and information and a lack of decision making, especially on *A.I.* and *Aryan Papers*, then one could assume that the opposite was the case on *Full Metal Jacket* and *Eyes Wide Shut*. However, the latter project had arguably been in development for nearly forty years, while *Full Metal Jacket*'s gestation took around seven years. So there must have been other factors at play that allowed Kubrick to produce these two films from development through to release. It may simply be that they had better scripts. Though that can't explain why so many of Kubrick's unmade projects have since been picked up for supposed development by film producers, including a proposed HBO *Napoleon* miniseries. Arguably, however, some of these projects are essentially using the Kubrick name to promote what are reworked, potentially wholly original, projects. What follows is a brief look at these final two films to try to broaden out the production and industrial contexts that led to their release.

Full Metal Jacket as an idea began to emerge around 1980, when Kubrick first came into contact with author and journalist Michael Herr and expressed a desire to make a film about the Vietnam War.[88] Herr had written a journalistic account of the war in his book *Dispatches* (1977), which served as a partial inspiration for the film. Kubrick conducted research throughout the early 1980s to try to locate a novel that would serve as the foundation of the film, including consulting Robert Flanagan's *Maggot* (1971); the novel, marketed as being "a ruthlessly honest novel of marine corps basic training, where the recruit is not a man but a Maggot," tells the story of new Marine Corps recruits subjected to abuse by a drill instructor on Parris Island in a bid to reprogram them as brutal killers.[89] The story is remarkably similar to the first act of Gustav Hasford's novel *The Short*

Timers (1979), the book that was used as the primary adaptation source for *Full Metal Jacket*.

By 1983, Kubrick submitted a treatment of *Full Metal Jacket* to Warner Bros. as part of his pitch to the company. The treatment read very much like an action film, telling the story of Joker (Matthew Modine) as he is in inducted as a Marine and then leaves to serve in Vietnam. The story is intercut with flashbacks to Joker's childhood throughout. The film ends on a bleak note when Joker is killed, with Kubrick describing how he would shoot the scene: Joker is riddled with bullets by an unseen sniper and, intercut with scenes of his eight-year-old self falling in mock agony as he plays with a toy gun, the adult Joker crumples to the ground. The images slow down to a freeze frame, "something like Capa's famous Spanish Civil War photograph of a man who has just been fatally shot but who is forever suspended in mid-fall by the camera."[90] Kubrick was referring to Capa's *The Falling Soldier* (1936), which reputedly captured the moment of death of a soldier at the Battle of Cerro Muriano, though the photograph's authenticity has long been debated. The treatment ends with Joker's funeral and a priest reciting A. E. Houseman's poem "Epitaph on an Army of Mercenaries" (1917).

The sentiment of the treatment pitched to Warner Bros., and the references to Capa and to Housman, hinted at Kubrick's desire to produce a visually poetic film, one that would elicit emotion and affect in the audience; it seems, according to a study of the literary sources of *Full Metal Jacket* by Michele Pavan Deana, that Kubrick wanted to "tell a story through the raw material of cinema, which is not dialogues and concepts, but pictures and, most of all, the emotions conveyed by actors and felt by the viewers."[91] This idea of an affective war film was underscored by Kubrick in his own notes: "Use the Shadow idea poetically. Dramatise it. Don't explain it!"[92] The concept Kubrick was referring to, the Shadow, was a psychoanalytical theory proposed by Carl Jung wherein all humans have an unconscious, unknown side to their personality—a dark inner personality, deemed as undesirable, dangerous, even primeval. It was a concept that Kubrick wanted to utilize from the very beginning of his collaboration with Michael Herr.[93]

These ideas of a poetic war film, one based on the psychology of the human, seemed to hark back to Kubrick's first attempt at a feature film, *Fear and Desire*. Was it possible that with *Full Metal Jacket* Kubrick was attempting to remake the idea that had underpinned his first feature effort, a film that he had come to essentially disown? Seen against this context, Kubrick's desire to produce *Full Metal Jacket* can be viewed as an attempt to finally make the war film he had long envisaged as well as an attempt to exorcise the demons of what he considered his amateur effort of *Fear and Desire*. This would suggest that a key motivation in producing *Full Metal Jacket* was one of artistic reformation, a correcting of past failures. Kubrick was in a position of control by the 1980s that he did not have in the early 1950s, along with the support of a major media conglomerate, allowing him to revisit his ideas of a poetic war film in a precise and controlled context. It's also striking how Kubrick was reiterating in handwritten notes how films needed to be visual. This was almost a return in itself to his earliest days when he used to write notes about what made a good film, always returning to the need for visuals and action. *Full Metal Jacket* was almost a return to Kubrick's roots as a producer in the 1950s. Seen against this backdrop, it could be argued that *Full Metal Jacket*'s gestation began not in 1980 but as early as 1950 and maybe even earlier.

The treatment Kubrick pitched to Warner Bros. executives also resonated with the production contexts and even political climate of the era. Shortly after the film had been pitched, *Full Metal Jacket* was announced as Kubrick's next project for Warner Bros. in January 1984.[94] The announcement was quickly followed by a series of open call adverts for amateur actors to submit audition tapes as part of a nationwide search for talent to play the marine recruits. Whether the open-call audition was more of a publicity stunt than a serious attempt to locate new talent, it did create momentum behind *Full Metal Jacket*, seeing it overtake other Kubrick projects that were in development at that time. And as the project did not begin shooting until autumn 1985, it allowed for wider production contexts to become clear, including the success of action films and Vietnam-themed combat films at the box office, many of which were couched in the nationalistic ideology of the Ronald Reagan era: *First Blood* (Kotcheff, 1982), *Conan the Barbarian* (Milius, 1982), *Conan the Destroyer* (Fleischer, 1984), *Red Dawn* (Milius, 1984), *Missing in Action* (Zito, 1984), *Rambo: First Blood Part II* (Cosmatos, 1985), *Rocky IV* (Stallone, 1985), and *Commando* (Lester, 1985). Many of these films feature overt machismo both in story, themes, and in the very actors starring in them, primarily Arnold Schwarzenegger and Sylvester Stallone. The muscle-bound appearance of the era's two biggest action stars even worked its way into *Full Metal Jacket*, with a caricature of sorts in the character Animal Mother (Adam Baldwin), a machine-gun-wielding marine who "needs someone to throw hand grenades at him for the rest of his life."

In some respects then *Full Metal Jacket* was Kubrick's Stallone-Schwarzenegger-Norris action film. And while Kubrick may have been satirizing the production cycles of the time, *Full Metal Jacket* also played to recognizable and marketable tropes. While Warner Bros. executives did not expect Kubrick to produce a *Rambo*-style picture, the project did provide the company with an exploitable angle. From renaming the film as *Full Metal Jacket*, with its overtones of masculinity and action, to making the phrase "Born to Kill" prominent on posters and utilizing a tie-in rap single, "I Wanna Be Your Drill Instructor," the promotion of *Full Metal Jacket* was one of the most straightforward of Kubrick's career. But it still wasn't the commercial blockbuster hit that perhaps Kubrick had hoped for. Kubrick realized how *Full Metal Jacket* was in competition with Oliver Stone's rival Vietnam War film *Platoon* (1986) and was eager to see a reissue of Hasford's *The Short Timers* in early 1987 "to exploit the interest in *Platoon*."[95] By 1988, the film had North American domestic rentals of $23 million, while *Platoon* had rentals of close to $70 million.[96] Without international rentals, which by 1988 were at $40 million, *Full Metal Jacket* would not have recouped its budget and marketing costs.[97] The kind of success that Kubrick was wanting to achieve—the Spielberg/Lucas levels of box office gross—were once again elusive.

The desire for box office success may have contributed to Kubrick's indecisiveness about what to produce for the second of his new three-picture contract with Warner Bros. By the early 1990s, Terry Semel was publicly admitting that there were other producers he favored more than Kubrick, most prominently Clint Eastwood. In an interview with Peter Biskind, Semel remarked that Eastwood was "the best producer I've ever worked with. He is more careful with our money than he is with his own."[98] Semel also revealed how Eastwood, who had creative and business autonomy over his films, had an arrangement whereby for every "personal" film he produced—less commercial fare such as *Honkytonk Man* (1982), *Bird* (1988), or *White Hunter Black Heart* (1990)—he would produce and direct a more box-office-orientated project.[99] Semel's preference was also probably borne out of a corporate responsibility to Warner Communications' shareholders. Power was increasingly concentrated in "banks and interlocking boards of directors" by the 1980s, who consolidated their political and economic ownership of companies like Warner Communications.[100] Responsible to these shareholders, and even influenced by them, Semel would have been required to advise his producers like Eastwood, and even Kubrick, on the profit potential of planned projects.

So did *Eyes Wide Shut* emerge out of an arrangement similar to that of Eastwood's? Possibly. It could well have been that, in return for producing and directing a more commercially orientated project, Kubrick expected to produce a personal film: *Eyes Wide Shut* was arguably his *most* personal film. Or it could have been that Kubrick was facing increasing pressure from Semel, who needed him to fulfill his three-picture contract. Or, more than likely, Kubrick realized that he had reached a point in his career where he had very few films left in him and that if he was ever to realize an adaptation of *Traumnovelle*, a book that had preoccupied him for over fifty years, it was now or never.

Michael Herr suggested that Kubrick had first read Schnitzler's *Traumnovelle* sometime in the mid-1950s. Kubrick had been in contact with Peter Schnitzler, grandson of Arthur, in 1959 when he had invited him to the set of *Spartacus*. The pair had apparently discussed adapting one of Schnitzler's novels, with Peter offering Kubrick the use of his grandfather's notebooks.[101] Robert Kolker and Nathan Abrams speculate that Kubrick may have even found a copy of the book in his father's library as a teenager.[102] However, what is perhaps more important to consider are Kubrick's repeated attempts to produce a film about sexual relationships. As discussed in part II of this book, Kubrick was attempting to develop projects based on such themes around the time of the incorporation of Harris-Kubrick Pictures through about 1957. Indeed, it's arguable that *Jealousy*, Kubrick's story of sexual fantasy and marital infidelity, was an early attempt at an adaptation of *Traumnovelle* (see chapter 4). The story is very close to that of *Traumnovelle*, with the main character, John Conrad, suffering visions of his wife's sexual encounters and contemplating revenge by sleeping with a stranger, something he is unable to go through with. *Jealousy* was even set in New York, just like *Eyes Wide Shut*. This correlates with how Kubrick had admitted to Anthony Burgess in 1986 that he had longed envisaged any adaptation of *Traumnovelle* to be set in a contemporary urban location.[103]

The idea for adapting *Traumnovelle* was repeatedly considered by Kubrick throughout the 1970s and 1980s. It was even announced as a potential project, titled *Rhapsody* (the title of the English translation of Schnitzler's novel), as part of his first three-picture contract with Warner Bros. in 1971.[104] This came at a time when Kubrick had been linked to a film about the porn industry, suggested by Terry Southern. Southern developed the idea into a novel, *Blue Movie* (1970), dedicated to "the great Stanley K." The novel was published a year after Andy Warhol's *Blue Movie* (1969), a film that featured explicit sex scenes and received a mainstream release and that precipitated a cycle of pornographic films. Most notable was *Deep Throat* (Damiano, 1972), which by 1973 had grossed over $3 million at the U.S. box office.[105] So successful was *Deep Throat* that it instigated the era of "porn chic," a period of mainstream, international success for pornographic films "when suddenly it was fashionable to stand in line at X-rated theatres" and new audiences were attending porn films who previously would not have considered doing so.[106] It is not unreasonable to suggest that Kubrick, a producer attuned to industrial and production contexts, wanted to take advantage of this porn chic wave; he apparently remarked to a French journalist that *Rhapsody* would be a "big-budget, big-cast porn film."[107] But *Rhapsody* did not come to be at that time, Kubrick perhaps warned off such an explicit genre by executives at Warner Bros. (and, some suggest, his wife, Christiane).[108]

But the idea for *Rhapsody* resurfaced once again following the release of *Barry Lyndon*. He had requested Gaby Blau, daughter of his lawyer Louis Blau, to write a concept for the story in 1976, this time set in London. Kubrick, however, was not convinced of her approach, deeming it a "very clever try," but passing on it.[109] The book remained on Kubrick's mind, reworking it in 1979 as a story about a porn film actress. One handwritten note by Kubrick suggested an adaptation that would feature a girl as a porn actress and that the main character of Bill, on discovering that she is starring in Mafia-financed porn films, is excited, believing he has found "the ultimate happiness." But the twist in the story is that the girl confesses that she wants to marry Bill, to have a family, and to make him a good wife.[110] The development of *Rhapsody* by the late 1970s and early 1980s seems to have veered toward the emerging genre of the erotic thriller, what Linda Ruth Williams describes as a "sexed-up formation of neo-noir [that] takes its cue from the sometimes transgressive sexuality of film noir proper . . . the genre also trades on the post-1970s development of softcore cinema."[111] While Williams attributes the genre starting proper with *Body Heat* (Kasdan, 1981) and *The Postman Always Rings Twice* (Rafelson, 1981), there had been earlier developments building toward these, including William Friedkin's *Cruising* (1980) and Paul Schrader's *American Gigolo* (1980) and *Hardcore* (1979). It was the latter film that Kubrick's reworked *Rhapsody* most closely matched, with its focus on the descent of a respectable businessman into the seedy underworld of the porn industry.

Kubrick seemed to be making concerted efforts to produce *Rhapsody* as a marketable film that would fit within wider production cycles and box office trends, perhaps in a bid to make it palatable to Warner Bros. Along with Anthony Frewin, Kubrick devised suggested promotional copy for *Rhapsody* in 1981—perhaps somewhat in jest—including tag lines such as "RHAPSODY—She had him, he had her, and together they had . . . her porno past"; "RHAPSODY—The film that asks the eternal question: 'that wasn't you in that adult video . . . uh, was it?'"; "RHAPSODY—she gave everything to him and to 20 million adult film viewers across the nation"; "Get it on with RHAPSODY, a film to come to grips with"; and "RHAPSODY—A tumescent love story of our time."[112]

Kubrick's renewed interest in *Rhapsody* in the early 1980s came at a time when he once again initiated contact with Peter Schnitzler, who was sending him research about *Traumnovelle* located in Vienna.[113] He also began obtaining as many reader reports as possible on the book, commencing in 1981 and running through until the early 1990s, with Empyrean's readers frequently being asked to consider the book.[114] Kubrick's repeated, almost obsessive request for reader reports seems to have been an attempt to solve narrative issues, specifically what he saw as being the ambiguities of the scenes at the orgy and also what he believed to be the "unrealistic" nature of the wife's confession of her sexual fantasies.[115] Kubrick also wanted to make the story more conspiratorial, with themes of power, particularly in relation to the orgy. In one notebook from 1989 he considered linking the film to ideas of Ted Kennedy;[116] the senator and presidential hopeful was involved in a car accident in 1969, what became known as the "Chappaquiddick incident," resulting in the death of the only other passenger, Mary Jo Kopechne. Kennedy fled the scene, leaving Kopechne trapped in the car to die and reporting the incident only over twenty-four hours later. The media immediately speculated about the relationship between Kennedy and Kopechne, making the link between Chappaquiddick and *Rhapsody* clear: the death of a woman at the hands of a powerful man in suspicious circumstances. This would become a central component of the eventual *Eyes Wide Shut*, in which Bill (Tom Cruise) believes a woman at the orgy he attends has been murdered and attempts to find out the truth.

The way in which Kubrick's adaptation of *Traumnovelle* was developing, in collaboration with author Frederic Raphael in the early 1990s, was within the wider political and social contexts of the United States. There was a growing list of sexual scandals in the country, with a media climate looking to expose politicians following the extramarital scandal that had ruined the presidential election chances of Democratic senator Gary Hart in 1988. Further scandals soon emerged, including a Hollywood prostitution ring run by Heidi Fleiss, who apparently was in possession of a "black book" that implicated some of the most powerful figures in Hollywood. In many respects, this was a context that was an extension of the erotic thriller but moving it into areas of power and fame and that was being explored in other films of the era, most notably *Basic Instinct* (Verhoeven, 1992). It is possible that Kubrick pitched the project in these terms to Warner Bros., and while *Eyes Wide Shut* was a much more earnest reflection of love, marriage, and sexual desire, it certainly wasn't promoted as such. Warner Bros. was adamant in developing a marketing campaign that reflected the star appeal of Tom Cruise and Nicole Kidman in what they termed "the erotic thriller from the legendary film director Stanley Kubrick."[117]

Conclusion

The later stages of Kubrick's career were marked by failure: *Napoleon*, *A.I.*, *Aryan Papers*, and others besides were left unmade. And while he certainly had other unmade projects to his name throughout his career, these projects were given serious consideration and even entered preproduction. Instead, their failure was largely a result of Kubrick's own control and micromanagement and the need for every available outcome to be presented to him before he could make a decision. This led to a marked decline, in terms of both Kubrick's output and his ability to even produce or direct anymore. Kubrick was clearly aware there was a problem and therefore gave thought to abdicating one aspect of his role, the responsibility of directing, and acting merely as a producer on *A.I.* and *Aryan Papers*.

The two films that were made during the last decade of his life, *Full Metal Jacket* and *Eyes Wide Shut*, were essentially legacy projects for Kubrick, by which I mean these were projects he wanted to produce for many years in one form or another. *Full Metal Jacket* was arguably a reworking of the war film he had wanted to make in 1950 and was perhaps a means of erasing the amateur efforts of *Fear and Desire*. As for *Eyes Wide Shut*, it was a film that he had long desired to produce and, perhaps sensing he had only one film left in him, finally entered production in the mid-1990s. It was also Kubrick's most personal film; maybe there was no real production context for the film but instead an artistic and intellectual obsession that needed to be realized. Upon seeing the final cut, Kubrick is reputed to have remarked that it was his best film. And in seeing it through to successful completion, Kubrick seems to have been relieved of an enormous burden. Just a week after screening the film for Terry Semel, Tom Cruise, and Nicole Kidman, Kubrick passed away in his sleep on March 7, 1999. *Eyes Wide Shut* was released posthumously.

Epilogue

This book is the culmination of my decade-long research on Stanley Kubrick. It brings together my thoughts, ideas, and feelings, but even after so long it still isn't complete. Despite having mined the Stanley Kubrick Archive and many other archives around the world, I've barely scratched the surface. But I came to the realization in early 2018 that I had to let go. Researching Kubrick had become an obsession. I needed to plough through ever more boxes, ever more archival material, all in the hope of finding the holy grail that would explain whom he was as an individual and the one document that would explain his rise and fall as a producer. I've never found it. And I never will. For while as a media historian I have the hindsight of tracing the evolution of a filmmaker, the truth is that Kubrick's life and career—like any life and career—was filled with halts, frustrations, twists, and turns. Kubrick had no grand plan, as such, but rather ambitions and intellectual motivations, all the while being influenced, shaped, and disrupted by wider structural forces of industrial, cultural, and political logic. Left behind in archives are the remnants of one producer's encounters with the capitalist forces of the American film industry.

If there was one document that I wish I could find, it would be the first three-picture contract between Kubrick and Warner Bros. from 1970. There are allusions and references to it in correspondence and other documents cited in this book, but the actual document itself is sealed away due to client-attorney privilege, along with much of the other legal documentation that was presided over by Kubrick's lawyer, Louis C. Blau. There are the phone calls too, of course; like any good producer, Kubrick conducted most of his business over the phone in the age before the internet, keeping his colleagues in conversation long into the night. Verbal deals, ideas, disagreements, inspiration, despair, all conveyed through the telephone. But the conversations are now merely fading memories of his still living friends, family members, and colleagues, leaving a large gap in our understanding of how Kubrick produced his films.

So where does this book leave Kubrick studies? Does it make any grand intervention? Will it advance understanding and debates, not only about Kubrick but concerning wider issues of power and control in the American film industry? I hope so, however incremental; otherwise I've failed. Its central argument—the rise and fall of Stanley Kubrick, brought about by crippling levels of control that he long sought to obtain—is controversial, no doubt. But the empirical research and the tracing of Kubrick's career alongside the industrial transformations of Hollywood indicate heavily that this was the case. The research conducted and the conclusions reached seek to disrupt the still dominant auteur myths—what one prominent Kubrick colleague of mine (who will remain nameless) has referred to as "this auteur bullshit"—that elevate Kubrick to the status of, to quote the title of Joseph Gelmis's book, "film director as superstar."[1] The problem with the auteur myth that surrounds Kubrick is how it can cloud our judgment of the practical realities of industry and perhaps even of Kubrick himself. I would suggest what research now needs to address is the "problem" with Kubrick, by which I mean his troubling practices as a producer, particularly his attitudes toward unionized labor. When making my own tentative inquiries about this subject with his friends and colleagues, the response has always been that he was creating "art," as if this somehow exempts someone (however great the films they produce may be) from rules around exploitation of workers and working hours. His correspondence with Robert O'Brien, for example, suggests Kubrick was seeking ways to extricate his productions from newly introduced union agreements and even blaming unions for the rapid increase in *2001: A Space Odyssey*'s budget. And what of Kubrick's lobbying of political parties in the 1970s? His attempts at intervening in new tax policies are disconcerting and speak to wider issues of private power and control among the country's elite. Kubrick, whatever his humble beginnings, was very much a part of the "elite" in the United Kingdom by the mid-1970s, which provided him with exceptional privilege and unprecedented levels of access and influence.

In many ways, this epilogue is my own coda as a researcher in Kubrick studies. My attention is turning elsewhere, not out of any rejection of Kubrick—I continue to love his work, and I am fascinated by the scholarly discourse that continues apace, to which I hope to contribute further—but because of questions this book itself has raised. Prominent among them, and obvious in the last chapter, is the question of the cultural and industrial logic of failure. Some may read the final chapter as a slight against Kubrick, suggesting he himself was a failure. But rather, it should be seen within the context of creative failure as a key characteristic of the media industries more broadly, with Kubrick presenting a fascinating case study on the topic. The litany of unmade films across his career, some even coming close to fruition (*Aryan Papers* chief among them), speak of a shadow history of his career: the Kubrick films—the Kubrick filmography—that might have been. It holds a fascinating grip over his fans' imaginations, with mock-up posters of *Napoleon*, *Aryan Papers*, and other projects appearing online, while any mention of supposed "lost" projects found among his papers generates considerable media attention. This interest is probably a result of a combination of a lack of Kubrick films generally, alongside the feverish social media afterlife Kubrick now has, with numerous fan groups, forums, and even official Instagram, Facebook, and Twitter accounts. The number of unmade Kubrick projects also raises questions as to *why* he didn't make them. But as a producer Kubrick was not unique in this regard, but more typical. Just ordinary. Peter Krämer first raised this issue in an article on *A.I. Artificial Intelligence*:

> While Kubrick was an extreme case of a filmmaker working on many projects that were never realised and radically reworking—during the story development process and later—those projects that he did turn into films, a more moderate version of this approach is characteristic of the American film industry as a whole (and the situation is likely to be similar in other countries). Indeed, unrealised film projects, as well as development trajectories which did not contribute a lot, or anything, to the films that were completed, have absorbed much of the creativity and a substantial portion of the financial investments of the American film industry.[2]

This "shadow cinema" raises the tantalizing prospect of the Hollywood that might have been.[3] But more important, the scale of unmade films and the lack of scholarly attention they have received suggest that the history, and thereby our understanding, of the American, British, and other film and television industries has barely been realized. And if a producer like Stanley Kubrick, with the control he wanted and achieved, had the amount of failures that he did, just what does it say about the industrial structures of the film industry as a whole?

This book set out to understand the issue of control, situating it within Kubrick's role as a producer. It traced his emergence as a producer, the ways in which he cemented his power base, and the detrimental impact that the control he wanted ultimately had on his business and creative processes. The implications for Kubrick studies are of some significance. But the book also shows that Kubrick was more than just an artist; he was a pragmatic businessman and producer who could adapt and change to ensure his longevity within a profit-orientated industry. If he hadn't been, he wouldn't have succeeded. Indeed, more than once his career came perilously close to a premature end. I would suggest that Kubrick's success was down to his ambition for control. And at the same time, it was control that brought about Kubrick's decline.

Appendix A
World Assembly of Youth Credits

●●●●●●●●●●●●●●●●●●●●

Title: *A Report on the First Triennial General Assembly of World Assembly of Youth at Cornell University, Ithaca, N.Y.*

Produced by News of the Day for World Assembly of Youth, Richard de Rochemont

Running time: 33 minutes and 28 seconds

Directors: D. Corbit Curtis and Richard Millett

Producer: Richard de Rochemont

Camera: George Stoetzel and George Hinners, with Rody Green, Leo Rossi, and T. Rickman

Sound: Anthony Girolami, with Fred Fenton and Abe Landau

Chief Electrician: Alfred Shaw

Editors: Lawrence Sherman, Gene Milford, and Robert Collison

Assistant Directors: H. O. Keith Ayling, Robert Daly, Sam Locke

The film received the approval of the Department of State on February 15, 1952.

Appendix B

Filmography

Flying Padre (1951), documentary
Produced by Burton Benjamin, Stanley Kubrick (uncredited)
Directed by Stanley Kubrick
Distributed by RKO-Pathé

Day of the Fight (1951), documentary
Produced by Jay Bonafield, Stanley Kubrick (uncredited)
Directed by Stanley Kubrick
Assistant Director Alex Singer
Distributed by RKO-Pathé

Mr. Lincoln (1952–1953), TV docudrama
Episode 1, "End of the Beginning"
Produced by Richard de Rochemont
Directed by Norman Lloyd
Second Unit Director Stanley Kubrick
Air date, November 16, 1952, CBS
Distributed by CBS

World Assembly of Youth (1952–1953), documentary
Produced by Richard de Rochemont
Directed by D. Corbit Curtis and Richard Millett
Stanley Kubrick's role unknown—stills photographer?
Distributed by News of the Day

Fear and Desire (1953)
Produced by Martin Perveler and Stanley Kubrick
Directed by Stanley Kubrick
Written by Howard Sackler

Distributed by Joseph Burstyn Inc.

The Seafarers (1953), documentary
Produced by Lester Cooper
Directed by Stanley Kubrick
Production company: Lester Cooper Productions
Distributed by the Seafarers' International Union

Shark Safari (ca. 1953)
Produced by James Atlee Phillips?
Directed by unknown
Release date unknown
Stanley Kubrick's role—dubbing assistant?

Killer's Kiss (1955)
Produced by Stanley Kubrick and Morris Bousel
Directed by Stanley Kubrick
Written by Howard Sackler
Production company: Minotaur Productions
Distributed by United Artists

The Killing (1956)
Produced by James B. Harris
Directed by Stanley Kubrick
Written by Stanley Kubrick, with additional dialogue by Jim Thompson
Production company: Harris-Kubrick Pictures Corporation
Distributed by United Artists

Paths of Glory (1957)
Produced by James B. Harris
Directed by Stanley Kubrick
Written by Stanley Kubrick, Calder Willingham, Jim Thompson
Production companies: Harris-Kubrick Pictures Corporation, Bryna Productions
Distributed by United Artists

Ilya Muromets / The Sword and the Dragon (1959)
Produced by Damir Vyatich-Berezhnykh, Joseph Harris, and Sig Shore
   (U.S. version)

Directed by Aleksandr Ptushko
Written by Mikhail Kochnev
Dubbing editing by Harris-Kubrick Pictures
Dubbing director James Landis
U.S. dubbed theatrical distributor: Valiant Films (1960)

Spartacus (1960)
Produced by Edward Lewis
Executive producer Kirk Douglas
Directed by Stanley Kubrick
Written by Dalton Trumbo
Production company: Bryna Productions
Distributed by Universal-International

Lolita (1962)
Produced by James B. Harris
Executive producer Eliot Hyman (uncredited)
Directed by Stanley Kubrick
Written by Vladimir Nabokov, James B. Harris, and Stanley Kubrick (uncredited)
Production companies: Harris-Kubrick Pictures Corporation, Seven Arts Productions, A.A. Productions, Transworld Pictures
Distributed by MGM

Dr. Strangelove, or How I Learned to Stop Worrying and Love the Bomb (1964)
Produced by Stanley Kubrick
Directed by Stanley Kubrick
Associate producer Victor Lyndon
Written by Stanley Kubrick, Terry Southern, Peter George
Production companies: Hawk Films and Polaris Productions
Distributed by Columbia

2001: A Space Odyssey (1968)
Produced by Stanley Kubrick
Directed by Stanley Kubrick
Associate producer Victor Lyndon
Written by Stanley Kubrick and Arthur C. Clarke
Production companies: Hawk Films and Polaris Productions
Distributed by MGM

A Clockwork Orange (1971)
Produced by Stanley Kubrick
Executive producers Si Litvinoff and Max Raab
Directed by Stanley Kubrick

Associate producer Bernard Williams
Written by Stanley Kubrick
Production companies: Hawk Films, Polaris Productions, Max L. Raab Productions, Si Litvinoff Film Productions
Distributed by Warner Bros. A Kinney Company

Barry Lyndon (1975)
Produced by Stanley Kubrick
Executive producer Jan Harlan
Directed by Stanley Kubrick
Associate producer Bernard Williams
Written by Stanley Kubrick
Production companies: Hawk Films, Peregrine
Distributed by Warner Bros.

The Shining (1980)
Produced by Stanley Kubrick
Executive producer Jan Harlan
Produced in association with the Producer Circle Company (Robert Fryer, Martin Richards, Mary Lea Johnson)
Directed by Stanley Kubrick
Written by Stanley Kubrick and Diane Johnson
Production companies: Hawk Films, Peregrine
Distributed by Warner Bros.

Full Metal Jacket (1987)
Produced by Stanley Kubrick
Coproducer Philip Hobbs
Executive producer Jan Harlan
Directed by Stanley Kubrick
Associate producer Michael Herr
Written by Stanley Kubrick, Michael Herr, Gustav Hasford
Production companies: Hawk Films, Natant
Distributed by Warner Bros.

Eyes Wide Shut (1999)
Produced by Stanley Kubrick
Executive producer Jan Harlan
Coproducer Brian Cook
Directed by Stanley Kubrick
Written by Stanley Kubrick and Frederic Raphael
Production companies: Hobby Films, Pole Star
Distributed by Warner Bros.

Acknowledgments

It's been a long journey for me in writing this book. I've spent over a decade of my life researching Kubrick and nearly two decades enthralled by his films. He has pervaded my existence for all that time, becoming almost an invisible friend. I've gotten to know him as I've sifted through boxes of his correspondence, or visited his family in St. Albans, or interviewed his closest colleagues. And the Kubrick I have grown to know was a man possessed by his work, dedicated to producing films that stimulated his intellect and reflected his philosophical and artistic passions. But of course the Kubrick I have grown to know is just one aspect of who he was; it is an identity that I have reconstructed from dusty archive boxes that can never represent the full history, personality, and complexity of who Stanley Kubrick was. I leave that to the biographers. And to his closest friends and family.

In researching and writing this book, I have developed many contacts across the globe, all of whom I am indebted to for their advice, feedback, and collaboration. Many people are perhaps not even aware of their invaluable contribution through off-the-cuff conversations at conferences or over a pint at the local pub. I endeavor to thank those people now.

First and foremost, I should thank Ian Hunter, my PhD supervisor and later my colleague. Ian has provided me with many valuable insights, tips, and suggestions along the way as well as even coming up with the title for this book. Ian has been a collaborator on many Kubrick ventures: we co-organized the conference "Stanley Kubrick: A Retrospective" held at De Montfort University in May 2016, which served as a catalyst for the Kubrick studies community that has since emerged. We also co-curated the exhibition "Stanley Kubrick: Cult Auteur," which was hosted at the Heritage Centre in Leicester from May to June 2016. And together we delivered the undergraduate module "Filmmakers: Stanley Kubrick" at De Montfort University for three years. Second, I wish to single out Peter Krämer, still the guru of Kubrick studies and a man who, however frustratingly, is always right! Peter has been instrumental in guiding my research and challenging my ideas. I know I am not alone in the field of film and media studies in owing a debt of gratitude to Peter.

I would like to also thank Nathan Abrams, Mick Broderick, Kate McQuiston, and Elisa Pezzotta, with whom I served as a co-organizer of the five-day international workshop "Life and Legacy, Studying the Work of Stanley Kubrick" (University of Leiden, July 15–19, 2019). Many collaborations have since emerged from those stimulating, exciting (and, yes, exhausting) five days. One moment sticks out: Dijana Metlic, whether she realizes it or not, offered me a nugget of advice that provided me the motivation I needed to finish this book. Thank you, Dijana. I am also thankful to the Nias-Lorentz Center in the Netherlands for providing the funding to facilitate "Life and Legacy."

I would like to thank Matt Melia for the feedback, insightful conversations, and many pints in London and other Kubrick adventures over the past few years. I am also indebted to the kindness of Filippo Ulivieri and Simone Odino, two of the finest Kubrick experts on the planet. They have patiently listened to and read my work over the last few years and, more important, have inspired me with their wisdom and expertise.

I also must thank the artist Matthew Needle for designing and providing the striking cover art for this book. Matthew's artwork is about creating alternative posters of classic Hollywood films (or what he calls pop-culture-inspired prints). If you haven't done so already, I would urge you to visit his website: needledesign.bigcartel.com.

Others who have provided me with support, guidance, insights, advice, interviews, assistance, and help have included Jan Harlan, James B. Harris, Gerald Fried, Anthony Frewin, Julian Senior, Joy Cuff, Chris "Fangorn" Baker, the Brian Aldiss family, Richard Daniels, Sara Mahurter, Georgina Orgill, the assistants who have worked at the Stanley Kubrick Archive over the past decade, Nash Sibanda, Cassie Brummitt, Kieran Foster, Laura Mee, Robert Kolker, Jim Russell, Vincent LoBrutto, Philippe Mather, John R. Waggener, who digitized the film *World Assembly of Youth*, the archive team at the American Heritage Center, University of Wyoming, the archive team at the Social Welfare History Archives, University of Minnesota, and Mary Huelsbeck of the Wisconsin Center for Film and Theater Research.

I want to thank the teams at Rutgers University Press and Westchester Publishing Services, including Nicole Solano, Vincent Nordhaus, Mary Ribesky, and Joseph Dahm. Their support has been invaluable in the production of this book.

The research for this book was made possible with funding provided by the European Association for American Studies.

Notes

Abbreviations

AHC	American Heritage Center, University of Wyoming
BAA	Brian Aldiss Archive, University of Liverpool
BFP	Bryan Forbes Papers, Margaret Herrick Library, Los Angeles
HPP	Harold Pinter Papers, British Library
JBH	James B. Harris Archive, private, Los Angeles
KDP	Kirk Douglas Papers, Wisconsin Center for Film and Theater Research
MHL	Margaret Herrick Library, Los Angeles
RDP	Richard De Rochemont Papers, University of Wyoming
SHA	Social Welfare History Archives, University of Minnesota
SKA	The Stanley Kubrick Archive, University of the Arts London
TNA	The National Archives, Kew Gardens

Introduction

1. See, among others, Michael Benson, *Space Odyssey: Stanley Kubrick, Arthur C. Clarke, and the Making of a Masterpiece* (New York: Simon & Schuster, 2019); Piers Bizony, *The Making of Stanley Kubrick's 2001: A Space Odyssey* (Cologne: Taschen, 2015); Alison Castle, *The Stanley Kubrick Archives* (Cologne: Taschen, 2008); and Filippo Ulivieri and Simone Odino, *2001 tra Kubrick e Clarke: Genesi, realizzazione e paternità di un capolavoro* (self-pub., Amazon, 2019).
2. "Dr. Mabuse No. 2: Kubrick's Mythological Image" (Kubrick Symposium, Deutsches Filmmuseum, July 21, 2018), www.youtube.com/watch?v=JzApr1Y74WA.
3. Derek Malcolm, "The Genius Who Outdid Hollywood," *Guardian*, March 8, 1999, 3.
4. Jonathan Romney, "The Eyes Still Have It," *Guardian*, March 12, 1999, A20.
5. Ronald Bergan, "Visions of Heaven and Hell," *Guardian*, March 8, 1999, 15.
6. Janet Maslin, "A Visionary, a Mind-Blower, Kubrick Never Failed to Stun," *New York Times*, March 14, 1999, AR30.
7. Romney, "Eyes Still Have It," A20.

8   "The Producer," *Observer*, March 14, 1999, F6.
9   The "decentring of Kubrick" was a phrase coined by Peter Krämer in his position paper "Marketing and Audiences" at the Life and Legacy, Studying the Work of Stanley Kubrick workshop, University of Leiden, July 15–19, 2019.
10 The Stanley Kubrick Archive is composed of boxes of varying volumes, each holding a range of documents and other artefacts. The original archive, deposited in 2007, takes up 800 linear meters of shelving. But this has probably expanded to around 900 linear meters after a further 100 boxes were recently donated. Estimates suggest there are around 36,000 boxes in the Stanley Kubrick Archive.
11 See Andrew Spicer, Anthony McKenna, and Christopher Meir, eds., *Beyond the Bottom Line: The Producer in Film and Television Studies* (New York: Bloomsbury, 2014).
12 Jon Lewis, ed., *Producing* (New Brunswick, NJ: Rutgers University Press, 2016), 1.

Chapter 1. The Beginning, 1928–1951

1   Gerald Fried, telephone interview, July 13, 2019.
2   Gary Hermalyn and Lloyd Ultan, "The Bronx," 2017, http://bronxhistoricalsociety.org/about/bronx-history/the-story-of-the-bronx/.
3   "Stanley Kubrick, at a Distance," *Washington Post*, June 28, 1987, F1.
4   Ibid., F5.
5   Philippe Mather, *Stanley Kubrick at Look Magazine* (Bristol: Intellect, 2013), 15–16.
6   Thomas Pryor, "Young Man with Ideas and a Camera," *New York Times*, January 14, 1951, X5.
7   Ibid.
8   Letter from Helen O'Brian to Stanley Kubrick, October 17, 1944, Wallet J, uncatalogued, SKA.
9   Ibid.
10 Mather, *Stanley Kubrick at Look Magazine*, 27.
11 Philippe Mather, "Stanley Kubrick and *Look* Magazine," in *Stanley Kubrick: Essays on His Life and Legacy*, ed. Gary Rhodes (Jefferson, NC: McFarland, 2008), 12.
12 Ibid.
13 Mather, *Stanley Kubrick at Look Magazine*, 21.
14 Letter from Henry to Stanley Kubrick, July 21, 1950, Wallet J, uncatalogued, SKA.
15 "Stanley Kubrick for *Look* Magazine," 2012, Library of Congress, https://www.loc.gov/rr/print/res/378_kubr.html.
16 Mather, "Stanley Kubrick," 11.
17 Mather, *Stanley Kubrick at Look Magazine*, 27.
18 Peter Krämer, "The Limits of Autonomy: Stanley Kubrick, Hollywood and Independent Filmmaking, 1950–53," in *American Independent Cinema*, ed. Geoff King, Claire Molloy, and Yannis Tzioumakis (London: Routledge, 2013), 157.
19 Henry to Kubrick, 1950, SKA.
20 Joseph Gelmis, *The Film Director as Superstar* (1970; repr., London: Pelican Books, 1974), 46.
21 Details of Kubrick's salary provided by Philippe Mather, email correspondence with author, July 22, 2019.
22 Jeremy Bernstein, "Projected Greatness," *Royal Photographic Journal* (September 2006 [1966]): 314–317.
23 Letter from Rex Carlton to Stanley Kubrick, August 8, 1950, Wallet J, uncatalogued, SKA.

24 "Chemical Bank (N.Y.) Freer Bankrolling," *Variety*, September 28, 1949, 15.
25 Ibid., 5.
26 Carlton to Kubrick, 1950, SKA.
27 Ibid.
28 "Judgment vs. Carlton for $55,800 on Pix Loan," *Variety*, August 1, 1951, 7.
29 "New Coin Hypos Indie Prod. 25%," *Variety*, September 28, 1949, 5.
30 James Naremore, "No Other Country but the Mind," *Masters of Cinema* pamphlet, *Fear and Desire* (DVD, 2013), 5–27.
31 R. M. Barsam, "'This Is America': Documentaries for Theaters, 1942–1951," *Cinema Journal* 12, no. 2 (1973): 22.
32 Ibid., 23.
33 Mather, *Stanley Kubrick at Look Magazine*, 247.
34 Stanley Kubrick, "Prizefighter," *Look*, January 18, 1949, 61–67.
35 Story outline and storyboard, *Day of the Fight*, Wallet K, uncatalogued, SKA.
36 Shooting breakdown, *Day of the Fight*, Wallet K, uncatalogued, SKA.
37 Rough action outline, *Day of the Fight*, Wallet K, uncatalogued, SKA.
38 *Day of the Fight* expenses, 1951, Wallet J, uncatalogued, SKA.
39 Letter from Thomas Orchard to Stanley Kubrick, August 31, 1950, Wallet J, uncatalogued, SKA.
40 Ibid.
41 Ibid.
42 "De Rochemont Signs Columbia Deal," *Boxoffice*, January 14, 1950, 14.
43 "March of Time Folds," *Variety*, July 11, 1951, 4.
44 Orchard to Kubrick, 1950, SKA.
45 "The Tattooed Stranger," American Film Institute, https://catalog.afi.com/Catalog/moviedetails/26519.
46 "Filmmaking in East Seen Hypoed by RKO-Pathe," *Variety*, July 19, 1950, 7.
47 "RKO Pathé to Produce 2 Features Annually," *Variety*, September 27, 1950, 5.
48 *Day of the Fight* expenses, 1951, SKA.
49 Krämer, "Limits of Autonomy," 156–157.
50 Fried, telephone interview.
51 The version of *Day of the Fight* held at the Library of Congress runs to sixteen minutes.
52 Barsam, "'This Is America,'" 24–27.
53 Letter from Fred Stadtmueller to Stanley Kubrick, October 3, 1950, Wallet J, uncatalogued, SKA.
54 RKO-Pathé and Stanley Kubrick agreement, October 5, 1950, Wallet J, uncatalogued, SKA.
55 Mather, *Stanley Kubrick at Look Magazine*, 247.
56 RKO-Pathé and Kubrick, 1950, SKA.
57 Letter from Stanley Kubrick to Camera Equipment Company, October 19, 1950, Wallet J, uncatalogued, SKA.
58 Fred Stadtmueller and Stanley Kubrick, October, 1950, Wallet J, uncatalogued, SKA.
59 Letter from Fred Stadtmueller to Stanley Kubrick, January 20, 1951, Wallet J, uncatalogued, SKA.
60 Letter from Fred Stadtmueller to Jay Bonafield, January 20, 1951, Wallet J, uncatalogued, SKA.
61 *Flying Padre* budget breakdown, Wallet J, uncatalogued, SKA.
62 Invoice from RKO-Pathé to Stanley Kubrick, November 22, 1950, Wallet J, uncatalogued, SKA.

63 "Flying Padre," *Boxoffice*, May 5, 1951, B14.
64 Pryor, "Young Man," X5.
65 Ibid., X5.
66 Ibid., X5.
67 Vincent LoBrutto, "The Written Word and the Very Visual Stanley Kubrick," in *Depth of Field: Stanley Kubrick, Film, and the Uses of History*, ed. Geoffrey Cocks, James Diedrick, and Glenn Perusek (Madison: University of Wisconsin Press, 2006), 31.

Chapter 2. The Unknown Early Years, 1951–1953

1 James Naremore, "No Other Country but the Mind," *Masters of Cinema* pamphlet, *Fear and Desire* (DVD, 2013), 7.
2 Prior to graduating from Howard Taft, Kubrick was taught by Herman Getter, a painter and avant-garde filmmaker who would screen his art films for Kubrick and Alexander Singer.
3 Gerald Fried, telephone interview, July 13, 2019.
4 Mick Broderick, "Kubrick on Screen," in *The Kubrick Legacy*, ed. Mick Broderick (London: Routledge Focus, 2019), 100.
5 Richard Suchenski, "Hans Richter," *Senses of Cinema*, no. 49 (February 2009), http://sensesofcinema.com/2009/great-directors/hans-richter/; Laura Marcus, "Introduction," in *Close Up: Cinema and Modernism*, ed. James Donald, Anne Friedberg, and Laura Marcus (Princeton, NJ: Princeton University Press, 2001), 240–241.
6 Broderick, "Kubrick on Screen," 102.
7 Letter from Wally to Stanley Kubrick, August 24, 1950, Wallet J, uncatalogued, SKA.
8 Ibid.
9 Thomas Pryor, "Young Man with Ideas and a Camera," *New York Times*, January 14, 1951, X5.
10 Nathan Abrams, "'America Is Home': *Commentary* Magazine and the Refocusing of the Community of Memory, 1945–60," *Jewish Culture and History* 3, no. 1 (2012): 46.
11 Howard Sackler, "E.A. Poe," *Commentary* 10, no. 5 (1950): 458.
12 Vincent LoBrutto, *Stanley Kubrick* (New York: Faber & Faber, 1998), 77.
13 Wally to Kubrick, August 24, SKA; Letter from Wally to Stanley Kubrick, June 25, 1950, Wallet J, uncatalogued, SKA.
14 Wally to Kubrick, June 25, SKA.
15 Naremore, "No Other Country," 14. See also Nathan Abrams, *Stanley Kubrick: New York Jewish Intellectual* (New Brunswick, NJ: Rutgers University Press, 2018), 31–32.
16 Letter from J. T. Gwynne to Stanley Kubrick, December 30, 1950, Wallet J, uncatalogued, SKA.
17 Peter Krämer, "The Limits of Autonomy: Stanley Kubrick, Hollywood and Independent Filmmaking, 1950–53," in *American Independent Cinema*, ed. Geoff King, Claire Molloy, and Yannis Tzioumakis (London: Routledge, 2013), 158–159.
18 "A 22-Year Old Producer," *New York Journal-American*, December 27, 1950, 16.
19 I. Q. Hunter, "*A Clockwork Orange*, Exploitation and the Art Film," in *Recycling Culture(s)*, ed. Sara Martin (Newcastle: Cambridge Scholars, 2008), 11–20.
20 James Naremore, "Stanley Kubrick and the Aesthetics of the Grotesque," *Film Quarterly* 60, no. 1 (2006): 4–14.
21 Hunter, "*A Clockwork Orange*, Exploitation and the Art Film," 11–12.

22 Notes on cinema by Stanley Kubrick, Wallet E, uncatalogued, SKA.
23 Krämer, "Limits of Autonomy," 159.
24 LoBrutto, *Kubrick*, 79–80.
25 Justin Stewart, "Kubrick's First Feature: Paul Mazursky Q&A on *Fear and Desire*," *Film Comment*, March 26, 2012, www.filmcomment.com/blog/kubricks-first-feature-paul-mazursky-qa-on-fear-and-desire/.
26 Krämer, "Limits of Autonomy," 159–160.
27 Stewart, "Kubrick's First Feature."
28 LoBrutto, *Kubrick*, 81–82.
29 Stanley Kubrick, "Statement on *Fear and Desire*," *Masters of Cinema* pamphlet, *Fear and Desire* (DVD, 2013), 29.
30 Krämer, "Limits of Autonomy," 160.
31 Letter from Stanley Kubrick to Mark Van Doren, June 28, 1952, Wallet J, uncatalogued, SKA.
32 Van Doren described the film as original, brilliant, and profound and claimed that "nothing like it has ever been done in a film before and it alone guarantees that the future of Stanley Kubrick is worth watching for those who want to discover high talent at the moment it appears" (Letter from Stanley Kubrick to Mrs. Cowles, July 6, 1952, Wallet J, uncatalogued, SKA).
33 Letter from Stanley Kubrick to Mark Van Doren, July 5, 1952, Wallet J, uncatalogued, SKA.
34 Letter from Stanley Kubrick to Antonio Petrucci, July 21, 1952, Wallet J, uncatalogued, SKA.
35 It is not entirely clear when Burstyn first became aware of *Fear and Desire*. Norman Kagan suggests that it was in November 1952, after Kubrick sent Burstyn a copy of the film (Kagan, *The Cinema of Stanley Kubrick* [New York: Continuum, 2003], 9). However, in an interview picked up off the UPI wire, Kubrick stated that "a friend who had seen the film told Mr. Burstyn he ought to take a look at it, and the next thing I knew he made an offer" ("Hollywood," *Mexia Daily News*, April 24, 1953, 6).
36 "Burstyn Sets 'Fugitive' Deals in 3 Countries," *Variety*, September 23, 1953, 15.
37 "Film Buyers Invited to View 'Fugitive' in Non-arty Situations," *Variety*, October 28, 1953, 5.
38 Ibid., 5.
39 Ibid., 5.
40 "Amateur-Made 'Little Fugitive' Cost $25,000," *Variety*, November 4, 1953, 3.
41 Paolo Usai, "Checkmating the General: Stanley Kubrick's *Fear and Desire*," *Image*, October 2, 2016, https://scrapsfromtheloft.com/2016/10/02/checkmating-the-general-stanley-kubricks-fear-and-desire/.
42 Roxy Theatre program, June 1953, SK/5/3, SKA. The program described *Fear and Desire* as follows: "Defenceless and tied to a tree, Virginia Leith, as the strange half-animal girl, faces the dramatic climax of 'Fear and Desire,' a film about four desperate men trapped in a forest." The film's double-bill partner, *The Brute*, was tagged merely as being "the story of a French prostitute."
43 "Feature Reviews," *Boxoffice*, May 2, 1953, B11.
44 Ibid., B11.
45 Ibid., B11.
46 Ibid., B12.
47 Ibid., B12.
48 Kristin Thompson and David Bordwell, *Film History: An Introduction* (New York: McGraw-Hill, 1994), 380.

49. Ibid., 380–381.
50. "Biography of Richard de Rochemont," https://rmoa.unm.edu/docviewer.php?docId=wyu-aho5940.xml#idp1327824.
51. "Richard de Rochemont, 78, Dies," *New York Times*, August 6, 1982, 11.
52. "Biography of Richard."
53. "Richard de Rochemont Seen Exiting Time Org.," *Variety*, July 11, 1951, 4.
54. "Ambassadors to Be Filmed by De Roch'm't," *Billboard*, August 9, 1952, 10.
55. "De Rochemont Planning Prod. with Benoit-Levy," *Variety*, December 19, 1951, 4.
56. "Transfilm and de Rochemont Sign a Pact," *Billboard*, July 5, 1952, 11.
57. "De Rochemont Moves," *Broadcasting*, June 30, 1952, 5.
58. "Indie TV Film Producers Gear Up for Windfall," *Variety*, October 8, 1952, 29.
59. Giles Scott-Smith, *Networks of Empire: The US State Department's Foreign Leader Program in the Netherlands, France and Britain 1950–70* (Brussels: Peter Lang, 2008), 224n40.
60. David Maunders, "Controlling Youth for Democracy: The United States Youth Council and the World Assembly of Youth," *Commonwealth Youth and Development* 1, no. 2 (2003): 22.
61. Frances Stonor Saunders, *Who Paid the Piper? The CIA and the Cultural Cold War* (London: Granta Books, 2000), 438–439.
62. Joël Kotek, "Youth Organisations as a Battlefield in the Cold War," *Intelligence and National Security* 18, no. 2 (2010): 168.
63. Neil Sheehan, "Foundations Linked to C.I.A. Are Found to Subsidize 4 Other Youth Organizations," *New York Times*, February 16, 1967, 26.
64. Ibid., 26.
65. *World Assembly of Youth*, Sub-Series 4, Box 9, RDP.
66. Background Information, 1951, United States Youth Council Records, Box 55, Folder 10, SWHA.
67. "63 Nations' Youth in a Minature U.N.," *New York Times*, August 6, 1951, 5.
68. "Youth Assembly Approves Aid Plan," *New York Times*, August 15, 1951, 11.
69. John Baxter, *Stanley Kubrick: A Biography* (London: HarperCollins, 1998), 51.
70. Ibid., 51.
71. A. H. Weiler, "By Way of Report," *New York Times*, June 29, 1952, X3.
72. "World Assembly of Youth," 1951, Series 5, Box 200, RDP.
73. Departments of State, Justice, Commerce, and the Judiciary Appropriations for 1953, U.S. Congress, 63.
74. Ibid., 63.
75. Weiler, "By Way of Report," X3.
76. Letter from J. M. Dent and Sons to Stanley Kubrick, September 2, 1952, Wallet J, uncatalogued, SKA.
77. Letter from J. M. Dent and Sons to Stanley Kubrick, September 11, 1952, Wallet J, uncatalogued, SKA.
78. J.M. Dent and Sons, September 2, SKA.
79. Letter from J. M. Dent and Sons to Stanley Kubrick, November 3, 1952, Wallet J, uncatalogued, SKA.
80. "At 92, a Film History Professor Keeps the Reels Rolling," *New York Times*, June 12, 1978, 16; "Museum Honors Arthur Mayer in His 85th Year" (press release, July 1971, Museum of Modern Art).
81. "Arthur L. Mayer, Film Exhibitor and Lecturer on Movie History," *New York Times*, April 15, 1981, 6.

82 "Coast's Stars Succumb to the Directing Urge," *New York Times*, July 15, 1951, X3; Letter from Peter Mayer to Stanley Kubrick, October 28, 1952, Wallet J, uncatalogued, SKA. The production plans for *The Alamo* fell through, and after Wayne left the project, the film was renamed *The Last Command* (1955).
83 *Jamaica Story*, September 1952, Wallet E, uncatalogued, SKA.
84 Letter from Peter Mayer to Stanley Kubrick, September 15, 1952, Wallet J, uncatalogued, SKA.
85 Ibid.
86 Ibid.
87 Mayer to Kubrick, October 28, SKA.
88 *The Ford Foundation Annual Report for 1952*, December 31, 1952, 45.
89 Ibid.
90 "'Omnibus' Sponsors Get Time Freedom," *Billboard*, November 8, 1952, 10.
91 The episodes were as follows: Episode 1: "End of the Beginning," aired November 16, 1952; Episode 2: "Nancy Hanks," aired November 20, 1952; Episode 3: "Growing Up," aired December 14, 1952; Episode 4: "New Salem," aired January 11, 1953; and Episode 5: "Ann Rutledge," aired February 8, 1953.
92 William Hughes, *James Agee, Omnibus, and "Mr Lincoln": The Culture of Liberalism and the Challenge of Television, 1952–1953* (Lanham, MD: Scarecrow Press, 2004), ix.
93 Ibid., 67–70.
94 *Ford Foundation Annual Report*, 9.
95 Hughes, *James Agee*, X
96 Ibid., 69–71.
97 Letter from Stanley Kubrick to the Cowles, July 5, 1952, Wallet J, uncatalogued, SKA.
98 Hughes, *James Agee*, 115, n15, 147.
99 "The Lincoln Story Breaks into TV," *Courier Journal*, October 26, 1952, SK/3/3, SKA.
100 "Dr. Mabuse No. 2: Kubrick's Mythological Image," Kubrick Symposium, Deutsches Filmmuseum, July 21, 2018, www.youtube.com/watch?v=JzApr1Y74WA.
101 LoBrutto, *Kubrick*, 84–85; "Norman Lloyd Interview," Television Foundation Academy, https://interviews.televisionacademy.com/interviews/norman-lloyd.
102 Ulivieri, "Dr. Mabuse."

Chapter 3. The New York "Film School," 1953–1955

1 Filippo Ulivieri, "From 'Boy Genius' to 'Barking Loon': An Analysis of Stanley Kubrick's Mythology," *Essais: Stanley Kubrick Nouveaux Horizons*, no. 4 (2017): 224.
2 Ibid., 232.
3 "Shark Safari," Wallet K, uncatalogued, SKA.
4 Telegram from James Atlee Phillips to Stanley Kubrick, April 23, 1953, Wallet K, uncatalogued, SKA.
5 "Phillip Atlee, 77, Dies," *New York Times*, May 30, 1991, 20.
6 Lee Server, *Encyclopedia of Pulp Fiction Writers* (New York: Facts on File, 2002), 212.
7 "David Atlee Phillips Dead at 65," *New York Times*, July 10, 1988, 24.
8 Server, *Encyclopedia*, 212.
9 Colour Service Company invoice, May 25, 1953, Wallet K, uncatalogued, SKA.
10 John Baxter, *Stanley Kubrick: A Biography* (London: HarperCollins, 1998), 51.
11 "Seafarers Union Fronts Nite Club in Brooklyn," *Variety*, September 17, 1952, 1.

12 "Lester Irving Cooper Is Dead," *New York Times*, June 13, 1985, B12.
13 Rough Cut Continuity, n.d., Wallet J, uncatalogued, SKA.
14 Drafts of the script are dated to mid-1953, Wallet K, uncatalogued, SKA. There are also notes for a story called "The Girl," set in New York and featuring a young girl and her abusive uncle. This could have been an early version of *Along Came a Spider*.
15 Minotaur Productions and Howard Sackler agreement, September 2, 1953, SK/6/1/1/2, SKA.
16 Letter from Stanley Kubrick to Morris Bousel, September 2, 1953, SK/6/1/6, SKA.
17 Minotaur Productions and Deluxe Lab Loan Agreement, September 17, 1953, SK/6/1/4, SKA.
18 Peter Krämer, "The Limits of Autonomy: Stanley Kubrick, Hollywood and Independent Filmmaking, 1950–53," in *American Independent Cinema*, ed. Geoff King, Claire Molloy, and Yannis Tzioumakis (London: Routledge, 2013), 162.
19 Bousel owned the Bousel Pharmacy in the Bronx.
20 Minotaur contracts file, September 1953, Wallet J, uncatalogued, SKA.
21 Minotaur Productions and Howard Sackler agreement, September 9, 1953, SK/6/1/1, SKA.
22 Minotaur and Deluxe Loan Agreement, SK/6/1/4, SKA.
23 Ibid.
24 "De Luxe Labs Splurge on Techni," *Variety*, December 2, 1953, 5.
25 "Million Tied Up by 20th-Fox in 2 Scientific Setups," *Variety*, February 28, 1951, 3.
26 Vincent LoBrutto, *Stanley Kubrick* (New York: Faber & Faber, 1998), 80.
27 Minotaur and Deluxe Loan Agreement, SK/6/1/4, SKA.
28 Minotaur Productions and Deluxe Laboratories Mortgage of Chattels, September 17, 1953, SK/6/1/3, SKA.
29 Ibid.
30 Ibid.
31 Notice of Irrevocable Authority for *The Nymph and the Maniac*, September 17, 1953, SK/6/1/8, SKA.
32 Ibid.
33 Ibid.
34 Consent to Execution of Loan Agreement, September 17, 1953, SK/6/1/3, SKA.
35 Gregory Downey, *Closed Captioning: Subtitling, Stenography, and the Digital Convergence of Text with Television* (Baltimore: Johns Hopkins University Press, 2008), 47.
36 Minotaur Productions and Titra Sound Corp Loan Agreement, September 19, 1953, SK/6/1/5, SKA.
37 Ibid.
38 Letter from Camera Equipment Company to Stanley Kubrick, February 17, 1955, SK/6/6/1, SKA.
39 Letter from Camera Equipment Company to Stanley Kubrick, February 23, 1955, SK/6/6/1, SKA.
40 A. H. Weiler, "New Drama 'Kiss Me, Kill Me' Filmed Here in Its Entirety," *New York Times*, May 23, 1954, X5.
41 *Killer's Kiss* Statement of Profit and Loss, July 30, 1960, SK/6/6/2, SKA.
42 Weiler, "New Drama," X5.
43 Gene D. Phillips, "*Killer's Kiss*," in *The Stanley Kubrick Archives*, ed. Alison Castle (Cologne: Taschen, 2005), 285.
44 *Killer's Kiss* Statement, SK/6/6/2, SKA.
45 Letter from Stanley Kubrick to Max Kenn, n.d., SK/6/1/6, SKA.

46 Minotaur Productions and IATSE Agreement, n.d., SK/6/1/6, SKA.
47 Ibid.
48 Schedule of Cost, *Killer's Kiss*, November 7, 1964, SK/6/6/2, SKA.
49 Ibid.
50 Letter from Stanley Kubrick to Nat Sobel, June 1, 1954, SK/6/7/1, SKA.
51 Blair Davis, *The Battle for the Bs: 1950s Hollywood and the Rebirth of Low-Budget Cinema* (New Brunswick, NJ: Rutgers University Press, 2012), 28.
52 Letter from Stanley Kubrick to James B. Harris, December 31, 1962, SK/1/2/2/2, SKA.
53 Robert Kolker, *The Altering Eye: Contemporary International Cinema* (Cambridge: Open Book, 2009), 5.
54 Davis, *Battle for the Bs*, 28.
55 Kristin Thompson and David Bordwell, *Film History: An Introduction* (New York: McGraw-Hill, 1994), 382.
56 Jonas Mekas, "Notes on the New American Cinema," in *Film Culture Reader*, ed. P. A. Sitney (New York: Cooper Square Press, 2000), 88.
57 Ibid., 88.
58 Ibid., 88.
59 "Need New Producers—Selznick," *Variety*, February 22, 1950, 63.
60 "Amateur-Made 'Little Fugitive' Cost $25,000," *Variety*, November 4, 1953, 3.
61 Mekas, "Notes on the New American Cinema," 90.
62 Ibid., 89.
63 Ibid., 89.
64 On set photographs, SK/6/8/5, SKA.
65 Phillips, "*Killer's Kiss*," 285.
66 Robert Kolker, *A Cinema of Loneliness* (New York: Oxford University Press, 2011), 111.
67 Ibid., 111.
68 Thomas A. Nelson, *Kubrick: Inside a Film Artist's Maze* (Bloomington: Indiana University Press, 2000), 29.
69 Emanuel Levy, *Cinema of Outsiders: The Rise of American Independent Film* (New York: New York University Press, 1999), 5.
70 Camera Equipment Company, February 23, SK/6/6/1, SKA.
71 "UA Buys *Killer's Kiss*," *Variety*, July 27, 1955, 3.
72 Schedule of Cost, *Killer's Kiss*, 1964.
73 "Fugitive Producers Financing Another Offbeat Film at 100G," *Variety*, May 4, 1955, 3.
74 Letter from Stanley Kubrick to A. H. Weiler, May 19, 1954, Wallet J, uncatalogued, SKA.
75 "Dr. Mabuse No. 2: Kubrick's Mythological Image," Kubrick Symposium, Deutsches Filmmuseum, July 21, 2018, www.youtube.com/watch?v=JzApr1Y74WA.
76 "Youngest Producer's First Film Opens Wed," September 18, 1955, Wallet J, uncatalogued, SKA.
77 Weiler, "New Drama," X5.
78 Sterling Note Book, Wallet E, uncatalogued, SKA.
79 Misc plot outlines, Wallet E, uncatalogued, SKA.
80 Minotaur headed paper, Wallet E, uncatalogued, SKA.
81 Outline, September 9, 1954, Wallet E, uncatalogued, SKA.
82 Ibid.
83 *The Cop Killer*, April 11, 1955, Wallet E, uncatalogued, SKA.
84 Ibid.
85 Ibid.

86 Ibid.
87 Ibid.
88 "Kept Girl's Body 8 Years," Wallet E, uncatalogued, SKA.
89 "UA Buys *Killer's Kiss*," 3.
90 "UA Grooms Young Producers," *Variety*, December 8, 1954, 5.
91 Ibid., 5.
92 Ibid., 5.
93 Ibid., 16.
94 "Picture Grosses," *Variety*, December 27, 1955, 8.
95 Ulivieri, "Dr. Mabuse."

Chapter 4. The New UA Team, 1955–1956

1 Nick Pinkerton, "Interview: James B. Harris," *Film Comment*, 2015, www.filmcomment.com/pages/interview-james-b-harris-part-one.
2 Gene D. Phillips and Rodney Hill, *The Encyclopedia of Stanley Kubrick: From Day of the Fight to Eyes Wide Shut* (New York: Checkmark Books, 2002), 144.
3 "New York Sound Track," *Variety*, July 29, 1959, 7.
4 "Short Scannings," *Billboard*, April 2, 1949, 18.
5 "Flamingo Films Inc.," *Billboard*, April 16, 1949, 22.
6 James B. Harris, interview with author, March 23, 2016.
7 "James Harris Partners with Kubrick for UA," *Variety*, August 3, 1955, 3.
8 "A Guide to TV Film Series Now Doing a Job for Their Sponsors," *Billboard*, May 28, 1955, 25–32.
9 "3 MPTV Execs May Revive Flamingo Co.," *Billboard*, October 31, 1953, 7.
10 Pinkerton, "Interview."
11 Harris interview.
12 "Yates Selling Control of Republic to Harris," *Variety*, September 11, 1957, 1.
13 Ibid.
14 Kenneth Hyman (1928–), son of Seven Arts founder Eliot Hyman (1904–1980), was appointed the executive vice president of Warner Bros–Seven Arts after the takeover of Warner Brothers by his father's company; David L. Wolper (1928–2010) was a significant documentary and television producer, most notably for the television series *Roots* (ABC, 1977); Steven J. Ross (1927–1992) was the CEO of Time Warner, parent company of Warner Bros.
15 Harris interview.
16 *The Killing* weekly cost summary, October 12, 1955, SK/8/2/2, SKA.
17 "James Harris Partners," 3.
18 Sterling Note Book, SKA.
19 Charles Waring, "Cigarettes and Alcohol—The Extraordinary Life of Jim Thompson," January 15, 2008, www.crimetime.co.uk/cigarettes-and-alchohol-the-extraordinary-life-of-jim-thompson/.
20 *The Killing* weekly cost summary, SKA.
21 Harris interview.
22 "Sam Jaffe, 98, Hollywood Agent," *New York Times*, January 19, 2000, 26.
23 Harris interview.
24 Letter from James B. Harris to David Stillman, June 1, 1956, JBH.
25 Harris interview; Eurist served as a production manager on other low-budget UA films, including *The Killer Is Loose* (1956) and *Dragon's Gold* (1954).
26 Harris to Stillman, JBH.

27. "The Big Bluff," *Variety*, July 13, 1955, 20.
28. "The Killer Is Loose," *Variety*, February 1, 1956, 6.
29. Harris interview; Vincent LoBrutto, *Stanley Kubrick* (New York: Faber & Faber, 1998), 115.
30. A. H. Weiler, "Screening the Local Motion Picture Scene," *New York Times*, September 11, 1955, X7.
31. A. H. Weiler, "By Way of Report," *New York Times*, June 26, 1955, X5; "Stan Kubrick Starts 'Clean Break' for UA," *Variety*, September 28, 1955, 24.
32. LoBrutto, *Kubrick*, 119–120.
33. Robert Kolker, *A Cinema of Loneliness* (New York: Oxford University Press, 2011), 110.
34. A. H. Weiler, "Precedent," *New York Times*, October 16, 1955, X5.
35. "Everybody's Sensitive," *Variety*, November 9, 1955, 5.
36. Edwin Schallert, "Vince Edwards Gains Star Rating," *Los Angeles Times*, October 7, 1955, B9.
37. Thomas Pryor, "M-G-M Signs Trio for 'High Society,'" *New York Times*, November 28, 1955, 27.
38. "Sterling Hayden's 'Bed' Closed Down," *Los Angeles Times*, November 28, 1955, A11.
39. Harris to Stillman, JBH.
40. "The New UA Team," *Variety*, March 21, 1956, 17.
41. Harris to Stillman, JBH.
42. Ibid.
43. Ibid.
44. Letter from Kay Proctor to Harris-Kubrick Pictures, October 29, 1956, SK/7/3/1, SKA.
45. Ibid.
46. Tino Balio, *United Artists: The Company That Changed the Film Industry* (Madison: University of Wisconsin Press, 1987), 158.
47. "'Killing,' 1st-Run Flop," *Variety*, August 29, 1956, 1.
48. See Mark Jancovich and Tim Snelson, "Horror at the Crossroads: Class, Gender and Taste at the Rialto Cinema (Times Square) in the 1940s," in *From the Grindhouse to the Arthouse: Highbrow and Lowbrow Transgression in Cinema's First Century*, ed. John Cline and Robert G. Weiner (New York: Scarecrow, 2010), 109–125.
49. "Art Back to U.S. Art Houses," *Variety*, December 30, 1959, 7.
50. "'Killing,' 1st-Run Flop," 1.
51. Ibid., 1.
52. Ibid., 1.
53. "Another Smartie Artie—Pitt Making a Killing with Same Name 'Dud,'" *Variety*, September 12, 1956, 4.
54. "Some World War I Cowards Theme of 'Glory' Film," *Variety*, August 1, 1956, 5.
55. Gavin Lambert, "The Killing," *Sight and Sound* 26, no. 2 (1956): 95.
56. "The Killing," *Variety*, May 23, 1956, 6.
57. Ibid., 6.
58. "New Master of the Thriller," *Manchester Guardian*, July 28, 1956, 3.
59. Letter from Stanley Kubrick to Jack Hamilton, June 18, 1956, JBH.
60. Letter from Stanley Kubrick to Bernard Newman, August 28, 1956, JBH.
61. Letter from Steve Noonan to F. A. Jones, June 19, 1956, SK/1/2/3/6/7, SKA.
62. "Kubrick and Harris," *Independent Film Journal*, June 30, 1956, 47.
63. Phillip Scheuer, "N.Y. Wonder Boys, Both 27, Produce Tense Melodrama," *Los Angeles Times*, April 1, 1956, E2.

64 Harris to Stillman, JBH.
65 Kubrick to Hamilton, JBH.
66 "Some World War I Cowards," 5.
67 James Fenwick, "A Production Strategy of Overdevelopment: Kirk Douglas's Bryna Productions and the Unproduced Viva Gringo," in *Shadow Cinema: Industrial and Production Contexts of Unmade Films*, ed. James Fenwick, David Eldridge, and Kieran Foster (New York: Bloomsbury, forthcoming).
68 "Freeman Speaks for Hollywood," *Variety*, May 23, 1956, 11.
69 Ibid., 11.
70 Fenwick, "Production Strategy."
71 Harris-Kubrick Pictures and Shelby Foote agreement, March 14, 1956, JBH.
72 Thomas Pryor, "Brynner Bow Set as Film Director," *New York Times*, April 5, 1956, 26.
73 Balio, *United Artists*, 160–162.
74 Ibid., 160.
75 Harris-Kubrick Pictures and Jim Thompson agreement, July 6, 1956, JBH.
76 Kubrick to Newman, JBH
77 Peter Lev, *The Fifties Transforming the Screen 1950–1959* (Berkeley: University of California Press, 2003), 198.
78 "Top Echelon Confers at Metro Studio," *Variety*, January 18, 1956, 7.
79 Ibid., 7.
80 "Call Top Hands at Metro; Tell 'Em Gotta Cut Costs," *Variety*, July 11, 1956, 5.
81 Ibid., 5.
82 Ibid.; Harris interview.
83 *The Famished Monkey*, Wallet E, uncatalogued, SKA.
84 *New York Story*, Wallet E, uncatalogued, SKA.
85 *Anxious Husband Prepares for His Bride*, Wallet E, uncatalogued, SKA.
86 Untitled idea, Misc Outlines, Wallet E, uncatalogued, SKA.
87 Stanley Kubrick MGM biography, SK/1/2/2/3, SKA.
88 Sterling note book, SKA.
89 *Jealousy*, Wallet E, uncatalogued, SKA.
90 *The Perfect Marriage*, Wallet E, uncatalogued, SKA.
91 *Married Man*, Wallet E, uncatalogued, SKA.
92 Letter from Stanley Kubrick to Gregory Peck, November 26, 1956, JBH. By 1956, Harris-Kubrick Pictures was represented by Ronnie Lubin of the Jaffe Agency.
93 Factors Influencing Movie Attendance, SK/1/2/2/3, SKA.

Chapter 5. New Modes of Producing, 1957–1959

1 Peter Lev, *The Fifties Transforming the Screen 1950–1959* (Berkeley: University of California Press, 2003), 2.
2 "UA Shows the Way!," *Independent Film Journal*, October 26, 1957, 28.
3 James B. Harris, interview with author, March 23, 2016.
4 Letter from James B. Harris to Stan Margulies, March 8, 1957, 23/19, KDP.
5 Memorandum of Understanding, Bryna Productions and Harris-Kubrick Pictures, January 9, 1957, 11/21, KDP.
6 James Fenwick, "'Look, Ma, I'm a Corporation!' United Artists and Kirk Douglas's Bryna Productions 1955–1959," in *United Artists Centenary Collection*, ed. Yannis Tzioumakis, Peter Krämer, Gary Needham, and Tino Balio (London: Routledge, forthcoming).

7   Harris to Margulies, March 8, 1957.
8   Memorandum of Understanding, January 9, 1957.
9   Principal Functions of Stan Margulies and Public Relations, 1959, 11/22, KDP.
10 Memorandum of Understanding, January 9, 1957.
11 Ibid.
12 Bryna Productions and Harris-Kubrick Pictures Agreement, February 6, 1957, 11/21, KDP.
13 Memorandum of Understanding, January 9, 1957.
14 Ibid.
15 James Fenwick, "Kirk Douglas and Stanley Kubrick: Reconsidering a Creative and Business Partnership," in *A Critical Companion to Stanley Kubrick*, ed. Elsa Colombani (Lanham, MD: Lexington Books, forthcoming).
16 Ibid.
17 Ibid.
18 Kubrick to Hamilton, JBH.
19 Christopher Isherwood, "Young American Writers," *Observer*, May 13, 1951, 7.
20 Letter from Kirk Douglas to Stanley Kubrick, February 13, 1957, 23/19, KDP.
21 Fenwick, "Kirk Douglas."
22 Douglas to Kubrick, February 13, 1957.
23 Ibid.
24 James Fenwick, "A Film 'Highly Offensive to Our Nation': Stanley Kubrick's *Paths of Glory* (1957), Censorship, and Militaristic Representations of Post-war Europe," in *Routledge Companion to European Cinema*, ed. Gábor Gergely and Susan Hayward (London: Routledge, forthcoming).
25 James Fenwick, "The Eady Levy, 'the Envy of Most Other European Nations': Runaway Productions and the British Film Fund in the Early 1960s," in *The Routledge Companion to British Cinema History*, ed. I. Q. Hunter, Laraine Porter, and Justin Smith (London: Routledge, 2017), 196.
26 "Freeman Speaks for Hollywood," *Variety*, May 23, 1956, 11.
27 Peter Krämer, "Stanley Kubrick and the Internationalisation of Post-war Hollywood," *New Review of Film and Television Studies* 15, no. 2 (2017): 250.
28 Letter from Stanley Kubrick to Hulki Saner, April 8, 1958, JBH.
29 "UA's $20-Mil for O'Seas Features," *Variety*, March 20, 1957, 3.
30 James Fenwick, "A Production Strategy of Overdevelopment: Kirk Douglas's Bryna Productions and the Unproduced Viva Gringo," in *Shadow Cinema: Industrial and Production Contexts of Unmade Films*, ed. James Fenwick, David Eldridge, and Kieran Foster (New York: Bloomsbury, forthcoming).
31 Press release, *Paths of Glory*, March 21, 1957, 23/19, KDP.
32 Press release, *Paths of Glory*, March 29, 1957, 23/19, KDP.
33 Letter from Stan Margulies to James B. Harris, April 18, 1957, 23/19, KDP.
34 Syd Stogel, Production Activities Report, 1957, SK/8/3/5/2, SKA.
35 Letter from Kirk Douglas to Stanley Kubrick, November 21, 1957, JBH.
36 *Paths of Glory*, Production Budget and Cost Report, May 1957, SK/8/6/3, SKA.
37 "Risks & Profits Both Sky-High, Sez Arthur Krim," *Variety*, June 11, 1958, 4.
38 Fred Hift, "The Company of the Independents: Ideas and Men Behind UA," *Variety*, June 24, 1959, 13.
39 Fred Hift, "UA: Budgets, Art & Sanity," *Variety*, June 3, 1959, 3.
40 Tino Balio, *United Artists: The Company That Changed the Film Industry* (Madison: University of Wisconsin Press, 1987), 93.

41 Hift, "Company of the Independents," 13.
42 Harris to Margulies, March 8, 1957.
43 Memo from Stan Margulies to Syd Stogel, March 21, 1957, 23/19, KDP.
44 Ibid.
45 Memo from Syd Stogel to Kirk Douglas, March 13, 1957, 23/19, KDP.
46 Letter from James B. Harris to Stan Margulies, March 30, 1957, 23/19, KDP.
47 Ibid.
48 Letter from Myers Beck to Stan Margulies, March 25, 1957, 23/19, KDP.
49 Letter from Stan Margulies to Myers P. Beck, March 27, 1957, 23/19, KDP.
50 Letter from Roger Lewis to Stan Margulies, December 3, 1957, 23/24, KDP.
51 Letter from Stan Margulies to Myers P. Beck, February 25, 1958, 23/25, KDP.
52 David Eldridge, *Hollywood's History Films* (London: I.B. Tauris, 2006), 54.
53 Richard Daniels, "Selling the War Film: Syd Stogel and the *Paths of Glory* Press Files," in *Stanley Kubrick: New Perspectives*, ed. Tatjana Ljujić, Peter Krämer, and Richard Daniels (London: Black Dog, 2015), 94.
54 Letter from Stan Margulies to Myers P. Beck, November 20, 1957, 23/24, KDP.
55 Beck to Margulies, March 25, 1957.
56 Letter from Stanley Kubrick to Myers P. Beck, February 17, 1958, 23/25, KDP.
57 Ibid.
58 Ibid.
59 Ibid.
60 Letter from Stan Margulies to Arnold Picker, January 25, 1957, 23/19, KDP.
61 Letter from Arnold Picker to Stan Margulies, January 29, 1957, 23/19, KDP.
62 Revised Campaign Projection, March 30, 1957, P.O.G. SK BOX, uncatalogued, SKA.
63 Fenwick, "Highly Offensive to Our Nation."
64 Picker to Margulies, January 29, 1957.
65 Fenwick, "Highly Offensive to Our Nation."
66 Letter from Stanley Kubrick to J. Siritsky, December 12, 1958, JBH.
67 Letter from Kirk to Sam Norton, May 25, 1957, 11/21, KDP.
68 Ibid.
69 Ibid.
70 Bryna and Harris-Kubrick agreement, February 6, 1957.
71 Letter from Sam Norton to Kirk Douglas, July 31, 1957, 11/21, KDP.
72 Bryna and Harris-Kubrick agreement, February 6, 1957.
73 "Dominating Douglas," *Picturegoer*, June 27, 1959, 6.
74 Letter from James B. Harris to Sam Norton, June 14, 1957, 11/21, KDP.
75 Harris interview.
76 Norton to Douglas, July 31, 1957.
77 Even though Harris-Kubrick Pictures continued to exist into 1963, it had been superseded in autumn 1962 by new production companies incorporated by Kubrick. See chapter 7 for more information.
78 Letter from Stanley Kubrick to George von Block, February 4, 1958, JBH.
79 Letter from Stan Margulies to Mac Reynolds, December 4, 1957, 56/11, KDP.
80 Ibid.
81 Press release, Public Relations, January 8, 1958, 56/11, KDP.
82 Fenwick, "Kirk Douglas."
83 Letter from James B. Harris to George von Block, February 4, 1958, JBH.
84 Fenwick, "'Look, Ma, I'm a Corporation!'"

85 Harris to Block, February 4, 1958.
86 Ibid.
87 Harris-Kubrick Pictures also considered developing television series, such as an adaptation of Arthur Carter's unproduced Broadway play, *Operation Madball*, produced as a film by Jed Harris in 1957; see Filippo Ulivieri, "Waiting for a Miracle: A Survey of Stanley Kubrick's Unrealized Projects," *Cinergie*, no. 12 (2017): 111.
88 Letter from Stanley Kubrick to George von Block, February 12, 1958, JBH.
89 A. H. Weiler, "By Way of Report," *New York Times*, February 16, 1958, X7.
90 Kubrick to Block, February 12, 1958.
91 Letter from Stanley Kubrick to Hollis Alpert, February 11, 1958, JBH.
92 Research 19th Century, 1958, uncatalogued, SK BOX, SKA.
93 Letter from James B. Harris to Sam Norton, March 11, 1958, 11/21, KDP.
94 Letter from Sam Norton to Marvin B. Meyer, March 15, 1958, 11/21, KDP.
95 Bryna Productions and Harris-Kubrick Pictures Termination and Release Agreement, May 1, 1958, 11/21, KDP.
96 Ibid.
97 Letter from Stanley Kubrick to Sheldon Wile, March 7, 1958, JBH.
98 Letter from Stanley Kubrick to Robert Hendrickson, May 7, 1958, JBH.
99 Letter from Columbia Pictures to Harris-Kubrick Pictures, December 23, 1958, JBH.
100 Kubrick to Wile, March 7, 1958,
101 Letter from James B. Harris to Sam Norton, August 4, 1958, JBH.
102 For more on *The German Lieutenant*, see Geoffrey Cocks, *The Wolf at the Door: Stanley Kubrick, History, and the Holocaust* (New York: Peter Lang, 2004), 151–154.
103 Letter from Stanley Kubrick to Paul Botica, February 2, 1959, JBH.
104 Letter from James B. Faichney to Stanley Kubrick, January 10, 1959; Letter from the Department of Justice to Harris-Kubrick Pictures, February 3, 1959, SK/18/4/2, SKA.
105 Letter from Stanley Kubrick to Audio Rarities, May 5, 1958, JBH.
106 Block to Kubrick, January 31, 1959, SK/18/4/3, SKA.
107 D-Mark budget, *The German Lieutenant*, January 1959, SK/18/4/2, SKA.
108 Block to Kubrick, January 31, 1959.
109 Kubrick to Botica, February 2, 1959.
110 Pennebaker Inc. and Harris-Kubrick Pictures Loan Agreement, September 26, 1958, JBH.
111 "Kubrick Quits Brando Picture," *Los Angeles Times*, November 20, 1958, B11.
112 Harris interview.
113 Harris-Kubrick Pictures and Joseph Harris agreement, October 31, 1958, JBH.

Chapter 6. Swords, Sandals, Sex, and Soviets, 1959–1962

1 Letter from Harris-Kubrick Pictures to Pennebaker Inc., January 8, 1959, JBH.
2 Telegram from Marlon Brando to Stanley Kubrick, February 28, 1959, SK/18/4/3, SKA.
3 U-I press release, May 19, 1958, 37/6, KDP. Douglas also approached David Lean.
4 Letter from Laurence Olivier to Edward Lewis, September 4, 1958, 33/3, KDP.
5 U-I press release, May 19, 1958.
6 "Kirk Is King," *Picturegoer*, June 28, 1958, 8–9.
7 "MCA Envelops Universal Lot," *Broadcasting*, December 22, 1958, 34.

8 "Universal Cutting Production in Half," *Variety*, September 17, 1958, 4.
9 U-I press release, May 19, 1958.
10 "Universal Cutting Production," 22.
11 James Russell, *The Historical Epic and Contemporary Hollywood: From Dances with Wolves to Gladiator* (New York: Continuum, 2007), 5.
12 U-I press release, May 19, 1958.
13 "MCA Envelops," 34.
14 Letter from Kirk Douglas to David Lean, January 24, 1958, 33/3, KDP.
15 James Fenwick, "A Production Strategy of Overdevelopment: Kirk Douglas's Bryna Productions and the Unproduced Viva Gringo," in *Shadow Cinema: Industrial and Production Contexts of Unmade Films*, ed. James Fenwick, David Eldridge, and Kieran Foster (New York: Bloomsbury, forthcoming).
16 Douglas Gomery, *The Hollywood Studio System: A History* (London: British Film Institute, 2005), 205–206.
17 Kirk Douglas, *The Ragman's Son* (London: Simon & Schuster, 1988), 326.
18 "Anthony Mann," *Variety*, October 8, 1958, 3.
19 "Kubrick Replaces Mann," *Variety*, February 18, 1959, 17. Bryna's official press release stated that Mann had "resigned" following "artistic differences" (Bryna press release, February 15, 1959, 37/6, KDP).
20 James B. Harris, interview with author, March 23, 2016.
21 "'Lolita' Bought by Screen Team," *New York Times*, September 13, 1958, 10.
22 Bryna Productions and Harris-Kubrick Pictures agreement, March 30, 1959, 11/21, KDP.
23 James Fenwick, "Kirk Douglas and Stanley Kubrick: Reconsidering a Creative and Business Partnership," in *A Critical Companion to Stanley Kubrick*, ed. Elsa Colombani (Lanham, MD: Lexington Books, forthcoming).
24 Ibid.
25 Harris-Kubrick Pictures Loan-Out Agreement, April 8, 1959, 35/4, KDP.
26 Memo from Edward Lewis to Jeff Asher, April 17, 1959, 11/21, KDP.
27 Harris-Kubrick Pictures Loan-Out Agreement, April 8, 1959.
28 Fiona Radford, "Having His Cake and Eating It Too: Stanley Kubrick and *Spartacus*," in *Stanley Kubrick: New Perspectives*, ed. Tatjana Ljujić, Peter Krämer, and Richard Daniels (London: Black Dog, 2015), 102.
29 Ibid., 103–109.
30 Memo from Kirk Douglas, April 29, 1959, 33/6, KDP.
31 Vincent LoBrutto, *Stanley Kubrick* (New York: Faber & Faber, 1998), 181–182.
32 Memo from Kirk Douglas to Marshall Green, February 25, 1959, 33/4, KDP.
33 Memo from Kirk Douglas to Ed Lewis, April 5, 1959, 33/4, KDP.
34 *Spartacus* Production Budget, February 10, 1960, 35/2, KDP.
35 Eugene Archer, "Hailed in Farewell," *New York Times*, October 2, 1960, X9.
36 Ibid., X9.
37 Philip Scheuer, "$12 Million Risk Taken by Douglas," *Los Angeles Times*, September 29, 1960, C9.
38 Ibid., C9.
39 Philip Scheuer, "Sequel Prepared for 'Sitting Pretty,'" *Los Angeles Times*, October 27, 1960, B13.
40 Archer, "Hailed in Farewell," X9.
41 Scheuer, "$12 Million Risk," C9.
42 Ibid., C9.
43 Archer, "Hailed in Farewell," X9.

44 James Howard, *Stanley Kubrick Companion* (London: B.T. Batsford, 1999), 69.
45 Harris-Kubrick Pictures Loan-Out Agreement, April 8, 1959.
46 Letter from James B. Harris to John Lewis, December 18, 1958, JBH.
47 Letter from James B. Harris to Boris Pasternak, January 8, 1959, JBH.
48 Letter from Kirk Douglas to Embassy of the USSR, March, 1958, 40/2, KDP.
49 "Communist View: Films Serve State," *Variety*, November 26, 1958, 1.
50 Ibid., 1.
51 "More Soviet Ballet Bought for Television," *Broadcasting*, June 29, 1959, 68.
52 James B. Harris, "Foreign Films Good Bet as the Thinking Man's Late Show," *Variety*, July 8, 1959, 32.
53 Ibid., 32.
54 "More Soviet Ballet," 68.
55 "Harris, Shore Set Soviet Pix Deals," *Variety*, June 24, 1959, 76.
56 "Private Enterprise & USSR Films," *Variety*, July 29, 1959, 3.
57 "Weak 'Hercules,'" *New York Times*, July 23, 1959, 32.
58 "Soviet's 'Muromets' Nabbed by Jos. Harris," *Variety*, September 23, 1959, 24.
59 "Harris, Shore Take Soviet Pic," *Variety*, May 25, 1959, 20.
60 Ibid.
61 "Sig Shore Handling Soviet 'Sword' Film," *Variety*, October 14, 1959, 7.
62 Letter from Stanley Kubrick to Joseph Harris, n.d., Wallet J, uncatalogued, SKA.
63 Letter from Joseph Harris to Stanley Kubrick, September 18, 1959, SK/8/7/2, SKA.
64 Ibid.
65 James Fenwick, "'A Commercial for God and the Space Program': *2001: A Space Odyssey* and the 1969 Moscow International Film Festival," *Les Éditions de l'École Polytechnique* (forthcoming).
66 Memo from Geoffrey Shurlock to Harris-Kubrick Pictures, October 24, 1956, MHL.
67 Letter from James B. Harris to Henry Miller, June 17, 1958, JBH.
68 Ibid.
69 Filippo Ulivieri has suggested that the likes of *Married Man*, *Jealousy*, and *The Perfect Marriage* could be early traces of *The Unfaithful Wife* (Life and Legacy, Studying the Work of Stanley Kubrick, general discussion, July 15–19, 2019, University of Leiden, Netherlands).
70 Receipts and Disbursements for Harris-Kubrick Pictures, 1962, SK/1/2/2/1, SKA.
71 *Laughter in the Dark* was eventually adapted by Vladimir Nabokov for a 1969 film of the same name, directed by Tony Richardson and starring Nicol Williamson and Anna Karina.
72 "Lolita B.O. Linked Up with Book's Notoriety," *Variety*, September 24, 1958, 2.
73 Ibid.
74 Letter from James B. Harris to Stanley Kubrick, October 22, 1959, SK/10/8/1, SKA.
75 John de St Jorre, *Venus Bound: The Erotic Voyage of the Olympia Press and Its Writers* (New York: Random House, 1994), 116–154.
76 James Fenwick, "X-Rating *Lolita* (1962): Canon L. John Collins, Stanley Kubrick and an 'Air of Sensationalism,'" *Journal of British Cinema and Television* (forthcoming).
77 "'Lolita' without Script Control Not for Us—WB," *Variety*, May 27, 1959, 17.
78 Ibid., 17.
79 "New York Sound Track," *Variety*, April 29, 1959, 4.
80 Tino Balio, *United Artists: The Company That Changed the Film Industry* (Madison: University of Wisconsin Press, 1987), 159.

81 Letter from Cecil Tennant to Stanley Kubrick, November 23, 1959, SK/10/8/1, SKA.
82 Letter from Laurence Olivier to Stanley Kubrick, December 15, 1959, SK/10/8/1, SKA.
83 Harris interview.
84 WGA Notice of Strike Action, November 5, 1959, SK/9/4/7, SKA.
85 "Writers Guild Wins Indie Producers," *Variety*, February 17, 1960, 2.
86 Harris to Kubrick, October 22, 1959.
87 Cable from James B. Harris to Stanley Kubrick, November 14, 1959, SK/10/8/1, SKA.
88 Ibid.
89 Harris to Kubrick, October 22, 1959.
90 Ibid.
91 Personal file, 1961, Wallet J, uncatalogued, SKA.
92 Harris interview.
93 James Fenwick, "The Eady Levy, 'the Envy of Most Other European Nations': Runaway Productions and the British Film Fund in the Early 1960s," in *The Routledge Companion to British Cinema History*, ed. I. Q. Hunter, Laraine Porter, and Justin Smith (London: Routledge, 2017), 192–193.
94 Ibid., 192.
95 "Seven Arts' $30,000,000 Stake in Pix," *Variety,* September, 14, 1960, 15.
96 Ibid., 1.
97 Ibid., 1.
98 Ibid., 1.
99 Ibid., 15.
100 Ibid., 15.
101 Letter from Stanley Kubrick to Peter Ustinov, May 20, SK/10/8/1, SKA.
102 Ibid.
103 Letter from Stanley Kubrick to Calder Willingham, December 11, 1959, SK/10/8/1, SKA.
104 Letter from Calder Willingham to Stanley Kubrick, December 14, 1959, SK/10/8/1, SKA.
105 Letter from Vera Nabokov to James B. Harris, August 12, 1959, SK/10/8/1, SKA.
106 Letter from Vera Nabokov to Stanley Kubrick, December 11, 1959, SK/10/8/2, SKA.
107 Letter from Vera Nabokov to Stanley Kubrick, December 31, 1959, SK/10/8/2, SKA.
108 Letter from Eliot Hyman to Harris-Kubrick Pictures, November 28, 1960, SK/10/8/1, SKA.
109 Ibid.
110 Ibid.
111 Letter from James B. Harris to Vera Nabokov, December 21, 1960, SK/10/8/1, SKA.
112 Ibid.
113 "Yes, They Did It: *Lolita* Is a Movie," *Life*, May 25, 1962, 97.
114 "Feature Reviews: Lolita," *Boxoffice*, June 25, 1962, 19. The Legion of Decency insisted that all advertising for *Lolita* had to clarify that the film was for those over eighteen only, but this also became an effective marketing tool in promoting the controversial nature of the film.
115 Gene D. Phillips, ed., *Stanley Kubrick Interviews* (Jackson: University Press of Mississippi, 2001, 88.
116 "Omaha Affiliate Refuses NBC-TV Spot for 'Adults Only' Movie," *Boxoffice*, August 27, 1962, 48.

117 Elena Gorfinkel, "Radley Metzger's 'Elegant Arousal': Taste, Aesthetic Distinction and Sexploitation," in *Underground U.S.A.: Filmmaking beyond the Hollywood Cannon*, ed. Xavier Mendik and Steven Schneider (London: Wallflower Press, 2002), 26–39.
118 Ibid., 39.
119 Letter from Stanley Kubrick to Eliot Hyman, August 4, 1961, SK/10/8/1, SKA.
120 Ibid.
121 Ibid.
122 "Pictures: All-Time Top Film Grossers," *Variety*, January 8, 1964, 69.
123 Letter from Leon Kaplan to Milton Shapiro, January 2, 1962, Box 11, Folder 21, KDP.
124 Harris interview.

Chapter 7. The Establishment of a Producing Powerhouse, 1962-1964

1 Receipts and Disbursements, Harris-Kubrick Pictures, 1962, SK/1/2/2/1, SKA.
2 Letter from Stanley Kubrick to James B. Harris, February 19, 1963, SK/1/2/2/2, SKA.
3 Ibid.
4 Ibid.
5 Letter from Stanley Kubrick to Nat Weiss, December 24, 1962, SK/11/9/112, SKA.
6 Kubrick to Harris, February 19, 1963.
7 Ibid.
8 Polaris Productions Incorporation Record, October 11, 1983, California State.
9 Polaris Productions and Stanley Kubrick agreement, October 14, 1962, SK/12/2/5, SKA.
10 Ibid.
11 Ibid.
12 "International Soundtrack," *Variety*, January 16, 1963, 22.
13 "CEA Drops Ideas for Cut-Off in Eady Levy," *Variety*, July 25, 1962, 12.
14 "Unions' Fears Allayed, British Film Industry Now Going 'International,'" *Variety*, January 10, 1962, 16.
15 Letter from Bromhead, Foster & Co Chartered Accountants to the Board of Trade, April 23, 1968, BT 335/28, TNA.
16 Ibid.
17 "Nat Weiss Ad-Pub Veep for Kubrick," *Variety*, December 19, 1962, 5, 19.
18 Letter from Nat Weiss to Stanley Kubrick, December 5, 1962, SK/11/9/111, SKA.
19 Letter from Stanley Kubrick to Nat Weiss, December 20, 1962, SK/11/9/111, SKA.
20 Letter from Roger Caras to Stanley Kubrick, August 31, 1966, SK/12/8/5, SKA.
21 "Obituaries: Nathan Weiss," *Variety*, July 21, 2008, 35.
22 "Book Review: The Cleopatra Papers," *Boxoffice*, October 21, 1963, 17.
23 "Ken Clark's 'Inner Sanctum' Crack at 'Cleo Papers,'" *Variety*, August 21, 1963, 4.
24 "Weiss: 'Let Kubrick Explain if My Papers Made Him Discharge Me,'" *Variety*, August 7, 1963, 7.
25 "Obituaries: Benn Reyes," *Variety*, December 11, 1968, 60.
26 Peter Krämer, "'Complete Total Final Annihilating Artistic Control': Stanley Kubrick and Post-war Hollywood," in *Stanley Kubrick New Perspectives*, ed. Tatjana Ljujić, Peter Krämer, and Richard Daniels (London: Black Dog, 2015), 48–61.
27 Notes on Polaris Productions Incorporated Agreement, June 26, 1964, SK/12/8/1/66, SKA.

28 Ibid.
29 "Kubrick, Harris and Seven Arts," *Variety*, May 23, 1962, 14.
30 Ibid., 14.
31 Letter from Stanley Kubrick to Nat Weiss, November 20, 1962, SK/11/9/111, SKA.
32 "New York Soundtrack," *Variety*, October 17, 1962, 4; "Latest in Mouthful Titles per Stan Kubrick," *Variety*, October 10, 1962, 4.
33 "Nat Weiss Ad-Pub," 5.
34 "Columbia Sets More Indie Productions," *Variety*, February 14, 1962, 17.
35 "Film Studio News," *Stage and Television Today*, October 25, 1962, 16.
36 Memo from W. L. G. LeBrun to Ron Phipps, November 5, 1962, SK/11/3/7, SKA.
37 Ibid.
38 Letter from W. L. G. LeBrun to Vic Lyndon, November 1, 1963, SK/11/9/68, SKA.
39 Letter from Vic Lyndon to Stanley Kubrick, November 9, 1963, SK/11/9/68, SKA.
40 "Mouse's B.O. Noise," *Variety*, December 14, 1960, 13.
41 James Fenwick, "The Eady Levy, 'The Envy of Most Other European Nations': Runaway Productions and the British Film Fund in the Early 1960s," in *The Routledge Companion to British Cinema History*, ed. I. Q. Hunter, Laraine Porter, and Justin Smith (London: Routledge, 2017), 193.
42 Terry Southern, "Notes from the War Room," *Grand Street*, 1994, www.criterion.com/current/posts/4125-notes-from-the-war-room.
43 Letter from Stanley Kubrick to James B. Harris, November 14, 1962, SK/1/2/2/2, SKA.
44 Letter from Stanley Kubrick to James B. Harris, November 19, 1962, SK/1/2/2/2, SKA.
45 Memo from W. L. G. LeBrun to Ron Phipps, March 21, 1963, SK/11/3/7, SKA; Statement of Dollars Cost, *Dr. Strangelove*, May 24, 1963, SK/11/3/7, SKA.
46 Letter from Stanley Kubrick to James B. Harris, February 8, 1963, SK/1/2/2/2, SKA.
47 Letter from James B. Harris to Stanley Kubrick, February 14, 1963, SK/1/2/2/2, SKA.
48 Letter from W. L. G. LeBrun to B. Birnbaum, August 16, 1963, SK/11/3/7, SKA.
49 Letter from Stanley Kubrick to James B. Harris, December 31, 1962, SK/1/2/2/2, SKA.
50 Robert Sklar, "Stanley Kubrick and the American Film Industry," *Current Research in Film* 4 (1988): 118.
51 Ibid., 118.
52 Lee Minoff, "Nerve Center for a Nuclear Nightmare," *New York Times*, April 21, 1963, X7.
53 Peter Krämer, "'To Prevent the Present Heat from Dissipating': Stanley Kubrick and the Marketing of *Dr. Strangelove* (1964)," *InMedia*, no. 3 (2013), https://journals.openedition.org/inmedia/634.
54 Minoff, "Nerve Center," X7.
55 Philip Scheuer, "Kubrick Explains 'Movie of Absurd,'" *Los Angeles Times*, May 2, 1963, 27.
56 "'Dr. Strangelove' Provokes Britons," *New York Times*, February 5, 1964, 29.
57 "What Makes Kubrick?," *Los Angeles Times*, February 9, 1964, C6.
58 "Debate over 'Strangelove' Film Echoes Happily at the Box Office," *New York Times*, February 10, 1964, 21.
59 Letter from Nat Weiss to Stanley Kubrick, November 23, 1962, SK/11/9/111, SKA.
60 Ibid.
61 Krämer, "'To Prevent the Present Heat from Dissipating.'"
62 Letter from Roger Caras to Stanley Kubrick, November 3, 1966, SK/12/8/5, SKA.

63 "Columbia Engineers 'The Victors' into Sub-run Showcase Pattern," *Variety*, February 12, 1964, 8.
64 "Plan-the-Push Panel for 'Dr. Strangelove,'" *Variety*, April 15, 1964, 21. In addition to the novelization, Kubrick also commissioned Bantam to publish a paperback of the *Dr. Strangelove* script in 1965 (Publishing contract, Bantam Books and Polaris Productions, June 23, 1965, SK/11/4/6, SKA).
65 Mick Broderick, *Reconstructing Strangelove: Inside Stanley Kubrick's "Nightmare Comedy"* (London: Wallflower Press, 2017), 8.
66 "How to Learn to Love World Destruction," *New York Times*, January 26, 1964, X13.
67 Letter from Allan, Foster, Ingersoll and Weber Inc., to Stanley Kubrick, September 4, 1964, SK/11/9/3, SKA.
68 Letter from James B. Harris to Stanley Kubrick, January 22, 1963, SK/1/2/2/2, SKA.

Chapter 8. Kubrick versus MGM, 1964–1969

1 "Big Picture Rentals of 1964," *Variety*, January 6, 1965, 39.
2 "All Time Top Grossers," *Variety*, January 6, 1965, 39, 67.
3 Letter from Stanley Kubrick to *Evening News*, 1963, SK/11/9/68, SKA.
4 Letter from Stanley Kubrick to Dick Hudson, October 13, 1964, SK/11/9/63, SKA.
5 Letter from Stanley Kubrick to Sylvia, October 21, 1964, SK/11/9/63, SKA.
6 Letter from Stanley Kubrick to Bryan Forbes, August 20, 1964, Folder 5, BFP.
7 Letter from Stanley Kubrick to Gerald Ayres, October 29, 1964, SK/18/4/3, SKA.
8 Letter from Stanley Kubrick to Steve McQueen, SK/18/4/3, SKA.
9 Memo Alan Sherwood to Stanley Kubrick, August 12, 1964, SK/18/4/3, SKA.
10 "Film Producer of James Baldwin's 'Charlie,'" *Variety*, October 21, 1964, 1.
11 Letter from Maurice Hatton to Stanley Kubrick, August 10, 1964, SK/11/9/94, SKA.
12 Letter from Stanley Kubrick to Herbert Biberman, July 20, 1964, SK/11/9/94, SKA.
13 Letter from Stanley Kubrick to Irving Allen, April 13, 1964, SK/11/9/100, SKA.
14 Letter from Stanley Kubrick to David Susskind, May 12, 1964, SK/11/9/94, SKA.
15 Letter from Stanley Kubrick to Ben Benjamin, July 20, 1964, SK/11/9/100, SKA.
16 Letter from Ronnie Lubin to Stanley Kubrick, March 14, 1963, SK/11/9/100, SKA.
17 Ibid.
18 Letter from Stanley Kubrick to Ronnie Lubin, August 18, 1964, SK/11/9/100, SKA.
19 Letter from Ray Lovejoy to Stan Hart, January 12, 1964, SK/11/9/75, SKA.
20 Ibid.
21 Letter from Stanley Kubrick to Michael Leigh, June 24, 1964, SK/11/9/76, SKA.
22 "6 Dramas on U.N. Planned for TV," *New York Times*, April 9, 1964, 63.
23 Simone Odino, "'God, It'll Be Hard Topping the H-Bomb': Kubrick's Search for a New Obsession in the Path from *Dr. Strangelove* to *2001: A Space Odyssey*," in *Understanding Kubrick's 2001: A Space Odyssey: Representation and Interpretation*, ed. James Fenwick (Bristol: Intellect, 2018), 24–25.
24 "Pause for Reflection with Peter Sellers," *New York Times*, October 25, 1964, X7.
25 "CBS-TV in Policy Statement about Xerox-UN 6 'Drama' Specials," *Variety*, April 15, 1964, 29.
26 Ibid., 29.
27 "Serling Play to Begin U.N. TV Series," *New York Times*, August 18, 1964, 63.
28 For a comprehensive account of the *Shadow on the Sun* project, see Odino, "'God, It'll Be Hard,'" 26–28.

29 *Shadow on the Sun* synopsis, R-KIVE 1, uncatalogued, SKA.
30 Letter from Ray Lovejoy to Ray Palmer, November 17, 1964, SK/11/9/63, SKA.
31 Odino, "'God, It'll Be Hard,'" 18.
32 Letter from Stanley Kubrick to Arthur C. Clarke, March 31, 1964, SKA.
33 Comparisons of *Dr. Strangelove* costs with *Journey Beyond the Stars*, August 26, 1964, SKA.
34 James Fenwick, "'A Commercial for God and the Space Program': *2001: A Space Odyssey* and the 1969 Moscow International Film Festival," *Les Éditions de l'École Polytechnique* (forthcoming).
35 Letter from Stanley Kubrick to Peter Sellers, June 30, 1964, SK/12/8/1/66, SKA.
36 James Fenwick, "Forging New Perspectives," in Fenwick, *Understanding Kubrick's 2001: A Space Odyssey*, 5.
37 Ibid.
38 Peter Krämer, *2001: A Space Odyssey* (London: British Film Institute, 2010), 29.
39 Piers Bizony, *The Making of Stanley Kubrick's 2001: A Space Odyssey* (Cologne: Taschen, 2014), 21.
40 Ariel Rogers, *Cinematic Appeals: The Experience of New Movie Technologies* (New York: Columbia University Press, 2013), 32–34.
41 Bizony, *Making of Stanley Kubrick's 2001*, 415.
42 Ibid., 417.
43 "Earnings Climb for MGM," *Boxoffice*, March 1, 1965, E1.
44 Ibid.
45 A. H. Weiler, "Beyond the Blue Horizon," *New York Times*, February 21, 1965, X9.
46 Krämer, *2001*, 32.
47 Letter from Robert O'Brien to Stanley Kubrick, March 3, 1965, uncatalogued, SKA.
48 Krämer, *2001*, 108.
49 Letter from Stanley Kubrick to Robert O'Brien, March 2, 1965, uncatalogued, SKA.
50 Draft contract, Polaris Productions and MGM, May 22, 1965, SK/12/2/5, SKA.
51 Telegram from Robert O'Brien to Stanley Kubrick, October 26, 1965, uncatalogued, SKA.
52 Telegram from Stanley Kubrick to Robert O'Brien, October 25, 1965, uncatalogued, SKA.
53 O'Brien to Kubrick, October 26, 1965.
54 "Personality: MGM Chief Robert O'Brien," *New York Times*, January 19, 1963, 13.
55 "Robert O'Brien Named M.P. Pioneer of 1965," *Boxoffice*, July 19, 1965, 5.
56 "Pro-O'Brien Ads Vex Levin Group," *Variety*, January 18, 1967, 3.
57 "Robert O'Brien Chapter-and-Verse Answer to Levin's Raps of MGM," *Variety*, May 25, 1966, 21.
58 "Robert O'Brien Sees Rising Earnings at MGM During Next Several Years," *Boxoffice*, August 1, 1966, 8.
59 "New Generation of Producers," *Variety*, June 24, 1959, 14.
60 Ibid., 14.
61 Ibid., 14.
62 "Studio Execs All Ad Experts," *Variety*, January 4, 1961, 7.
63 "Robert Cohn Stresses Manpower," *Boxoffice*, August 17, 1964, W-2.
64 "Studio Execs All Ad Experts," 36.
65 Ibid., 36.
66 Ibid., 36.
67 "Paramount Expands Promotion Dept.," *Boxoffice*, July 11, 1966, 3.
68 Ibid., 3.

69 "Columbia's New Merchandising Plan," *Boxoffice*, July 10, 1961, 8.
70 Ibid., 8.
71 Ibid., 8.
72 "Eight from Columbia," *Boxoffice*, March 2, 1964, 26.
73 "Columbia's New Merchandising Plan," 8.
74 Ibid., 8.
75 Ibid., 8.
76 Ibid., 8.
77 "Studio Execs All Ad Experts," 7.
78 Ibid.
79 "New Generation of Producers," 14.
80 Vincent Canby, "Producer's Ego vs. Distrib's," *Variety*, November 3, 1965, 5.
81 Ibid., 5.
82 Ibid., 5.
83 Ibid., 5.
84 Draft contract, Polaris Productions and MGM, SK/12/2/5, SKA.
85 Letter from Robert O'Brien to Stanley Kubrick, March 3, 1965, uncatalogued, SKA.
86 "Roger Caras to Kubrick," *Variety*, June 9, 1965, 13.
87 "Caras, Roger," *American National Biography*, www.anb.org/articles/15/15-01308.html.
88 "Chatter: Broadway," *Variety*, May 23, 1956, 90.
89 "Shifting of Roger Caras," *Variety*, February 8, 1961, 64.
90 "Roger Caras Is Named Ass't to Joyce Selznick at Col.," *Boxoffice*, August 27, 1962, E4.
91 "Ken Clark's 'Inner Sanctum' Crack at 'Cleo Papers,'" *Variety*, August 21, 1963, 4.
92 "Merchandising Session on 'Neighbor Sam,'" *Boxoffice*, June 29, 1964, E1.
93 "Columbia Saturation Bookings on Moon," *Boxoffice*, November 2, 1964, 11.
94 Ibid., 11.
95 "Ferguson Advocates Two-Year Campaigns," *Boxoffice*, May 10, 1965, 11.
96 Ibid., 11.
97 "*2001: A Space Odyssey* Interview Series: Ivor Powell," http://blog.tvstoreonline.com/2014/07/2001-space-odyssey-interview-series.html.
98 Letter from Nat Weiss to Stanley Kubrick, December 5, 1962, SK/11/9/111, SKA.
99 Letter from Ray Lovejoy to Roger Caras, July 5, 1966, SK/12/8/3/31, SKA.
100 Letter from Roger Caras to Ray Lovejoy, July 12, 1966, SK/12/8/3/31, SKA.
101 Memo from Stanley Kubrick to Roger Caras, July 11, 1966, SK/12/8/5, SKA.
102 Letter from Roger Caras to Stanley Kubrick, July 14, 1966, SK/12/8/5, SKA.
103 Cable from Stanley Kubrick to Roger Caras, December 27, 1966, SK/12/8/5, SKA.
104 "Ferguson Quits MGM; Terrell Succeeds," *Boxoffice*, January 7, 1950, 10.
105 "MGM Appoints Terrell Eastern Publicity Mgr," *Boxoffice*, December 13, 1952, 22.
106 "Exploitation, Publicity Combined at Metro under Dan Terrell," *Variety*, December 10, 1952, 17.
107 "Weiss: 'Let Kubrick Explain If My Papers Made Him Discharge Me,'" *Variety*, August 7, 1963, 7.
108 Ibid., 7.
109 Ibid., 7.
110 "Columbia Expanding Its Field Promotion Force," *Boxoffice*, August 12, 1963, 12.
111 "Ramsay, Terrell Top MGM Ad-Pub, Marketing Group," *Variety*, April 24, 1963, 7.
112 "MGM Appoints Segal Assistant to Terrell," *Boxoffice*, October 4, 1965, 9.
113 Ibid., 9.

114 "MGM Launches Large Scale Promotions for 'The V.I.P.s,'" *Boxoffice*, August 5, 1963, B2.
115 Ibid.
116 Letter from Roger Caras to Stanley Kubrick, October 11, 1965, SK/12/8/5, SKA.
117 Letter from Stanley Kubrick to Roger Caras, December 15, 1965, SK/12/8/5, SKA.
118 Caras to Kubrick, October 11, 1965.
119 Ibid.
120 Letter from Tom Buck to Mort Segal, January 11, 1967, SK/12/8/2/33, SKA.
121 Ibid.
122 Peter Krämer, "'A Film Specially Suitable for Children': The Marketing and Reception of *2001: A Space Odyssey* (1968)," in *Family Films in Global Cinema: The World beyond Disney*, ed. Noel Brown and Bruce Babington (London: I.B. Tauris, 2015), 40–43.
123 Letter from Stanley Kubrick to Robert O'Brien, April 27, 1967, uncatalogued, SKA.
124 Caras to Kubrick, October 11, 1965.
125 Ibid.
126 Ibid.
127 Ibid.
128 Letter from Roger Caras to Stanley Kubrick, October 26, 1965, SK/12/8/5, SKA.
129 Ibid.
130 Letter from Roger Caras to Arthur Pincus, December 21, 1965, SK/12/6/8, SKA.
131 Ibid.
132 Ibid.
133 Letter from Roger Caras to Sid Balkin, August 9, 1965, SK/12/8/2/45, SKA.
134 Letter from Roger Caras to Chuck Hollister, June 2, 1965, SK/12/8/2/45, SKA.
135 Letter from Roger Caras to Stanley Kubrick, June 2, 1965, SK/12/8/2/45, SKA.
136 Letter from Roger Caras to Stanley Kubrick, August 26, 1965, SK/12/8/2/45, SKA.
137 Letter from Roger Caras to Stanley Kubrick, August 31, 1966, SK/12/8/5, SKA.
138 Ibid.
139 See Kathrina Glitre, "Conspicuous Consumption: The Spectacle of Widescreen Comedy in the Populuxe Era," in *Widescreen Worldwide*, ed. John Belton, Sheldon Hall, and Steven Neale (Bloomington, IN: John Libbey, 2010), 133–143.
140 "2001—The Watch of the Future," *Vogue*, November 15, 1966, 78.
141 By January 1966, Kubrick was already half a million dollars over budget. In a bid to preserve his reputation with Robert O'Brien, he attributed 80 percent of the overspend to set construction and the other 20 percent to a loss of working hours brought about by a new union agreement, which he argued had resulted in thirty minutes working time being lost per day. In addition, a second union agreement, negotiated by the ACTT, had led to an increase in wages and overtime. Together, this had resulted in Kubrick's overspend (though he did admit to also having written an inaccurate budget). Kubrick was using the union agreements as a way of mitigating the embarrassment of being so grossly over budget so early in the production (Letter from Stanley Kubrick to Robert O'Brien, January 23, 1966, uncatalogued, Robert O'Brien File, SKA).
142 Letter from Roger Caras to Robert Cartwright, August 16, 1965, SK/12/8/2/45, SKA.
143 Caras to Kubrick, August 26, 1965.
144 Letter from Ray Lovejoy to Roger Caras, August 10, 1965, SK/12/8/3/31, SKA.
145 Caras to Kubrick, August 26, 1965.
146 Letter from Roger Caras to Victor Lyndon, October 20, 1965, SK/12/8/3/34, SKA.

147 Letter from Roger Caras to Stanley Kubrick, August 13, 1965, SK/12/8/2/45, SKA.
148 Letter from Roger Caras to Stanley Kubrick, December 27, 1966, SK/12/8/5, SKA.
149 Letter from Roger Caras to Stanley Kubrick, July 14, 1966, SK/12/8/5, SKA.
150 Letter from Roger Caras to Stanley Kubrick, November 29, 1966, SK/12/8/5, SKA.
151 Letter from Roger Caras to Stanley Kubrick, December 5, 1966, SK/12/8/5, SKA.
152 Letter from Stanley Kubrick to Robert O'Brien, June 7, 1967, uncatalogued, SKA.
153 Caras to Kubrick, November 29, 1966.
154 Letter from Stanley Kubrick to Robert O'Brien, June 9, 1967, uncatalogued, SKA.
155 Ibid.
156 Ibid.
157 Letter from Robert O'Brien to Stanley Kubrick, July 11, 1967, uncatalogued, SKA.
158 Kubrick to O'Brien, June 9, 1967.
159 Letter from Stanley Kubrick to Robert O'Brien, July 22, 1967, uncatalogued, SKA.
160 Ibid.
161 Letter from Roger Caras to Stanley Kubrick, November 3, 1966, SK/12/8/5, SKA.
162 Ibid.
163 Ibid.
164 Letter from Roger Caras to Stanley Kubrick, July 15, 1966, SK/12/8/5, SKA.
165 Letter from Roger Caras to Stanley Kubrick, October 12, 1966, SK/12/8/5, SKA.
166 Letter from Roger Caras to Stanley Kubrick, October 14, 1966, SK/12/8/5, SKA.
167 "Beaucoup Secrecy (Not Just Publicity) on Kubrick's '2001,'" *Variety*, April 3, 1968, 7.
168 Ibid.
169 Ibid.
170 Cable from Stanley Kubrick to Roger Caras, March 22, 1967, SK/12/8/2/248, SKA.
171 Cable from Benn Reyes to Stanley Kubrick, April 26, 1967, SK/12/8/2/249, SKA.
172 "Benn F. Reyes Appointed V-P for Two Companies," *Boxoffice*, July 3, 1967, 6.
173 Cable from Benn Reyes to Stanley Kubrick, May 1, 1967, SK/12/8/5, SKA.
174 Letter from Roger Caras to Dan Terrell, April 7, 1967, SK/12/8/2/47, SKA.
175 "Late-Starting and Uniquely-Motivated Selling Campaign for MGM's 2001," *Variety*, February 28, 1968, 7.
176 "MGM Launches 'Space Odyssey' Ad Campaign," *Independent Film Journal*, March 2, 1968, 18.
177 "Late-Starting and Uniquely-Motivated Selling Campaign," 7.
178 Ibid., 7.
179 Ibid., 7.
180 Ibid., 7.
181 Letter from Roger Caras to Stanley Kubrick, April 5, 1967, SK/12/8/2/47, SKA.
182 Ibid.
183 Buck to Segal, January 11, 1967.
184 "Metro Leans on Kubrick's 'Odyssey,'" *Variety*, December 13, 1967, 5.
185 Peter Krämer, "Audience Responses to *2001: A Space Odyssey* in the Late 1960s," *Participations* 6, no. 2 (2009): 240–259.
186 "'2001' as Grist for Coffee Cup Debate," *Variety*, April 24, 1968, 29.
187 R. Barton Palmer, "*2001*: The Critical Reception and the Generation Gap," in *Stanley Kubrick's 2001: A Space Odyssey: New Essays*, ed. Robert Kolker (Oxford: Oxford University Press, 2006), 14.
188 "Late-Starting and Uniquely-Motivated Selling Campaign," 7.
189 Letter from James B. Harris to Stanley Kubrick, January 22, 1963, SK/1/2/2/2, SKA.
190 Robert Sklar, "Stanley Kubrick and the American Film Industry," *Current Research in Film* 4 (1988): 118.

Chapter 9. Kubrick and Warner Bros., 1970-1980

1. James Fenwick, "Kubrick and Production," in *The Bloomsbury Companion to Stanley Kubrick*, ed. I. Q. Hunter and Nathan Abrams (London: Bloomsbury, forthcoming).
2. "Dr. Mabuse No. 2: Kubrick's Mythological Image," Kubrick Symposium, Deutsches Filmmuseum, July 21, 2018, www.youtube.com/watch?v=JzAprIY74WA.
3. Ibid.
4. Letter from Roger Caras to Stanley Kubrick, July 22, 1966, SK/12/8/5, SKA,
5. Ibid.
6. "Kubrick's $205,000 Buy of Metro Shares; Ticket Orders for '2001' Perky," *Variety*, March 6, 1968, 4.
7. Isadore Barmash, *Welcome to Our Conglomerate—You're Fired* (Washington, DC: Beard Books, 1971), 150.
8. "Kubrick's $205,000 Buy of Metro Shares," 4.
9. "Kubrick's Stock Buy," *Variety*, February 28, 1968, 7.
10. "Pro-O'Brien Ads Vex Levin Group," *Variety*, January 18, 1967, 3.
11. Ibid., 3.
12. Ibid., 3.
13. Robert Sklar, "Stanley Kubrick and the American Film Industry," *Current Research in Film* 4 (1988): 118.
14. "Pro-O'Brien Ads Vex Levin Group," 3.
15. "Back to the Proxy Wars for MGM," *Broadcasting*, July 28, 1969, 46.
16. Jerry Markham, *A Financial History of Modern U.S. Corporate Scandals: From Enron to Reform* (London: M.E. Sharpe, 2006), 272.
17. Barmash, *Welcome to Our Conglomerate*, 150.
18. "Inside Stuff—Pictures," *Variety*, July 24, 1968, 11.
19. "Chatter—Paris," *Variety*, August 7, 1968, 62; Romanian Film Studios, *Napoleon*, SK/1/1/2, SKA.
20. "New York Soundtrack," *Variety*, October 9, 1968, 24.
21. Jan Harlan, interview with author, January 21, 2016.
22. "Kubrick's Napoleon to United Artists," *Variety*, January 15, 1970, 21.
23. Ibid.
24. "Rival Film Projects Hit New High," *Variety*, June 11, 1969, 46.
25. David Cook, *Lost Illusions: American Cinema in the Shadow of Watergate and Vietnam, 1970–1979* (Berkeley: University of California Press, 2000), 71.
26. "KK Calls for Cuts at MGM," *Observer*, November 23, 1969, 4.
27. "Streamlined MGM Due as Aubrey Cuts 'Fat,'" *Independent Film Journal*, December 23, 1969, 6.
28. "KK Calls for Cuts," 4.
29. "Dreamy Cheapness of 'Rider,'" *Variety*, December 10, 1969, 5.
30. Ibid., 5.
31. Cook, *Lost Illusions*, 71.
32. "Obituaries: The Man Who Rebuilt WB," *Variety*, September 2, 2002, 51.
33. "Ashley Cites Production Program, Continuing High WB Earnings," *Boxoffice*, February 23, 1970, 8.
34. Ibid., 8.
35. "Press Peek at Calley," *Variety*, April 22, 1970, 7.
36. "Pledges Kinney Alert WB Team & Tight Budgets," *Variety*, February 18, 1970, 15.
37. "Kinney Hails All Popular Media as Big Payoff in Coming Leisure," *Variety*, January 13, 1971, 5.

38 "WB Tally," *Variety*, September 16, 1970, 4.
39 "Pledges Kinney Alert," 15.
40 "Kubrick's WB Deal," *Variety*, February 4, 1970, 22.
41 A. H. Weiler, "Kubrick to Adapt 'A Clockwork Orange' for Screen," *New York Times*, February 3, 1970, 36.
42 Ibid., 36.
43 Susskind's production was left unproduced. Brian De Palma's *Casualties of War* (1989) was later based on an altered version of Lang's novel.
44 "Ken Russell's Next," *Variety*, April 1, 1970, 3.
45 "Kinney Defends Warner Actions," *New York Times*, February 18, 1970, 69.
46 "Huxley Drama to be Film," *New York Times*, August 19, 1969, 18.
47 "WB Acceptance of X for 'The Devils,'" *Variety*, July 14, 1971, 5.
48 "Trade Ponders: X the Key to B.O.," *Variety*, February 25, 1970, 1.
49 "Slowed, Not Sloughed, Brit," *Variety*, December 24, 1969, 52.
50 Letter from Si Litvinoff to Stanley Kubrick, February 6, 1970, SK/13/8/5/12, SKA.
51 *A Clockwork Orange* Production Analysis, 1970, Box 2, uncatalogued, SKA.
52 Ibid.
53 Interoffice Warner Bros. Memo from Clive Parsons to Mike Baumohl, 1970, SK/13/8/5/10, SKA.
54 Ibid.
55 Memo from Sidney Kiwitt to Frank Wells, June 3, 1970, SK/13/8/5/10, SKA.
56 Ibid.
57 "Obituaries: The Man Who Rebuilt WB," 51.
58 "Ashley Cites Production Program," 8.
59 Harlan interview.
60 Fenwick, "Kubrick and Production."
61 Gene D. Phillips, ed., *Stanley Kubrick Interviews* (Jackson: University Press of Mississippi, 2002), 189.
62 Telex from Stanley Kubrick to Frank Wells, January 2, 1977, Suspension File—Cable TV, uncatalogued, SKA.
63 Memo from Frank Wells to Sidney Kiwitt, June 19, 1970, SK/13/8/5/10, SKA.
64 Parsons to Baumohl, 1970.
65 Serenella Zanotti, "Auteur Dubbing: Translation, Performance and Authorial Control in the Dubbed Versions of Stanley Kubrick's Films," in *Reassessing Dubbing: Historical Approaches and Current Trends*, ed. Irene Ranzato and Serenella Zanotti (Amsterdam: John Benjamins, 2019), 80.
66 Ibid.
67 Serenella Zanotti, "Investigating the Genesis of Translated Films: A View from the Stanley Kubrick Archive," *Perspectives* 27, no. 2 (2019): 201.
68 Memo from Robert Timms to Frank Pierce, January 8, 1977, Suspension File—Cable TV, uncatalogued, SKA.
69 Fax from Stanley Kubrick to Frank Pierce, January 23, 1977, Suspension File—Cable TV, uncatalogued, SKA.
70 Fax from Stanley Kubrick to Frank Pierce, January 20, 1977, Suspension File—Cable TV, uncatalogued, SKA.
71 Gerald Fried, telephone interview, July 13, 2019.
72 Ibid.
73 Catriona McAvoy, "Creating *The Shining*: Looking Beyond the Myths," in *Stanley Kubrick New Perspectives*, ed. Tatjana Ljujić, Peter Krämer, and Richard Daniels (London: Black Dog, 2015), 294.

74. Letter from Jan Harlan to Creative Management International, October 17, 1975, SK/14/10/10/1, SKA.
75. "Hollywood Production Pulse," *Variety*, September 1, 1971, 20.
76. "Kubrick Hero of Warner Meet," *Variety*, February 16, 1972, 4.
77. Based on the official film credits.
78. Harlan interview.
79. Bernard Williams, Unit Memo, July 17, 1970, SK/13/3/1, SKA.
80. Bernard Williams Unit Memo, December 30, 1970, SK/13/3/1, SKA.
81. Letter from John Mackey to Stanley Kubrick, December 10, 1971, SK/13/8/3/1, SKA.
82. Letter from Stanley Kubrick to Bryan Loftus, December 21, 1971, SK/13/8/3/1, SKA.
83. Ibid.
84. Declan McGrath, "Moments of Transcendence: An Interview with John Boorman," *Cineaste* 40, no. 2 (2015): 33.
85. "Mike Kaplan Vamoose of MGM for Kubrick," *Variety*, March 24, 1971, 21.
86. "Kubrick: A Marketing Odyssey," *Guardian*, November 2, 2007, www.theguardian.com/film/2007/nov/02/marketingandpr.
87. Peter Krämer, "'A Film Specially Suitable for Children': The Marketing and Reception of *2001: A Space Odyssey* (1968)," in *Family Films in Global Cinema: The World beyond Disney*, ed. Noel Brown and Bruce Babington (London: I.B. Tauris, 2015), 43–47.
88. "Catholics Doubt '2001' for Kids," *Variety*, April 17, 1968, 7.
89. "The Ultimate Trip," *Variety*, July 17, 1968, 49.
90. "How Stanley Kubrick Kept His Eyes on the Budget, Down to the Orange Juice," www.moviefone.com/2012/02/19/how-stanley-kubrick-budget/.
91. "Kubrick: A Marketing Odyssey."
92. "How Stanley Kubrick Transformed the Modern Box-Office Report," *Huffington Post*, January 10, 2012, www.huffingtonpost.com/mike-kaplan/stanley-kubrick-box-office_b_1195323.html.
93. Ibid.
94. "50 Top-Grossing Films," *Variety*, May 7, 1969, 15.
95. Cinema Ticket Sales, General Business and Personal Materials, SK/1/2/3/8/6, SKA.
96. Memo from Stanley Kubrick to Leo Greenfield, June 28, 1971, SK/13/8/5/10, SKA.
97. Memo from Leo Greenfield to Stanley Kubrick, June 28, 1971, SK/13/8/5/10, SKA.
98. Letter from Mike Kaplan to Richard Lederer, October 22, 1971, F117, MHL.
99. Ibid.
100. Ibid.
101. Letter from Stanley Kubrick to Ian Ballantine, December 20, 1971, SK/13/8/3/6, SKA.
102. "Stills 'Graphicize' Stan Kubrick Book," *Variety*, July 26, 1972, 12.
103. Deborah Allison, "Paging Inspector Callahan: The Novel Adventures of Dirty Harry," *Literature/Film Quarterly* 44, no. 1 (2016): 5.
104. "'Super Fly' Principals Win Big Payoff," *Variety*, January 17, 1973, 30.
105. "How Stanley Kubrick Kept His Eyes on the Budget, Down to the Orange Juice," www.moviefone.com/2012/02/19/how-stanley-kubrick-budget/.
106. *Orange Times*, summer 1972, CWO R-KIVE 1, uncatalogued, SKA.
107. Open letter from Stanley Kubrick, 1969, uncatalogued, SKA.
108. "How Stanley Kubrick Shot His Own Newsweek Cover," *Huffington Post*, February 8, 2012, www.huffingtonpost.com/mike-kaplan/kubrick-newsweek-cover_b_1263300.html.

109 *Newsweek*, January 3, 1972.
110 *A Clockwork Orange* press book, 1971, 1–2.
111 "Ross Concedes 'Lyndon' Flop," *Variety*, May 12, 1976, 3.
112 "*The Shining*," *Variety*, January 28, 1981, 15.
113 "The Sixth Annual Grosses Gloss," *Film Comment* 17, no. 2 (1981): 64.
114 Harmetz, "How Does Hollywood Decide if a Film Is a Hit?," *New York Times*, June 2, 1981, C7.
115 "WB Wants Stiff Terms for Stan Kubrick's 'Shining,'" *Variety*, September 19, 1979, 5.
116 "What Were 1980's Most Popular Movies?," *New York Times*, January 19, 1981, C13.
117 "Kubrick Extruded," *Variety*, November 28, 1973, 6.
118 Letter from Stanley Kubrick to John Calley, April 30, 1975, SK/14/6/8, SKA.
119 Key Worries of Filming, *Barry Lyndon*, May 21, 1973, SK/143/11, SKA.
120 Telex from Stanley Kubrick to Frank Wells, February 1, 1977, Suspension File—Cable TV, uncatalogued, SKA.
121 *Barry Lyndon* Media Plan, SK/14/7/26, SKA.
122 Ibid.
123 *Barry Lyndon* Radio Promotion, January 30, 1976, SK/14/7/21, SKA.
124 Ibid.
125 *Barry Lyndon* Valentine's invitation, SK/14/7/21, SKA.
126 Warner Bros. Interoffice Memo, *Barry Lyndon* book, October 27, 1975, SK/14/7/21, SKA.
127 Ibid.
128 Memo from Lige Brien to Leo Wilder, February 12, 1976, SK/14/7/21, SKA.
129 Telex from Frank Wells to Stanley Kubrick, February 1, 1977, Suspension File—Cable TV, uncatalogued, SKA.
130 "The Shining" (1976), *Kirkus Reviews*, January 1, 1976.
131 "Kubrick to Make 'Occult' Movie," *Screen International*, June 18, 1977, 92.
132 "WB Wants Stiff Terms," 5.
133 Letter from Michael Edwards to Jan Harlan, October 26, 1981, SK/15/8/1, SKA.
134 "WB Wants Stiff Terms," 5.
135 Draft press release, February 12, 1981, SK/15/8/5, SKA.
136 Telex from Frank Wells to Stanley Kubrick, October 22, 1975, SK/14/10/20, SKA.
137 Letter from Stanley Kubrick to Peter Knecht, July 28, 1975, SK/14/10/20, SKA.
138 Letter from Stanley Kubrick to Peter Knecht, July 21, 1975, SK/14/10/20, SKA.
139 Howard Glennerster, "Why Was a Wealth Tax for the UK Abandoned? Lessons for the Policy Process and Tackling Wealth Inequality," *Journal of Social Policy* 41, no. 2 (2012): 238.
140 Ibid., 239.
141 Draft letter, Stanley Kubrick, February 13, 1975, Future of British Film Industry, uncatalogued, SKA.
142 Letter from John Woolf to Stanley Kubrick, May 23, 1975, Future of British Film Industry, uncatalogued, SKA.
143 Letter from Stanley Kubrick to John Woolf, June 7, 1975, Future of British Film Industry, uncatalogued, SKA.
144 Letter from Stanley Kubrick to John Woolf, May 14, 1975, Future of British Film Industry, uncatalogued, SKA.
145 Letter from Stanley Kubrick to Geoffrey Howe, May 23, 1977, Future of British Film Industry, uncatalogued, SKA. Kubrick's interactions with the Conservative Party should not be misconstrued as betraying his political persuasions. Kubrick

was courting a range of powerful UK political figures and was even good friends with Michael Foot, the Labour Party leader from 1980 to 1983.
146 See Peter Krämer, *A Clockwork Orange* (Basingstoke, UK: Palgrave Macmillan, 2011), 111–112, 117–118.
147 Letter from Bob Webster to Myron Karlin, September 22, 1977, Clockwork UK 76–78, uncatalogued, SKA.
148 Ibid.
149 Telex from Stanley Kubrick to Myron Karlin, October 4, 1977, Clockwork UK 76–78, uncatalogued, SKA.
150 Telex from Stanley Kubrick, November 1, 1977, Clockwork UK 76–78, uncatalogued, SKA.
151 Undated note, CWO R-KIVE 1, uncatalogued, SKA.
152 Letter from Julian Senior to Albert Salem, November 11, 1976, SK/14/5/4/2, SKA.

Chapter 10. The End, 1980–1999

1 "Dateline Hollywood," *Washington Post*, January 26, 1984, B7.
2 Richard Daniels, "The Stanley Kubrick Archive: A Filmmaker's Legacy," *Screening the Past*, no. 42 (2017), www.screeningthepast.com/2017/09/the-stanley-kubrick-archive-a-filmmakers-legacy/.
3 Draft outline *Job*, May 28, 1971, Jan's Office Box 4, uncatalogued, SKA.
4 Anthony Frewin, email correspondence with author, March 16, 2016.
5 Ibid.
6 Anthony Frewin, Empyrean Films, June 4, 1990, SK/1/2/3/2/85, SKA.
7 Anthony Frewin, Empyrean Films, September 22, 1990, SK/1/2/3/2/85, SKA.
8 Anthony Frewin, Empyrean Films, April 29, 1991, SK/1/2/3/2/85, SKA.
9 Development breakdown for *The Crying of Lot 49*, SK/1/2/12/1/2/4, SKA.
10 Ibid.
11 Option agreement, *Déricourt* file, August 23, 1989, SK/18/4/3, SKA.
12 *Eric Brighteyes* synopsis, August, 1982, SK/18/4/2, SKA.
13 "Finding and Developing the Story," Stanley Kubrick Archive Oral History Project, www.youtube.com/watch?v=Lx49KEJxUF0&feature=youtu.be.
14 See, for example, Theatrical Distribution Analysis, May 14, 1975, SK/14/5/4/1, SKA; Theatrical Distribution Map, SK/14/5/4/7, SKA; and Initial Marketing Strategy Plan, 1992, SK/1/2/3/8/3, SKA.
15 Aldiss has said that Kubrick first contacted him in 1974, but archival evidence suggests that the relationship didn't commence until 1975 and was initiated by Aldiss.
16 Letter from Brian Aldiss to Stanley Kubrick, November 7, 1975, Letters of Interest, uncatalogued, SKA.
17 Letter from Brian Aldiss to Stanley Kubrick, July 7, 1976, Letters of Interest, uncatalogued, SKA.
18 Letter from Stanley Kubrick to Brian Aldiss, August 3, 1976, Letters of Interest, uncatalogued, SKA.
19 Fax from Brian Aldiss to Merv Binss, BWA/3/4, BAA.
20 William Beard, "'A.I.' or, The Agony of Steven Spielberg," *Cineaction*, April 2005, 5.
21 Aldiss to Binss.
22 "Re Stanley Kubrick and 'Supertoys,'" BWA/1/3/4/3, BAA.
23 Ibid.
24 Aldiss to Binss.

25. "Re Stanley Kubrick."
26. Ibid.
27. Ibid.
28. Letter from Brian Aldiss to Sharon Baker, 1982, BWA/3/3, BAA.
29. Breakdown of *Supertoys*, Bob Shaw, December 20, 1989, Jan's Office Box 4, uncatalogued, SKA; *A.I.* treatment, Brian Aldiss, 1990, *A.I.* Box A, uncatalogued, SKA.
30. Chris Baker, email correspondence with author, October 17, 2016.
31. Letter from Ned Gorman to Stanley Kubrick, April 12, 1994, *A.I.* Box A, uncatalogued, SKA.
32. Email from Stanley Kubrick to Steven Spielberg, July 29, 1993, Letters of Interest, uncatalogued, SKA.
33. Letter from Steven Spielberg to Stanley Kubrick, May 7, 1996, Letters of Interest, uncatalogued, SKA.
34. Peter Krämer, "Adaptation as Exploration: Stanley Kubrick, Literature, and *A.I. Artificial Intelligence*," *Adaptation* 8, no. 3 (2015): 380.
35. "Interview with Brian Aldiss," Red Carpet News, www.youtube.com/watch?v=ffxS6hH2omA.
36. Geoffrey Cocks, *The Wolf at the Door: Stanley Kubrick, History, and the Holocaust* (New York: Peter Lang, 2004), 150.
37. The UK and U.S. intelligence agencies doubted Operation Long Jump was ever a credible plan, citing the unreliability of Soviet intelligence.
38. Letter from Niels Larsen to Stanley Kubrick, n.d., Brown Wallet J, uncatalogued, SKA.
39. Letter from Niels Larsen to Stanley Kubrick, April 30, 1969, Brown Wallet J, uncatalogued, SKA.
40. Pinter was in the process of adapting Marcel Proust's *In Search of Lost Time* and was seeking Kubrick's advice on the project. Kubrick, who had previously considered an adaptation of Proust's book with Harris-Kubrick Pictures, advised Pinter to take the project to the BBC (Letter from Stanley Kubrick to Harold Pinter, August 6, 1982, MS 88880/6/26, HPP; Letter from Harris-Kubrick Pictures re. *In Remembrance of Things Past*, July 24, 1959, JBH).
41. Letter from Stanley Kubrick to Harold Pinter, June 11, 1982, MS 88880/6/36, HPP.
42. Jan Harlan, interview with author, January 21, 2016.
43. Veit Harlan was the uncle of Jan Harlan and became a leading director of propaganda for Joseph Goebbels. His most notorious film was *Jud Süß* (1940). Harlan was later tried, but acquitted, of crimes against humanity for directing the film.
44. Harlan interview.
45. Geoffrey Cocks, "The Hinting: Holocaust Imagery in Kubrick's *The Shining*," *Psychohistory Review* 16, no. 1 (1985): 115–136.
46. Geoffrey Cocks, "Indirected by Stanley Kubrick," *Post Script* 32, no. 2 (2013): 20.
47. Ibid., 20.
48. *Aryan Papers* Production Plan, July 10, 1991, Aryan Papers Box 1, uncatalogued, SKA.
49. Ibid.
50. "Hollywood's Most Secret Agent," *New York Times*, July 9, 1989, 24.
51. Michael Ovitz, *Who Is Michael Ovitz?* (London: W. H. Allen, 2018); "How *Schindler's List* and *Jurassic Park* Came to Be," CBS News, www.cbsnews.com/news/book-excerpt-who-is-michael-ovitz-how-schindlers-list-and-jurassic-park-came-to-be/.

52 "Prolific U Plans 24 Films for '90," *Variety*, May 10, 1989, 34.
53 Paula Parisi, "The Intelligence Behind A.I.," *Wired*, www.wired.com/1997/01/ffai/.
54 Ibid.
55 "Spielberg Has H'Wood on Hook," *Variety*, November 18, 1991, 53.
56 *Aryan Papers* breakdown, February 4, 1992, *Wartime Lies* Box 4, uncatalogued, SKA.
57 *Aryan Papers* draft treatment, June 12, 1992, SK/18/2/1/6, SKA.
58 *Aryan Papers* draft treatment, October 5, 1992, SK/18/2/1/7, SKA.
59 Jan Harlan correspondence with Louis Begley, September 9–19, 1991, *Aryan Papers* Box 2, uncatalogued, SKA.
60 *Aryan Papers* Production Plan.
61 Fax from Jeff Berg, November 3, 1992, *Aryan Papers* Box 1, uncatalogued, SKA.
62 Fax from Richard Attenborough to Stanley Kubrick, February 16, 1993, Letters of Interest, uncatalogued, SKA.
63 Fax from Stanley Kubrick to Richard Attenborough, February 16, 1993, Letters of Interest, uncatalogued, SKA.
64 Attenborough was eventually able to cast Mazzello in *Shadowlands*.
65 Fax from Philip Hobbs to Amsterdam Studio, September 5, 1991, *Aryan Papers* Box 1, uncatalogued, SKA.
66 Harlan interview.
67 "Kubrick's Got His Next Pic," *Variety*, April 5, 1993, 24B.
68 Letter from Stanley Kubrick to Jeff Berg, December 4, 1992, SK/18/2/4/2, SKA.
69 "Kubrick's Got His Next Pic," 24B.
70 Letter from Jan Harlan to Rick Senat, May 22, 1993, SK/18/2/5/3/4, SKA.
71 Ibid.
72 "Big Buck Bonanza in Local Shoots," *Variety*, August 16, 1993, 28.
73 Ibid., 28.
74 Ibid., 28.
75 Ibid., 28.
76 Fax from Jilly Nissler to Jan Harlan, April 8, 1993, SK/18/2/5/3/4, SKA.
77 An alternative production schedule was proposed, with a start date of January 3, running for twenty-one weeks until May 28 (Shooting schedule, *Aryan Papers* Box 1, uncatalogued, SKA).
78 "Essential Steps," n.d., SK/18/2/5/3/4, SKA.
79 Letter from Jan Harlan to S.J. Berwin & Co., May 20, 1993, SK/18/2/5/3/4, SKA.
80 Letter from Jan Harlan to Rick Senat, May 22, 1993, SK/18/2/5/3/4, SKA.
81 "Big Buck Bonanza," 28.
82 Note from Jan Harlan to Stanley Kubrick, May 30, 1993, SK/18/2/5/3/4, SKA.
83 Eastern European weather forecasts, Tony Frewin, *Wartime Lies* Box 4, uncatalogued, SKA.
84 Letter from Jan Harlan to Tamara Holoubkova, November 18, 1993, *Wartime Lies* Box 4, uncatalogued, SKA.
85 Kubrick made notes of directors he thought capable of realizing *Aryan Papers*, including Egon Günther, director of the German film *Morenga* (1985) (*Aryan Papers* Production Plan).
86 Harlan interview.
87 Letter from Tom Cruise to Stanley Kubrick, August 8, 1994, Letters of Interest, uncatalogued, SKA.
88 Michael Herr, *Kubrick* (London: Picador, 2000), 6.
89 *Maggot*, FMJ Box 5, uncatalogued, SKA.

90 *Full Metal Jacket* treatment, 1983, FMJ Box 7, uncatalogued, SKA.
91 Michele Pavan Deana, "Epicentre of an Earthquake: The Literary Sources of *Full Metal Jacket*," *Historical Journal of Film, Radio and Television* 37, no. 3 (2017): 400.
92 "Sit and Talk," FMJ Box 7, uncatalogued, SKA.
93 Herr, *Kubrick*, 6–7.
94 "Dateline Hollywood," *Washington Post*, January 26, 1984, B7.
95 Letter from Stanley Kubrick to Gustav Hasford, March 24, 1987, FMJ Box 5, uncatalogued, SKA.
96 "Big Rental Films of '87," *Variety*, January 20, 1988, 19.
97 "Lucky 7 Reap Record Rentals for Warner International," *Variety*, January 16, 1988, 1.
98 Terry Gross, "Eastwood's *Letters from Iwo Jima*," in *Clint Eastwood Interviews*, ed. Robert Kapsis and Kathie Coblentz (Jackson: University Press of Mississippi, 1999), 204.
99 Ibid., 204–205.
100 Chris Jordan, *Movies and the Reagan Presidency: Success and Ethics* (Westport, CT: Praeger, 2003), 36–37.
101 James Fenwick, "A Day at the Archives . . . the Stanley Kubrick Archives," December 5, 2017, http://iamhist.net/2017/12/stanley-kubrick-archives/.
102 Herr, *Kubrick*, 7; Robert Kolker and Nathan Abrams, *Eyes Wide Shut: Stanley Kubrick and the Making of His Final Film* (New York: Oxford University Press, 2019), 14.
103 Letter from Stanley Kubrick to Anthony Burgess, April 23, 1986, EWS RKIVE 1, uncatalogued, SKA.
104 "Warners Moving Forward on Major Prods. To Roll in Europe and U.S.," *Variety*, July 28, 1971, 3.
105 Nicola Simpson, "Coming Attractions: A Comparative History of the Hollywood Studio System and the Porn Business," *Historical Journal of Film, Radio and Television* 24, no. 4 (2004): 645.
106 Ibid., 644–645.
107 Kolker and Abrams, *Eyes Wide Shut*, 30.
108 Christopher Forsley, "Stanley Kubrick Wanted a Taste of Terry Southern's Lamb-Pit," *Vice*, January 16, 2013, www.vice.com/en_us/article/dp49pz/stanley-kubrick-wanted-a-taste-of-terry-southerns-lamb-pit.
109 *Rhapsody* story concept, August 4, 1976, EWS Box 11, uncatalogued, SKA.
110 Handwritten notes, EWS Box 11, uncatalogued, SKA.
111 Linda Ruth Williams, "A Woman Scorned: The Neo-Noir Erotic Thriller as Revenge Drama," in *Neo-Noir*, ed. Mark Bould, Kathrina Glitre, and Greg Tuck (London: Wallflower Press, 2009), 169.
112 *Rhapsody* promotional copy, November 28, 1981, EWS R-KIVE 1, uncatalogued, SKA.
113 Letter from Peter Schnitzler to SK, July 22, 1981, EWS Box 11, uncatalogued, SKA.
114 See, for example, Blue Folder—Reader's Reports, 1981/1982, EWS R-KIVE 1, uncatalogued, SKA; Empyrean Films, Files 1 and 2, SK/1/2/3/2/35, SKA; Black File, Reader's Reports, Letters of Interest, uncatalogued, SKA.
115 Kubrick to Burgess, April 23, 1986; Black File, Reader's Reports.
116 *Rhapsody*, Kubrick Working Copy, August 21, 1989, EWS R-KIVE 1, uncatalogued, SKA.
117 Marketing Plan, *Eyes Wide Shut*, n.d., SK/17/5/6, SKA.

Epilogue

1 Joseph Gelmis, *The Film Director as Superstar* (New York: Doubleday, 1970).
2 Peter Krämer, "Adaptation as Exploration: Stanley Kubrick, Literature, and *A.I. Artificial Intelligence*," *Adaptation* 8, no. 3 (2015): 381.
3 James Fenwick, David Eldridge, and Kieran Fosters, eds., *Shadow Cinema: Industrial and Production Contexts* (New York: Bloomsbury, forthcoming).

Select Bibliography

Archives

Aldiss, Brian. Archives. Special Collections and Archives. University of Liverpool.
Ballantine Books. Archive. Columbia University Libraries, New York.
Board of Trade and Department of Trade and Industry Records. The National Archives. Kew, London.
Collins, L. J. Papers. Lambeth Palace Library, London.
de Rochemont, Richard. Papers. American Heritage Center. University of Wyoming.
Douglas, Kirk. Papers. Wisconsin Historical Society. University of Wisconsin–Madison.
Dunn, Linwood G. Papers. Margaret Herrick Library of Motion Picture Arts and Sciences, Los Angeles.
Forbes, Bryan. Papers. Margaret Herrick Library of Motion Picture Arts and Sciences, Los Angeles.
Kubrick, Stanley. Archive. Archives and Special Collections Centre. University of the Arts London.
Peck, Gregory. Papers. Margaret Herrick Library of Motion Picture Arts and Sciences, Los Angeles.
Pinter, Harold. Archive. Western Manuscripts. British Library, London.
Production Code Administration Records. Motion Picture Association of America. Margaret Herrick Library, Los Angeles.
United Artists. Corporation Records. Wisconsin Historical Society. University of Wisconsin–Madison.
United States Youth Council Records. Social Welfare History Archives. University of Minnesota.
Weiser, Marty. Papers. Margaret Herrick Library of Motion Picture Arts and Sciences, Los Angeles.

Books

Abrams, Jerold J., ed. *The Philosophy of Stanley Kubrick*. Lexington: University Press of Kentucky, 2007.

Select Bibliography

Abrams, Nathan. *Stanley Kubrick: New York Jewish Intellectual*. New Brunswick, NJ: Rutgers University Press, 2018.

Agel, Jerome. *The Making of Kubrick's "2001."* New York: New American Library, 1970.

Balio, Tino, ed. *The American Film Industry*. 2nd ed. Madison: University of Wisconsin Press, 1985.

———. *United Artists: The Company That Changed the Film Industry*. Madison: University of Wisconsin Press, 1987.

Baxter, John. *Stanley Kubrick: A Biography*. London: HarperCollins, 1998.

Begley, Louis. *Wartime Lies*. New York: Knopf, 1991.

Bizony, Piers. *The Making of Stanley Kubrick's 2001: A Space Odyssey*. Cologne: Taschen, 2014.

Bordwell, David, Janet Staiger, and Kristen Thompson. *The Classical Hollywood Cinema: Film Style and Mode of Production to 1960*. London: Routledge, 1985.

Broderick, Mick. *Reconstructing Strangelove: Inside Stanley Kubrick's "Nightmare Comedy."* London: Wallflower Press, 2017.

———, ed. *The Kubrick Legacy*. New York: Routledge, 2019.

Burgess, Anthony. *A Clockwork Orange*. London: Heinemann, 1962.

Castle, Alison, ed. *The Stanley Kubrick Archives*. Cologne: Taschen, 2005.

Chapman, James, Mark Glancy, and Sue Harper, eds. *The New Film History: Sources, Methods, Approaches*. Basingstoke: Palgrave Macmillan, 2007.

Chion, Michel. *Kubrick's Cinema Odyssey*. London: British Film Institute, 2001.

Clarke, Arthur C. *Expedition to Earth*. 1953. Reprint, London: New English Library, 1983.

———. *The Sentinel*. 1951. Reprint, Glasgow: Voyager, 2000.

———. *2001: A Space Odyssey*. London: Hutchinson, 1968.

Cocks, Geoffrey. *The Wolf at the Door: Stanley Kubrick, History, and the Holocaust*. New York: Peter Lang, 2007.

Cocks, Geoffrey, James Diedrick, and Glenn Perusek, eds. *Depth of Field: Stanley Kubrick, Film, and the Uses of History*. Madison: University of Wisconsin Press, 2006.

Coëgnarts, Maarten. *Film as Embodied Art: Bodily Meaning in the Cinema of Stanley Kubrick*. Brookline, MA: Academic Studies Press, 2019.

Cook, David. *Lost Illusions: American Cinema in the Shadow of Watergate and Vietnam, 1970–1979*. Berkeley: University of California Press, 2000.

Corliss, Richard. *Lolita*. London: British Film Institute, 1994.

Coyle, Wallace. *Stanley Kubrick: A Guide to References and Resources*. Boston: G. K. Hall, 1980.

D'Alessandro, Emilio, and Filippo Ulivieri. *Stanley Kubrick and Me: Thirty Years at His Side*. New York: Arcade, 2012.

Davis, Blair. *The Battle for the Bs: 1950s Hollywood and the Rebirth of Low-Budget Cinema*. New Brunswick, NJ: Rutgers University Press, 2012.

Douglas, Kirk. *I Am Spartacus! Making a Film, Breaking the Blacklist*. New York: Open Road, 2012.

———. *The Ragman's Son*. London: Simon & Schuster, 1988.

Elsaesser, Thomas. *The Persistence of Hollywood: From Cinephile Moments to Blockbuster Memories*. New York: Routledge, 2012.

Falsetto, Mario, ed. *Perspectives on Stanley Kubrick*. New York: G. K. Hall, 1996.

———. *Stanley Kubrick: A Narrative and Stylistic Analysis*. 2nd ed. Westport, CT: Praeger, 2001.

Fenwick, James, ed. *Understanding Kubrick's 2001: A Space Odyssey: Representation and Interpretation*. Bristol: Intellect, 2018.

García-Mainar, Luis M. *Narrative and Stylistic Patterns in the Films of Stanley Kubrick*. New York: Camden House, 2000.

Gelmis, Joseph. *The Film Director as Superstar*. Garden City, NY: Doubleday, 1970.
Hunter, I. Q. *Cult Film as a Guide to Life: Fandom, Adaptation and Identity*. London: Bloomsbury, 2016.
Jenkins, Greg. *Stanley Kubrick and the Art of Adaptation: Three Novels, Three Films*. Jefferson, NC: McFarland, 1997.
Kagan, Norman. *The Cinema of Stanley Kubrick*. New York: Holt, Rinehart and Winston, 1972.
Kolker, Robert, ed. *A Cinema of Loneliness*. 4th ed. New York: Oxford University Press, 2011.
———. *The Extraordinary Image: Orson Welles, Alfred Hitchcock, Stanley Kubrick, and the Reimagining of Cinema*. New Brunswick, NJ: Rutgers University Press, 2016.
———. *Stanley Kubrick's 2001: A Space Odyssey: New Essays*. New York: Oxford University Press, 2006.
Kolker, Robert, and Nathan Abrams. *Eyes Wide Shut: Stanley Kubrick and the Making of His Final Film*. New York: Oxford University Press, 2019.
Krämer, Peter. *A Clockwork Orange*. Basingstoke, UK: Palgrave Macmillan, 2011.
———. *Dr. Strangelove; or How I Learned to Stop Worrying and Love the Bomb*. London: British Film Institute, 2014.
———. *The New Hollywood: From Bonnie and Clyde to Star Wars*. New York: Wallflower Press, 2005.
———. *2001: A Space Odyssey*. London: British Film Institute, 2010.
Krohn, Bill. *Stanley Kubrick*. London: Phaidon Press, 2010.
Kuberski, Philip. *Kubrick's Total Cinema: Philosophical Themes and Formal Qualities*. London: Bloomsbury, 2012.
Kubrick, Stanley. *Stanley Kubrick's A Clockwork Orange*. New York: Ballantine Books, 1972.
Lev, Peter. *The Fifties Transforming the Screen 1950–1959*. Berkeley: University of California Press, 2003.
Lewis, Jon, ed. *Producing*. New Brunswick, NJ: Rutgers University Press, 2016.
Ljujić, Tatjana, Peter Krämer, and Richard Daniels, eds. *Stanley Kubrick: New Perspectives*. London: Black Dog, 2015.
LoBrutto, Vincent. *Stanley Kubrick*. London: Faber & Faber, 1997.
Luckhurst, Roger. *The Shining*. London: British Film Institute, 2013.
Mather, Philippe. *Stanley Kubrick at Look Magazine: Authorship and Genre in Photojournalism and Film*. Bristol: Intellect, 2013.
McQuiston, Kate. *We'll Meet Again: Musical Design in the Films of Stanley Kubrick*. New York: Oxford University Press, 2013.
Mee, Laura. *The Shining*. Leighton Buzzard: Auteur, 2017.
Naremore, James. *On Kubrick*. London: British Film Institute, 2007.
Pezzotta, Elisa. *Stanley Kubrick: Adapting the Sublime*. Jackson: University Press of Mississippi, 2013.
Phillips, Gene D., ed. *Stanley Kubrick Interviews*. Jackson: University Press of Mississippi, 2001.
Phillips, Gene D., and Rodney Hill. *The Encyclopaedia of Stanley Kubrick: From Day of the Fight to Eyes Wide Shut*. New York: Checkmark Books, 2002.
Pramaggiore, Maria. *Making Time in Stanley Kubrick's Barry Lyndon: Art, History, and Empire*. New York: Bloomsbury, 2015.
Prince, Stephen. *A New Pot of Gold: Hollywood under the Electronic Rainbow 1980–1989*. Berkeley: University of California Press, 2000.
Reichmann, Hans-Peter, ed. *Stanley Kubrick*. Frankfurt: Deutsches Filmmuseum, 2007.
Rhodes, Gary D., ed. *Stanley Kubrick: Essays on His Films and Legacy*. Jefferson, NC: McFarland, 2008.

Schnitzler, Arthur. *Traumnovelle: Dream Story*. 1926. Reprint, London: Penguin, 2004.
Spicer, Andrew, A. T. McKenna, and Christopher Meir, eds. *Beyond the Bottom Line: The Producer in Film and Television Studies*. London: Bloomsbury, 2014.
Stoehr, Kevin L. *Nihilism in Film and Television*. Jefferson, NC: McFarland, 2006.
Ulivieri, Filippo, and Simone Odino. *2001 between Kubrick and Clarke: The Genesis, Making and Authorship of a Masterpiece*. Independent, 2019.
Walker, Alexander. *Kubrick Directs*. London: Davis-Poynter, 1972.
Winkler, Martin, ed. *Spartacus: Film and History*. Chichester: Wiley-Blackwell, 2008.

Journal Articles and Book Chapters

Abrams, Nathan. "An Alternative New York Jewish Intellectual: Stanley Kubrick's Cultural Critique." In *Stanley Kubrick: New Perspectives*, edited by Tatjana Ljujić, Peter Krämer and Richard Daniels, 62–79. London: Black Dog, 2015.
——. "Becoming a Macho Mensch: Stanley Kubrick, *Spartacus* and 1950s Jewish Masculinity." *Adaptation* 8, no. 3 (2015): 283–296.
——. "A Jewish American Monster: Stanley Kubrick, Anti-Semitism and *Lolita* (1962)." *Journal of American Studies* 49, no. 3 (2015): 541–556.
——. "What Was HAL? IBM, Jewishness and Stanley Kubrick's *2001: A Space Odyssey* (1968)." *Historical Journal of Film, Radio and Television* 37, no. 3 (2017): 416–435.
Bernstein, Matthew. "The Producer as Auteur." In *Auteurs and Authorship: A Reader*, edited by Barry K. Grant, 180–189. Oxford: Blackwell, 2008.
Broderick, Mick, Joy McEntee, and James Fenwick. "Missing Links: Exploring Traces of Kubrick's Unknown Early Work." *Senses of Cinema* (forthcoming).
Church, David. "The Cult of Kubrick." *Offscreen* 10, no. 5 (2006). www.offscreen.com/view/cult_kubrick.
Cocks, Geoffrey. "Bringing the Holocaust Home: The Freudian Dynamics of Kubrick's *The Shining*." *Psychoanalytic Review* 78, no. 1 (1991): 103–125.
——. "A Quality of Obsession Considerably Further East: The Holocaust in the Cinema of Stanley Kubrick." *Shofar: Interdisciplinary Journal of Jewish Studies*, no. 28 (2010): 72–85.
Egan, Kate. "Precious Footage of the Auteur at Work: Framing, Accessing, Using, and Cultifying Vivian Kubrick's Making the Shining." *New Review of Film and Television Studies* 13, no. 1 (2015): 63–82.
Fenwick, James. "*A Clockwork Orange*: Anthony Burgess's (1962) Black Comedy and Stanley Kubrick's Violent Grotesque (1971)." In *Major Genres, Forms, and Media in British Literature*, edited by Katy Stavreva. Farmington Hills, MI: Gale Researcher, 2018.
——. "'A Commercial for God and the Space Program': *2001: A Space Odyssey* and the 1969 Moscow International Film Festival." *Les Éditions de l'École Polytechnique* (forthcoming).
——. "Curating Kubrick: Constructing New Perspective Narratives in Stanley Kubrick Exhibitions." *Screening the Past*, no. 42 (2017). www.screeningthepast.com/2017/09/curating-kubrick-constructing-new-perspective-narratives-in-stanley-kubrick-exhibitions/.
——. "The Eady Levy, 'the Envy of Most Other European Nations': Runaway Production and the British Film Fund in the Early 1960s." In *The Routledge Companion to British Cinema History*, edited by I. Q. Hunter, Laraine Porter, and Justin Smith, 191–199. Abingdon, UK: Routledge, 2017.
——. "*Eyes Wide Shut*." In *The Encyclopaedia of Sexism in American Cinema*, edited by Salvador Jimenez Murguía, Erica Dymond, and Kristina Fennelly, 110–115. Lanham, MD: Rowman & Littlefield, 2020.

———. "'Freddie, Can You Talk?' The Ethics of Betrayal in Frederic Raphael's Memoir *Eyes Wide Open.*" In *British Autobiography in the 20th and 21st Centuries*, edited by Sara Herbe and Gabriele Linke, 39–57. Heidelberg: Universitätsverlag, 2017.

———. "Kirk Douglas and Stanley Kubrick: Reconsidering a Creative and Business Partnership." In *A Critical Companion to Stanley Kubrick*, edited by Elsa Colombani. Lanham, MD: Lexington Books, forthcoming.

———. "Kubrick and Production." In *Stanley Kubrick Companion*. New York: Bloomsbury, forthcoming.

———. "'Let This Be Kubrick's Final Word. Do You Hear Us Warner Bros.?' Fan Reaction to *Eyes Wide Shut* (1999) and the Death of a Cult-Auteur." *Journal of Fandom Studies* 5, no. 3 (2018): 21–32.

———. "'Look, Ma, I'm a Corporation!' United Artists and Kirk Douglas's Bryna Productions 1955–1959." In *United Artists*, edited by Yannis Tzioumakis, Peter Krämer, Gary Needham, and Tino Balio, 94–111. London: Routledge, 2020.

———. "A Production Strategy of Overdevelopment: Kirk Douglas's Bryna Productions and the Unproduced *Viva Gringo!*" In *Shadow Cinema: Industrial and Production Contexts*, edited by James Fenwick, David Eldridge, and Kieran Foster. New York: Bloomsbury, forthcoming.

Fenwick, James, I. Q. Hunter, and Elisa Pezzotta, eds. "The Stanley Kubrick Archive: A Dossier of New Research." Special issue, *Historical Journal of Film, Radio, and Television* 37, no. 3 (2017).

———, eds. "Stanley Kubrick: A Retrospective." Special issue, *Cinergie*, no. 12 (2017). https://doi.org/10.6092/issn.2280-9481/7341.

Hunter, I. Q. "*A Clockwork Orange*, Exploitation and the Art Film." In *Recycling Culture(s)*, edited by Sara Martin, 96–103. Newcastle: Cambridge Scholars, 2008.

———. "From Adaptation to Cinephilia: An Intertextual Odyssey." In *Science Fiction Across Media: Adaptation/Novelization*, edited by Thomas Van Parys and I. Q. Hunter, 43–63. Canterbury: Gylphi Limited, 2013.

———, ed. "Kubrick and Adaptation." Special Issue, *Adaptation* 8, no. 3 (2015). https://doi.org/10.1093/adaptation/apv026.

Jaunas, Vincent, and Jean-François Baillon, eds. "Stanley Kubrick Nouveaux Horizons." Special issue, *Essais* hors série (2017).

Kerr, Paul. "'A Small, Effective Organization': The Mirisch Company, the Package-Unit System, and the Production of *Some Like It Hot*." In *Billy Wilder, Movie-Maker: Critical Essays on the Films*, edited by Karen McNally, 117–131. Jefferson, NC: McFarland, 2011.

Krämer, Peter. "Adaptation as Exploration: Stanley Kubrick, Literature, and *A.I. Artificial Intelligence*." *Adaptation* 8, no. 3 (2015): 372–382.

———. "'Dear Mr. Kubrick': Audience Responses to *2001: A Space Odyssey* in the Late 1960s." *Participations* 6, no. 2 (2009): 240–259.

———. "'A Film Specially Suitable for Children': The Marketing and Reception of *2001: A Space Odyssey* (1968)." In *Family Films in Global Cinema: The World beyond Disney*, edited by Noel Brown and Brice Babington, 37–52. London: I.B. Tauris, 2015.

———. "The Limits of Autonomy: Stanley Kubrick, Hollywood and Independent Filmmaking, 1950–53." In *American Independent Cinema: Indie, Indiewood and Beyond*, edited by Geoff King, Claire Molloy, and Yannis Tzioumakis, 153–164. London: Routledge, 2013.

———. "'Movies That Make People Sick': Audience Responses to Stanley Kubrick's *A Clockwork Orange* in 1971/72." *Participations* 8, no. 2 (2011): 416–430.

———. "Spielberg and Kubrick." In *A Companion to Steven Spielberg*, edited by Nigel Morris, 195–211. Malden, MA: Wiley-Blackwell, 2017.

———. "Stanley Kubrick and the Internationalisation of Post-war Hollywood." *New Review of Film and Television Studies* 15, no. 2 (2017): 250–269.

———. "Stanley Kubrick: Known and Unknown." *Historical Journal of Film Radio and Television* 37, no. 3 (2017): 373–395.

———. "'To Prevent the Present Heat from Dissipating': Stanley Kubrick and the Marketing of *Dr. Strangelove* (1964)." *InMedia*, no. 3 (2013). http://inmedia.revues.org/634.

Martino, Caterina. "Pictures of *2001: A Space Odyssey* in the Stanley Kubrick Archive." *Photography and Culture* 9, no. 1 (2016): 79–87.

Mather, Philippe. "Stanley Kubrick: Photography and Film." *Historical Journal of Film, Radio and Television* 26, no. 2 (2006): 203–214.

Naremore, James. "Stanley Kubrick and the Aesthetics of the Grotesque." *Film Quarterly* 60, no. 1 (2006): 4–14.

Sanders, Terry B. "The Financing of Independent Feature Films." *Quarterly of Film, Radio, and Television* 9, no. 4 (1955): 380–389.

Sklar, Robert. "Stanley Kubrick and the American Film Industry." *Current Research in Film* 4 (1988): 114–124.

Ulivieri, Filippo. "From 'Boy Genius' to 'Barking Loon': An Analysis of Stanley Kubrick's Mythology." *Essais* hors série (2017): 221–242.

———. "Waiting for a Miracle: A Survey of Stanley Kubrick's Unrealised Projects." *Cinergie*, no. 12 (2017). http://doi.org/10.6092/issn.2280-9481/v6-n12-2017.

Index

2001: A Space Odyssey, 1, 46, 124, 132, 136–139, 143–151, 155–158, 164–166, 169, 171, 182, 198; budget, 136–137, 151; *Journey Beyond the Stars*, 136–138; merchandising, 132, 145–148, 150–151; publicity, 142–151, 166; release, 150–151, reviews, 151

Academy Awards, 52, 70, 130, 151
Agee, James, 17, 40–42
A.I. Artificial Intelligence, 179–183, 186, 189–190, 196, 199
Aldiss, Brian, 182–183
American film industry, 15–18, 20, 24, 26, 30–31, 33–35, 39–40, 48–49, 51–55, 57–58, 66, 68, 70–73, 77, 79, 83–85, 88, 92, 100, 105–107, 122, 126, 129, 130–132, 137, 139–140, 142–144, 156–160, 168, 188–189, 192, 197, 199
Aryan Papers, 179–181, 183–190, 196, 198–199
Ashley, Ted, 159–162, 164, 166, 170–172, 176, 179

Ballantine Books, 168
Ballard, Lucien, 68
Bantam Books, 129
Barry Lyndon, 163–164, 169–174, 181, 194; adaptation, 170, 172; publicity, 171–172; release, 172.
Bass, Saul, 86, 145
Beck, Myers P., 85–87

Begley, Louis, 183–186
Benjamin, Burton (*see also* Flying Padre), 22, 25
Bergman, Ingrid, 5
Blau, Joseph D., 65
Blau, Louis C., 65, 121, 138, 180, 194, 197
The Blind Mirror, 74
Bonafield, Jay (*see also* RKO-Pathé), 20–22
Bousel, Morris, 47–50, 58
Brando, Marlon, 69, 89, 96, 99, 108
The British Film Fund Agency (*see also* Eady Levy), 111, 122, 125–126
British film industry, 110–111, 122, 125–126, 132, 174–175, 198–199
Bryna Productions, 80–82, 84–86, 89–91, 93, 98–99, 101–102, 104, 115–116
Burgess, Anthony, 160, 168, 194
Burning Secret, 72, 74, 107
Burstyn, Joseph, 27, 33, 34, 39, 52–53, 58, 64

Calley, John, 132, 159–162, 164, 166, 170–172, 176, 179
Camera Equipment Company, 19, 22, 49, 54
Caras, Roger, 123–124, 129, 132, 140, 142–151, 156
Carlton, Rex (*see also* Laurel Films), 16–17
Cartier, Walter, 18
Central Intelligence Agency (C.I.A.), 36–37, 45
Cinerama, 137, 148–149, 170

249

Clarke, Arthur C., 92, 94, 136–137, 149, 183; *The Sentinel*, 136
Clean Break, 65–66
A Clockwork Orange, 159–161, 163–169, 171–173, 175–176, 182; adaptation, 160; budget, 160, 165–166; distribution, 167; novelization, 167–168; production, 160, 165; promotion, 167–168; UK distribution, 175–176
Cobb, Humphrey, 74, 82
Columbia Pictures, 5, 19, 95, 119, 122, 124–126, 128–130, 139–142, 149, 160
Conrad, Joseph, 29, 38–40, 66; *Heart of Darkness*, 29
Cooper, Lester Irving, 46
The Cop Killer, 56–57, 65
Cowles, John (*see also* Ford Foundation), 42
Cowles, Mike (*see also Look* magazine), 15, 42
Cruise, Tom, 185, 190, 195–196

Dancigers, Óscar, 40
Dassin, Jules, 53
Day of the Fight, 11, 18–21, 23–24, 27, 29, 37, 50
Deluxe Laboratories, 48–49, 54
De Rochemont, Louis, 16–17, 19
De Rochemont, Richard, 7, 15, 17, 19–20, 24–25, 27, 29, 32–33, 35–38, 40–43, 46, 58
Douglas, Kirk, 6, 24, 45, 50, 63, 77–86, 88–93, 96–104, 115–116, 122
The Down Slope, 73
Dr. Strangelove, 5, 120, 124–133, 135, 140, 142, 171, 182; budget, 124, 126–127, 136–137; casting, 125–126; development, 124–125; distribution, 129; novelization, 129; publicity, 127–129, 140; reception, 127–129, 131; script, 124–126
Dullea, Keir, 149

Eady levy, 111, 122, 125–126, 138, 175
Empyrean Films, 119, 180–181, 195
Engel, Morris, 33, 52–54
Essex Universal, 64
Evans, Walker, 17
Eyes Wide Shut, 76, 108, 178–179, 190, 193–196; development, 193–196; publicity, 195–196;

Fast, Howard, 99
Fear and Desire, 2, 11, 13, 14, 16–36, 38, 42, 44, 46–48, 51–52, 64, 71, 191, 196; budget, 31; distribution, 32–35, 44; exploitation, 30–31, 34; postproduction, 31–32, 45; reviews, 34
Flamingo Films, 64–65, 68, 104–105
Flying Padre, 11, 21–24, 29, 37
Foote, Shelby, 73–74
Ford Foundation (*see also Mr. Lincoln*), 40–42
Frewin, Anthony, 119, 180, 195
Fried, Gerald, 12, 20, 21, 27, 50, 164
Full Metal Jacket, 178–179, 183, 190–193, 196; publicity, 192–193; release, 192–193; script, 191–192

George, Peter, 129
The German Lieutenant, 95, 135, 184
Goldwyn, Samuel, 30, 39
Graziano, Rocky, 19

Harlan, Jan, 156, 158, 164–165, 169, 181, 183, 186–190
Harlan, Veit, 184–185
Harris-Blau Group, 65, 96
Harris, James B., 3, 6, 24, 51, 63–73, 77–78, 80–82, 84–86, 89–102, 104–106, 108–116, 119–121, 124–127, 141; cultural network, 64–65, 68, 77–78, 104, 110–111, 120; early career, 64; Flamingo Films, 64, 105; meets Kubrick, 64–65; television distribution, 64–65
Harris, Joseph, 64–66, 96–97, 99, 104–107, 120
Harris-Kubrick Pictures Corporation, 3, 11, 63–74, 77, 80–83, 85–86, 90–99, 102–113, 115–116, 119–121, 124–127, 129, 135, 156, 180, 184, 193; dissolution, 89–90, 119–121; incorporation, 63, 65; management, 64–67, 69–70, 73–74, 77, 80–82, 84, 89–90, 93–97, 99, 101–102, 104, 110–111, 119–121; production strategy, 64–68, 71–75, 77, 80, 89–98, 101, 107–108, 111, 114–115; unmade films, 66, 72–77, 80, 82, 90–97, 104, 107–108
Hasford, Gustav, 190
Hawk Films, 6, 120–122, 125–126, 129, 138–139, 142–143, 148, 165–166, 183; incorporation, 121, 129
Hayden, Sterling, 58, 67, 69, 126, 138
Herr, Michael, 186, 190–191
Hyman, Eliot, 111, 113
Hyman, Kenneth, 65, 110–111

I Stole $16,000,000, 90–93, 96
Ilya Muromets, 105–106

Jealousy, 74–76, 193–194
Johnson, Diane, 163

Kaplan, Mike, 123, 166–168
Kidman, Nicole, 196
Killer's Kiss, 26, 44, 46–55, 57–58, 71–72, 126; budget, 47–51, 53; locations, 49–50, 53; sale, 49–50, 54; script, 47, 50
The Killing, 56, 63–64, 66–71, 73–74, 77, 81, 96, 114–116, 126; budget, 66–67; casting, 67; production, 68–69; publicity, 68–70; release, 70–72; reviews, 71–72; script, 66
King, Stephen, 163, 173
Krim, Arthur (*see also* United Artists), 85
Kubrick, Barbara, 12
Kubrick, Christiane, 87, 169
Kubrick, Gertrude, 12–13
Kubrick, Jack, 12–14, 18, 23, 76–77
Kubrick, Stanley: adaptation, 16, 18, 21–22, 24, 29, 38–39, 65–66, 72–73, 91–92, 94, 99, 104, 107, 133–136, 163, 172, 179–185, 193–195; agent, 67, 80, 100; awards, 70, 130, 151; birth, 11–12; British film industry, 2–4, 7, 110–111, 122, 125–126, 137–138, 174–175; childhood, 12–14; contracts, 16–17, 22–23, 31, 39, 47–49, 58, 80–81, 89–90, 93, 96, 98–99, 101–102, 110–111, 115–116, 121, 124–125, 138–139, 141–142, 156, 159, 161–163, 169, 173, 178, 185–186, 197; cultural networks, 17, 24, 27–29, 35–36, 39–43, 50, 58–59, 63, 77–78, 81, 93, 120, 132; death, 2–3, 196; documentary, 7, 15–25, 27, 33, 36, 38, 58; dubbing, 1, 45, 49, 99, 106–107, 163–164, 176; early career, 7, 11, 13–43, 58–59; education, 13–14, 18, 27–28; failure, 23, 32–34, 38, 43, 77, 93–94, 96–97, 132, 155–156, 158–159, 164, 176–177, 183, 189–191, 193, 196, 198–199; film festivals, 33–34, 96, 106; as filmgoer, 12–13, 15, 31, 39; at *Look* magazine, 1, 6, 11, 14–15, 17–19, 23–24, 26–27, 33, 42, 56; myth, 2–4, 23–24, 30, 32, 42–43, 54, 128, 149–151, 155–156, 168–169, 198; in New York, 11–14, 17, 27–28, 30–31, 44, 47, 49–56, 75–76, 124; overseas production, 39–40, 83–84, 92, 95–97, 110–111, 120, 137, 158–159, 181, 187–189; photography, 13–15, 17–19, 21–23, 38, 42, 53, 58; self-promotion, 2, 11–12, 14, 23–24, 28, 30, 32, 37, 42–45, 54–55, 58, 69, 88–89, 91, 102–103, 122–125, 127–130, 132, 150–151, 155–156, 168–169, 173; television, 25, 36–38, 40–44, 64, 135–136; trade unions, 5, 24, 50, 91–92, 109–110, 122, 125, 198; unmade films, 7, 24, 38–40, 55–57, 72–77, 80, 82, 90–97, 104, 107–108, 133–136, 155–160, 179–190, 193–196, 198–199; wealth (income), 11, 15–16, 18, 23–24, 27, 32, 34–35, 38, 45–46, 50, 58, 63–64, 96–97, 102, 125, 156–157, 174–175, 198; as writer, 18, 24, 27–29, 47, 51, 55–57, 66, 75, 82, 91, 93, 107–108, 111–112, 160, 186, 188
Kubrick studies, 2, 4, 26, 198–199

Laughter in the Dark, 107–108
Laughton, Charles, 100, 103, 116
Laurel Films (*see also* Carlton, Rex), 16–17
Leith, Virginia, 30
Levitt, Helen, 17, 42, 52
Litvinoff, Si, 160
Lloyd, Norman (see also *Mr. Lincoln*), 40–43
Loeb, Janice, 17, 33, 52
Lolita, 63, 98–99, 101–102, 107–116, 120, 125–127, 131, 141, 171; box office, 115; budget, 109, 111; casting, 109–110; censorship, 108–109, 111–114; distribution, 112, 114; production, 110; publicity, 103, 113–114, 127; reputation, 101, 108–109, 113–114; script, 108, 111–113
Look magazine, 1, 6, 11, 14–15, 17–19, 21–24, 26–27, 33, 38, 42, 56, 58, 71, 148
Lovejoy, Ray, 137, 143, 147
Lunatic at Large, 66
Lyndon, Victor, 125
Lyon, Sue, 111, 113–114, 119–120

Mann, Anthony, 101
The March of Time, 15–16, 18–20, 24–25, 35–36
Margulies, Stan, 80, 84–88, 99
Married Man, 74–77, 107
Mason, James, 77, 111
Mayer, Arthur, 33, 39, 52, 58
Mayer, Peter, 39–40
Mazursky, Paul, 27, 30–31

Music Corp of America (MCA) (see also Wasserman, Lew), 93, 100–101, 109
Metz, Toba, 27–28, 31
Minotaur Productions, 46–49, 51, 54, 110
Mosby's Rangers, 92–93
Motion Picture Association of America (MPAA), 83, 94, 111–112, 123
MGM, 5, 30, 63, 72–74, 79, 114, 119, 122, 127, 132, 137–139, 141–151, 156–159, 166–167
Mr. Lincoln, 7, 17, 27, 40–43

Nabokov, Vera, 112
Nabokov, Vladimir, 99, 101, 107–108, 110, 112, 114
Napoleon, 155, 157–161, 170, 190, 196, 199
The New York school, 17, 28, 30, 33–34, 42, 44, 51–54
Nicholson, Jack, 173
Norton, Sam, 89–90

O'Brian, Helen, 14
O'Brien, Robert, 132, 137–139, 142–145, 148, 151, 157, 198
Olivier, Laurence, 5, 99, 100, 103, 109, 116
Olympia Press, 101, 108, 114
Omnibus (see also Ford Foundation), 40–42
One-Eyed Jacks, 96, 99
Ovitz, Michael, 185–186, 190

Paramount Pictures, 30, 39, 72, 79, 139–140, 158, 170
Paths of Glory, 63–64, 66, 72, 74, 77, 80–89, 95–96, 102, 108, 115–116, 141, 163; budget, 84–85; political sensitivities, 83, 88–89; production, 83; publicity, 84–89; script, 82–83
Peck, Gregory, 77, 89, 93
Perfect Marriage, 74–76, 107
Perveler, Martin, 13, 28–30, 32, 47, 58
Polaris Productions, 6, 120–125, 127–130, 132, 135, 137–138, 142–151, 166–168; incorporation, 121, 129, 131; vice president, 122–124, 132, 142, 145, 149–150, 161, 166–167
producer studies, 4–6
Production Code Administration (PCA), 107, 113
Public Relations Ltd (see also Margulies, Stan), 80–81, 85–88, 91, 119, 122

Raphael, Frederic, 195
Reyes, Benn, 119, 123–124, 150
Richter, Hans, 28, 30–31
RKO-Pathé, 18, 20–23, 25, 29
RKO Studios, 72
Ross, Steve, 65, 132, 159, 169

Sackler, Howard O., 27–29, 47, 50
Schary, Dore, 72, 74, 77
Schindler's List, 185–188
Schnitzler, Arthur, 76, 155–156, 181, 194
Scott, George C., 129
The Seafarers, 26, 44–46
Sellers, Peter, 111, 125–129, 134, 136–137
Semel, Terry, 132, 179, 186, 190, 193, 196
Seven Arts Productions, 63, 78, 110–115, 119–120, 124–125, 127, 159
Shark Safari, 45–46
The Shining, 3, 76, 163, 169–170, 172–173, 179, 185; distribution, 169–170, 173; publicity, 172–173
Shore, Sig, 104–106, 114, 168
Silvera, Frank, 31, 40, 46
Singer, Alexander, 13–15, 17–19, 24, 27, 64
Sobotka, Ruth, 50, 68, 75–76
Southern, Terry, 126, 194
Spartacus, 63, 89, 96–105, 109, 116, 126, 131, 149, 184; budget, 100, 102; casting, 99–100; director, 100–102, 104; publicity, 102–103; production, 102; reception, 104; script, 99
Spielberg, Steven, 171, 179, 181–183, 185–188, 193
Stadtmueller, Fred (see also *Flying Padre*), 21–23

The Stanley Kubrick Archive, 4, 5, 35, 45, 48, 108, 162, 178–179, 197
Stogel, Syd, 84–85
Terrell, Dan, 143–146, 148–150, 158, 166
Thackeray, William Makepeace, 170, 172
Thompson, Jim, 66, 74, 82
Titra Sound Corporation, 49
trade unions, 5
Traumnovelle (see also Schnitzler, Arthur), 76, 156, 181, 193–195
Trumbo, Dalton, 99
Twentieth Century Fox, 48, 74, 79, 122–123, 140, 158

United Artists (UA), 5, 44, 48, 54–55, 57–58, 63, 65–73, 79 81, 83–88, 109, 111, 114–115, 119, 139, 141, 156, 158, 160
Universal, 63, 98–102, 156
Ustinov, Peter, 77, 100, 103, 111, 116

Van Doren, Mark, 32
Vitalite Film Corporation (*see also* Harris, Joseph), 105–106

Warner Bros., 5, 13, 72, 106, 109, 132, 155–156, 158–165, 167–180, 186–197

Wasserman, Lew, 93, 100–101
Wayne, John, 40, 45, 93
Weiss, Nat, 121–123, 125, 127–130, 143
White, Lionel, 65–66
Willingham, Calder, 74, 77, 82, 96, 107, 112
World Assembly of Youth, 7, 27, 36–38
The Writer's Guild of America (WGA), 109–110

Youngstein, Max, 67, 69–72, 86–87

Zweig, Stefan, 72, 74

About the Author

JAMES FENWICK is a senior lecturer in media at Sheffield Hallam University. He is the editor of *Understanding Kubrick's 2001: A Space Odyssey: Representation and Interpretation* and the coeditor of *Shadow Cinema: Industrial and Production Contexts*. He has written numerous book chapters and journal articles on Stanley Kubrick, Kirk Douglas, and unmade film and television. He is currently working on a series of projects about the media industries and media representations of Sheffield.